# Lecture Notes in Computer Science 14212

The series Lecture Notes in Computer Science (LNCS), including its subseries Lecture Notes in Artificial Intelligence (LNAI) and Lecture Notes in Bioinformatics (LNBI), has established itself as a medium for the publication of new developments in computer science and information technology research, teaching, and education.

LNCS enjoys close cooperation with the computer science R & D community, the series counts many renowned academics among its volume editors and paper authors, and collaborates with prestigious societies. Its mission is to serve this international community by providing an invaluable service, mainly focused on the publication of conference and workshop proceedings and postproceedings. LNCS commenced publication in 1973.

Bedir Tekinerdogan · Catia Trubiani ·
Chouki Tibermacine · Patrizia Scandurra ·
Carlos E. Cuesta
Editors

# Software Architecture

17th European Conference, ECSA 2023
Istanbul, Turkey, September 18–22, 2023
Proceedings

 Springer

*Editors*
Bedir Tekinerdogan (ID)
Wageningen University
Wageningen, The Netherlands

Chouki Tibermacine (ID)
LIRMM
University of Montpellier
Montpellier, France

Carlos E. Cuesta (ID)
Superior de Ingeniería Informática
Rey Juan Carlos University
Mostoles, Madrid, Spain

Catia Trubiani (ID)
Computer Science
Gran Sasso Science Institute
L'Aquila, Italy

Patrizia Scandurra (ID)
DIGIP
University of Bergamo
Dalmine, Italy

ISSN 0302-9743          ISSN 1611-3349 (electronic)
Lecture Notes in Computer Science
ISBN 978-3-031-42591-2          ISBN 978-3-031-42592-9 (eBook)
https://doi.org/10.1007/978-3-031-42592-9

This Springer imprint is published by the registered company Springer Nature Switzerland AG
The registered company address is: Gewerbestrasse 11, 6330 Cham, Switzerland

Paper in this product is recyclable.

# Preface

The European Conference on Software Architecture (ECSA) is the premier European software architecture conference, providing researchers, practitioners, and educators with a platform to present and discuss the most recent, innovative, and significant findings and experiences in the field of software architecture research and practice.

The special theme for the 17th edition of ECSA was "Software Architectures for Engaging Responsibility". We are interested in learning about how software architecture principles and practices are evolving and being applied to engage software architects in societal and environmental responsibility. This raises questions such as: What are current research and practice results in developing and evolving software architecture principles for systems that include responsible design solutions? What are current research and practice results in developing and evolving software architecture principles for promoting responsibility in different domains such as collaborative, autonomous, and heterogeneous systems, as well as other emerging applications? What are good/bad examples and case studies in the context of responsible software architectures? How have software architecture courses changed to accommodate responsibility in design decisions, team skills, and underlying technologies?

This edition of ECSA was held during September 18–22, 2023, as an in-person event taking place in the beautiful and historic city of Istanbul in Turkey. The core technical program included five sessions that blended contributions from the research, industry, and tools & demonstration tracks, plus three keynote talks. Moreover, ECSA 2023 offered a doctoral symposium track. ECSA 2023 also encompassed workshops on diverse topics related to the software architecture discipline, such as context-aware, autonomous and smart architectures, agility with microservices programming, formal approaches for advanced computing systems, designing and measuring security in software architectures, quality in software architectures, and digital twin architectures.

For ECSA 2023, we received 71 submissions for research and industrial full papers. For the second time, this year the ECSA research track followed a double-blind review process. Each paper received three reviews. Based on the recommendations of the Program Committee, we accepted 16 papers as full papers and 9 additional papers as short papers. Hence the acceptance rate for full papers was 22% for ECSA 2023. The conference attracted papers (co-)authored by researchers, practitioners, and academics from 28 countries (Argentina, Australia, Austria, Belgium, Brazil, Canada, Chile, China, Colombia, Czech Republic, Denmark, France, Germany, Greece, India, Italy, Japan, The Netherlands, Peru, Poland, Portugal, South Korea, Spain, Sweden, Switzerland, Turkey, the UK, and the USA).

The main ECSA program had three keynotes. Our first speaker, Virginie Corraze, is Associate Director at Amadeus, in charge of Engineering Quality & Sustainability. She has 25+ years of experience in IT travel, in both commercial and R&D organizations. Virginie and her team interact with the Amadeus engineering community (8,000 members) to ensure sustainability and quality are part of all engineering practices. Our second speaker, Flavio Oquendo, is a Full Professor of Computing and a research director on Formal Approaches to Software Architecture at the IRISA Research Institute (UMR CNRS 6074), France. He has been a recipient of the Research Excellence Award from the Ministry of Research and Higher Education (France), having been promoted to the rank of Distinguished Full Professor, named by the Section of Computing of the National Council of Universities. Our third speaker, Birgit Penzenstadler, is an Associate Professor at the joint Department of Computer Science and Engineering at Chalmers University of Technology and Gothenburg University, Sweden, as well as an Adjunct Professor at the Lappeenranta University of Technology, Finland. She has been investigating resilience and sustainability from the point of view of software engineering during the past ten years, working on a body of knowledge and concepts of how to support sustainability from within Requirements Engineering.

We are grateful to the members of the Program Committee for their valuable and timely reviews. Their efforts formed the basis for a high-quality technical program for ECSA 2023. We would like to thank the members of the Organizing Committee for successfully organizing the event with several tracks, as well as the workshop organizers, who made significant contributions to this year's successful event.

We thank our sponsor Springer, who funded the best paper award of ECSA 2023 and supported us by publishing the proceedings in the Lecture Notes in Computer Science series. Finally, we thank the authors of all the ECSA 2023 submissions and the attendees of the conference for their participation.

We thank the software architecture community for their support, and for continuing to advance the field of software architecture through their scientific submissions to ECSA.

July 2023

Bedir Tekinerdogan
Catia Trubiani
Chouki Tibermacine
Patrizia Scandurra
Carlos E. Cuesta

# Organization

## General Chair

Bedir Tekinerdogan — Wageningen University, The Netherlands

## Steering Committee

| | |
|---|---|
| Paris Avgeriou | University of Groningen, The Netherlands |
| Thais Batista | Federal University of Rio Grande do Norte, Brazil |
| Stefan Biffl | Vienna University of Technology, Austria |
| Tomas Bures | Charles University, Czech Republic |
| Laurence Duchien | CRIStAL, University of Lille, France |
| Carlos E. Cuesta | Rey Juan Carlos University, Spain |
| David Garlan | Carnegie Mellon University, USA |
| Ilias Gerostathopoulos | Vrije Universiteit Amsterdam, The Netherlands |
| Paola Inverardi | University of L'Aquila, Italy |
| Patricia Lago | Vrije Universiteit Amsterdam, The Netherlands |
| Grace Lewis | Carnegie Mellon Software Engineering Institute, USA |
| Ivano Malavolta | Vrije Universiteit Amsterdam, The Netherlands |
| Raffaela Mirandola | Politecnico di Milano, Italy |
| Henry Muccini | University of L'Aquila, Italy |
| Elena Navarro | University of Castilla-La Mancha, Spain |
| Flavio Oquendo (Chair) | IRISA, University of South Brittany, France |
| Ipek Ozkaya | Carnegie Mellon University, USA |
| Jennifer Pérez | Technical University of Madrid, Spain |
| Bedir Tekinerdogan | Wageningen University, The Netherlands |
| Chouki Tibermacine | University of Montpellier, France |
| Catia Trubiani | Gran Sasso Science Institute, Italy |
| Danny Weyns | KU Leuven, Belgium |

## Program Co-chairs

| | |
|---|---|
| Chouki Tibermacine | University of Montpellier, France |
| Catia Trubiani | Gran Sasso Science Institute, Italy |

# Program Committee

| | |
|---|---|
| Jesper Andersson | Linnaeus University, Sweden |
| Vasilios Andrikopoulos | University of Groningen, The Netherlands |
| Paolo Arcaini | National Institute of Informatics, Japan |
| Hernan Astudillo | Universidad Técnica Federico Santa María, Chile |
| Justus Bogner | University of Stuttgart, Germany |
| Paris Avgeriou | University of Groningen, The Netherlands |
| Muhammad Ali Babar | University of Adelaide, Australia |
| Rami Bahsoon | University of Birmingham, UK |
| Luciano Baresi | Politecnico di Milano, Italy |
| Thais Batista | Federal University of Rio Grande do Norte, Brazil |
| Steffen Becker | University of Stuttgart, Germany |
| Alessio Bucaioni | Mälardalen University, Sweden |
| Radu Calinescu | University of York, UK |
| Matteo Camilli | Politecnico di Milano, Italy |
| Jan Carlson | Mälardalen University, Sweden |
| Carlos E. Cuesta | Rey Juan Carlos University, Spain |
| Rogério de Lemos | University of Kent, UK |
| Elisabetta Di Nitto | Politecnico di Milano, Italy |
| Daniele Di Pompeo | University of L'Aquila, Italy |
| Khalil Drira | LAAS-CNRS, France |
| Ghizlane El Boussaidi | École de Technologie Supérieure, Canada |
| António Rito Silva | University of Lisbon, Portugal |
| Filipe Figueiredo Correia | University of Porto, Portugal |
| Matthias Galster | University of Canterbury, New Zealand |
| David Garlan | Carnegie Mellon University, USA |
| Ilias Gerostathopoulos | Vrije Universiteit Amsterdam, The Netherlands |
| Robert Heinrich | Karlsruhe Institute of Technology, Germany |
| Sebastian Herold | Karlstad University, Sweden |
| Jasmin Jahic | University of Cambridge, UK |
| Andrea Janes | FHV Vorarlberg University of Applied Sciences, Austria |
| Anne Koziolek | Karlsruhe Institute of Technology, Germany |
| Patricia Lago | Vrije Universiteit Amsterdam, The Netherlands |
| Valentina Lenarduzzi | University of Oulu, Finland |
| Grace Lewis | Carnegie Mellon Software Engineering Institute, USA |
| Lukas Linsbauer | ABB Corporate Research, Germany |
| Marin Litoiu | York University, Canada |
| Antónia Lopes | University of Lisbon, Portugal |
| Ivano Malavolta | Vrije Universiteit Amsterdam, The Netherlands |

| Tommi Mikkonen | University of Helsinki, Finland |
| Raffaela Mirandola | Politecnico di Milano, Italy |
| Henry Muccini | University of L'Aquila, Italy |
| Elena Navarro | University of Castilla-La Mancha, Spain |
| Evangelos Ntentos | University of Vienna, Austria |
| Pablo Oliveira Antonino | Fraunhofer IESE, Germany |
| Flavio Oquendo | IRISA (UMR CNRS) - Univ. Bretagne-Sud, France |
| Ipek Ozkaya | Carnegie Mellon University, USA |
| Patrizio Pelliccione | Gran Sasso Science Institute, Italy |
| Jennifer Perez | Universidad Politécnica de Madrid (UPM), Spain |
| Ana Petrovska | Technical University of Munich, Germany |
| Diego Pérez | Linnaeus University, Sweden |
| Riccardo Pinciroli | Gran Sasso Science Institute, Italy |
| Maryam Razavian | Eindhoven University of Technology, The Netherlands |
| Salah Sadou | IRISA (UMR CNRS) - Univ. Bretagne-Sud, France |
| Riccardo Scandariato | Hamburg University of Technology, Germany |
| Patrizia Scandurra | University of Bergamo, Italy |
| Bradley Schmerl | Carnegie Mellon University, USA |
| Lionel Seinturier | University of Lille, France |
| Jacopo Soldani | University of Pisa, Italy |
| Romina Spalazzese | Malmö University, Sweden |
| Christos Tsigkanos | University of Bern, Switzerland |
| Katja Tuma | Vrije Universiteit Amsterdam, The Netherlands |
| Elisa Yumi Nakagawa | University of São Paulo, Brazil |
| Christelle Urtado | IMT Mines Alès, France |
| Dimitri Van Landuyt | KU Leuven, Belgium |
| Rainer Weinreich | Johannes Kepler University Linz, Austria |
| Danny Weyns | KU Leuven, Belgium |
| Anna Wingkvist | Linnaeus University, Sweden |
| André van Hoorn | University of Hamburg, Germany |
| Andrzej Zalewski | Warsaw University of Technology, Poland |

## Organizing Committee

### Industrial Track Co-chairs

| Carlos E. Cuesta | Rey Juan Carlos University, Spain |
| Patrizia Scandurra | University of Bergamo, Italy |

**Workshops Co-chairs**

Hasan Sozer                     Özyeğin University, Turkey
Romina Spalazzese               Malmö University, Sweden

**Tools and Demos Co-chairs**

Rami Bahsoon                    University of Birmingham, UK
Matthias Galster                University of Canterbury, New Zealand

**Doctoral Symposium Co-chairs**

Muhammad Ali Babar              University of Adelaide, Australia
Danny Weyns                     KU Leuven, Belgium

**Journal-First Chair**

Henry Muccini                   University of L'Aquila, Italy
Uwe Zdun                        University of Vienna, Austria

**Proceedings Chair**

Jasmin Jahic                    University of Cambridge, UK

**Publicity Chair**

Elisa Yumi Nakagawa            University of São Paulo, Brazil

**Local Chair**

Mert Özkaya                     Yeditepe University, Turkey

**Web Chair**

Deniz Akdur                     Aselsan, Turkey

**Virtualization Chair**

Sezer Gören Uğurdağ            Yeditepe University, Turkey

**Registration Chair**

Esin Onbaşıoğlu                    Yeditepe University, Turkey

**Student Volunteer Co-chairs**

Egehan Asal                        Yeditepe University, Turkey
Sevde Şimşek                       Yeditepe University, Turkey

## Additional Reviewers

Joran Leest                        Max Scheerer
Elvin Alberts                      Leif Bonorden
Sylvain Vauttier                   Dominik Fuchß
Calum Imrie                        Vaclav Struhar
Tobias Dürschmid                   Adel Taweel
Sinem Getir                        Samir Ouchani
Farnaz Fotrousi                    Cédric Eichler

# Abstract of Keynotes

# The Trek Towards Sustainability - Truth, Tale, or Transition?

Birgit Penzenstadler

Chalmers University of Technology and Gothenburg University, Sweden
birgitp@chalmers.se

**Abstract.** You may have heard about sustainability and the Sustainable Development Goals and the Global Reporting Initiative that now requires bigger companies to adjust their reporting in order to increase transparency. At the same time, you may have a funky feeling that there's quite a bit of hot air and greenwashing going on around there. So how do we truly transition towards more sustainability? Why may we also want to think about more resilience? And what inner transition is required to make this big outer shift? In this talk, I give a brief (necessarily incomplete) overview of the last decade of sustainability research in and outside of software engineering and sketch a vision of what's to come if we truly embrace a transition, and what may happen if we don't.

# Green IT: How You Can Take Action Now

Virginie Corraze

Amadeus, France
vcorraze@amadeus.com

**Abstract.** The younger generations seek a sense of purpose in their work, while the pace of climate change is increasing, with the IT industry playing a significant role in this acceleration through its carbon footprint. Now is the time to take accountability and prioritize sustainability in all engineering activities, to generate a positive influence and reduce the environmental impact of IT and in particular as a software architect. Join the session to gain knowledge on the fundamentals of green IT, learn Amadeus' feedback practices on deploying green practices in an IT organization, and ways to integrate sustainable development in your daily work.

# Software Architecture in the Era of Collective Intelligence: The Rise of Systems-of-Systems

Flavio Oquendo

IRISA Research Institute, France
flavio.oquendo@irisa.fr

**Abstract.** This keynote addresses why and how software architecture plays a central role in building collective intelligence in a rising class of complex systems, enabled by pervasive connectivity. De facto, different enabling technologies have progressively made possible to interconnect software-intensive systems that were independently developed, operated, managed, and evolved, yielding a new kind of complex system, i.e., a system that is itself composed of systems, the so-called "system-of-systems". By its very nature, a software-intensive system-of-systems is architected to exhibit "collective intelligence", very often opportunistically while operating in open environments. This is the case of systems-of-systems found in different areas as diverse as automotive, aeronautics, energy, healthcare, manufacturing, and transportation. In this context, safety is of paramount necessity since various aspects of our lives and livelihoods are becoming progressively dependent on those systems-of-systems. In this keynote, I will present the challenges facing research on software architecture to address the building of artificial collective intelligence in systems-of-systems, while enforcing safety. I will discuss the discriminating characteristics of systems-of-systems when compared with single (even very large) systems from the software architecture perspective. Especially, I will analyze why novel architectural approaches are needed to handle the complexity of software-intensive systems-of-systems in particular regarding the architectural challenges implied by self-organization and emergent behavior, the two key features for supporting collective intelligence. I will survey novel solutions for architecting systems-of-systems based on supervenience for achieving intelligent collective behavior and illustrate their applications in the field of driving automation for connected and automated vehicles. I will conclude by identifying the guarantees of correctness of the proposed approaches for architecting safe systems-of-systems, based on formal description and verification techniques dealing with dynamicity and uncertainty.

# Contents

**Artificial Intelligence and Autonomous Systems**

**Software Architecture Implementation and Deployment**

## Software Architecture Documentation

# Quality in Software Architectures

# Supporting the Exploration of Quality Attribute Tradeoffs in Large Design Spaces

J. Andres Diaz-Pace[1]([✉]) [iD], Rebekka Wohlrab[2] [iD], and David Garlan[3] [iD]

[1] ISISTAN Research Institute, CONICET and UNICEN University,
Tandil, Buenos Aires, Argentina
`andres.diazpace@isistan.unicen.edu.ar`
[2] Department of Computer Science and Engineering,
Chalmers University of Gothenburg, Gothenburg, Sweden
`wohlrab@chalmers.se`
[3] Software and Societal Systems Department, Carnegie Mellon University,
Pittsburgh, PA, USA
`garlan@cs.cmu.edu`

**Abstract.** When designing and evolving software architectures, architects need to consider large design spaces of architectural decisions. These decisions tend to impact the quality attributes of the system, such as performance, security, or reliability. Relevant quality attributes might influence each other and usually need to be traded off by architects. When exploring a design space, it is often challenging for architects to understand what tradeoffs exist and how they are connected to architectural decisions. This is particularly problematic in architectural spaces generated by automated optimization tools, as the underlying tradeoffs behind the decisions that they make are unclear. This paper presents an approach to explore quality-attribute tradeoffs via clustering and visualization techniques. The approach allows architects to get an overview of the main tradeoffs and their links to architectural configurations. We evaluated the approach in a think-aloud study with 9 participants from academia and industry. Our findings show that the proposed techniques can be useful in understanding feasible tradeoffs and architectural changes affecting those tradeoffs in large design spaces.

**Keywords:** Quality attribute tradeoffs · Architecture exploration

## 1 Introduction

Designing and evolving a software architecture is usually a challenging activity, as architects need to consider large design spaces that arise from alternative architectural decisions [4,7]. These decisions tend to have an impact on quality attributes of the system (e.g., performance, security, or reliability requirements), which might interact with each other. For example, achieving excellent performance and reliability at a low cost and with high security is often unfeasible. In

B. Tekinerdogan et al. (Eds.): ECSA 2023, LNCS 14212, pp. 3–19, 2023.
https://doi.org/10.1007/978-3-031-42592-9_1

practice, stakeholders make tradeoffs between the quality attributes of interest, which in turn affect the decisions that the architect can choose for the system.

This architectural decision problem can be seen as one of multi-objective optimization [1,15], in which making a set of decisions (and avoiding others) produces an architectural configuration that fulfills a set of quality attribute goals to varying degrees. However, in large design spaces, it is often difficult for humans to assess how good a set of architectural decisions is for the relevant quality attributes and what tradeoffs those decisions entail. To assist architects, several tools for automated architecture generation and optimization have been proposed [1,3,9,16,17], which can search through a wide range of configurations and recommend the most promising ones (e.g., those closer to the Pareto front for the relevant quality measures). An architectural configuration is shaped by the decisions being selected (e.g., deploying a service on a device, or inserting an intermediary between components). An architect normally takes a given configuration as the starting point and then relies on an optimization tool for generating and assessing alternative configurations. In some cases, different configurations might be connected to similar tradeoffs. Conversely, in other cases, small variations in a configuration might lead to different tradeoffs. However, in existing tools, the reasons why a generated configuration fulfills a set of quality attributes are normally opaque to architects. This limitation negatively affects their interactions with the tool and the exploration of architectural alternatives.

The concerns above call for forms of explaining a design space [20] to humans, which are currently not supported in optimization tools. This paper presents an approach to explain tradeoff spaces using clustering and visualization techniques. Clustering is used to find groups of configurations sharing similar quality-attribute characteristics (i.e., making similar tradeoffs). Furthermore, configurations are linked to each other based on a distance measure that considers the decisions (or architectural changes) to transition from one configuration to a neighborhood of alternatives. Along with this process, different charts are used to visualize prototypical configurations within a particular group, or to identify differences between groups. The proposed techniques enable us to summarize a large amount of information about quality attributes and related decisions. Thus, we help architects to quickly explore a design space and increase their confidence in the solutions generated by a tool.

To evaluate our approach, we performed a think-aloud study with 9 participants from industry and academia. The goal was to assess how the proposed techniques support architects in understanding tradeoffs and associated decisions within a space. Although at initial stages, we found that our techniques can be beneficial in large design spaces, allowing users to identify key tradeoffs, reason about architectural changes affecting them, and explore related alternatives.

## 2   Example: A Client-Server Design Space

For illustration purposes, let's assume a simple client-server architecture as schematized in Fig. 1 (left). The relevant quality attributes are performance, reliability, and cost. Client requests go through a load balancer that assigns them to service instances (on the server side) for processing. Service instances can be deployed on two physical devices. Each device is assumed to have a capacity to host up to six service instances. The two devices differ in their hardware characteristics: *device*1 is a low-end device while *device*2 is a high-end device, which affects their processing and reliability capabilities. In this setting, the processing time for incoming requests depends on the number of service instances, regardless of their deployment. For reliability, the probability of successfully executing a request is maximized when both devices are used or decreases otherwise.

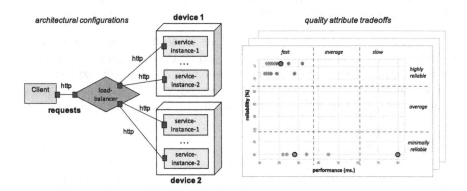

**Fig. 1.** Simple client-server style and associated tradeoffs.

To quantify the levels of performance, reliability and cost, let's assume that predefined analysis models are provided [15]. These models rely on both the structure and additional properties of a configuration (e.g., device cost, service failure probability, etc.) to compute a variety of measures. For instance, a cost model that sums up the individual costs of all the active services and devices might estimate a total cost of $70 for a configuration. Analogously, models for the processing time and failure probability of a configuration are devised.

In an architectural configuration, the decisions refer to the specific number of service instances and devices being active. As a result, this space has a total of 48 possible configurations with different tradeoffs. For example, the chart of Fig. 1 (right) shows that configurations with fast response times for processing the requests might have either low or high reliability. However, not all combinations of performance and reliability are feasible in this space. In general, it is not always obvious for the architect to determine what tradeoffs a given configuration is associated with and how the quality measures are correlated with each other.

## 3   Requirements for Tradeoff Explainability

For explaining tradeoff spaces, it is crucial to understand the information needs that stakeholders have. In particular, we focus on the questions that architects might pose when trying to reason about architectural configurations, design

decisions, and quality-attribute tradeoffs. First, to select an appropriate configuration, it is important to get an overview of the kinds of tradeoffs that exist
in a design space. Afterwards, the corresponding configurations can be assessed
individually, along with alternatives having similar or different tradeoffs. In this
work, we consider the following questions:

- **Q1**: What are the categories of feasible tradeoffs in a given design space?
- **Q2**: What architectural configurations are representative of each category of
  tradeoffs? What are the key decisions behind those configurations?
- **Q3**: For a given configuration, which alternatives lead to similar tradeoffs?
- **Q4**: For a given configuration, which alternatives lead to different tradeoffs?

We argue that, by answering these questions, tradeoffs can be understood and
the design space can be quickly explored to arrive at one or more configurations
that make appropriate tradeoffs. The requirements of a tradeoff explainability
approach are thus to: answer Q1–Q4, provide a sufficient level of usability, and
be understandable to stakeholders with basic architecture knowledge.

## 4   Approach

We propose a framework that involves three stages, as outlined in Fig. 2. The
output of the first two stages is a repository that enables the creation of a
dashboard with visualizations (called explanation charts) for the architect.

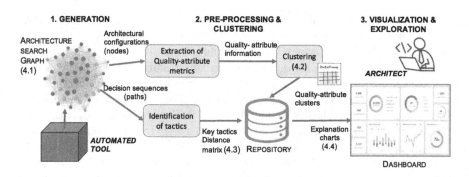

**Fig. 2.** Stages of the proposed framework.

First, there is an *exploration stage*, in which a (large) number of architectures
is generated (or sampled) by an automated optimization tool. This stage must
be executed beforehand. Each architectural instance comprises both the architectural configuration and its quality-attribute values. This information is represented by a search graph, which connects an initial architectural configuration
to the various configurations that can be derived from it by applying predefined
decisions. Next, during the *pre-processing and clustering stage*, the information

from the architectural instances is split into two parts. The quality-attribute values are grouped to derive clusters. To do this, a combination of discretization (of numerical values) and clustering techniques is used. The sequences of decisions (paths in the graph) leading to each configuration are identified, and the important decisions for the tradeoffs are then determined. Furthermore, decisions serve to compute a distance metric between sequences. All the artifacts are stored in a repository. Finally, the *visualization stage* provides a set of explanation charts for the architect to get insights on the tradeoff space.

## 4.1   Design Representation Using a Search Graph

We consider a multi-objective architecture optimization [4], and assume an *architectural space* for a family of systems that encompasses all possible architectural configurations in terms of a (finite) set of *design decisions*. More formally, let $DS = \{A_0, A_1, A_2, ..., A_n\}$ be a design space with $n$ architectural configurations in which each $A_i$ corresponds to a (valid) configuration that results from a sequence of predefined decisions $A_i = < d_{1i}, d_{2i}, ..., d_{mi} >$. Each $d_{ij} = 1$ if the decision was made (for configuration $A_i$) or 0 otherwise.

In this work, we restrict the possible decisions to *architectural tactics* [5]. An architectural tactic is a design transformation that affects parts of an architectural configuration to improve a particular quality attribute. In our example, a tactic is to deploy a service instance on a given device in order to increase the system performance. Note that the same tactic might have an effect on other quality attributes (e.g., cost). From this perspective, the configurations in $DS$ are linked to one another through the application of tactics. $DS$ can be visualized as a directed graph in which each node represents a configuration, while an edge between two nodes $A_i$ and $A_j$ captures a tactic leading from the former to the latter. A distinctive node $A_0$ refers to the initial configuration.

In general, an automated tool will be responsible for exploring the design space and generating a (large) graph of configurations. The techniques for populating $DS$ might include specific architectural tools [1], evolutionary algorithms [3,6], or model checkers such as Prism [7,14], among others. Since enumerating all the configurations available in the design space is usually computationally unfeasible, only a subset of those configurations will be generated. Our framework does not depend on the tool or the specific search technique, as long as it can expose the decisions being applied for each configuration.

We require a configuration $A_i$ to be assessed with respect to multiple quality attributes (objectives) by means of quantitative measures [15]. Let $QAS = < O_1, O_2, ..., O_k >$ be a *quality-attribute space* with $k$ objectives in which each $O_k$ represents a quality metric (e.g., latency, failure probability, or cost) associated with some architectural configuration. That is, an evaluation function $f : DS \rightarrow QAS$ maps a configuration to a multi-valued vector in $\Re^k$.

## 4.2   Clustering of the Quality-Attribute Space

To understand the possible tradeoffs, architects need a succinct representation of the quality-attribute space. A suitable technique for this purpose is *clustering* [22], which is a Machine Learning technique for grouping a set of instances in such a way that instances in the same group (or cluster) are more similar to each other than to those in other groups. To do so, a similarity criterion needs to be established. In our case, an instance refers to the quality-attribute vector for a configuration $A_i$. For the similarity criterion, we rely on the Euclidean distance between vectors (although other metrics could be used).

We are interested in cohesive clusters that capture the main tradeoffs available in the space. To this end, classical algorithms such as *k-means* or *agglomerative clustering* [22] can be applied. In both algorithms, the number of desired clusters is specified beforehand, and the quality of the resulting clusters is assessed with metrics such as the silhouette coefficient [22]. This coefficient assesses the (average) cohesion and separation of a set of clusters, by measuring how similar instances are for their own cluster compared to the other clusters.

Once clusters are identified, we assign a label to each cluster that reflects the quality attributes being traded off in a way that humans can more easily understand. Specifically, we select the cluster *centroid*, which is computed as the mean of the vectors belonging to the cluster. Examples of three clusters were shown in Fig. 1 (right) with their centroids marked. Since a centroid is a numeric vector, we transform it into a label by means of a discretization procedure which partitions the range of values of each quality attribute into an ordinal (or Likert-like) scale. In Fig. 1, the partitioning is indicated by the dotted lines that map to levels of satisfaction (e.g., *fast*, *average*, or *slow* for performance). The cluster label results from the concatenation of the quality-attribute levels of the cluster centroid. In our example using a 3-point scale, the orange cluster gets labeled as *fast/minimally-reliable*, the blue cluster gets *fast/highly-reliable*, and the green cluster gets *slow/minimally-reliable*. Note that after the clustering and discretization, the quality-attribute space is reduced to three groups of tradeoffs. The number of architectural configurations belonging to each cluster might vary, depending on the design space being considered.

## 4.3   Distance Between Architectural Configurations

An architectural configuration in the search graph is the result of applying specific tactics to the initial architecture. The optimization tool progressively applies different tactics to derive alternative configurations. Thus, a configuration $A_i$ can be represented by a *sequence of tactics* $S_i = < t_{1i}, t_{2i}, ..., t_{mi} >$, which comes from the shortest path between the initial node and a particular node (with a valid configuration) in the search graph. Coming back to our client-server example, we can consider a tactic *increaseCapacity(?device)* that deploys (and activates) a new service on a given device[1]. Instantiations of this tactic for specific devices

---

[1] A tactic *decreaseCapacity(?device)* that reverses the effects of adding a service to a device can be also considered in the graph.

(*device*1, *device*2) will then label the edges of the graph. Note that we consider the sequences as shorter paths in the graph because all the tactics in the example involve "atomic" configuration changes. If more complex tactics were available, other criteria for determining the paths to each alternative should be considered.

By representing configurations as sequences of decisions, we can assess the distance between two configurations in terms of their delta of changes [3]. Given a pair of configurations $A_i$ and $A_i$, which are derived from sequences $S_i$ and $S_j$ respectively, we model their distance as a function of the differences in the tactics made for $S_i$ and $S_j$. Our approach currently uses a version of the *hamming distance*[2] [10], although other metrics could be employed. A distance matrix for all tactic sequences is computed in the *pre-processing stage* (Fig. 2).

When the architect wants to explore alternatives for a configuration $A_x$, all configurations are sorted based on their distance to $A_x$, and the top-k results with the shortest distance are returned. Upon the architect's request, filters can be applied to select: only configurations within a particular cluster, configurations belonging to all clusters, or configurations that exclude a predefined cluster. For instance, Fig. 3 shows the distances between three configurations resulting from two clusters from our example. Configurations $A$ and $C$ are assumed to share the same cluster, while configuration $B$ belongs to a different cluster. The labels associated with each configuration refer to its quality-attribute characteristics (which might slightly differ from those of the cluster centroid). For example, as shown in Fig. 3, one could sacrifice response time (e.g., due to cost concerns) by moving from $A$ towards $C$, which both decreases the number of active services and uses a cheaper device for them. Alternatively, one could make changes to

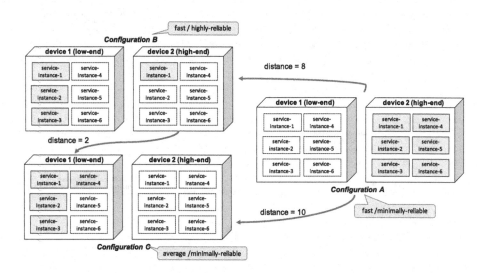

**Fig. 3.** Alternative configurations and tradeoffs based on decision changes.

---

[2] In case of sequences of different lengths, we pad the shorter sequence with a special *noOp()* tactic that makes no changes to the architectural configurations.

$A$ so as to reach $B$, which offers both higher reliability and smaller response time, because services are deployed in two devices. Alternative $C$ causes a slight variation in the tradeoff of $A$ for performance and reliability, while alternative $B$ leads to a better tradeoff for both qualities. In general, intermediate configurations might need to be traversed (in the graph) to move between two particular alternatives. Note also that the distances refer to changes in the design space, rather than to cluster differences in the quality-attribute space.

### 4.4   Explanation Charts

In the *visualization stage*, the architect goes through a series of charts that shed light on different aspects of the design space. This exploratory process is structured as a suggested workflow of activities. Each activity involves a specific chart targeted to answer questions Q1-Q4. The four available charts are illustrated in Fig. 4. The suggested order for an architect to use them is clockwise, as indicated by the numbers in the figure. The charts were designed and adjusted iteratively by the authors, according to the notion of *pretotypes* [19], which allows one to test ideas at a low cost before building a (prototype) tool.

   We briefly describe below the main characteristics of each chart type:

1. **Quality-attribute prototypes.** This radar chart displays the values of the cluster centroids with respect to the quality attribute goals. As the initial view, it presents the main tradeoffs of the quality-attribute space to the

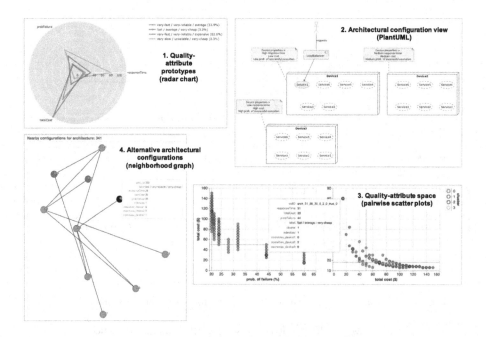

**Fig. 4.** Types of explanation charts.

architect, using the centroids as representative instances (or prototypes) of the feasible tradeoffs. This chart is intended to address **Q1**. The chart legend additionally shows the labels and the percentage of architectural configurations (from the whole space) per cluster.

2. **Architectural configuration view**. To focus on a given prototype or cluster (from chart #1), the architect can inspect one or more architectural configurations related to that cluster. This is motivated by the need to drill down into the structure of configuration and its underlying decisions. The chart targets **Q2** and enables an understanding of the design space. Here, we use PlantUML for our client-server example, although the notation is dependent on the architectural models being captured by the space.

3. **Quality-attribute space.** This chart gives a detailed view of all the architectural configurations, their contributions to the different quality-attribute measures, and how configurations are grouped into clusters. It complements chart #1 by showing all possible tradeoffs, in order to address **Q1** and **Q2**. This chart is interactive, allowing architects to select specific points and display basic information about the configurations or cluster labels.

4. **Alternative architectural configurations**. After the insights exposed by the previous charts, the architect might want to understand how to move from a given configuration to another with different quality-attribute characteristics. This chart creates an interactive graph that takes a target configuration and connects it to a set of nearby configurations that result from making "small" changes to the decisions for the target configuration. The alternative configurations might belong either to the same cluster as the target or to different clusters. This graph chart seeks to address **Q3** and **Q4**. The target can be any configuration from charts #1 or #3. The construction of the graph is based on the architectural distance described in Sect. 4.3.

## 5  Study Design

To evaluate the effectiveness of our explanation framework, we applied it to an extended version of the client-server problem presented in Sect. 2 in two ways: (i) exploring and assessing configuration variants and tradeoffs using a pre-generated space, and (ii) conducting a think-aloud study to evaluate our findings and the role of the explanation charts[3].

### 5.1  Client-Server Design Space

We set a client-server style with up to three available servers (devices), each with a capacity to deploy a maximum of six services. To model tradeoffs between performance (latency), reliability (probability of failure), and cost (total deployment expenditure), we assigned different characteristics to each device, in terms of high-end hardware (i.e., very good processing capabilities, low failure rate,

---

[3] Notebook: https://shorturl.at/jyCX3 - Tasks: https://shorturl.at/lHU08.

and high cost), mid-range hardware, and low-end hardware (i.e., minimum processing capabilities, higher failure rate, and low cost). The decisions in this space include: (i) adding one (active) service to any device, or (ii) removing an already-deployed service from a device. The choice of the device depends on its hardware characteristics.

We departed from an initial configuration with no services allocated to devices, and ran an optimization procedure based on the Prism model checker [14]. This way, we generated a large number of architectural configurations for our system to evaluate the feasibility of the proposed framework. In principle, other search strategies (e.g.,, evolutionary algorithms) could have been used, as the approach is mostly independent of how the optimization part is implemented.

## 5.2   User Study

The think-aloud method is a technique to investigate problem-solving processes and participants' cognitive models [12], in which participants vocalize their thought process while working on a task. We chose a think-aloud study because it can provide insights into how the clustering and visualization techniques proposed in our framework can facilitate the participants' architectural reasoning.

The study consisted of a series of design sessions with 9 participants from both academia and industry. The selected participants had various roles in their organizations (e.g., university faculty, researcher, PhD student, industry practitioner, and senior engineer) and varying degrees of architectural knowledge and experience (from 2 to more than 20 years in the architecture field). All sessions were recorded and had a duration of 45 min approximately.

A session involved four phases: introduction, learning, testing, and post-mortem. The session started with an introduction to the architectural problem, and was facilitated by one of the authors. As mentioned above, this problem was based on the design space already investigated (Sect. 5.1). After the introduction, there was a learning phase in which the participant assumed the role of an architect and was asked to explore the space of quality-attribute trade-offs and candidate configurations by means of the explanation charts. For this phase, we provided a *Jupyter* notebook in *Google Colab* that included predefined Python functions for a user to load the space as a dataset and generate the charts. Furthermore, some Python functions admit parameters to adjust the chart behavior (e.g., the name of the architectural configuration to be inspected, or the number of alternatives to show in the graph). We decided not to include the quality-attribute space chart (pairwise scatter plots) in this study, since it provides detailed information about the clusters but can be complex to grasp for unfamiliar users. To avoid long sessions, we considered it could be substituted by the radar and graph charts in the interviews, without losing much information.

The effectiveness of the charts was assessed during the testing phase, in which a set of glitch detection tasks and prediction tasks was presented to the participant [11]. In the glitch detection tasks, the subjects identify things that are wrong in a system or explanation; while in the prediction tasks, the subjects have to predict the results of certain design decisions and explain their predictions. Both kinds of tasks referred to design situations based on the presented charts. These tasks enabled us to analyze the participant's reasoning process and whether it was aided by the mechanisms of the explanation charts.

At the end, we conducted a short questionnaire to measure the satisfaction levels of the participants when using the charts. To do this, we used a list of Likert-scale questions. Apart from satisfaction, we also focused on the participants' expectations as well as on areas of improvement for the framework.

## 6   Findings

For our client-server example, Prism returned a graph with a design space of 342 configurations. Each configuration was evaluated with (simplified) analytical models to estimate values of cost, latency, and probability of failure. A visual inspection of the resulting tradeoff space showed that it had enough diversity and coverage. Figure 5 depicts both the design and quality-attribute spaces. Each path in the graph is a sequence of design decisions. The sequence length to move between configurations ranges from 1 to 18 decisions.

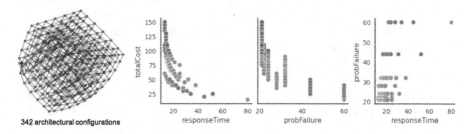

**Fig. 5.** Design space (graph) and quality-attribute space (pairwise scatter plots) for the client-server space. Colors refer to the clusters exposing four tradeoffs.

In the clustering process, we sought a balance between having a small number of clusters and achieving a high silhouette coefficient. We applied hierarchical clustering with four clusters, which yielded a silhouette coefficient of 0.52. The obtained clusters have unique combined labels, which are derived from a discretization of the ranges for each quality attribute into five bins. In principle, this discretization enables 125 possible tradeoffs, but only 19 of them were reachable in the space. Thus, our clustering reduced the tradeoff space in $\approx 80\%$.

For the user study, we categorized the findings according to the chart types, focusing on the understandability of the charts (and the design space thereof) as well as on participants' satisfaction. An overview of the questions and answers from the post-mortem questionnaire is given in Fig. 6. The participants indicated that they were generally satisfied with the information conveyed by the charts. During the learning phase, all participants were able to understand the purpose of the three charts, and to use them for architectural reasoning in the testing phase. Most glitches were detected by the participants. The most difficult glitches and prediction tasks were those related to the graph chart, particularly for less experienced participants.

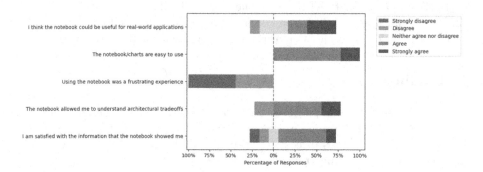

**Fig. 6.** Likert-scale answers of participants of the user study.

The radar chart was judged as the easiest to use by most participants. During the testing phase, it was perceived as straightforward to apply. This might be due to the fact that architects are often exposed to similar charts. In fact, other visualization tools [9] have proposed radar charts for tradeoffs. A PhD student stated: *"The radar chart with the clusters shows you quite easily what types of solutions are the most likely ones to satisfy your needs"*. As for the labels, they were intuitive for the participants, although some asked questions about the value ranges for the labels, and moreover, about the quality-attribute thresholds that should be considered in order to weight each cluster prototype. On the downside, some participants argued that despite the chart provides an overview of the tradeoffs, it did not seem actionable with respect to decision-making.

The architectural configuration chart was used by participants to drill down into the architectural structure of a particular prototype. Participants usually did not explore more than one configuration with the chart. During the testing phase, the annotations on the devices were a key element for detecting glitches. This might suggest that enriching architectural views with quality-attribute annotations can help design reasoning. However, this aspect likely depends on the size and architectural notation used for the views. Along this line, one researcher noted: *"If I had a system with dozens of components, where there is only a slight difference between configuration A and configuration B when I'm looking at the alternatives, it'll take me much longer to understand what the differences are between these alternatives, and I'd have to trust more the tool to do the job right ... I might need something that shows me the differences between the architectures"*.

When it comes to the graph chart, we observed mixed impressions. A number of participants found the chart difficult to interpret and use later in the glitch detection and prediction tasks. This situation was evident for those participants with less architecture experience. For instance, the implications of the decisions made when transitioning from one configuration to another were not easy to be reasoned about. Despite this complexity, other participants argued that it was useful to explore alternatives by means of small configuration changes. One practitioner said: *"The graph was probably the most challenging to use but also potentially getting to be the most powerful"*. Another participant stated: *"[The graph chart] shows me a what-if analysis ... it lets me do an analysis of different tactics and look at what is their impact in terms of the tradeoffs I would get"*. We collected suggestions to enhance this chart, such as: clarifying the tactic names in the edges, linking the nodes to architectural views (configurations), and (again) adding quality-attribute thresholds. During the learning phase, three participants raised questions about the effort or complexity (e.g., development cost, or deployment cost) of applying the decisions shown in the graph.

Overall, we can conclude that the charts were effective in helping to expose the tradeoffs of the space, and to a lesser extent, in helping the participants reason about decisions affecting those tradeoffs. Having a better focus on the decisions that architects could make is one of the areas of improvement that we identified from the user study. In retrospect, our findings indicate that the information shown in the notebook provides insights about the tradeoffs and configurations, but it might lack contextual information about the problem that the architect is trying to solve. In this regard, one practitioner said during a session: *"I'm trying to arrive at a decision, not just see that there are tradeoffs"*. Furthermore, two practitioners mentioned that the charts should be integrated with tools that architects and developers use in their daily work (e.g., infrastructure as code, dashboards, or IDEs) for assessing options and making decisions.

## 6.1   Threats to Validity

*Internal Validity.* The results of the clustering process depend on both the characteristics of the quality-attribute space and the (hyper-)parameters used for the algorithm (e.g., choosing the number of clusters). The cluster boundaries might not be always clean. Furthermore, using the cluster centroid (and its associated label) to characterize the tradeoffs of all the cluster members is an approximation. Not all the instances belonging to a cluster might have the same tradeoff posed by the centroid, and thus slight tradeoff variations might appear in the space. In the client-server example, applying other clustering algorithms (e.g., k-medoids) could produce different results. All these factors can affect the participants' interpretation of the radar chart and parts of the graph chart. The graph chart relies on both the tactic sequences for each configuration and a distance criterion for sequences. The sequences can be seen as proxies for representing the configurations, but they omit some architectural characteristics. Thus, the sequences were a good representation for our client-server example, but they might fall short for dealing with other architectural styles. Regarding the architectural distance, we implemented a hamming distance under the assumption that all the tactics have the same weight (or involve a similar amount of changes). This might not hold if a different set of tactics is considered.

*Construct Validity.* When talking about concepts like "tradeoffs" or "software architecture", our participants might have different interpretations as to what they mean. Especially due to their abstract nature, these constructs can be difficult to understand. To mitigate the threat, we discussed the example scenario and concepts at the beginning of the interviews. We asked our participants to describe the scenario in their own words to understand their ways of thinking about tradeoff-related issues. In case they were unsure, we gave explanations of the key constructs and ensured that our views were aligned.

*Conclusion Validity.* While we did not aim to arrive at statistically significant results, conclusion validity is still relevant for our study. The reliability might have been compromised by having a sample of nine participants with limited time to work with the notebook during the sessions. Collecting data from a larger number of participants would have led to more information and richer feedback about the framework. To mitigate this, we aim to be transparent about our research method and study materials. We thoroughly discussed and refined the materials to avoid issues such as potentially incoherent structure, overly complex visualizations, or poor wording in tasks and questions.

*External Validity.* The automated generation of a large graph of alternatives, which also includes the information required by our framework (e.g., decisions applied at each step, quality-attribute values for each alternative), can be challenging and might not feasible (or accurate) for any system or optimization algorithm. This aspect might prevent the exploitation of the techniques presented in the paper. Furthermore, our study does not have a broad generalizability, as it was exercised on a small architectural problem. The goal was to present a think-aloud study focusing on the practical usage of the explainability charts by humans. We selected the participants trying to achieve a coverage of different profiles. Involving different participants helped us get a variety of perspectives on the topic and strengthen external validity. Another threat is the presence of the authors, who assumed a central role in developing the notebook and facilitating the sessions. These factors might lead to the participants responding more positively. As mitigation, we stressed that they should openly share their thoughts and that improvement suggestions were welcome. Our results indicate that the participants followed these instructions and shared criticisms.

# 7    Related Work

Several tools for automated architecture optimization that generate a set of alternatives have been proposed [1,3]. These tools work mostly as black boxes, and their internal search space is not comprehensible by humans. As a result, architects might not trust the proposed architecture candidates. Recent approaches, like *SQuAT-Viz* [9] and *Voyager* [16], have investigated visualization techniques for helping architects to understand tradeoffs, and have also evaluated their usability. Among other techniques, *SQuAT-Viz* [9] uses radar charts and scatter plots for the quality-attribute space, although they show all possible combinations of tradeoffs. *Voyager* [16], in turn, combines tradeoff analysis with architectural structure visualizations alongside, highlighting the need to connect these two spaces, which is a shared concern with our framework. *Voyager* does not consider strategies for reducing the size of the quality-attribute space (e.g., via clustering) or navigating related configurations (e.g., like our graph chart).

Other authors have attempted to explain tradeoff spaces using dimensionality reduction and clustering techniques. For instance, Camara et al. [8] propose PCA (Principal Component Analysis) loading plots to relate quality-attribute and architectural variables. In the robot planning domain [20], contrastive explanations of tradeoffs have been developed. This kind of explanations compares a selected policy to Pareto-optimal alternative plans and describes their quality-attribute impact on the user. Also in the planning domain, Wohlrab et al. [21] complement the PCA plots of Camara et al. [8] with clustering and decision trees. The usage of the clusters differs from our framework, as they refer to policies sharing similar characteristics and provide a high-level tradeoff explanation. The clustering process is applied on top of the loading plots, which often implies some information loss when transforming the space to a 2D representation. Furthermore, clusters are explained using bar charts showing feature means, which might not be an intuitive visualization for humans. These works center on information reduction techniques for the design space, but user studies about their effectiveness have not been reported yet.

The *GATSE* tool [17] allows architects to visually inspect *AADL* (Architecture Analysis and Description Language) models from a previously computed dataset. It offers several visualizations to support quality-attribute analyses of AADL models (e.g., via a Pareto diagram), enabling the architect to focus on regions of the quality-attribute space to narrow down or deepen the search for alternatives. This interaction mechanism is called "design by shopping".

Kinneer and Herzig [13] investigate metrics of dissimilarity and clustering for a set of spacecraft architectures within a space mission domain. Since a large number of architecture candidates are automatically synthesized, but some candidates might be similar to each other, the architect has to waste time sifting through the space. Thus, a clustering process based on PAM (Partitioning Around Medoids) is proposed to group the architectures and select a representative instance from each group. The clustering is tied to the notion of distance between architectures. Based on user studies that identify correlations between clustering and human judgements, the authors highlight the role of human perception when different stakeholders explore the space.

## 8 Conclusions

In this paper, we discussed some requirements for improving an architect's understanding of design spaces regarding the interplay between tradeoffs and architectural decisions. To this end, we presented an approach that relies on clustering and visualization techniques. An initial version of our framework was evaluated on an architectural problem with a think-aloud study. This study confirmed our hypothesis that design spaces can be summarized to a handful of quality-tradeoffs and related architectural decisions, and also provided us with feedback to improve the explanation charts and underlying techniques. This suggests more focus on characterizing the architecture space, which has received less attention in the literature in comparison to the quality-attribute space.

As future work, we plan to test our framework for larger design spaces, whether generated by existing optimization tools [3,17] or by humans [18]. As the spaces grow larger, mechanisms to extract the main paths of decisions and tradeoffs will become increasingly important. We think that the notion of "policy summaries" [2] can be adapted to work with the graphs of alternatives (within the architectural space) to extract a sub-graph of decisions that contribute the most to the quality attributes of interest for the architect or stakeholders.

**Acknowledgments.** This work was partially supported by the Wallenberg AI, Autonomous Systems and Software Program funded by the Knut and Alice Wallenberg Foundation. It was also supported by project PICT-2021-00757.

# References

1. Aleti, A., Buhnova, B., Grunske, L., Koziolek, A., Meedeniya, I.: Software architecture optimization methods: a systematic literature review. IEEE Trans. on Soft. Eng. **39**(5), 658–683 (2013)
2. Amir, O., Doshi-Velez, F., Sarne, D.: Summarizing agent strategies. Auton. Agent. Multi-Agent Syst. **33**(5), 628–644 (2019). https://doi.org/10.1007/s10458-019-09418-w
3. Arcelli, D., Cortellessa, V., D'Emidio, M., Di Pompeo, D.: Easier: an evolutionary approach for multi-objective software architecture refactoring. In: 2018 IEEE Int. Conf. on Software Architecture (ICSA), pp. 105–10509 (2018). https://doi.org/10.1109/ICSA.2018.00020
4. Bachmann, F., Bass, L., Klein, M., Shelton, C.: Designing software architectures to achieve quality attribute requirements. IEEE Proc. Softw. **152**, 153–165 (2005)
5. Bass, L., Clements, P., Kazman, R.: Software Architecture in Practice. SEI Series in Software Engineering, Addison-Wesley (2003)
6. Busch, A., Fuchß, D., Koziolek, A.: PerOpteryx: automated improvement of software architectures. In: 2019 IEEE International Conference on Software Architecture Companion (ICSA-C), pp. 162–165 (2019). https://doi.org/10.1109/ICSA-C.2019.00036
7. Cámara, J., Garlan, D., Schmerl, B.: Synthesizing tradeoff spaces of quantitative guarantees for families of software systems. J. Syst. Softw. **152**, 33–49 (2019)
8. Cámara, J., Silva, M., Garlan, D., Schmerl, B.: Explaining architectural design tradeoff spaces: a machine learning approach. In: Biffl, S., Navarro, E., Löwe, W., Sirjani, M., Mirandola, R., Weyns, D. (eds.) ECSA 2021. LNCS, vol. 12857, pp. 49–65. Springer, Cham (2021). https://doi.org/10.1007/978-3-030-86044-8_4
9. Frank, S., van Hoorn, A.: SQuAT-Vis: visualization and interaction in software architecture optimization. In: Muccini, H. (ed.) ECSA 2020. CCIS, vol. 1269, pp. 107–119. Springer, Cham (2020). https://doi.org/10.1007/978-3-030-59155-7_9

10. Hamming, R.W.: Error detecting and error correcting codes. Bell Syst. Tech. J. **29**(2), 147–160 (1950). https://doi.org/10.1002/j.1538-7305.1950.tb00463.x
11. Hoffman, R.R., Mueller, S.T., Klein, G., Litman, J.: Metrics for explainable AI: Challenges and prospects. arXiv preprint arXiv:1812.04608 (2018)
12. Jaspers, M.W., Steen, T., van den Bos, C., Geenen, M.: The think aloud method: a guide to user interface design. Int. J. Med. Inf. **73**(11), 781–795 (2004). https://doi.org/10.1016/j.ijmedinf.2004.08.003
13. Kinneer, C., Herzig, S.J.I.: Dissimilarity measures for clustering space mission architectures. In: Proceedings of the 21th ACM/IEEE International Conference on Model Driven Engineering Languages and Systems, pp. 392–402. MODELS 2018, ACM, New York, USA (2018). https://doi.org/10.1145/3239372.3239390
14. Kwiatkowska, M., Norman, G., Parker, D.: PRISM 4.0: verification of probabilistic real-time systems. In: Gopalakrishnan, G., Qadeer, S. (eds.) CAV 2011. LNCS, vol. 6806, pp. 585–591. Springer, Heidelberg (2011). https://doi.org/10.1007/978-3-642-22110-1_47
15. Martens, A., Koziolek, H., Becker, S., Reussner, R.: Automatically improve software architecture models for performance, reliability, and cost using evolutionary algorithms. In: Proceedings of the 1st Joint WOSP/SIPEW International Conference on Performance Engineering, pp. 105–116. ACM, New York, USA (2010). https://doi.org/10.1145/1712605.1712624
16. Mashinchi, J., Cámara, J.: *Voyager*: software architecture trade-off explorer. In: Muccini, H. (ed.) ECSA 2020. CCIS, vol. 1269, pp. 55–67. Springer, Cham (2020). https://doi.org/10.1007/978-3-030-59155-7_5
17. Procter, S., Wrage, L.: Guided architecture trade space exploration: fusing model based engineering amp; design by shopping. In: 2019 ACM/IEEE 22nd International Conference on Model Driven Engineering, Languages and Systems (MODELS), pp. 117–127 (2019)
18. Sanchez, C.C., Capilla, R., Staron, M.: Estimating the complexity of architectural design decision networks. IEEE Access **8**, 168558–168575 (2020). https://doi.org/10.1109/ACCESS.2020.3023608
19. Savoia, A.: The Right It: Why So Many Ideas Fail and How to Make Sure Yours Succeed. Harper-Collins (2019)
20. Sukkerd, R., Simmons, R., Garlan, D.: Tradeoff-focused contrastive explanation for MDP planning. In: Proceedings of 29th IEEE International Conference on Robot & Human Interactive Communication. Virtual (September 2020)
21. Wohlrab, R., Cámara, J., Garlan, D., Schmerl, B.: Explaining quality attribute tradeoffs in automated planning for self-adaptive systems. J. Syst. Softw. **198**, 111538 (2023). https://doi.org/10.1016/j.jss.2022.111538
22. Xu, D., Tian, Y.: A comprehensive survey of clustering algorithms. Ann. Data Sci. **2**, 165–193 (2015)

# Tool Support for the Adaptation of Quality of Service Trade-Offs in Service- and Cloud-Based Dynamic Routing Architectures

Amirali Amiri[1,2(✉)] and Uwe Zdun[1]

[1] University of Vienna, Software Architecture Group, Vienna, Austria
Uwe.Zdun@univie.ac.at
[2] University of Vienna, Doctoral School Computer Science, Vienna, Austria
Amirali.Amiri@univie.ac.at

**Abstract.** Dynamic routing is an essential part of service- and cloud-based applications. Routing architectures are based on vastly different implementation concepts, such as API Gateways, Enterprise Service Buses, Message Brokers, or Service Proxies. However, their basic operation is that these technologies dynamically route or block incoming requests. This paper proposes a new approach that abstracts all these routing patterns using one adaptive architecture. We hypothesize that a self-adaptation of the dynamic routing is beneficial over any fixed architecture selections concerning reliability and performance trade-offs. Our approach dynamically self-adapts between more central or distributed routing to optimize system reliability and performance. This adaptation is calculated based on a multi-criteria optimization analysis. We evaluate our approach by analyzing our previously-measured data during an experiment of 1200 h of runtime. Our extensive systematic evaluation of 4356 cases confirms that our hypothesis holds and our approach is beneficial regarding reliability and performance. Even on average, where right and wrong architecture choices are analyzed together, our novel architecture offers 9.82% reliability and 47.86% performance gains.

**Keywords:** Self-Adaptive Systems · Dynamic Routing Architectures · Service- and Cloud-Based Applications · Reliability and Performance Trade-Offs · Prototypical Tool Support

## 1 Introduction

Dynamic routing is common in service- and cloud-based applications, for which different techniques are available. These techniques range from simple strategies, e.g., request routing based on load balancing, to more complex routing, such as

This work was supported by FWF (Austrian Science Fund), projects IAC$^2$: I 4731-N, API-ACE: I 4268.

checking for compliance with regulations. Assume a company has to comply with a regulation that the data of European customers have to be stored and processed on European servers based on the General Data Protection Regulation[1]. In such a case, Dynamic Routers [17] can update the data-flow paths at runtime to ensure compliant data handling. Multiple dynamic-routing architectural patterns are provided for service- and cloud-based environments. These patterns include centralized routing, e.g., using an API Gateway [27] or an Enterprise Service Bus [10], and distributed routing using multiple Dynamic Routers [17] or Sidecars [20,27] to make local routing decisions.

The dynamic-routing architectures are based on vastly different implementations. However, they all route or block requests essentially. There is a possibility to change these patterns, e.g., from centralized to distributed routing, by adjusting the number of routers in a service- and cloud-based system. To do so, we should monitor the quality-of-service measures and make architectural decisions. So far, the trade-offs of reliability and performance measures in cloud-based dynamic routing have not been specifically and extensively studied. Reliability and performance in relation are essential for designing routing architectures. This factor must be considered because changing the routing schema to improve performance, e.g., by adding more routers for parallel processing of requests, may lead to a decrease in system reliability as more points of a crash are introduced to a system (empirically validated in [3]).

Our study is motivated by example scenarios, such as assuming a sudden reliability decrease is observed in a software system by adding services to the system for the parallel processing of requests (increasing the performance). In such a situation, time is important to reconfigure the system to meet the quality criteria required for the application. An automatic adaptation can yield benefits not only in time and effort overheads for the management of the system but also in reliability and performance trade-offs. Thus, we study the research questions:

**RQ1:** *Can we find an optimal configuration of routers that automatically adapts the reliability and performance trade-offs in dynamic routing architectures based on monitored system data at runtime?*

**RQ2:** *What is the architecture of a supporting tool that analyses the system at runtime and facilitates the reconfiguration of a dynamic routing application using the optimal configuration solution?*

**RQ3:** *How do the reliability and performance predictions of the chosen optimal solution compare with the case where one architecture runs statically?*

---

[1] https://gdpr.eu.

The contributions of this paper are three-fold. Firstly, we propose an adaptive-routing architecture that automatically adjusts the quality-of-service trade-offs. Secondly, we introduce an analytical model of performance that is generalizable to dynamic-routing applications and analyze the trade-offs of reliability and performance. Finally, we provide a prototypical tool that generates deployment artifacts for reconfiguring a dynamic-routing application. Additionally, our tool provides a visualization environment for users to study different configurations without generating additional artifacts.

The structure of the paper is as follows: Sect. 2 presents the overview of our approach. Section 3 explains the proposed architecture in detail, presenting our performance model and the trade-off analysis. Section 4 provides the tool that supports our architectural concepts. Section 5 presents the evaluation of the presented approach, and Sect. 6 discusses the threats to the validity of our research. We study the related work in Sect. 7 and conclude in Sect. 8.

## 2      Approach Overview

The proposed architecture in this paper is based on Monitor, Analyze, Plan, Execute, Knowledge (MAPE-K) loops [4,5,19]. Our adaptive architecture automatically changes between different dynamic-routing patterns by reconfiguring service- and cloud-based applications according to an optimization analysis [2]. We define a *router* as an abstraction for any controller component that makes routing decisions, e.g., an API Gateway [27], an Enterprise Service Bus [10], or Sidecars [20,27]. Our approach changes the number of routers, i.e., changes between different configurations moving from a centralized approach with one router to a distributed system with more routers (or vice versa) to adapt based on the need of an application.

**Metamodel.** Figure 1 presents the metamodel of our architecture. A *Model* describes multiple elements. *Host* is any execution environment, either physical or virtual. Each *Component* is deployed on (up to) one *Host* at each point in time. *Request* models the request flow, linking a source and a destination component. There are several different component types. *Clients* send *Client Requests* to *API Gateways*. The gateways send *Internal Requests* to *Routers* and *Services*.

*Configurator Components* perform the reconfiguration, and *Reconfigurable Components* are the adaptation targets of our architecture. *Monitor* observes reconfigurable components and the requests that pass the gateways. *Manager* manages the control flow of the reconfiguration by calling *Infrastructure as Code (IaC)* to update the infrastructure, or *Scheduler* to reschedule the containers. *Visualizer* provides visualizations of the architectural configurations.

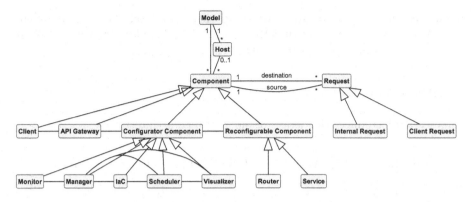

**Fig. 1.** Metamodel of the Adaptive Architecture

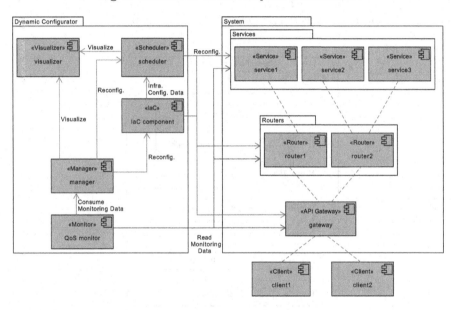

**Fig. 2.** Component Diagram of an Example Configuration (dashed lines represent the data flow and solid lines the reconfiguration control flow.)

**Example of a Routing Configuration.** Figure 2 presents a component diagram of a sample configuration, in which dashed lines represent the data flow and solid lines the reconfiguration control flow of an application. As shown, clients access the system via a gateway that publishes monitoring data to the Quality-of-Service (QoS) monitor component. The configuration manager observes the monitoring data and triggers a reconfiguration. Moreover, the manager can communicate with the visualizer component to visualize the current architecture configuration. The manager calls the IaC component if infrastructure changes are needed. IaC reconfigures the infrastructure and triggers the scheduler to reschedule the containers. Alternatively, if there is no need for infrastructure reconfiguration, the manager directly triggers the scheduler. After a reconfiguration, the scheduler can call the visualizer.

# 3   Approach Details

This section introduces the details of our proposed architecture.

## 3.1   Reconfiguration Activities of the Dynamic Configurator

Figure 3 shows the reconfiguration activities of the dynamic configurator. The QoS monitor reads monitoring data and checks for reconfiguration, e.g., when degradation of reliability and performance metrics are observed. Moreover, the reconfiguration can be triggered periodically or manually by an architect. When a

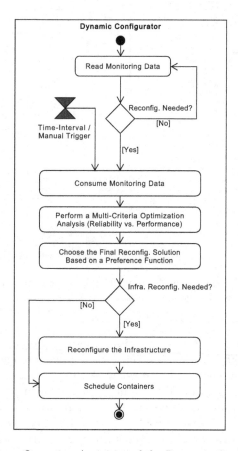

**Fig. 3.** Reconfiguration Activities of the Dynamic Configurator

reconfiguration is triggered, the reconfiguration manager consumes the monitoring data, performs a multi-criteria optimization analysis [2], and chooses a final reconfiguration solution. Either the IaC component is triggered to reconfigure the infrastructure or the scheduler reschedules the containers. Our architecture is based on MAPE-K loops [4,5,19]. The QoS monitor implements the *monitor* and *analyze* stages, the manager develops the *plan* step, and the IaC component and the scheduler realize the *execute* step. We use our models as *knowledge*.

### 3.2 Analytical Models

**Reliability Model** Based on Bernoulli processes [31], request loss during router and service crashes can be modeled as follows [3]:

$$R = \frac{\lfloor \frac{T}{CI} \rfloor \cdot cf \cdot \sum_{c \in Com} CP_c \cdot d_c}{T} \tag{1}$$

In this formula, request loss is defined as the number of client requests not processed due to a failure, such as a component crash. Equation 1 gives the request loss per second as a metric of reliability by calculating the expected value of the number of crashes. Having this information, we sum all the requests received by a system during the downtime of a component and divide them by the observed system time $T$. We model the crash interval as $CI$ that is the interval during which we check for a crash of a component. To clarify, $CI$ is the time between two consecutive health checks when the heartbeat pattern [18] or the health check API pattern [26] are used. $cf$ is the incoming call frequency based on requests per second (r/s). $Com$ is the set of components, i.e., routers and services. $CP_c$ is the crash probability of each component, and $d_c$ is the average downtime of a component after it crashes.

**Performance Model.** We model the average processing time of requests per router as a performance metric. This metric is important as it allows us to study the quality of service factors, such as the efficiency of architecture configurations. The total number of client requests, i.e., *Req*, is the call frequency $cf$ multiplied by the observed time $T$:

$$Req = cf \cdot T \tag{2}$$

The number of processed requests is the total number of client requests minus the request loss. Let $P$ be performance. The average processing time of requests per router is given as follows:

$$P = \frac{T}{n_{rout}(Req - R)} \tag{3}$$

Using Eqs. 1 to 3, the average processing time is the following:

$$P = \frac{T}{n_{rout} \cdot cf \left(T - \lfloor \frac{T}{CI} \rfloor \cdot \sum_{c \in Com} CP_c \cdot d_c\right)} \tag{4}$$

**Model Validations.** To empirically validate our models, we ran an experiment of 200 runs with a total of 1200 h of runtime (excluding setup time) [3]. We had a private cloud setting with three physical nodes and installed virtual machines with eight cores and 60 GB of system memory. Each router or service was containerized in a Docker[2] container. Moreover, to ensure generalizability, we duplicated our experiment on Google Cloud Platform[3] and empirically validated our results (see below for experiment cases). We compared our analytical reliability and performance model with our empirical results using the mean absolute percentage error [31]. With more experiment runs, we observed an ever-decreasing error, converging at 7.1%. Our analytical performance model yielded a low error rate of 0.5%, indicating the very high accuracy of our model. We also evaluated our models using the mean absolute error, the mean square error, and the root mean square error, which confirmed our results.

**Parameterization of Model to Experiment Values.** In our experiment, we defined $n_{serv}$ and $n_{rout}$ as the number of services and routers to study their effects. We had three levels for the number of services, i.e., $n_{serv} \in \{\ 3, 5, 10\ \}$. Based on our experience and a survey of existing cloud applications in the literature and industry, the number of cloud services directly dependent on each other in a call sequence is usually rather low. Moreover, we had four levels for incoming call frequencies, i.e., $cf(r/s) \in \{\ 10, 25, 50, 100\ \}$. The call frequency of $cf = 100\,r/s$, or even lower numbers, is chosen in many studies (see, e.g., [13,30]). Therefore, we chose different portions between 10 to 100 $r/s$. We studied three architecture configurations, i.e., centralized routing ($n_{rout} = 1$), completely distributed routing with one router per each service ($n_{rout} = n_{serv}$), and a middle ground with three routers ($n_{rout} = 3$). Therefore, we have $n_{rout} \in \{\ 1, 3, n_{serv}\ \}$. Overall, we evaluated our model in 36 experiment cases.

We also defined some constants as follows: We observed the system for $T = 600\ s$ in each experiment case, had a crash interval of $CI = 15\ s$, and studied uniform crash probabilities and downtimes for all components as $CP_c = 0.5\%$ and $d_c = 3\ s$, respectively. These values are system-specific and can be updated based on different infrastructures. Considering these experiment cases, we can parameterize our general reliability model in $r/s$ (presented by Eq. 1) and performance model in $ms$ (given by Eq. 4) as follows:

$$R = cf \cdot 0.001(n_{serv} + n_{rout}) \tag{5}$$

$$P = \frac{1000}{n_{rout} \cdot cf(1 - 0.001(n_{serv} + n_{rout}))} \tag{6}$$

---

[2] https://www.docker.com.
[3] https://cloud.google.com/.

**Multi-criteria Optimization (MCO) Analysis.** In our approach, the reconfiguration between the architecture configurations is performed automatically based on an MCO analysis [2]. Consider the following optimization problem: An application using the proposed architecture has $n_{serv}$ services and is under stress for a period of time with the call frequency of $cf$. To optimize reliability and performance, the system can change between different architecture configurations dynamically by adjusting $n_{rout}$, ranging from a centralized routing ($n_{rout} = 1$) and up to the extreme of one router per service ($n_{rout} = n_{serv}$).

We use the notations $R_{n_{rout}}$ and $P_{n_{rout}}$ to specify the reliability and performance of an architecture configuration by its number of routers. For instance, only configuring one router $R_1$ indicates the reliability model of centralized routing, and configuring $n_{serv}$ routers (i.e., $R_1, \ldots, R_{n_{serv}}$) indicates completely distributed routing. Let $R_{th}$ and $P_{th}$ be the reliability and performance thresholds. The MCO question is: Given a $cf$ and $n_{serv}$, what is the optimal number of routers that minimizes request loss and average processing time for requests per router without the predicted values violating the respective thresholds?

$$Minimize$$
$$R_{n_{rout}} \tag{7}$$
$$P_{n_{rout}} \tag{8}$$

---

**Algorithm 1:** Reconfiguration Algorithm

---

**Input**: $R_{th}$, $P_{th}$, performanceWeight

$R_{n_{rout}}, P_{n_{rout}}, cf, n_{serv} \leftarrow$ **readMonitoringData()**

routersRange $\leftarrow$ **MCO**$(cf, n_{serv}, R_{n_{rout}}, P_{n_{rout}}, R_{th}, P_{th})$

reconfigSolution $\leftarrow$ **preferenceFunction**(routersRange, performanceWeight)

**reconfigureRouters**(reconfigSolution)

**function** preferenceFunction(range, PW)
**begin**

    length $\leftarrow$ max(range) - min(range) +1

    floor $\leftarrow$ $\lfloor$ PW * length $\rfloor$

    **if** *floor == max(range)* **then**

        **return** max(range)

    **else if** *floor == 0* **then**

        **return** min(range)

    **else**

        **return** floor + min(range) -1

    **end**

**end**

---

$$Subject\ to$$
$$R_{n_{rout}} \leq R_{th} \tag{9}$$
$$P_{n_{rout}} \leq P_{th} \tag{10}$$
$$1 \leq n_{rout} \leq n_{serv} \tag{11}$$

Typically, there is no single answer to an MCO problem. Using the above MCO analysis, we find a range of $n_{rout}$ configurations that all meet the constraints. One end of this range optimizes reliability and the other performance. We need a preference function so our approach can automatically select a final $n_{rout}$ value.

**Preference Function.** An architect defines an importance vector that gives weights to reliability and performance. The preference function instructs the proposed architecture to choose a final $n_{rout}$ value in the range found by the MCO analysis based on this importance vector. Let us consider an example: When performance is of the highest importance to an application, an architect gives the highest weight, i.e., 1.0, to performance and the lowest weight, i.e., 0.0, to reliability. Thus, the preference function chooses the highest value on the $n_{rout}$ range to choose more distributed routing. This reconfiguration results in processing client requests in parallel, giving a higher performance.

**Automatic Reconfiguration.** As shown in Fig. 2, the QoS monitor reads the monitoring data from the API Gateway and feeds this information to the reconfiguration manager. This manager reconfigures the infrastructure or reschedules the containers. Algorithm 1 presents our reconfiguration algorithm. The QoS monitor triggers the reconfiguration algorithm, e.g., whenever reliability or performance metrics degrade. Time intervals, manual triggering or change in the incoming load can also be used to trigger the algorithm if more appropriate than metrics degradation. Note that `reconfigureRouters(reconfigSolution)` performs the final reconfiguration based on the chosen solution by either reconfiguring the infrastructure using the IaC component or rescheduling the containers using the container scheduler. Our supporting tool provides a simple implementation.

## 4   Tool Overview

We developed a prototypical tool to demonstrate our adaptive architecture, which is available in our online artifact[4]. Figure 4 shows the tool architecture. We provide two modes, i.e., deployment and visualization. In the case of deployment, our tool generates artifacts in the form of Bash[5] scripts and configuration files, e.g., infrastructure configuration data to be used by an IaC tool. These

---

[4] The online artifact of our study can be anonymously downloaded from https://zenodo.org/record/7944823.

[5] https://www.gnu.org/software/bash/.

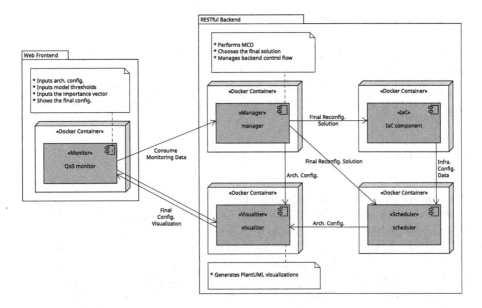

**Fig. 4.** Tool Architecture Diagram

scripts can schedule containers using the Docker technology[6]. We also provide a visualization environment that only generates diagrams using PlantUML[7].

The frontend of our application provides the functionalities of the QoS monitor, i.e., to specify architecture configurations as well as model elements such as reliability and performance thresholds. This information is sent to the manager component in the backend that finds the final reconfiguration solution (see Algorithm 1). The manager sends this solution to the IaC component and the scheduler to generate deployment artifacts. A visualization is then created in the backend and shown in the frontend. The frontend is implemented in React[8] and the backend is developed in Node.js[9] as a RESTful application.

The tool flow of our application is as follows: An architect gives the architecture configuration by entering the number of services and routers. Users also specify model thresholds, call frequency of client requests, and performance weight. A reconfiguration is triggered when metrics degradation is observed, according to timers or manually. When reconfiguration is triggered, the backend performs an MCO analysis and chooses a final reconfiguration solution. If the deployment mode is chosen, deployment artifacts will be generated. The reconfiguration visualization is then created and shown.

---

[6] https://www.docker.com/.

[7] https://plantuml.com/.

[8] https://reactjs.org/.

[9] https://nodejs.org/.

# 5    Evaluation

In this section, we evaluate our architecture by comparing the reliability and performance predictions to the empirical results of our experiment (see Sect. 3.2). The proposed architecture is neither specific to our infrastructure nor our cases. We use our empirical data set in our online artifact (see footnote 4) to evaluate our approach.

## 5.1    Evaluation Cases

We systematically evaluate our proposed architecture through various thresholds and importance weights for reliability and performance. We compare our model predictions with our 36 experiment cases (see Sect. 3.2 for the rationale behind choosing them). That is, we compare with three fixed architecture configurations, i.e., $n_{rout} \in \{ 1, 3, n_{serv} \}$ and three levels of services, i.e., $n_{serv} \in \{ 3, 5, 10 \}$. We consider four levels of call frequencies, i.e., $cf \in \{ 10, 25, 50, 100 \}$ $r/s$. Regarding reliability and performance thresholds, we start with very tight reliability and very loose performance thresholds so that only centralized routing is acceptable. We increase the reliability and decrease the performance thresholds by 10% in each step so that distributed routing becomes applicable.

To find the starting points, we consider the worst-case scenario of our empirical data. Equation (1) informs that a higher $n_{serv}$ results in a higher expected request loss. In our experiment, the highest number of services is ten. With $n_{serv} = 10$, the worst-case reliability for centralized routing and completely distributed routing ($n_{rout} = 10$) is 1.1 and 2.0 $r/s$, respectively. Regarding performance, for the case of $n_{serv} = 10$, we investigate our predictions to find a range where a reconfiguration is possible. The lowest possible performance prediction is 33.7 $ms$, and the highest is 101.1 $ms$. We adjust these values slightly and take our boundary thresholds as follows. We analyze step-by-step by increasing the reliability threshold and decreasing the performance threshold by 10% as before.

$$1.1 \leq R_{th} \leq 2.0 \ r/s \tag{12}$$

$$35 \leq P_{th} \leq 100 \ ms \tag{13}$$

We start with an importance weight of 1.0 for reliability and 0.0 for performance. We decrease the reliability importance and increase the performance weight by 10% in each iteration. Overall we evaluate 4356 systematic evaluation cases: 36 experiment cases, 11 importance weight levels, and 11 thresholds. To support reproducibility, the evaluation script and the evaluation log detailing information about each case are provided in the online artifact of our study (see footnote 4).

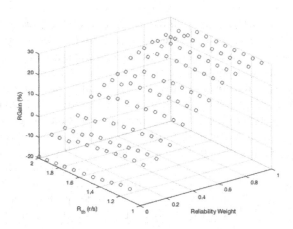

(a) Reliability Gain

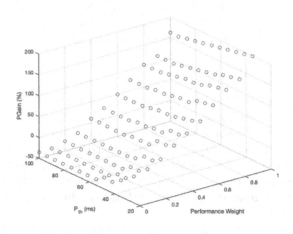

(b) Performance Gain

**Fig. 5.** Reliability and Performance Gains of our Adaptive Architecture Compared to Fixed Architecture Configurations ( $n_{rout} \in \{ 1, 3, n_{serv} \}$ )

## 5.2   Results Analysis

We define reliability gain, i.e., $RGain$, and performance gain, i.e., $PGain$, as the average percentage differences of our predictions compared to those of fixed architectures, i.e., $n_{rout} \in \{ 1, 3, n_{serv} \}$. These formulas are based on the Mean Absolute Percentage Error (MAPE), widely used in the cloud QoS research [31].

$$RGain = \frac{100\%}{n} \cdot \sum_{c \in Cases} \frac{R_c - R_{n_{rout}}}{R_{n_{rout}}} \qquad (14)$$

$$PGain = \frac{100\%}{n} \cdot \sum_{c \in Cases} \frac{P_c - P_{n_{rout}}}{P_{n_{rout}}} \qquad (15)$$

Remember $R_{n_{rout}}$ and $P_{n_{rout}}$ are reliability and performance predictions (see the MCO analysis in Sect. 3.2). *Cases* are our experiment cases, so $n = 36$.

Figure 5 shows the reliability and performance gains compared to the predictions of fixed architecture configurations, i.e., without adaptations. Our adaptive architecture provides improvements in both reliability and performance gains. As more importance is given to the reliability of a system, i.e., reliability weight increases, our architecture reconfigures the routers so that the gain in reliability rises, as shown by Fig. 5a. Regarding performance, the same trend can be seen in Fig. 5b. A higher performance weight results in a higher performance gain. On average, when cases with correct and incorrect architectural choices are analyzed together, our adaptive architecture provides 9.82% and 47.86% reliability and performance gains, respectively. A higher gain for performance compared to reliability is expected. To clarify, studying Eqs. 5 and 6 informs that changing the number of routers has a higher effect on the performance than a system's reliability. We define performance as the average processing time of requests per router. Having a higher number of routers to process the requests in parallel divides the average processing time by more routers. However, only the sum of the number of services and routers affects the reliability.

## 6    Threats to Validity

Regarding *construct validity*, we used request loss and the average processing time of requests per router as reliability and performance metrics, respectively. While this is a common approach in service- and cloud-based research (see Sect. 7), the threat remains that other metrics might model these quality attributes better, e.g., a cascade of calls beyond a single call sequence for reliability [22], or data transfer rates of messages which are $m$ byte-long for performance [21]. More research, probably with real-world systems, is required for this threat to be excluded.

Regarding *Internal validity*, our adaptive architecture abstracts the controlling logic component in dynamic routing under a router concept to allow interoperability between different implementation technologies. In a real-world system, changing between these technologies is not always an easy task, but it is not impossible either. In this paper, we provided a scientific proof-of-concept based on an experiment with the prototypical implementation of these technologies. The threat remains that changing between these technologies in a real-world application might have other impacts on reliability and performance, e.g., network latency increasing processing time.

Regarding *External validity*, we designed our novel architecture with generality in mind. However, the threat remains that evaluating our approach based on another infrastructure may lead to different results. To mitigate this thread, we systematically evaluated the proposed architecture with 4356 evaluation cases (see Sect. 5 for details). Moreover, the results might not be generalizable beyond the given experiment cases of 10–100 requests per second and call sequences of length 3–10. As this covers a wide variety of loads and call sequences in cloud-based applications, the impact of this threat should be limited.

Regarding *Conclusion validity*, as the statistical method to evaluate the accuracy of our model's predictions, we defined reliability and performance gains based on the Mean Absolute Percentage Error (MAPE) metric [31] as it is widely used and offers good interpretability in our context.

## 7 Related Work

Architecture-based approaches [12,31] employ probabilistic analytical models such as discrete-time Markov chains (DTMCs) [11] and Queueing Networks (QNs) [29]. Some papers use high-level architectural models such as profile-extended UML [23] or Palladio [7,8] models that are simulated or transformed into analytical models. These works are based on the observation that a system's reliability and performance depend on those of each component, along with the interplay between them. Pitakrat et al. [24] use architectural knowledge to predict how a failure propagates to other components based on Bayesian networks.

Other studies introduce service- and cloud-specific reliability models. For instance, Wang et al. [32] propose a DTMC model for analyzing system reliability based on constituent services. Grassi and Patella [15] propose an approach for reliability prediction that considers the decentralized and autonomous nature of services. Zheng and Lyu [34] propose an approach that employs past failure data to predict a service's reliability. However, none of these approaches focuses on major routing architectural patterns in service- and cloud-based architectures; they are rather based on a very generic model concerning the notion of service. Moreover, numerous approaches have been proposed that study architecture-based performance prediction. Spitznagel and Garlan [29] present a general architecture-based model for performance analysis based on QNs.

Architecture-based MCO [2] builds on top of these prediction approaches and the application of architectural tactics to search for optimal architectural candidates. Example MCO approaches supporting reliability and performance is ArcheOpterix [1], PerOpteryx [9], and SQuAT [25]. Sharma and Trivedi [28] present an architecture-based unified hierarchical model for software reliability, performance, security, and cache behavior prediction. This is one of the few studies that consider performance and reliability. Like our study, those works focus on supporting architectural design or decision-making. In contrast to our work, they do not focus on specific kinds of architecture or architectural patterns. Our approach focuses on service- and cloud-based dynamic routing.

Finally, our approach is related to self-adaptive systems, which typically use MAPE-K loops [4,5,19] and similar approaches to realize adaptations. Our approach is based on the MAPE-K loop structure and extends such approaches with support specific to the cloud- and service-based dynamic routing architectures. Similarly, auto-scalers for the cloud [6,33], which promise stable QoS and cost minimization when facing changing workload intensity, and in general research on cloud elasticity [14,16] are related to our work. Our approach is similar to auto-scaling but performs the adaptation only for the dynamic routers. Major contributions of our approach are that, in contrast to the existing related work, it considers reliability and performance trade-offs together and focuses on specific architectural patterns for dynamic routing in service- and cloud-based architectures. By focusing on runtime adaptations, we defined a targeted model and a reconfiguration algorithm, which is hard to consider in the generic case.

# 8   Conclusions

In this paper, we set out to answer whether we can find an optimal configuration of routers that automatically adapts the reliability and performance trade-offs in dynamic routing architectures based on monitored system data at runtime (**RQ1**), what the architecture of a supporting tool that analyses the system at runtime and facilitates the reconfiguration of a dynamic routing application using the optimal configuration solution is (**RQ2**), and how the reliability and performance predictions of the chosen optimal solution compare with the case where one architecture runs statically (**RQ3**).

For **RQ1**, we proposed a routing architecture that dynamically self-adapts between different routing patterns based on the need of an application. For **RQ2**, we provided a prototypical tool that analyzes different inputs and creates deployment artifacts. This tool also provides visualizations to study different architecture configurations. For **RQ3**, we systematically evaluated our approach using 4356 evaluation cases based on the empirical data of our extensive experiment of 1200 h of runtime (see Sect. 5). The results confirms that the proposed architecture can adapt the routing pattern in a running system to optimize reliability and performance. Even on average, where cases with the right and the wrong architecture choices are analyzed together, our approach offers a 9.82% reliability gain and a 47.86% performance gain. For our future work, we plan to apply our novel architecture to real-world applications.

# References

1. Aleti, A., Björnander, S., Grunske, L., Meedeniya, I.: ArcheOpterix: an extendable tool for architecture optimization of AADL models. In: ICSE 2009 Workshop on Model-Based Methodologies for Pervasive and Embedded Software, MOMPES 2009, pp. 61–71. IEEE (2009)
2. Aleti, A., Buhnova, B., Grunske, L., Koziolek, A., Meedeniya, I.: Software architecture optimization methods: a systematic literature review. IEEE Trans. Software Eng. **39**(5), 658–683 (2013)
3. Amiri, A., Zdun, U., van Hoorn, A.: Modeling and empirical validation of reliability and performance trade-offs of dynamic routing in service- and cloud-based architectures. In: IEEE Transactions on Services Computing (TSC) (2021)
4. Arcaini, P., Riccobene, E., Scandurra, P.: Modeling and analyzing MAPE-K feedback loops for self-adaptation. In IEEE/ACM 10th International Symposium on Software Engineering for Adaptive and Self-Managing Systems, pp. 13–23 (2015)
5. Arcaini, P., Riccobene, E., Scandurra, P.: Formal design and verification of self-adaptive systems with decentralized control. ACM Trans. Auton. Adapt. Syst. (TAAS) **11**(4), 1–35 (2017)

6. Bauer, A., Herbst, N., Spinner, S., Ali-Eldin, A., Kounev, S.: Chameleon: a hybrid, proactive auto-scaling mechanism on a level-playing field. IEEE Trans. Parallel Distrib. Syst. **30**(4), 800–813 (2018)
7. Becker, S., Koziolek, H., Reussner, R.: Model-based performance prediction with the palladio component model. In: Proceedings of the 6th International Workshop on Software and Performance, WOSP 2007, pp. 54–65. ACM (2007)
8. Brosch, F., Koziolek, H., Buhnova, B., Reussner, R.: Architecture-based reliability prediction with the palladio component model. IEEE Trans. Softw. Eng. **38**(6), 1319–1339 (2011)
9. Busch, A., Fuchss, D., Koziolek, A.: PerOpteryx: automated improvement of software architectures. In: IEEE International Conference on Software Architecture ICSA Companion 2019, pp. 162–165. IEEE (2019)
10. Chappell, D.A.: Enterprise Service Bus. O'Reilly, Sebastopol (2004)
11. Cheung, R.C.: A user-oriented software reliability model. IEEE Trans. Softw. Eng. **SE-6**(2), 118–125 (1980)
12. Cortellessa, V., Di Marco, A., Inverardi, P.: Model-based software performance analysis, Springer (2011). https://doi.org/10.1007/978-3-642-13621-4
13. Dean, D.J., Nguyen, H., Wang, P., Gu, X.: PerfCompass: toward runtime performance anomaly fault localization for infrastructure-as-a-service clouds. In: 6th USENIX Workshop on Hot Topics in Cloud Computing (HotCloud 14) (2014)
14. Galante, G., de Bona, L.C.E.: A survey on cloud computing elasticity. In: 2012 IEEE Fifth International Conference on Utility and Cloud Computing, pp. 263–270. IEEE (2012)
15. Grassi, V., Patella, S.: Reliability prediction for service-oriented computing environments. IEEE Internet Comput. **10**(3), 43–49 (2006)
16. Herbst, N.R., Kounev, S., Reussner, R.: Elasticity in cloud computing: what it is, and what it is not. In: 10th International Conference on Autonomic Computing (ICAC 13), pp. 23–27 (2013)
17. Hohpe, G., Woolf, B.: Enterprise Integration Patterns. Addison-Wesley, Boston (2003)
18. Homer, A., Sharp, J., Brader, L., Narumoto, M., Swanson, T.: Cloud Design Patterns. Microsoft Press (2014)
19. Iglesia, D.G.D.L., Weyns, D.: MAPE-K formal templates to rigorously design behaviors for self-adaptive systems. ACM Trans. Auton. Adapt. Syst. (TAAS) **10**(3), 1–31 (2015)
20. Jamshidi, P., Pahl, C., Mendonça, N.C., Lewis, J., Tilkov, S.: Microservices: the journey so far and challenges ahead. IEEE Softw. **35**(3), 24–35 (2018)
21. Kratzke, N.: About microservices, containers and their underestimated impact on network performance. arXiv preprint arXiv:1710.04049 (2017)
22. Nygard, M.: Release It!: Design and Deploy Production-Ready Software. Pragmatic Bookshelf, Raleigh (2007)
23. Petriu, D., Shousha, C., Jalnapurkar, A.: Architecture-based performance analysis applied to a telecommunication system. IEEE Trans. Softw. Eng. **26**(11), 1049–1065 (2000)
24. Pitakrat, T., Okanović, D., van Hoorn, A., Grunske, L.: Hora: architecture-aware online failure prediction. J. Syst. Softw. **137**, 669–685 (2018)
25. Rago, A., Vidal, S.A., Diaz-Pace, J.A., Frank, S., van Hoorn, A.: Distributed quality-attribute optimization of software architectures. In: Proceedings of the 11th Brazilian Symposium on Software Components, Architectures and Reuse, SBCARS 2017, pp. 7:1–7:10. ACM (2017)

26. Raj, P., Raman, A., Subramanian, H.: Architectural Patterns: Uncover Essential Patterns in the Most Indispensable Realm. Packt Publishing, Birmingham (December 2017)
27. Richardson, C.: Microservice architecture patterns and best practices. https:// microservices.io/index.html (2019)
28. Sharma, V.S., Trivedi, K. S.: Architecture based analysis of performance, reliability and security of software systems. In: Proceedings of the 5th International Workshop on Software and Performance, WOSP 2005, pp. 217–227, New York, USA (2005). Association for Computing Machinery
29. Spitznagel, B., Garlan, D.: Architecture-based performance analysis. In: Proceedings of the 1998 Conference on Software Engineering and Knowledge Engineering. Carnegie Mellon University (June 1998)
30. Sukwong, O., Sangpetch, A., Kim, H.S.: SageShift: managing SLAs for highly consolidated cloud. In: 2012 Proceedings IEEE INFOCOM, pp. 208–216 (2012)
31. Trivedi, K.S., Bobbio, A.: Reliability and Availability Engineering: Modeling, Analysis, and Applications. Oxford University Press, Oxford (2017)
32. Wang, L., Bai, X., Zhou, L., Chen, Y.: A hierarchical reliability model of service-based software system. In: 2009 33rd Annual IEEE International Computer Software and Applications Conference. vol. 1, pp. 199–208, July 2009
33. Zhang, F., Tang, X., Li, X., Khan, S.U., Li, Z.: Quantifying cloud elasticity with container-based autoscaling. Future Gener. Comput. Syst. **98**, 672–681 (2019)
34. Zheng, Z., Lyu, M.R.: Collaborative reliability prediction of service-oriented systems. In: 2010 ACM/IEEE 32nd International Conference on Software Engineering. vol. 1, pp. 35–44, May 2010

# Architecture-Based Attack Path Analysis for Identifying Potential Security Incidents

Maximilian Walter[(✉)], Robert Heinrich, and Ralf Reussner

KASTEL – Institute of Information Security and Dependability, Karlsruhe Institute
of Technology (KIT), Karlsruhe, Germany
{maximilian.walter,robert.heinrich,ralf.reussner}@kit.edu

**Abstract.** Analyzing attacks and potential attack paths can help to identify and avoid potential security incidents. Manually estimating an attack path to a targeted software element can be complex since a software system consists of multiple vulnerable elements, such as components, hardware resources, or network elements. In addition, the elements are protected by access control. Software architecture describes the structural elements of the system, which may form elements of the attack path. However, estimating attack paths is complex since different attack paths can lead to a targeted element. Additionally, not all attack paths might be relevant since attack paths can have different properties based on the attacker's capabilities and knowledge. We developed an approach that enables architects to identify relevant attack paths based on the software architecture. We created a metamodel for filtering options and added support for describing attack paths in an architectural description language. Based on this metamodel, we developed an analysis that automatically estimates attack paths using the software architecture. This can help architects to identify relevant attack paths to a targeted component and increase the system's overall security. We evaluated our approach on five different scenarios. Our evaluation goals are to investigate our analysis's accuracy and scalability. The results suggest a high accuracy and good runtime behavior for smaller architectures.

**Keywords:** Attack Propagation · Software Architecture · Attack Path

## 1 Introduction

As a society, we digitize various aspects of our lives with new smart devices. This covers different sectors, such as the health sector with a wide variety of

This work was supported by the German Research Foundation (DFG) under project number 432576552 (FluidTrust), by funding from the topic Engineering Secure Systems of the Helmholtz Association (HGF), by KASTEL Security Research Labs, by "Kerninformatik am KIT (KiKIT)" funded by the Helmholtz Association (HGF), and by the German Federal Ministry of Education and Research (BMBF) grant number 16KISA086 (ANYMOS).

B. Tekinerdogan et al. (Eds.): ECSA 2023, LNCS 14212, pp. 37–53, 2023.
https://doi.org/10.1007/978-3-031-42592-9_3

eHealth services, the energy sector with smart meters, or production processes with Industry 4.0. Internet of Things (IoT) devices are the foundation for most of these sectors. These devices exchange data with a wide range of possible services, such as cloud services, thereby building a large and complex network of heterogeneous devices and services.

Often, these devices or services contain vulnerabilities. However, not only IoT devices are affected but also the backend of these systems, such as cloud services or typical company networks with outdated Windows versions [12]. These vulnerabilities can be chained in so-called *advanced persistent threats (APT)* and build complex attack paths and potentially enable attackers to reach critical components, such as payment components [26] or even turn off critical infrastructure, such as the power grid [9].

Analyzing these systems for attack paths is complicated since different devices often have different vulnerabilities. Moreover, these vulnerabilities may manifest in diverse areas of the system, including hardware resources, network resources, and various software components. Therefore, it is essential to model different areas of the system to estimate the potential impact of any vulnerabilities effectively. Software architecture can provide the means to model these different areas. An attack path is then a list of compromised architectural elements. Moreover, a software architecture model may facilitate system analysis, even in cases where a running system is unavailable. Therefore, it enables secure system design and management during development and periods of downtime, such as following an attack or maintenance. Notably, this concept aligns with the principles outlined in the new OWASP Top Ten element "Insecure Design" [18], highlighting that security threats are often embedded within the system design and, therefore, the software architecture. Furthermore, a modeled software architecture enables the creation of what-if scenarios to analyze and find the best solution by modeling and analyzing different scenarios. Existing attack propagation approaches, such as Bloodhound[1], mainly focus on one aspect, such as the Active Directory, or only use a network topology, which often does not contain information regarding software components or deployments. Finally, given the high number of vulnerable elements in many systems, it is not uncommon that there are many possible attack paths that attackers could exploit. In such cases, effective vulnerability management is necessary. One solution is to prioritize and select the most relevant attack paths for mitigation. Therefore, meaningful filter operations are necessary to identify relevant paths. Besides vulnerabilities, attackers may exploit access control policies to gain access to various architectural elements. Once an attacker has gained access to an element, they may use this element to launch further attacks on other elements. Therefore, it is crucial to consider vulnerabilities and access control to develop a comprehensive security analysis for identifying combined attack paths. These attack paths help then to identify potential security incidents, which are multiple unwanted *security events* that threaten the system [11].

---

[1] https://bloodhoundenterprise.io/.

In Walter et al. [33], we developed a metamodel and analysis to tackle some of these problems. However, we focused on the propagation of one attacker from one initial breach point in the software architecture. In contrast, this work focuses on creating multiple attack paths leading to one targeted element in the software architecture. This enables architects to identify potential security risks to critical components. For instance, a software architect could be interested in whether an attack path from an externally accessible component, such as a web service, to a confidential database exists. In addition, this approach estimates the used attacks based on the modeled vulnerabilities and the filtering options. It does not require the concrete modeling of the attacker's capabilities and knowledge as the previous approach [33]. Our contributions to this paper are: **C1** We extended an architectural vulnerability metamodel by adding support for modeling multiple attack paths leading to a target element and support for filtering options. This enables architects to select attack paths based on the relevant properties, such as the complexity of the used attacks. **C2** Based on the new extended metamodel, we developed an attack path generation. It generates multiple attack paths to a targeted element and can consider filter options. These filters can help software architects to identify relevant attack paths based on the paths' properties. Additionally, the filters fasten the calculation since they reduce the problem size. In contrast to existing approaches (see Sect. 5), we consider fine-grained access control policies and vulnerabilities based on the software architecture for attack paths leading to one targeted element. The derived attack paths can help software architects to harden the system.

We evaluated our approach on five scenarios based on real-world breaches and research cases. The investigated properties are accuracy and scalability. The results indicate a high accuracy and acceptable overall runtime for smaller systems. The paper is structured as follows. We describe our metamodel and the attack path generation in Sect. 2 and Sect. 3. The evaluation follows in Sect. 4. Afterward, we discuss related work in Sect. 5. Finally, Sect. 6 concludes the paper.

## 2    Modeling Attack Paths and Path Selection

In Walter et al. [33], we provide a metamodel extension for the Palladio Component Model (PCM) [21] to model access control properties and vulnerabilities. PCM is an architecture description language (ADL) which supports the component-based modeling and analysis for different quality properties, such as confidentiality or performance [21,25]. We also used the approach to estimate the criticality of the accessed data [34] and analyze different usage and misuse scenarios [32]. The main idea of their approach is to reuse the existing vulnerability classifications Common Weakness Enumeration (CWE) [7], Common Vulnerabilities and Exposure (CVE) [5] and Common Vulnerability Scoring System (CVSS) [6] to describe the vulnerabilities during an attack propagation. These are commonly used to classify vulnerabilities and their attributes can be found in public databases, such as the US National Vulnerability Database (NVD). We also developed an approach to derive the architecture and vulnerabilities automatically [15].

We will explain our approach based on the running example from Walter et al. [33]. Figure 1 illustrates the components, devices, and network entities. The example is settled in an Industry 4.0 setting. It contains a technician who can maintain a machine by accessing a terminal. The machine stores its data on an external storage. This scenario is modeled by three components (`Terminal`, `Machine`, `ProductionDataStorage`). Each of these components is deployed on its own hardware device. A local network connects each hardware device. Additionally, the storage device contains one additional component, which contains confidential data about the production process. For simplicity reasons, we reduced the number of access control policies to two. The `StorageServer` and `TerminalServer` are only accessible by a user with the role `Admin`. Additionally, in our case, we have one vulnerability for the `TerminalServer`. In this scenario, the goal or the target of the attacker is to find potential attack paths, leading to the `ProductStorage` since this component contains confidential data.

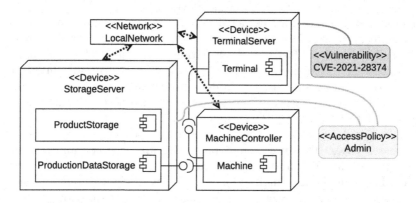

**Fig. 1.** Running Example with a vulnerable TerminalServer and Access Control policies based on Walter et al. [33]

Figure 2 illustrates the extended vulnerability metamodel. The gray elements are the original metamodel elements [33], the black ones are PCM elements, and the white elements are the new elements. For simplicity reasons, we left out non-relevant elements for this approach. The complete metamodel can be found in our dataset [35]. The main element to integrate vulnerabilities in PCM is the `Vulnerability` class. It annotates `LinkingResources` for network resources, `ResourceContainers` for hardware devices and `AssemblyContexts` for instantiated components with vulnerability information. This element is implemented by two concrete elements the `CWEVulnerability` and the `CVEVulnerability`. The `CWEVulnerability` describes more general vulnerabilities based on a CWE class, and the `CVEVulnerability` describes a concrete vulnerability. The relationship between CVE and CWE is not represented in the model excerpt but is included in the metamodel. The `Vulnerability` has attributes, such as the attack vector (the location from which a vulnerability is exploitable) or the gained attributes through the exploitation.

While our previous metamodel can already model vulnerabilities and access control properties, the output is restricted to one attack propagation graph for a list of concrete attacks. It cannot represent different attack paths leading to a target or attacks limited by their properties. Hence, we need to add support for different attack paths. Additionally, for identifying the relevant attack paths, we need to add support for finding the relevant attack paths.

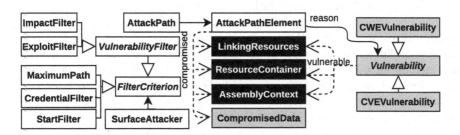

**Fig. 2.** Excerpt of the extended metamodel with filters (white elements are new elements, gray ones are taken from Walter et al. [33], and black ones are taken from PCM)

The starting point for an attack path is the attack's initial start point, and the targeted element is the element an attack wants to infiltrate. In our running example (Fig. 1), the targeted element is the `ProductStorage`. It is, therefore, the element to which all the attack paths should lead. The start point of the list is connected by its elements to the targeted element. The connection is realized by vulnerabilities or exploited credentials. The attack path is represented with the `AttackPath` element. The actual path elements are modeled as a list of `AttackPathElements`. Each `AttackPathElement` describes a compromised architectural element and stores the reason for the compromisation.

With the extension to the metamodel so far, our analysis can calculate attack paths leading to one targeted element based on the modeled software architecture. However, even in our small example, this could lead to many irrelevant attack paths. For instance, for our running example, we get an attack path to the targeted element for every architectural element, resulting in seven paths. In larger systems, this might be even more. Many attack paths may be irrelevant because they demand initial knowledge about specific credentials. For instance, in our running example, there is an attack path from the `MachineController` to the `ProductStorage` over the `StorageServer`. However, this path would require the knowledge of the `Admin` credentials. Usually, a system architect might assume that the admin's credentials might be secure. Therefore, the attack path can sometimes be considered irrelevant.

The selection of relevant paths is realized by filtering. We currently support five filter options. The common abstract element to model attack path filters is the `FilterCriterion`. The filters are then realized as child elements, allowing an easy metamodel extension for new filters. The first filter is the `MaximumPath` filter, and it restricts the path length of the found attack paths. This property can also be found in related approaches, such as [20]. This is beneficial if software architects are only interested in short attack paths because they may be simpler than longer paths. As described, in some cases, it is beneficial to restrict the initial usage of credentials. This is represented by the `CredentialFilter`. Suppose the software architect is only interested in an attack path from certain elements, such as in our running the externally accessible `Terminal`, to the target element. They can use the `StartElement` filter in that case.

The last two filters (`ImpactFilter`, `ExploitFilter`) use properties of the vulnerability for filtering. Hence, they are grouped together with the common parent `VulnerabilityFilter` element. Because the initial metamodel does not include all CVSS properties, we added the following: 1. *AttackComplexity* describes how complex it is to exploit the vulnerability. 2. *UserInteraction* describes that the attacker needs additional support from the user to exploit the vulnerability. 3. *IntegrityImpact* is the impact regarding integrity. 4. *AvailablityImpact* is the impact regarding availability. A more detailed description of the properties can be found in [6]. The `ExploitFilter` filters attacks based on the attackVector, attackComplexity, UserInteraction. This enables an architect to find only attack paths to a targeted element, which contains easily exploited vulnerabilities. This can be helpful in considering different attacker types. The `ImpactFilter` filters out vulnerabilities of a certain impact, such as only attack paths that affect the confidentiality of a system.

The different filters are then selected in the `SurfaceAttacker`. It stores a list of the filter criteria. Additionally, it contains the information necessary to calculate an attack path by storing the targeted element.

## 3   Attack Path Identification

Based on a modeled software architecture, our approach can identify attack paths leading to a targeted element. We identify the potential attack paths based on an attack graph. In contrast to our previous work [33], the attack graph contains all the vulnerabilities as long as they do not share the filtered properties. The graph is especially not limited by a set of specified attacks. Figure 3 illustrates an attack graph based on our running example. The graph consists of vertices, which are the vulnerable architectural elements. In our case, these are elements from the type `LinkingResource`, `ResourceContainer`, and `AssemblyContext`. The edges are possibilities to compromise a vertex from another vertex. For this, the original architectural elements represented by the vertex need to be connected. For instance, this could be the network connection like in our running example with the `MachineController` to the `Terminal-Server`. Additionally, the edges have three types. The first type models the necessary credentials to access a vertex. For instance, in our running example, the `TerminalServer` is connected with the `MachineController` and the `Admin`

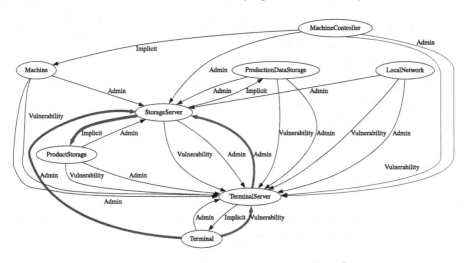

**Fig. 3.** Attack Graph of the running example with attack path p1 in red and attack path p2 in blue (Color figure online)

property gives access to the `TerminalServer`. Therefore, there is a directed edge from the `MachineController` to the `TerminalServer` with the label `Admin`. The second edge type models vulnerabilities, which can be exploited on the target vertex. For instance, the `Terminal` is deployed on the `TerminalServer` and the `TerminalServer` is vulnerable to `CVE-2021-28374`. Therefore, a vulnerability edge exists between `Terminal` and `TerminalServer`. In our illustration, we renamed `CVE-2021-28374` with vulnerability. However, in the analysis, the edge still has the information about its vulnerability. The last edge type is implicit edges. These are edges between a `ResourceContainer` and the components deployed on it. Here, we assume that a compromised hardware automatically compromises the underlying software. For instance, in our running example, the `ProductStorage` is deployed on the `StorageServer`. Hence, there is a directed implicit edge from `StorageServer` to the `ProductStorage`.

Algorithm 1 illustrates the graph creation process in more detail. For the graph creation, we need the software architecture (`arch`) and the selected filters (`fil`). We first create an empty graph (l. 2) and then iterate over all relevant architectural elements (`ResourceContainer`, `AssemblyContext`, `LinkingResource`). For each element, we identify the connected neighbors (l. 4). Afterwards, we iterate over the neighbors and identify how they are connected. If the neighbor element is deployed on the current element, we add an implicit edge (l. 6/7). If the neighbor has access control policies, we add an edge containing this policy. The last step is to identify whether the neighbor has a vulnerability (l. 12). If it has at least one vulnerability, we iterate over all the vulnerabilities of the neighbor. We check whether each vulnerability's attack vector is within the connection vector to the current architectural element (l. 14). Besides the attack vector, we also check whether the vulnerability can be filtered based on the use

**Algorithm 1.** Simplified Attack Graph Creation
***
1: **procedure** ATTACKGRAPHCREATION(arch,fil)
2:    $g := emptyGraph()$
3:    **for all** $res := arch.getElements$ **do**
4:        $neighbours := getConnectedElements(res)$
5:        **for all** $n := neighbours$ **do**
6:            **if** $isDeployment(res, n)$ **then**
7:                $g.createImplicitEdge(res, n)$
8:            **end if**
9:            **if** $n.hasACPolicy()$ **then**
10:                $g.createACEdge(res, n)$
11:            **end if**
12:            **if** $n.hasVulnerability()$ **then**
13:                **for all** $vul = n.getVulnerability()$ **do**
14:                    **if** $isInAVector(vul.AVector())$ &&
15:                    $fil.notFiltered(vul)$ **then**
16:                        $g.createVEdge(res, n, vul)$
17:                    **end if**
18:                **end for**
19:            **end if**
20:        **end for**
21:    **end for**
22: **end procedure**
***

of VulnerabilityFilters. For instance, a ExploitFilter with a selected high complexity would create an attack graph that contains only vulnerabilities with low attack complexity. This is helpful in scenarios where software architects want only to consider low-complexity attacks.

Based on this attack graph, the attack paths are calculated by calculating the path from a node to the targeted node. An attack path is a sequence of nodes that are connected by edges. It has a starting node and a target node from the targeted architectural element. For instance, based on the attack graph in Fig. 3, an attack path (p1) with the targeted element ProductStorage could be: Terminal $\xrightarrow{\text{Admin}}$ StorageServer $\xrightarrow{\text{Implicit}}$ ProductStorage The attack path is also highlighted in red in Fig. 3. Besides the start point, the path on the graph and the endpoint, an AttackPath also contains a set of initially required credentials. These can be calculated by first getting all required credentials. The required credentials are all credentials that are on the edge of an attack path. In our running example, this is the Admin. Afterward, all credentials gained during the attack path are removed. The rest are then the initially required credentials. Since we do not gain any credentials in our example path, the Admin attribute is in the initial required set.

The actual attack path is calculated by first determining the start nodes. The start nodes are all nodes except the target node. If a StartFilter exists, only these elements are start nodes. Afterward, the analysis calculates paths to the target node. The path finding invalidates solutions, which require the filtered credentials as initial credentials. However, it supports the gaining of credentials during the path. Therefore, the path can contain the filtered credential. After a path is found, we check for the length of the path. We discard it if it exceeds the length specified in the `MaximumPath` filter. Otherwise, we add the path to the list of attack paths. For our running example with the `ProductStorage` as a target, we get seven attack paths, including our previous example, p1. However, not all are reasonable. For instance, the attack path from the `StorageServer` only exploits the deployment relationship. A software architect can specify a start filter to get a better solution. We choose a `StartFilter` containing only the `Terminal` since external technicians can access it. Then the output is only the attack path p1. However, this attack path requires that the attacker knows the `Admin` credentials since it is an initially required credential. While an attacker could have it at the beginning, in general, we assume that an attacker does not have the knowledge. Therefore, we create a `CredentialFilter` with the `Admin`. If we run our analysis now, we get the following attack path (p2): `Terminal` $\xrightarrow{Vulnerability}$ `TerminalServer` $\xrightarrow{Admin}$ `StorageElement` $\xrightarrow{Implicit}$ `ProductStorage`. The path is highlighted in blue. This attack path still uses the `Admin` credential but gains it by exploiting the vulnerability and, therefore, does not require it from the start. A software architect can then use the resulting attack path and consider mitigating the attack path or accepting the risk.

## 4   Evaluation

We structure our evaluation using the Goal Question Metric [3] approach. Afterward, we will explain our evaluation scenarios, design and discuss our results, threats to validity, and limitations.

*Goals, Questions, Metrics.* The first evaluation goal **G1** is to investigate accuracy. Accuracy is an important property that is also investigated in other related approaches, such as [10,25]. The evaluation question **Q1** is: *How accurately does the analysis identify the attack paths?* This question is important since a low accuracy suggests that our analysis does not work adequately and that the attack paths might be meaningless for software architects. Our metrics are precision (p), recall (r) [31] and the harmonic middle F1 of both: $p = \frac{t_p}{t_p + f_p}$ $r = \frac{t_p}{t_p + f_n}$ $F1 = 2\frac{p*r}{p+r}$. The $t_p$ are true positives, meaning correctly detected attack paths. $f_p$ are false positives that are attack paths, which are actually no attack paths and $f_n$ false negatives are not found attack paths. Higher values are better.

Our second goal **G2** is to evaluate the scalability of the approach. The number of architectural elements is increasing due to trends like IoT. Furthermore, new vulnerabilities are discovered continuously during the system's lifespan. Hence, continuously searching for the system's existing attack paths is necessary. One possible solution is to conduct checks similar to integration tests as recommended by [24]. Typically, these tests run daily. Therefore, it is required that the analysis is completed within a few hours. Our questions are: **Q2.1** *How does the*

*runtime of the graph creation behave with an increasing number of elements?*
**Q2.2** *How does the runtime of the path finding behave with an increasing number of elements?* We split the evaluation into two questions to investigate the goal in more detail. Q2.1 investigates the part where the analysis transforms the software architecture in an attack graph, and Q2.2 then covers identifying an attack path on a given attack graph. The G2's metric is the relation between runtime and input elements.

*Evaluation Scenarios.* We answer our evaluation question based on five scenarios. Two scenarios (Target, Power Grid) are based on real-world system breaches. One scenario is based on the research case TravelPlanner [14] and one scenario is based on the cloud case study from [2]. The last scenario is based on our running example. The Target, Power Grid and TravelPlanner scenarios are also used in Walter et al. [33]. Hence, the architectural models are the same. Using these scenarios for our evaluation increases the insight and illustrates the applicability and comparability of our approach. Table 1 illustrates some characteristics of the evaluation scenarios. It contains the name of the scenario, the number of instantiated components (abbrev. comp), the number of hardware resources (abbrev. hard.), the number of linking resources (network) and the number of potential attack paths. In addition, it contains the evaluation results for G1.

**Table 1.** Characteristic of the evaluation scenarios and results for accuracy goal

| Scenario | comp. | hard. | network | paths | $p$ | $r$ | $F1$ |
|---|---|---|---|---|---|---|---|
| Target | 7 | 6 | 2 | 14 | 1.00 | 1.00 | 1.0 |
| Power Grid | 9 | 8 | 2 | 16 | 1.00 | 0.88 | 0.93 |
| Cloud Storage | 11 | 16 | 4 | 14 | 1.00 | 1.00 | 1.00 |
| TravelPlaner | 4 | 3 | 3 | 1 | 1.00 | 1.00 | 1.00 |
| Maintenance | 4 | 3 | 1 | 7 | 1.00 | 0.86 | 0.92 |

Our first scenario is a scenario based on the Target breach, which involved attackers stealing access credentials from a supplier to access Targets's billing business backend. Afterward, they exploited different vulnerabilities in other components to gain access to unencrypted credit card data. The model is based on [19,26]. It contains POS devices, FTP storage servers, and databases annotated with vulnerabilities, as they were components compromised in the Target breach [26]. These elements are segregated by the supplier in a separate network. The targeted element is one POS device. The second scenario is based on the cyberattack on the Ukrainian Powergrid in 2015, which resulted in a widespread power outage. The model relies on the report of [9] and covers the attack propagation from the back-office network to the ICS network. The target is the circuit breakers in the ICS network. The third scenario is a research case study for threat modeling in a cloud environment [2]. In contrast to the previous scenarios, it is not a real-world system breach. However, the software architecture is based on concepts and ideas from real-world products. It resembles a cloud storage environment. We manually created a PCM model based on the description for the first proposed cloud infrastructure. Here, the targeted element is a database. The fourth scenario is the confidentiality research case study TravelPlanner [14]. It is used to evaluate different security analyses, such as [25,33]. The previous scenarios are based on real-world breaches or inspired by real-world cloud centers. Therefore, the attacker behavior was given by the case. This case study lets us define the attacker's behavior in more detail. The case is a simple mobile application to book flights. It has four entities: customer, credit card center, travel agency, and airline. The fifth scenario is our running example, the maintenance scenario.

*Evaluation Design.* For the accuracy analysis, we used the five scenarios. We manually determined the number of attack paths for each scenario based on their descriptions. We tried to find an attack path from each architectural element (excluding the targeted element) to the targeted element. For the attack paths, we used the vulnerabilities and potentially found credentials. However, we excluded as initial credentials all credentials so that an attack path needs to either find the necessary credentials or need to exploit a vulnerability. This is beneficial to get more complicated attack paths than otherwise the attack path could be just using the root or admin credentials. For each scenario, we then manually checked whether each attack path was a valid attack path. An attack path is valid if it is a list of connected vulnerable elements from the start point to the target and each vulnerability can be exploited by the attacker. If it is a valid path, we count it as $t_p$. If it is not a valid path, we count it as $f_p$. If we found for one architectural element an attack path and the analysis did not show an attack path, we counted this as $f_n$. Based on these values, we then calculate $p$, $r$ and $F1$ for each scenario.

For analyzing the scalability, we first identified the influencing factors. We separate this along Q2.1 and Q2.2. For Q2.1, based on our algorithm 1, the most influencing factors are l. 3, 5, and 13 because of their loops. The other lines, 2, 4, 6–12,14–17, are not relevant. For l. 3,5, the relevant attributes are the architectural elements (l. 3 and l. 5). For l. 13, it is the vulnerabilities for an architectural element. For the former, we choose to scale along the number of connected resource containers. This creates a linked chain of vulnerable resource containers and creates a worst-case scenario for the graph creation. The behavior for architectural elements is similar in the algorithm, so the analysis time should be similar. We did not investigate the scaling along the number of vulnerabilities for one architectural element because, usually, the number for one element is not very high. We measured the runtime starting from the graph creation with the already loaded PCM models till the attack graph is returned. We scaled by the power of 10 from $10^1$ elements to $10^5$ elements. Regarding Q2.2, the relevant factors are the number of edges between distinct nodes and the path length. We achieve the first by choosing the scaling along the `ResourceContainer`. For the second, we use a start filter and set it to the first element in the chained elements, and the target element is the last. This will force a worst-case scenario for a single path. We assume that software architects are more interested in only a filtered list for bigger architectures. For instance, similar to our running example with the `Terminal`, they are only interested in paths from externally accessible components to certain internal components. Here, we measured the time after the attack graph from Q2.1 is created till one attack path is returned. For both, we repeated each measurement five times and calculated the average to avoid outliers. We performed one warm-up analysis and run the analysis on a Debian 11 VM with 21 AMD Opteron Processor 8435 with 62.5 GB RAM.

*Results and Discussion Accuracy.* The last three columns in Table 1 show the evaluation results for G1. For each scenario, we get the perfect precision of 1.00. This means that every attack path of the analysis was an actual attack path regarding our manual comparison. We archived these perfect results since the cases are small, and we focused on a restricted model with no dependencies to unknown behavior, which simplifies the results. Regarding the recall, we archive in the Cloud Storage, Target, and TravelPlanner scenarios the perfect results of 1.00 and also an F1 score of 1.00. This means that our analysis can find all the attack paths from our manual comparison in these scenarios, and they are valid attack paths. However, in the Power Grid, our analysis missed two attack paths and in the Maintenance scenario, one attack path. Therefore, we only have a recall of 0.88 and 0.86 in these scenarios. The F1 score is 0.93 and 0.92. The missed attack paths can be traced back to our usage of simple paths during the attack path creation. For simplicity and performance reasons, the attack paths are loopless and do not contain duplicates. However, in the missed cases, it would be necessary to have loops to get the required credentials. For instance, in the maintenance scenario, the attack path from the `TerminalServer` would require one self-loop to get the necessary credentials.

*Results and Discussion Scalability.* Figure 4 illustrates the scalability results. The horizontal axis shows the number of resource containers and the vertical axis shows the runtime in ms. The blue line with circles is the graph creation and the red line with the boxes is the path finding. Both axes use a logarithmic scale. The runtime of both functions is very close together. For 10 elements, the graph creation needs around 26 ms and the path finding around 42 ms. It then slowly increases till around $10^3$ elements with 597 ms (graph creation) and 693 ms (path finding). From there, the runtime grows longer until it takes around $5.7 \times 10^6$ ms (graph creation) and $5.6 \times 10^6$ ms (path finding) for $10^5$ elements. This summarizes to a runtime of around 3 h. The scalability behavior is not ideal. However, the runtime should still be sufficient for the usage in daily analysis runs. In addition, the model sizes with $10^5$ elements are quite high. Usually, the model sizes are smaller. Even in bigger architectures like in IoT environments, the architecture can be reduced by grouping similar elements, for instance, when there are groups of sensors connected to the same backend.

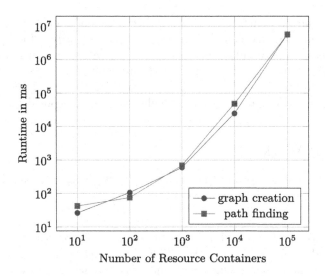

**Fig. 4.** Scalability results for increasing number of resource containers

*Threats to Validity.* We structure our threats to validity on the guidelines for case study validity from Runeson and Höst [22].

*Internal Validity* is that only the expected factors influence the results. Our evaluation depends on the modeled system as input and the results reflecting modeled properties. Especially since we also manually created the reference output. We tried to lower the risk by using real-world breaches and literature to create the reference output. For the scalability, other factors, such as the general system usage, could affect the runtime. To avoid this, we repeated the experiment 5 times and ran it on a separate VM. We used multiple real-world breach and research scenarios in our evaluation to ensure the *External Validity* of our results. While we modeled systems are small, we covered all relevant model elements for our extension and analysis features. While scalability may vary with different architectural elements, our internal handling of elements should produce similar results. *Construct Validity* is about the validity of the investigated properties for the intended goal. In our case, the properties are the metrics, and the goal is the evaluation goals. To lower the threat, we used the GQM approach, which illustrates the connection between goals and metrics. For accuracy, we use precision, recall and F1. These metrics are often used to describe the accuracy in different related architectural approaches such as [25,33]. Therefore, we assume the metrics to be appropriate and the risk to be low. The scalability metric is a simple runtime metric and similar metrics are used in related approaches, such as [20]. *Reliability* discusses how reproducible the results are by other researchers. We use metrics to answer our evaluation question, avoiding subjective interpretation and increasing reproducibility. Besides the metrics, we also provide a dataset [35] for others to verify the results.

*Limitations.* Our approach requires an architecture model and the manual creation of the vulnerability model. Our approach can identify attack paths only based on known vulnerabilities. In addition, it can only be used to identify mitigation locations, but does not support advanced mitigations, such as trusted execution environments. While we already consider the involvement of third parties in our filter, the actual attack calculation does not consider it besides in the filtering.

## 5    Related Work

We divided the related work in the section of *Policy Analysis*, *Model-based Confidentiality Analysis* and *Attacker Modeling*.

*Policy Analysis.* Our approach analyzes access control policies to estimate the necessary credentials for an attacker. Other approaches can consider various other policy quality aspects. One policy analysis approach is Margrave [8], which can calculate change impact on policies. Another policy analysis is Turkmen et al. [30], which uses SMT internally to analyze policies for different properties, such as change impact and attribute hiding. In summary, all the approaches mentioned focus on policy analysis, not attack propagation.

*Model-driven Security Analyses.* Our approach uses model-driven concepts for generating the attack paths. UMLSec [13] extends UML with security properties. It adds different analysis types, such as secure communication link, fair exchange, and confidentiality. Additionally, they include an attacker model for checking the security requirements. In contrast, our approach focuses on the attack path generation. Another UML extension for security is SecureUML [17]. They focussed on access control. So far, they do not support attack propagation or attack path generation. There exist various approaches which analyze information flow or access control based on some model, such as SecDFD [29], and Data-centric Palladio [25]. In contrast, both use dataflow definitions, but do not consider attack paths calculation. Attacker-related approaches are the Sparta approach [27], Berger et al. [4] or Cyber Security Modeling Language (CySeMoL) [28]. The first two are dataflow analyses in threat detection. In contrast to our approach, these focus on single threat detection and not combining different vulnerabilities/threats to attack paths. CySeMoL [28] calculates potential attack paths but does not use a fine-grained access control system.

*Attacker Modeling.* Schneier [23] introduced the idea of attack trees, which are used in many approaches to model attacker behavior [16]. Polatidis et al. [20] present an approach for attack path generation. Other approaches are, for instance, Aksu et al. [1] and Yuan et al. [36]. In contrast to our approach, all the mentioned approaches use a network layer perspective instead of a component-based software architecture and do not consider fine-grained access control policies.

# 6    Conclusion

We proposed an approach for generating potential attack paths to a targeted architectural element. Our presented metamodel extension enables architects to model filtering options for attack paths and specify targeted elements. In contrast to Walter et al. [33], our attack analysis provides multiple attack paths to the targeted elements and can remove non-relevant paths by using the filter options. The evaluation indicates that our approach can find in several scenarios attack paths with high accuracy and for smaller systems within a reasonable time. Our approach can help to identify potential weak spots in the software architecture. Software architects can use this information to add mitigation mechanisms to harden the system and prevent attacker propagation. In the future, we want to investigate the problem with the missing attack paths in the evaluation. Additionally, we want to consider mitigation approaches and combine the approach with dataflow analyses similar to [34].

**Acknowledgement.** We like to thank Jonathan Schenkenberger, who helped to implement this approach during his Master's thesis.

# References

1. Aksu, M.U., et al.: Automated generation of attack graphs using NVD. In: Proceedings of the Eighth ACM Conference on Data and Application Security and Privacy (CODASPY), pp. 135–142. ACM (2018)
2. Alhebaishi, N., et al.: Threat modeling for cloud data center infrastructures. In: Foundations and Practice of Security, pp. 302–319 (2016)
3. Basili, G., et al.: The goal question metric approach. Encyclopedia of Software Engineering (1994)
4. Berger, B.J., Sohr, K., Koschke, R.: Automatically extracting threats from extended data flow diagrams. In: Caballero, J., Bodden, E., Athanasopoulos, E. (eds.) ESSoS 2016. LNCS, vol. 9639, pp. 56–71. Springer, Cham (2016). https://doi.org/10.1007/978-3-319-30806-7_4
5. CVE. https://cve.mitre.org/. Accessed 11 Jan 2022
6. CVSS SIG. https://www.first.org/cvss/. Accessed 11 Jan 2022
7. CWE. https://cwe.mitre.org/. Accessed 11 Jan 2022
8. Fisler, K., et al.: Verification and change-impact analysis of access-control policies. In: International Conference on Software Engineering 2005, p. 196 (2005)
9. Hamilton, B.A.: Industrial Cybersecurity Threat Briefing. Tech. rep., p. 82
10. Heinrich, R., et al.: Architecture-based change impact analysis in cross-disciplinary automated production systems. JSS **146**, 167–185 (2018)
11. ISO: Information technology. en. Standard ISO/IEC 27000:2018, Geneva, CH (2018)
12. Johns, E.: Cyber Security Breaches Survey 2021: Statistical Release (2021)
13. Jürjens, J.: UMLsec: extending UML for secure systems development. In: Jézéquel, J.-M., Hussmann, H., Cook, S. (eds.) UML 2002. LNCS, vol. 2460, pp. 412–425. Springer, Heidelberg (2002). https://doi.org/10.1007/3-540-45800-X_32
14. Katkalov, K.: Ein modellgetriebener Ansatz zur Entwicklung informationsflusssicherer Systeme. doctoral thesis, Universität Augsburg (2017)

15. Kirschner, Y.R., et al.: Automatic Derivation of Vulnerability Models for Software Architectures. In: IEEE 20th International Conference on Software Architecture Companion (ICSA-C), pp. 276–283 (2023)
16. Kordy, B., et al.: DAG-based attack and defense modeling: don't miss the forest for the attack trees. Comput. Sci. Rev. **13–14**, 1–38 (2014)
17. Lodderstedt, Torsten, Basin, David, Doser, Jürgen.: SecureUML: a UML-based modeling language for model-driven security. In: Jézéquel, Jean-Marc., Hussmann, Heinrich, Cook, Stephen (eds.) UML 2002. LNCS, vol. 2460, pp. 426–441. Springer, Heidelberg (2002). https://doi.org/10.1007/3-540-45800-X_33
18. OWASP Top Ten Web Application Security Risks — OWASP. https://owasp.org/www-project-top-ten/. Accessed 11 Jan 2022
19. Plachkinova, M., Maurer, C.: Security breach at target. J. Inf. Syst. Educ. **29**(1), 11–20 (2018)
20. Polatidis, N., et al.: From product recommendation to cyber-attack prediction: generating attack graphs and predicting future attacks. Evolving Syst. **11**(3), 479–490 (2020)
21. Reussner, R., et al.: Modeling and Simulating Software Architectures - The Palladio Approach. MIT Press, Cambridge (2016). isbn: 9780262034760
22. Runeson, P., Höst, M.: Guidelines for conducting and reporting case study research in software engineering. Empirical Softw. .ineering **14**(2), 131 (2008)
23. Schneier, B.: Attack trees. Dr. Dobb's J. **24**(12), 21–29 (1999)
24. Securing the Software Supply Chain: Recommended Practices Guide for Developers, p. 64. Cybersecurity and Infrastructure Security Agency (CISA) (2022)
25. Seifermann, S., et al.: detecting violations of access control and information flow policies in data flow diagrams. J. Syst. Softw. **184**, 111138 (2021)
26. Shu, X., et al.: Breaking the Target: An Analysis of Target Data Breach and Lessons Learned. arXiv:1701.04940 [cs] (2017)
27. Sion, L., et al.: Solution-aware data flow diagrams for security threat modeling. In: Symposium on Applied Computing, pp. 1425–1432. ACM (2018)
28. Sommestad, T., et al.: The cyber security modeling language: a tool for assessing the vulnerability of enterprise system architectures. IEEE Syst. J. **7**(3), 363–373 (2012)
29. Tuma, K., et al.: Flaws in flows: unveiling design flaws via information flow analysis. In: International Conference on Software Architecture, pp. 191–200 (2019)
30. Turkmen, F., den Hartog, J., Ranise, S., Zannone, N.: Analysis of XACML policies with SMT. In: Focardi, R., Myers, A. (eds.) POST 2015. LNCS, vol. 9036, pp. 115–134. Springer, Heidelberg (2015). https://doi.org/10.1007/978-3-662-46666-7_7
31. Van Rijsbergen, C., and Van Rijsbergen, C.: Information Retrieval. Butterworths (1979). isbn: 9780408709293
32. Walter, M., and Reussner, R.: Tool-based attack graph estimation and scenario analysis for software architectures. In: European Conference on Software Architecture 2022 Tracks and Workshops (accepted, to appear)
33. Walter, M., et al.: Architectural attack propagation analysis for identifying confidentiality issues. In: International Conference on Software Architecture (2022)
34. Walter, M., et al.: Architecture-based attack propagation and variation analysis for identifying confidentiality issues in Industry 4.0. at - Automatisierungstechnik **71**(6), 443–452 (2023)
35. Walter, M., et al.: Dataset: Architecture-based Attack Path Analysis for Identifying Potential Security Incidents. https://doi.org/10.5281/zenodo.7900356

36. Yuan, B., et al.: An attack path generation methods based on graph database. In: 2020 IEEE 4th Information Technology, Networking, Electronic and Automation Control Conference (ITNEC), pp. 1905–1910 (2020)

# Carving Sustainability into Architecture Knowledge Practice

Markus Funke[✉][iD] and Patricia Lago[iD]

Vrije Universiteit Amsterdam, Amsterdam, The Netherlands
m.t.funke@vu.nl

**Abstract.** In the daily work of a software architect, knowledge is ubiquitous. In addition to technical expertise, architecture knowledge (AK) also requires practical experience in the representation, communication, and management of architectural decisions. However, there is a pressing need to also incorporate sustainability aspects, i.e., capturing decisions towards software systems that are environmentally, economically, and socially balanced in the long term. With this study, we aim to provide a review of AK concepts and their representation and communication from a practical point of view. Having this understanding, we explore where sustainability can be applied in daily practice and how we can address sustainability in architecture processes in the future. The paper presents an empirical study conducted in an industrial context encompassing a questionnaire survey with 32 participants and semi-structured interviews with 15 practitioners; both groups are from a major bank in the Netherlands. Based on the insights gained from combining our findings, we (i) provide a map of applied concepts for communicating and representing AK in a large enterprise, and (ii) discuss potential avenues for carving sustainability into current software architecture practice.

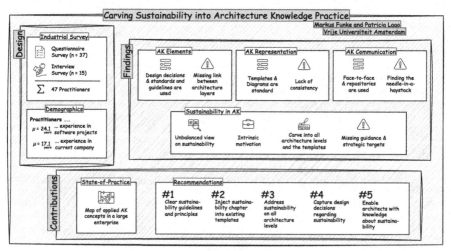

**Graphical Abstract.**

We thank the architects participating in this survey; Antony Tang, John Klein, and Rich Hilliard for discussions on current state-of-research; and Haben Birhane Gebreweld for executing the questionnaire survey.

B. Tekinerdogan et al. (Eds.): ECSA 2023, LNCS 14212, pp. 54–69, 2023.
https://doi.org/10.1007/978-3-031-42592-9_4

# 1   Introduction

Software Architecture entails the systematic organisation of various software components to construct a comprehensive system [13] and facilitate the reasoning about a given system [3]. In the present day, the life cycle of software has a holistic impact on an enterprise and thus demands consideration on multiple layers of its business operations. To preserve the reasoning and information about the overarching system across all layers, documentation is a crucial part [8]. It facilitates the documentation of knowledge during the design process, i.e., architecture knowledge (AK), enabling the recording of decisions for future reference and leveraging past experience to improve future decisions [1].

Although AK is a well-established field in software engineering, the concept of sustainability has gained significant attention only in recent times [4]. Software sustainability is a multidimensional concept that involves environmental, social, economic, and technical dimensions [17]. Despite the increasing attention given to sustainability, practitioners lack reusable guidelines and consolidated knowledge to integrate sustainability into their daily work [16]. We aim to highlight the critical role of AK across all different layers of architecture and propose the incorporation of software sustainability into existing AK methods. This integration contributes to achieving sustainable development goals.

Following the problem statement we need to bridge the gap between isolated techniques for software sustainability and their application in professional practice. First, we need to know the state-of-practice of software AK and how professionals understand and already support sustainability in their daily work. With these insights, we can either improve current practice on AK or propose recommendations to incorporate sustainability. By combining our findings from an extensive survey in a major bank in the Netherlands encompassing a questionnaire with 35 practitioners and 15 semi-structured interviews, our main **contributions** of this research are twofold: **(i)** we provide an overview of applied AK concepts in a large organisation; **(ii)** we use this understanding to discuss recommendations for applying sustainability.

In the remainder of this section we first provide the background; then we discuss related studies. In Sect. 2 we outline our study goal and describe the applied methodology. Section 3 presents the main findings which are then discussed in Sect. 4. Threats to validity are examined in Sect. 5, while Sect. 6 closes this paper.

## 1.1   Background

**Architecture Knowledge.** Throughout this study, we use the definition of AK according to Kruchten et al. [12] as:

> *Architectural knowledge consists of architecture design as well as the design decisions, assumptions, context, and other factors that together determine why a particular solution is the way it is.*

Additionally, in our work we particularly highlight the distinction between AK representation and AK communication. The former, **AK representation**, aims at capturing and preserving knowledge in a certain form. While the latter, **AK communication**, describes how the knowledge is disclosed between involved stakeholders. Figure 1 depicts our view on the interaction of the AK artifacts as a mental model. We can observe that various AK representation methods *express* AK. Such representation *identifies* multiple stakeholders by capturing their concerns and interests in the particular knowledge. While stakeholders have a certain *interest* in the AK, they acquire the knowledge by *using* certain communication methods.

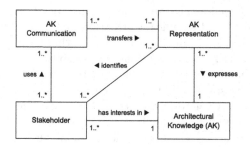

**Fig. 1.** Architecture knowledge mental model - *Process view*

We can compare our mental-model with the different "AK management philosophies" defined by Ali Babar et al. [1]. The authors differentiate between "explicit and tacit knowledge" and between "application-generic and application-specific knowledge". While this view can be considered as the *knowledge view*, i.e., from the knowledge perspective, we define our AK mental model as the *process view*, i.e., from the stakeholder perspective. The knowledge view illustrates how the knowledge itself *moves* within the different categories; our process view, instead, illustrates how the knowledge is *utilised* by the actual stakeholders. This view emphasises the utilisation of AK in an industrial context and is considered throughout the rest of our study.

**Software and Sustainability.** The need for addressing sustainability in architecture has led to various approaches, techniques, and tools for designing [14,15], evaluating [10], and improving [20] the sustainability of software systems. To the best of our knowledge, however, those emerging approaches appear in isolation without consideration of embedding them in industrial practice.

When we call for balanced sustainability in software architecture, we seek to achieve a harmonious and equitable consideration of the four sustainability dimensions [17] into the design and development of software systems. We recognise that software is a multi-faceted concept which requires a construct of inter-dimensional trade-offs. Those trade-offs demand to be considered at design time, i.e., in software architecture, to align the software with sustainability goals.

## 1.2   Related Studies

There are few studies that examine the use of AK in professional practice. Malavolta et al. [18] consider architecture modeling languages (AL) as representation tool for AK and conduct a study on the strengths and limitations of these languages by surveying 49 practitioners and identifying their needs and requirements for future AL. Our study goes beyond AK representation and also examines AK elements and communication methods.

In facing AK from the knowledge management perspective (AKM) [1], Capilla et al. [5] determine what industry needs by analysing state-of-the-art AKM tools. The authors raise questions identifying barriers for using those tools and documenting architecture in practice. Even though the focus of this research relies on AKM tools, we are able to build up on this research and reuse for instance certain interview questions for our work.

Dasanayake et al. [7] conduct a case study in an industrial setting to investigate how architecture decisions are made in practice and to improve the decision-making process. The study entails 10 interviews in three companies, revealing that the experts do not follow a systematic approach. The study also finds that the practitioners are willing to adopt lightweight solutions to enhance their decision processes. While the study partially aligns with our goal of comprehensively embracing the entire AK process, it primarily focuses on decision-making.

The studies discussed above have made partial contributions to our research, but none of them have specifically aimed to incorporate sustainability into current practice using AK. Andrikopoulos et al. [2] conduct a systematic mapping study to explore software architecture together with sustainability and find that current research has neglected the holistic viewpoint by focusing on particular sustainability-related dimensions. Lago et al. [16] conduct a more practical study by examining the needs of both researchers and practitioners regarding "architecting for sustainability". The study uncovers barriers to implement sustainability, such as the lack of understanding among practitioners on how to translate sustainability into their own work.

## 2   Methodology

To encourage reproducibility and enhance the reliability of our results, we provide an online replication package[1] containing the anonymized data and results related to this paper.

### 2.1   Study Objective and Questions

The **goal** of this study is twofold. First, we want to provide a review to software architects and the research community about AK and its representation and communication in an industrial context. This understanding helps us in our second goal, i.e., to explore *where* and *how* sustainability can be addressed in the future. We identify two main research questions (RQs) and three sub-questions:

---

[1] Replication package: https://github.com/S2-group/ECSA23-AKCR-rep-pkg.

RQ1 *How is AK represented and communicated in practice?*
    *RQ1.1 What are the elements that are represented and communicated?*
    *RQ1.2 How is architecture knowledge represented?*
    *RQ1.3 How is architecture knowledge communicated?*
    We investigate current professional practice about AK by executing our
    research together with a major bank in the Netherlands. The industrial
    context helps us in creating a holistic view on what the state-of-practice is
    regarding AK. We create a map of a large enterprise and their AK elements
    (e.g., decisions and principles), representation methods (e.g., diagrams and
    viewpoints), and communication practices (e.g., corporate platforms and
    workshops). This helps us in understanding the daily work of architects.
RQ2 *How can sustainability aspects be represented and communicated in soft-*
    *ware architecture?*
    Building upon the practical insights about AK identified in RQ1 we are
    able to propose recommendations on how sustainability can be incorpo-
    rated into daily practice. Based on the additionally uncovered impediments
    we can establish the current needs in order to achieve balanced sustain-
    ability.

## 2.2  Study Design

To answer our RQs, we organize our research process in four steps (see Fig. 2).
    **Exploratory Review.** In Step (1) we build the necessary understanding
about architecture documentation, representation, communication, and AK in
general. We talk to three researchers in the field of AK. We enrich those insights
by consulting background literature and books (e.g., [1,3,6]). This understanding
helps us in the subsequent steps to bootstrap our qualitative research.

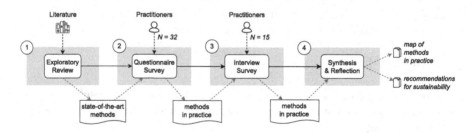

**Fig. 2.** Study Design

**Questionnaire Survey.** In Step (2) we construct a series of questions to
operationalize our RQs. The questions are related to AK practices, supplemented
with commonly used demographic questions. The questionnaire comprises 34
questions in total. With 24 open questions and the rest as guiding and closed
questions, we facilitate a candid expression of our participants' unique experiences. The survey guide can be found in the replication package.

Following the design, we first execute a pilot survey with five experts to check the quality of the survey and eliminate potential pitfalls. Then, we determine the main population. Based on the objectives of our research, we determine software architects and similar roles (e.g., domain architects, cloud architects, etc.) as our target population. Based on an internal mailing list and the team leads we generate a draft list of 145 architects. After eliminating redundant names and removing the architects needed for an extensive interview in Step (3) we arrive at a population with 124 architects. The survey is conducted using Qualtrics[2] and designed to be anonymous to alleviate concerns about judgment or consequences. We reach out to the 124 architects via email and received 45 (39 %) survey responses. After removing the 13 responses that refused consent or dropped after completing the demographics part, the total population counts 32 architects (N = 32).

**Interview Survey.** The aim of Step (3) is to gain in-depth insights from the experts and follow up on the results from the questionnaire. Again, the complete interview guide can be found online. The interview comprises 21 questions in total, all of them designed as open-questions. Most questions are adopted from the questionnaire survey. However, some questions are combined to better fit in an interview setting. It is accepted and especially appreciated if the interview flow lead to other questions or guides the discussion into other directions. The interviewees are selected following purposeful sampling based on two conditions: (i) interviewee has a leading role in the organisation, e.g., manager or head-of, and (ii) interviewee is not part of the questionnaire survey. The leading role allows us to ask more detailed questions of the representatives of an entire group of architects. Further, we do not only select software architects, but rather a broader range of architects including architects with a higher level focus, e.g., enterprise architects or business architects. In total we contacted 21 practitioners, and 15 accepted our invitation (N = 15). To determine the length and flow of the interview, we use three experts as pilots. These are included in our final data set as the structure and questions did not change and only a few questions were improved in terms of phrasing.

**Synthesis and Reflection.** To understand the current practice of AK and uncover potential hooks for sustainability, the final Step (4) synthesises the data gained from both the questionnaire and the interviews.

*Data collection and organisation.* As the questionnaire is executed online, the collected data is exported automatically into spreadsheets. The answers are not edited. In contrast, all interviews are conducted virtually via Microsoft Teams, audio recorded, and transcribed. The transcriptions are cleaned from emotions and mumbled speech.

*Coding and Vertical Analysis.* The questionnaire data are pre-coded per question. Those results are used in preparation for the in-depth interviews, e.g., in form of follow-up questions. As both the questionnaire spreadsheets and the interview transcripts follow a similar structure, they are coded together by the first author and validated by the second author following coding techniques for

---

[2] QualtricsXM: https://www.qualtrics.com.

qualitative data analysis [19]. We start with an initial set of coding categories derived by the RQs (i.e., provisional coding [19]), which are then revised and/or extended (i.e., open coding [19]). We use ATLAS.ti[3] as qualitative data analysis tool. The output of this step are the results in Sect. 3. We structure our results according to the identified themes, codes, and sub-codes as shown in Table 2.

*Horizontal Analysis and Reflection.* To gain further insights from the data, we investigate the responses across our two RQs via horizontal analysis [9]. Our goal is to merge the insights related to AK with those regarding sustainability, and identify potential avenues and gaps for addressing sustainability in AK practice. We reflect on our results by organising all findings in one comprehensive table. The table contains the results from the coding and vertical analysis and the emerged insights from the horizontal analysis. Insights are then turned into recommendations and discussed in several brainstorming sessions between the researchers. To find further practical connections or insights, we additionally discuss this set of recommendations together with two experts from our industrial partner in two informal meetings; one expert related to the higher level of architecture (i.e., Lead of Senior Architects) and one related to the lower level of architecture (i.e., Domain Architect). We summarise our results from this final step in our Discussion in Sect. 4.

## 3   Main Findings and Results

As in our study design outlined, the coding procedure is identical for both the interviews and the questionnaire survey. After saturation, four themes emerged with 12 codes in total (cf. Table 2). Each code has several sub-codes with more granular results. The complete code-book is available in the replication package. Due to space restrictions, we present and analyse the top sub-codes selected based on their highest frequency - if applicable.

The given frequencies indicate the population who answered a certain question. Not all participants responded to every item in the survey. Items may have been left empty or filled with blanks because the expert was reluctant to answer, did not understand it, or had personal time constraints. If a substantial proportion of respondents did not answer a question, this is mentioned in our analysis. All results and frequencies refer to the data from both interviews and questionnaire; only when significant, we distinguish between the two.

### 3.1   Demographics

The demographics of our participants is outlined in Table 1. Our entire population comprises 47 participants with 32 from the questionnaire survey and 15 from the interviews. As outlining all different job titles would not reveal strong insights due the variety of titles in a large enterprise, we clustered the participants into either *high-level* or *low-level* architecture. The former, *high-level*,

---

[3] ATLAS.ti: https://atlasti.com.

includes jobs like Enterprise-, Business-, or Governance Architect; all operating towards the strategic level of architecture. The latter, *low-level*, includes roles like Solution-, Domain-, or Data Architect; all operating towards the operational level of architecture. For the interviews, we sought balance to complement the questionnaire with its majority on the low-level. We acknowledge that the high-level architecture has a substantial influence on the low-level. Thus, we aim to complement our insights from both levels.

We notice that 42 participants (89%) have engaged in software projects for more than 10 years, with their experience ranging from 11 to 41 years. This suggests that the results obtained were derived from experts who possess extensive and valuable experience gained from a long industrial career. With working for the same company of more than 17 years on average (arithmetic mean), we guarantee that the majority of the experts have profound understanding of the processes in their organisation, leading us to reliable results.

**Table 1.** Demographics of participants. **I** = Interview; **Q** = Questionnaire; $\Sigma$ = Summation of Interview and Survey Participants; $\overline{years}$ = Arithmetic mean

| (a) Architecture Level | | | | (b) Experience in software | | | | (c) Experience in current organisation | | | |
|---|---|---|---|---|---|---|---|---|---|---|---|
| | | | | **Years** | **I** | **Q** | **Σ** | **Years** | **I** | **Q** | **Σ** |
| **Level** | **I** | **Q** | **Σ** | 1 - 5 | 1 | 0 | 1 | 1 - 5 | 3 | 6 | 9 |
| High-Level | 7 | 5 | 12 | 6 - 10 | 1 | 3 | 4 | 6 - 10 | 2 | 8 | 10 |
| Low-Level | 8 | 27 | 35 | 11 - 20 | 3 | 10 | 13 | 11 - 20 | 6 | 3 | 9 |
| | | | | 21 - 30 | 7 | 8 | 15 | 21 - 30 | 3 | 9 | 12 |
| | | | | 31 - 41 | 3 | 11 | 14 | 31 - 41 | 1 | 6 | 7 |
| | | | | $\overline{years}$ | 23.5 | 24.4 | 24.1 | $\overline{years}$ | 15.3 | 18.0 | 17.1 |

### 3.2 Architecture Knowledge Elements

Most participants provided definitions that reflected our understanding of AK. However, a few participants shared unique perspectives:

> *"Skills to guide a particular solution landscape in a certain context. This is not a library: it is fluid and keeps developing with every problem I address. Because I have been doing this for a long time, books and trainings are hardly needed, unless big new innovations [...]"* (Q_ID-31)

Besides the general understanding of AK, our interest is especially focused on what kind of knowledge elements the experts keep in their professional context and if they could think of any elements which would support their daily work.

**Elements.** While the majority referred to well known elements as part of their daily work, i.e., (i) architecture design decisions, (ii) standards and guidelines, and (iii) principles, we also found the blueprint (n = 11) mentioned as a driving"element". Although we have not considered this as a separate element,

**Table 2.** Results clustered by themes, codes, and sub-codes *(extract)*

(a) RQ1: on AK representation and communication

| | | | |
|---|---|---|---|
| **Theme-1 - RQ1.1 AK Elements** | **Elements** | | |
| | [1.1.1] | *Design-decisions are a central element* | (n = 19) |
| | [1.1.2] | *Standards and guidelines are a central element* | (n = 15) |
| | [1.1.3] | *Architecture principles are a central element* | (n = 13) |
| | **Impediments** | | |
| | [1.2.1] | *Missing link between architecture levels* | (n = 16) |
| | [1.2.2] | *Missing business architecture* | (n = 5) |
| | [1.2.3] | *Missing information about the context* | (n = 5) |
| **Theme-2 - RQ1.2 AK Representation** | **Methods** | | |
| | [2.1.1] | *Architecture description templates* | (n = 45) |
| | [2.1.2] | *Architecture diagrams* | (n = 34) |
| | [2.1.3] | *Guidelines and Standards* | (n = 10) |
| | **Standards** | | |
| | [2.2.1] | *ArchiMate* | (n = 34) |
| | [2.2.2] | *TOGAF* | (n = 14) |
| | **Impediments** | | |
| | [2.3.1] | *Knowledge is not captured consistently* | (n = 19) |
| | [2.3.2] | *Need for more standards* | (n = 7) |
| **Theme-3 - RQ1.3 AK Communication** | **Methods** | | |
| | [3.1.1] | *Face-to-face is used for communicating* | (n = 30) |
| | [3.1.2] | *Corporate Repositories are a major communication channel* | (n = 26) |
| | [3.1.3] | *The Architecture Review Board is a central element* | (n = 13) |
| | **Stakeholders** | | |
| | [3.2.1] | *Architects are the communication bridge* | (n = 35) |
| | **Impediments** | | |
| | [3.3.1] | *Knowledge is like finding the needle-in-a-haystack* | (n = 6) |
| | [3.3.2] | *Tacit knowledge remains implicit* | (n = 4) |

(b) RQ2: on carving sustainability into AK practice

| | | | |
|---|---|---|---|
| **Theme-4 - RQ2 Sustainability** | **Definition** | | |
| | [4.1.1] | *Unbalanced view on sustainability* | (n = 21) |
| | [4.1.2] | *Comparison with economic costs* | (n = 13) |
| | **Daily Work** | | |
| | [4.2.1] | *Sustainability by intrinsic motivation* | (n = 19) |
| | [4.2.2] | *Sustainability is addressed unconsciously* | (n = 11) |
| | [4.2.3] | *Usage of dashboards* | (n = 5) |
| | **Where and How to inject?** | | |
| | [4.3.1] | *Low level architecture; Bottom-up* | (n = 11) |
| | [4.3.2] | *High level architecture; Top-down* | (n = 10) |
| | [4.3.3] | *Architecture Description Templates* | (n = 14) |
| | **Impediments** | | |
| | [4.4.1] | *Missing awareness about strategic targets* | (n = 28) |
| | [4.4.2] | *Missing guidance on how to implement sustainability* | (n = 9) |
| | [4.4.3] | *Lack of knowledge about sustainability* | (n = 5) |

as it implies the entire architecture design [3], it is worth mentioning that the design is treated as a holistic AK element by the experts.

**Impediments.** It appears that there might be a demand (n = 16) for a better link beyond the specific architecture documents to (i) the other architecture levels, (ii) the business itself, and (iii) the broader context. We identify that as a need for developing new AK elements that better capture the context and link various architecture views to various stakeholders and the business.

> *"[...] we tend to develop views that are understood by architects (which gives grip on the architecture), but less meaningful for (other) stakeholders, linking architecture views to (non architectural) views of different stakeholders is now lacking. We tend to speak our own language and not the language of different stakeholders."* (Q_ID-4)

In our interviews we tried to better understand this need. We found that indeed, only on the higher level of architecture documents, there are elements (e.g., diagrams) that explicitly outline the relationship to the business models. At the lower level this connection is not made explicit and the link to the underlying system architecture is lost.

> *"If we distinguish enterprise architecture and domain architecture what we have in the bank, and then also the lower level [...] system architecture, that linkage is missing. [...] what I would suggest is that we co-create the domain architecture also with the system architecture. So, certain chapters in the template would be created from the domain architect, while others would be created from the system architect. This would lead to one joint-deliverable and enable collaboration"* (I_ID-10)

### 3.3  Architecture Knowledge Representation

**Methods.** Not surprisingly, 45 experts (95%) referred to architecture description templates and 34 (72%) to diagrams as their method to represent AK. However, most of the experts used their corporate synonyms to refer to a template. For instance, the professionals distinguish between Solution Intents to describe the actual change and architecture of an intended solution on the low-level; and Future State Architecture to represent the envisioned state incorporating strategic goals on the high-level. Nevertheless, all documents are based on one common template. Interestingly, only five experts mentioned views and viewpoints. Recent emerging methods such as Architecture Description Records (ADRs)[4] or C4-model[5] haven been mentioned only once.

**Standards.** Highly related to the methods are standard notations and languages to represent AK. ArchiMate[6] was mentioned 32 times (72%) as standard architecture modeling language. However, at the same time, especially during the interviews, we also recognised impediments regarding ArchiMate:

---

[4] ADRs: https://cognitect.com/blog/2011/11/15/documenting-architecture-decisions.

[5] C4-model: https://c4model.com.

[6] ArchiMate: https://www.opengroup.org/archimate-forum/archimate-overview.

*"The point with ArchiMate is it's not easy to understand for people who don't know the notation [...] I think the knowledge of ArchiMate is really decreasing in the organization [...]"* (I_ID-06)

The experts mentioned also methods which cannot be considered as standards (n = 9) such as PowerPoint or "Diagram.net" diagrams. This underlines the deep integration of "boxes-and-lines" tools into the daily work.

**Impediments.** We uncovered that the architecture is currently not consistently represented and captured throughout the bank. This conclusion derives from contradicting results: 19 experts (40%) answered our question about consistency with *no*, while 23 (48%) answered with *yes*. When differentiating between architecture layers, only 16% of high-level architects report a lack of complete consistency across the organisation, while nearly 50% of low-level architects affirm or deny this, respectively. This might be an indicator that the high-level architects are not aware of the lack in consistency on the lower-levels. However, we do also acknowledge the fluid transition between the layers which is in line with the findings from Capilla et al. [5] that consistency in AK is context dependent.

### 3.4    Architecture Knowledge Communication

**Methods.** Similar to the results of AK representation methods, the discovered methods in AK communication are in line with our understanding on how AK is communicated. While 26 experts (55%) use their corporate repositories (e.g., Microsoft SharePoint or Confluence) as main communication tool, the majority mentioned face-to-face knowledge exchange in form of scheduled or informal meetings as well as meetings in a workshop setup. The Architecture Review Board (ARB) is used to evaluate all architecture description documents and assess how well they conform to the company's fundamental principles. We consider the ARB as a central communication element since the knowledge represented and captured in the documents is complemented with tacit knowledge during the review sessions.

**Stakeholders.** Overall we got diverse answers regarding the stakeholders the architects have to communicate their knowledge. The responses vary from product owner or managers to people who build the architecture, the DevOps team, or the platform team. However, if we consider the role of our expert and match the named roles to their level, in 74% of the cases we observe that it is always *"the level below you, and the level above you"* (I_ID-04). This conclusion confirms the results from Kruchten [11] as they see the architecture role as "communication bridge" between different levels.

**Impediments.** While we did not encounter any significant obstacles in the communication process, a subset of experts (n = 6) expressed the concern AK may be scattered across various repositories. Although only a small number of participants (n = 4) reported implicit tacit knowledge, it may still pose a challenge due to the frequent reliance on face-to-face communication as a primary instrument for sharing information.

## 3.5 Sustainability

**Definition.** Among respondents, 25 linked environmental factors (e.g., energy efficiency) and 21 linked technical factors (e.g., longevity) to IT sustainability. Thirteen experts connected sustainability directly to economic costs. These findings highlight an imbalanced perspective and limited understanding of the sustainability dimensions. The participants tend to focus either on single dimensions or merge concerns from different dimensions.

*"[...] reducing footprints, reducing energy, reducing the use of resources in general - almost equals to reducing costs."* (I_ID-07)

**Daily Work.** Nineteen experts expressed a personal interest in IT sustainability and intrinsic motivation to address it in their daily work. We reached that conclusion based on participants' missing awareness about strategic targets pertaining sustainability (n = 28), coupled with frequent mentions (n = 25) of sustainability practices in their daily tasks (e.g., selecting energy-efficient solutions during the design process or incorporating quality attributes regarding sustainability).

*"I do something from an intrinsic motivation. So how can I from a data management perspective contribute to the sustainability agenda of [anonymised], maybe the IT sustainability agenda as well?"* (I_ID-17)

Interestingly, 15 respondents reported that they did not consider sustainability in their daily work; however, they later mentioned some sustainability-related tasks in their professional routine. The incorporation of sustainability aspects contradicts their awareness of sustainability. This indicates a possibly-unconscious consideration of sustainability.

**Where and How to inject?** We also leveraged the participants' experience to understand where and how sustainability could be considered in their daily work. While 11 architects suggest that sustainability should be integrated into the low-level, i.e., the solution design, 10 experts consider the high-level as the right starting level, i.e., enterprise architecture. The most frequent answer regarding the *how* was to embed sustainability into the architecture description templates, i.e., the Solution Intent.

*"In the solution intent by using quality attributes. I see sustainability as an aspect of the solution, like security"* (Q_ID-12)

**Impediments.** The majority of experts (59%) are not aware of the sustainability targets in their organisation. This points to a problem in both representing and communicating the two strategic targets on all architecture levels: target (i) *lower the Co2 footprint*, and target (ii) *circular IT assets*.

When asked what would be necessary or what hinders the experts in addressing sustainability, some respondents indicated missing guidance on how to leverage sustainability. This guidance should be either in form of concrete architecture guidelines and standards, tangible strategic goals, and a clear definition of what sustainability means. This reflects the findings from Lago et al. [16].

*"We need to have some guidelines, what sustainability requirements we see as a bank or what we have as a bank. [...] So we would need some hooks."* (I_ID-11)

## 4  Discussion

In the previous section, results give an overview of AK professional practice in a large-scale enterprise, which helps us achieve our first research goal and answer RQ1. Building on these results, we now turn to our second goal. We conducted a horizontal analysis between RQ1 and RQ2 and identified a list of 14 recommendations. Due to space limitations, we discuss those five that have been prioritised in the two informal meetings (cf. Section 2.2). The complete list is available online. Each recommendation is labeled **R-1** through **R-5** and comes with a boxed example of a specific AK method and the equivalent application of sustainability. The example entails the "as-is" state describing the current situation in the bank[7]; the "to-be" state exemplifies our vision towards achieving sustainable architecture in current practice. All recommendations are grounded on the evidence found during the interviews and questionnaire. We link the recommendations to our findings presented in Sect. 3.

**R-1:** Repositories contain architecture standards and guidelines developed at a high-level. These standards provide the necessary knowledge about specifications that solutions or documents must conform to, while guidelines represent the recommended course of action. This enables a valuable opportunity to also establish principles and guidelines related to sustainability to guide the architecture design process. We can reuse current practices and ensure that sustainability is not addressed unconsciously, while also providing the required guidance.

| **R-1:** Clear Sustainability Guidelines and Principles | |
|---|---|
| ⊘ **as-is state** | ⚡ **to-be state** |
| Guideline for Databases<br>Security related:<br>*"D1: Direct links between databases are not allowed in order to achieve isolation."* | Guideline for Sustainability<br>Cloud related:<br>*"S1: Auto-scaling of cloud application needs to be enabled by default."* |
| **Evidence:** *[1.1.2]; [1.1.3]; [4.2.2]; [4.4.2]* | |

**R-2:** Given that AK is largely represented in templates and diagrams, we recommend utilizing these templates to add a new chapter dedicated to sustainability assessments and persistently storing sustainability knowledge. Initially, this chapter could include diagrams (e.g., [14]), a sustainability assessment (e.g., [15]), and the adherence to sustainability standards and guidelines (see R-1). By treating sustainability in the same manner as other important chapters such as *security*, it can be effectively integrated into the architecture document. We acknowledge that adding a new chapter may increase the size of

---

[7] The "as-is" states are based on real-world examples; however, they have been generalised to avoid disclosing sensitive information.

the template, but if sustainability is a part of a company's strategy, it requires the same level of attention as other strategic concerns.

**R-2:** Inject a sustainability chapter into existing templates

| ⊘ **as-is state** | ⚡ **to-be state** |
|---|---|
| **Template outline** | **Template outline** |
| *1) Stakeholders* | *...* |
| *2) Solution Architecture* | *5) Sustainability Assessment* |
| *3) Architecture Compliance* | *5a) Sustainability by Design* |
| *4) Architecture Decisions* | *5b) Adherence to Sustainability* |
| | *Standards and Guidelines* |

**Evidence:** *[2.1.1]; [2.1.2]; [4.3.1]; [4.3.2]; [4.3.3]*

**R-3:** Given the importance of architecture design-decisions in the current AK practice, we propose capturing sustainability-related design-decisions.

**R-3:** Design Decisions regarding sustainability need to be captured

| ⊘ **as-is state** | ⚡ **to-be state** |
|---|---|
| *"The new process will be migrated without code optimizations due to increased complexity and risks."* | *"[...] We are accepting the high computation and energy consumption and therefore apply auto-scaling to compensate this trade-off."* |

**Evidence:** *[1.1.1]; [4.3.3]*

**R-4:** Based on the current architecture process, it is crucial to address sustainability on all levels and translate individual requirements for each level. However, we face two challenges: (i) the need for new or revised AK elements to better connect the different architecture levels, and (ii) the need for clear guidance on how to address sustainability throughout all levels. To make an immediate impact, we suggest a "bottom-up" approach, starting with the low-level, while also implementing a "top-down" approach on the high-level to ensure lasting effects on future solutions.

**R-4:** Sustainability needs to be addressed on all architecture levels

⊘ **as-is state**          ⚡ **to-be state**

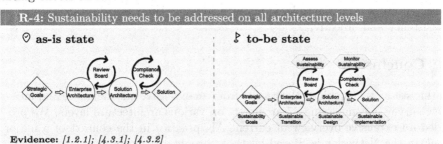

**Evidence:** *[1.2.1]; [4.3.1]; [4.3.2]*

**R-5:** Given the critical importance of understanding sustainability in general, we see the repositories currently used (e.g., Microsoft SharePoint) as an opportunity to provide experts with the necessary knowledge. Similar to the e-learning tutorials available on architecture, crucial information about sustainability can also be communicated. This knowledge transfer is particularly important for members of the ARB, as it is the highest instance assessing new designs.

**R-5:** Enable architects with knowledge about sustainability

| ◊ as-is state | ♭ to-be state |
|---|---|
| E-learning on Architecture: *"This virtual class explains the way of working around Enterprise Architecture and how the organisation works towards a solid architecture."* | E-learning on Sustainability: *"This virtual class explains the way of working around sustainability-aware architecture towards achieving our sustainability targets."* |

**Evidence:** *[3.1.2]; [4.1.1]; [4.1.2]; [4.4.3]*

## 5   Threats to Validity

**External Validity.** To increase the adoption of our recommendations, we phrased them in a generic manner for potential reuse, dependent on the AK practices in other enterprises. To further improve the generality of our findings, we clearly describe the context and methodology of our study. Additionally, we selected a diverse population with an average of 24.1 years of experience in software projects and 17.1 years of experience in the company. We also asked participants if they were aware of any AK methods that were exclusively valid in their banking context, and the majority (n = 31) responded *no*. Based on this response and their long experience in software in general, we derive that our results are applicable and generally known beyond our specific context.

**Internal Validity.** To ensure the validity of our survey findings, we acknowledge potential threats due to cultural differences, organizational culture, time and project pressure, and the design of the questionnaire. To address these issues, we carefully designed our survey guides based on existing literature and expert opinions, and conducted a pilot study to test the questions. Additionally, we collected data from multiple sources and triangulated the findings to ensure consistency and objectivity.

## 6   Conclusion

In this study, we combined the results from an extensive questionnaire and interview survey encompassing 47 architects on various architecture layers. We provided an extensive overview of current AK practice in the context of a major bank in the Netherlands. Based on those insights we propose concrete recommendations on how sustainability can be addressed and integrated. With those recommendations we contribute a major building block towards the overarching need: providing practical guidance on architecting software systems that are sustainable-balanced and creating awareness for a sustainability-aware architecture process in professional practice. In the future, we aim to first deriving insights from other domains, and then apply our recommendations in a real-world setting using an action research approach, with the goal of contributing our findings to both the research community and practitioners.

# References

1. Ali Babar, M., Dingsøyr, T., Lago, P., van Vliet, H.: Software Architecture Knowledge Management. Springer, Berlin Heidelberg (2009)
2. Andrikopoulos, V., Boza, R.D., Perales, C., Lago, P.: Sustainability in Software Architecture: A Systematic Mapping Study. In: 48th Euromicro Conference on Software Engineering and Advanced Applications (SEAA), IEEE (2022)
3. Bass, L., Clements, P., Kazman, R.: Software Architecture in Practice, 4th edn. Sei Series in Software Engineering, Addison-Wesley (2021)
4. Calero, C., et al.: 5Ws of green and sustainable software. Tsinghua Sci. Technol. **25**(3) (2020)
5. Capilla, R., Jansen, A., Tang, A., Avgeriou, P., Babar, M.A.: 10 years of software architecture knowledge management: Practice and future. J. Syst. Softw. **116**, 191–205 (2016)
6. Clements, P., et al.: Documenting Software Architectures: Views and Beyond. SEI Series in Software Engineering, Addison-Wesley (2003)
7. Dasanayake, S., Markkula, J., Aaramaa, S., Oivo, M.: Software Architecture Decision-Making Practices and Challenges: An Industrial Case Study. In: 24th Australasian Software Engineering Conference, IEEE (2015)
8. Ding, W., Liang, P., Tang, A., van Vliet, H.: Knowledge-based approaches in software documentation: a systematic literature review. Inform. Softw. Technol. **56**(6), 545–567 (2014)
9. Kasunic, M.: Designing an Effective Survey. Carnegie-Mellon Univ Pittsburgh PA Software Engineering Inst, Tech. rep. (2005)
10. Koziolek, H.: Sustainability evaluation of software architectures: A systematic review. In: Proceedings of the Joint ACM SIGSOFT Conference and Symposium on Quality of Software Architectures and Architecting Critical Systems, ACM (2011)
11. Kruchten, P.: What do software architects really do? J. Syst. Softw. **81**(12), 2413–2416 (2008)
12. Kruchten, P., Lago, P., van Vliet, H.: Building Up and Reasoning About Architectural Knowledge. In: Quality of Software Architectures, vol. 4214, Springer, Berlin Heidelberg (2006)
13. Kruchten, P., Obbink, H., Stafford, J.: The Past, Present, and Future for Software Architecture. IEEE Software **23**(2), 22–30 (2006)
14. Lago, P.: Architecture Design Decision Maps for Software Sustainability. In: 41st International Conference on Software Engineering: Software Engineering in Society (ICSE-SEIS), IEEE (2019)
15. Lago, P., Condori-Fernandez, N.: The Sustainability Assessment Framework. SAF) toolkit, Instruments to help sustainability-driven software architecture design decision making (2022)
16. Lago, P., Greefhorst, D., Woods, E.: Architecting for Sustainability. In: EnviroInfo (2022)
17. Lago, P., Koçak, S.A., Crnkovic, I., Penzenstadler, B.: Framing sustainability as a property of software quality. Commun. ACM **58**(10), 70–78 (2015)
18. Malavolta, I., Lago, P., Pelliccione, P., Tang, A.: What industry needs from architectural languages: a survey. IEEE Trans. Softw. Eng. **39**(6) (2013)
19. Saldaña, J.: The Coding Manual for Qualitative Researchers. SAGE (2016)
20. Vos, S., Lago, P., Verdecchia, R., Heitlager, I.: Architectural Tactics to Optimize Software for Energy Efficiency in the Public Cloud. In: ICT4S, IEEE (2022)

# Guidance Models for Designing Big Data Cyber Security Analytics Systems

Faheem Ullah[✉] and Muhammad Ali Babar

The Centre for Research on Engineering Software Technologies, The University of Adelaide,
Adelaide, Australia
{faheem.ullah,ali.babar}@adelaide.edu.au

**Abstract.** Big Data Cyber Security Analytics (BDCA) systems leverage big data technologies to collect, store, and analyze a large volume of security event data for detecting cyber-attacks. Architecting BDCA systems is a complex design activity, which involves critical decisions about the selection of architectural tactics for the satisfaction of various quality goals. Software architects need to consider associated dependencies, constraints, and impact on quality goals, which makes the design process quite challenging. To facilitate the design process, we propose guidance models for supporting the systematic design of BDCA systems. The guidance models facilitate architects to map functional and non-functional requirements for BDCA systems to a set of architectural tactics.

**Keywords:** Security · Big Data · Architectural Tactic · Design

## 1 Introduction

The amount of digital data produced is enormously increasing with around 41 Zettabytes data created in 2019 (as compared to 2 Zettabytes in 2010), which is expected to reach 149 Zettabytes in 2024 [1]. Such an enormous growth in data generation has fueled the role of big data technologies (e.g., Hadoop and Spark) in various domains such as healthcare, business analytics, and smart environments. Like other domains, the traditional systems in cyber security (such as Intrusion Detection System (IDS) and malware detector system) are unable to cope with the increasing volume, velocity, and variety of security event data (e.g., NetFlows) [2]. For example, an organization as large as HP generates around 1 trillion security events per day and a continuous network traffic of merely 1 Gbps can make an IDS obsolete [2]. Therefore, these traditional systems are supported with big data technologies, which has given birth to **Big Data Cyber Security Analytics (BDCA)** systems. A BDCA system is defined as "*A system that leverages big data tools for collecting, storing, and analyzing a large volume of security data to protect organizational networks, computers, and data from unauthorized access, damage, or attack*" [3].

The growing interest in BDCA systems motivated us systematically review and synthesize the State-of-the-Art (SOTA) architectures for BDCA systems [3], which revealed several useful findings: (i) a set of architectural tactics that are used to achieve different quality goals (e.g. response time) (ii) the tactics have associated constraints and impacts

B. Tekinerdogan et al. (Eds.): ECSA 2023, LNCS 14212, pp. 70–80, 2023.
https://doi.org/10.1007/978-3-031-42592-9_5

on multiple quality attributes and (iii) the selection and implementation of tactics varies among the reviewed BDCA systems. In the context of this study, an architectural tactic is a reusable design strategy that helps to achieve a particular quality attribute. A follow up empirical study [4] of ours on BDCA showed that the effectiveness of the tactics depends upon several factors such as the quality of security event data, the employed algorithms, and the execution mode of a system (e.g., standalone or distributed). These findings underline the inherent complexities in the design of a BDCA system. Such complexities make it challenging to understand the underlying design dependencies, constraints, and impact of quality goals, and subsequently make informed design decisions.

Building on the findings of our previous studies [3, 4], we present guidance models for designing BDCA systems. The guidance models are associated with different BDCA design phases such as data engineering and feature engineering. The guidance models map the problem space (requirements) to the solution space (tactics) and reveal the dependencies, constraints, quality implications, and implementation option for the tactics. The models are expected to guide software architects in mapping functional and non-functional requirements for BDCA systems to a set of architectural tactics. This way, the architects can select the most optimal set of tactics that best satisfy the quality goals, dependencies, and associated constraints.

## 2 Research Approach

The type model characterizes the elements of the guidance model and the relationship among the elements. The type model has been developed based on the guidelines provided in [5] and taking inspirations from the state-of-the-art on guidance models in various domains such as Cyber-foraging [6] and Microservices [7]. Our type model is presented in Fig. 1, which divides the design process into a problem space and a solution space. The problem space specifies the requirements (both functional and non-functional) and the solution space employs architectural tactics to address the requirements. The bold-headed arrow between a tactic and a requirement indicates that a particular tactic can be used to satisfy the requirement(s). Since BDCA systems use machine learning models to classify security event data into malicious and benign classes, the tactics are divided into three types based on whether a tactic is used in the training phase, testing phase, or both. The tactics used in the training phase are specified by the green box with a dotted borderline, in testing phase by the green box with a solid borderline, and in both training and testing phases by the green box with no borderline. Furthermore, some tactics are generic best practice, some are adopted for use in BDCA systems, and some are only applicable to BDCA systems. Such classification of tactics is specified in Fig. 1 by the symbols for each tactic – '*' generic tactic, '#' adopted for BDCA systems, and 'Δ' specific to BDCA systems.

If there are any risks or conditions associated with enabling a tactic to satisfy the requirement, these are represented as constraints. A relation between a tactic and requirement(s) has some implications for various Quality Attributes (QA). These implications are denoted as + QA, -QA, + + QA, -- QA, and + -QA in Fig. 1. The ' +' specifies a positive impact on a particular QA, '-' specifies a negative impact, ' + +' specifies a strong positive impact, '- -' QA specifies a strong negative impact, and ' + -' specifies

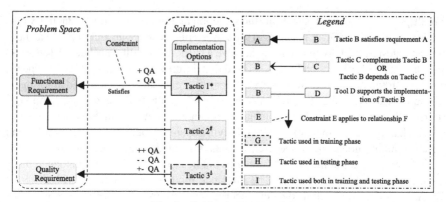

**Fig. 1.** Guidance Type Model

a potential for both positive and negative impact. The light-headed arrow between two tactics specifies that a tactic (tactic 1) requires or depends upon another tactic (tactic 2) for its incorporation in a design. In other words, a tactic (tactic 2) complements another tactic (tactic 1). Dependency and complementation are two different sides of the same relationship. However, dependency is an undesirable quality and complementation is a desirable quality. For example, if the incorporation of a tactic (say tactic-X) requires the incorporation of other three tactics in the system, the architect must incorporate all four tactics. On the other hand, if a tactic (say tactic-Y) does not require the incorporation of another tactic (i.e., tactic-Y is not dependent on another tactic), the architect can leverage only one tactic i.e., tactic-Y for a particular decision. Hence, tactic-Y is better (in terms of utility) than tactic-X. Similarly, a tactic that supports/complements the incorporation of other tactics in the system's design is better than a tactic that does not. The line between a tactic and the associated implementation option specifies that the mentioned tool/technology can be used for the implementation of the tactic.

We have developed the guidance models based a systematic analysis of the 74 BDCA systems' architectures reported in [3]. Based on the previous studies [3, 4], the functional requirements of a BDCA system are divided into five phases. These phases are data engineering, feature engineering, process engineering, data processing, and data post-processing. First, tactics are selected to address these functional requirements, which are then accompanied by tactics for satisfying non-functional requirements/quality (e.g., scalability and reliability).

## 3   Guidance Models

This section presents the guidance models for various BDCA design areas.

### 3.1   Data Engineering

Figure 2 presents the guidance model for data engineering. The tactics instantiated during the data engineering aims to preprocess and clean the collected data. The **Removal of Duplicates** tactic removes duplicate records from the training data to ensure that

Machine Learning (ML) model is not biased towards learning more frequent behaviors. The existence of a large number of duplicates prevents a model from learning the rare behaviors that indicate dangerous attacks [8]. The tactic *reduces training time* by reducing data size and *improves accuracy* by ensuring the development of an unbiased ML model. The tactic requires that the functionality responsible for removal of duplicates should not be computationally expensive. The tactic can be implemented using the NullWritable class in Hadoop library. The **Handling Missing Values** tactic detects the records with the values missing for some features (e.g., protocol type). Such records create a substantial amount of bias for subsequent data analysis. Upon detection, the tactic either removes the record or implants a new value for the feature using the data imputation technique. The tactic improves *accuracy* but *reduces the training time*. Some common tools for data imputation include NORM, SOLAS, and SAS. The **Removal of Incorrect Data** tactic discards records with future values that are not suitable for security analytics. For example, -20 is not a suitable value for number_of_bytes feature in a record. The tactic *improves accuracy* with a negligible *increase in response time*. The tactic requires careful formulation of rules (e.g., number_of_bytes > 0) for detecting incorrect values. The **Removal of Valueless Data tactic** discards data that does not contribute to detecting attacks. For instance, zero-byte flows are collected by a network sniffer;

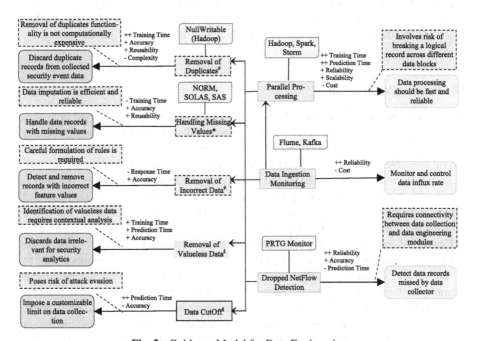

**Fig. 2.** Guidance Model for Data Engineering

Such data is only used in TCP/IP handshaking and does not have any relevance to attack detection [9]. Similarly, image data captured as URL suffixes with JPEG or JPG needs to be discarded [10]. The tactic *improves response time* by reducing data size.

The **Data CutOff tactic** imposes a customizable limit on data to be collected for each network connection or process. For example, only collecting the first 15 Kbytes of a network connection or storing data pertaining only to the first 100 s of the execution of a process. This tactic reduces the size of data to *reduce prediction time*. However, the tactic carries a risk of evading an attack if an attacker plans the execution of an attack after the customizable limit [11]. All five tactics associated with functional requirements depends on Parallel Processing tactic to manage the distribution of processing among computing nodes and Data Ingestion Monitoring tactic to prevent node failures by controlling data influx into a system. The **Parallel Processing** tactic *improves response time, scalability, and reliability*, however, it *increases the operation cost* of a system. The tactic involves a minor risk of breaking a record across different blocks during data partitioning. The tactic depends on Data Ingestion Monitoring tactic and Dynamic Load Balancing tactic for preventing node crash and balancing the load among nodes. The tactic is implemented using big data frameworks such as Hadoop and Spark. The **Data Ingestion Monitoring** tactic improves *reliability* by keeping a constant check on data ingestion rate, however, it also complicates the deployment of a system. The tactic is implemented using Flume or Kafka servers. **The Dropped NetFlow Detection** tactic detects records that are missed by a data collection tool (e.g., Wireshark). The tactic monitors the sequence number of records and if found out of order, a message is flagged. The tactic *improves reliability* by ensuring data is collected in its entirety and *increases response time* due to the monitoring cost. The tactic requires connectivity between data collection and data engineering modules. PRTG monitor is a tool for implementing this tactic.

## 3.2   Feature Engineering

Figure 3 presents a guidance model for feature engineering. The tactics used in feature engineering aim to select, generate, and/or transform features in the collected security event data. The **Feature Selection** tactic selects the most relevant features out of the several available features in data. The security event data often consists of many features as evident from 41 features in KDD and 82 features in CICIDS2017 dataset. Not all the features contribute to attack detection. Therefore, the irrelevant features are discarded to reduce data size and complexity, which eventually leads to *improved accuracy* and *reduced response time*. However, discarding features in situations where the number and nature of features continuously change (e.g., in dynamic networks) can harm the accuracy of a system. The **Feature Generation** tactic generates new features from.

the existing features to either improve accuracy or reduce data dimensionality. For example, Rathore et al., [12] sum source_bytes and destination_bytes to generate a new feature number_of_bytes. The tactic *improves accuracy*, however, the impact on response time depends upon whether the overall number of features is increased or decreased after the feature generation. An increase in the number of features increases response time and vice versa. This tactic *increases the overall complexity* of a system and requires a lightweight feature generation mechanism to achieve improvement in response time. The **Feature Transformation** tactic enhances security data in a way that an ML model can efficiently analyze data to detect suspicious cyber activities. For instance, the features'

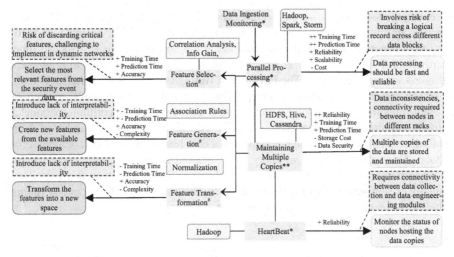

**Fig. 3.** Guidance Model for Feature Engineering

values can be transformed into a range of 0 to 1 to help an ML model to discriminate between malicious and benign access requests. This tactic *improves accuracy but increases response time* and *complexity*. Some common techniques for implementing this tactic includes normalization, bucketing, and one hot encoding. All the three tactics associated with the functional requirements depend on Parallel Processing and Maintaining Multiple Copies tactics. The Parallel Processing tactic distributes the processing for feature engineering among nodes. The **Maintaining Multiple Copies** tactic stores and maintains multiple copies of the data processed in this phase. These choices address the *issue of node failure* and *improve response time*. This tactic increases the attack surface by exposing the data on multiple fronts and *increases storage cost*. The tactic requires connectivity among nodes hosting data replicas and introduce data inconsistencies. The tactic relies on **Heartbeat** to check connectivity and health of the nodes that share data replicas.

### 3.3 Process Engineering

Process engineering ensures effective data processing in the subsequent phase (i.e., data processing). The guidance model for process engineering is shown in Fig. 4, which employs two tactics (i.e., ML Algorithm Selection and Parameter Tuning). The two most important factors for effective security analytics are input data quality and the employed ML algorithm [13]. Therefore, **ML Algorithm Selection** tactic assesses the applicability of various ML algorithms (e.g., Naïve Bayes and K-means) to select the most suitable algorithm to be employed in the subsequent phase. The algorithms are assessed based on their time complexity, incremental update capacity, attack detection accuracy, online/offline mode, and generalization capability. The tactic *improves accuracy and usability* by ensuring to select the algorithm that generates highly accurate and interpretable results. The impact on response time depends upon the time consumed in the selection process vs the time gained from the efficiency of the selected algorithm.

Moreover, the tactic *increases the overall complexity* of the BDCA system. The tactic requires careful trade-off among various quality attributes [13]. For example, an algorithm may generate more accurate results but at the cost of increased response time. Distributed ML libraries (such as Apache Mahout and MLlib) are used to implement and assess various algorithms. The **Parameter Tuning** tactic tunes the parameters (e.g., weights in a regression model) and hyperparameters (number of clusters in K-means) for the algorithms and frameworks (e.g., Hadoop). In addition to ML algorithms, parameter tuning is important for the underlying frameworks. For example, the number of Map and Reduce jobs, buffer size, and the number of data replicas need to be configured for Hadoop. This tactic *improves accuracy* with potential for both increase and decrease in response time. Furthermore, it *decreases the usability* of a system as a user must manually or semi-manually tune the parameters. Techniques for ML parameter tuning include Grid search and Bayesian optimization.

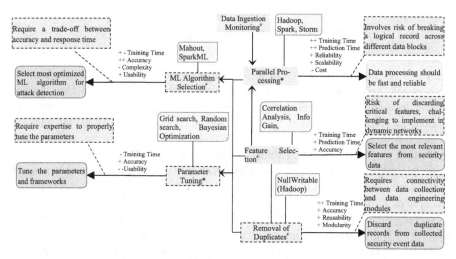

**Fig. 4.** Guidance Model for Process Engineering

## 3.4 Data Processing

The guidance model for data processing is shown in Fig. 5. This phase uses two tactics for detection of attacks. The **Anomaly-based Detection** tactic is the most crucial tactic, which uses an ML model to detect cyber behavior that deviates from normal behavior. Anomaly-based detection is very effective in detecting zero-day attacks [14]. The efficient use of this tactic *improves accuracy, response time, and generality* of a BDCA system. The tactic relies on ML algorithm selection and Parameter Tuning tactics to ensure effective selection and execution of ML algorithms and frameworks. The key disadvantage of this tactic is the potential to *generate many false positives*. Apache Mahout, MLlib, and Distributed Weka are some of the libraries used for implementation of ML algorithms used in anomaly detection. The **Signature-based Detection** tactic detects known attacks based on their attack signatures. The tactic *improves accuracy* only for known attacks by reducing false alarms and is faster as compared to anomaly-based detection. However, this tactic not only *increases the overall complexity* but also poses a *challenge of interoperability* between anomaly-based detection and signature-based detection. This concern is more severe in cases where a signature-based detection is an open-source tool such as BRO and SNORT. Signature-based detection is unable to detect zero-day attacks. Moreover, this tactic requires frequent updates of attack signatures to be able to detect newly introduced attacks. For updating the signatures, this tactic uses **Attack Pattern Updation** tactic that (semi) automatically updates the signatures used by the signature-based detection tactic. Both the tactics in data processing phase depend upon **Result Polling and Optimized Notification** tactic, which optimizes the delay in feeding results from mappers to reducers. This way Mapper nodes do not have to wait for predefined time limit rather they can notify the Reducer as soon as the Mapper results are ready. This tactic *improves response time* but makes nodes more vulnerable to failure.

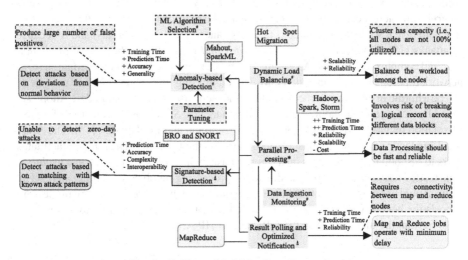

**Fig. 5.** Guidance Model for Data Processing

### 3.5 Data Post-Processing

The guidance model for post-processing is presented in Fig. 6. This phase processes the generated alerts to remove (any) false positives, correlate the alerts to reveal sophisticated attacks, and rank them to facilitate users in responding to them. The **False Positive Reduction** tactic uses mining techniques (e.g., clustering and classification) to learn about true positive and false positive from various features (e.g., IP address and protocol) of alerts [15]. The learnt characteristics are then used to classify future alerts. This tactic *improves accuracy* but *increases prediction time* due to extra processing. The tactic requires ground truth in the form of labels to mine insight from previous alerts. The

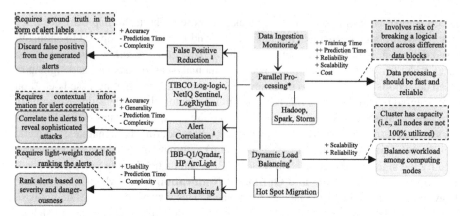

**Fig. 6.** Guidance Model for Data Post-processing

tactic depends upon Anomaly-based Detection tactic for alert generation. The **Alert Correlation** tactic correlates alerts based on logical relations to generate attack scenarios that help reveal sophisticated attacks (e.g., Advanced Persistent Threats) and root cause of attacks [15]. This tactic *improves accuracy and generality* at the cost of *prediction time* and complexity of a BDCA system. This tactic requires contextual information (e.g., network topology) to correlate alerts. Moreover, missing links and/or pre and post alerts can be a hurdle in efficient alert correlation. The tactic uses alerts generated by Anomaly-based Detection and Signature-based Detection tactics. Some commercial tools for alert correlation include TIBCO Log-logic, NetIQ Sentinel, and LogRhythm [15]. The **Alert Ranking** tactic ranks the final list of alerts based on their severity. The ranking facilitates users to respond to severe alerts on a priority basis, which *improves a system's usability*. This tactic *increases response time* due to the processing involved in ranking alerts. The tactic should use a lightweight ranking model otherwise the intensive ranking processing cancels the benefit gained through prioritized response to severe alerts. Some example tools for ranking alerts are IBB-Q1/QRadar and HP ArcSight [15].

## 4   Related Work

Guidance models recently attracted a lot of attention from the SE community. MacLean et al., [16] introduced Questions-Option-Criteria (QOC) approach, which provides a basis for guidance models. The QOC approach maps questions (problem space) to the options (solutions space). Other similar work include guidance models for cyber-foraging [6], microservices [7], and cloud computing [17]. Sabry et al., [18] report a survey aimed at quantifying the importance of various quality attributes and satisfying them using well-known tactics. Soliman et al., [19] proposes a design approach for making decisions related to the selection of technologies based on their impacts on a system's architecture. Al-Naeem et al., [20] proposed a quality-driven approach to quantitatively compares various technological options for designing systems. Xu et al., [21] presented decision models for designing Blockchain-based systems. To the best of our knowledge, ours is the first effort to propose guidance models for designing BDCA systems.

# 5 Conclusions

We proposed guidance models for designing BDCA systems. The guidance models provide guidance on various design considerations (e.g., implications on quality goals). The guidance models do not attempt to replace an architect rather aims to enable the architect to consider a variety of factors (e.g., QA and dependencies) in decision making and end up with a BDCA design that is optimal, traceable and justifiable. We plan to evaluate whether or not the models are correct and how useful these are for the practitioners in terms of helping them to design BDCA system. The evaluation will be carried out through a user study with practitioners.

# References

1. Holst, A.: Volume of data/information created worldwide from 2010 to 2024. Statistica (2020)
2. Cardenas, et al.: Big data analytics for security. IEEE Secur. Priv. **11**(6), 74–76 (2013)
3. Ullah, F., Babar, M.A.: Architectural tactics for big data cybersecurity analytics systems: a review. J. Syst. Softw. (2019)
4. Ullah, F., Babar, M.A.: An architecture-driven adaptation approach for big data cyber security analytics. Int. Conf. Softw. Architect. (ICSA) (2019)
5. Weinreich, R., Groher, I.: Software architecture knowledge management approaches and their support for knowledge management activities: a systematic literature review. Inf. Softw. Technol. **80**, 265–286 (2016)
6. Lewis, G.A., Lago, P., Avgeriou, P.: A decision model for cyber-foraging systems. Conf. Softw. Architect. (WICSA), (2016)
7. Haselböck, S., Weinreich, R., Buchgeher, G.: Decision guidance models for microservices: service discovery and fault tolerance. Conf. Eng. Comput.-Based Syst. (2017)
8. Chen, T., Zhang, X., Jin, S., Kim, O.: Efficient classification using parallel and scalable compressed model and its application on intrusion detection. Expert Syst. Appl. (2014)
9. Zhao, et al.: I-can-mama: integrated campus network monitoring and management. In: Network Operations and Management Symposium (2014)
10. Tian, J.-W., Qiao, H., Li, X., Tian, Z.: A statistical threat detection method based on dynamic time threshold. In: International Conference on Computer and Communications (2016)
11. Zhen, C.: Cloud computing-based forensic analysis for collaborative network security management system (2013)
12. Rathore, M.M., Ahmad, A., Paul, A.: Real time intrusion detection system for ultra-high-speed big data environments. J. Supercomput. **72**(9), 3489–3510 (2016)
13. Buczak, A.L., Guven, E.: A survey of data mining and machine learning methods for cyber security intrusion detection. IEEE Commun. Surv. Tutorials **18**(2), 1153–1176 (2016)
14. Bhuyan, M.H., Bhattacharyya, D.K., Kalita, J.K.: Network anomaly detection: methods, systems and tools. IEEE Commun. Surv. Tutorials **16**(1), 303–336 (2014)
15. Hubballi, N., Suryanarayanan, V.: False alarm minimization techniques in signature-based intrusion detection systems: a survey. Comput. Commun. **49**, 1–17 (2014)
16. MacLean, A., Young, R.M., Bellotti, V.M., Moran, T.P.: Questions, options, and criteria: elements of design space analysis. Hum. Comput. Interact. **6**(3–4), 201–250 (1991)
17. Zimmermann, O., Wegmann, L., Koziolek, H., Goldschmidt, T.: Architectural decision guidance across projects-problem space modeling, decision backlog management and cloud computing knowledge. In: Conference on Software Architecture (2015)
18. Sabry, A.E.: Decision model for software architectural tactics selection based on quality attributes requirements. Procedia Comput. Sci. **65**, 422–431 (2015)

19. Soliman, M., Riebisch, M., Zdun, U.: Enriching architecture knowledge with technology design decisions. In: Working IEEE/IFIP Conference on Software Architecture (2015)
20. Al-Naeem, T., Gorton, I., Babar, M.A., Rabhi, F., Benatallah, B.: A quality-driven systematic approach for architecting distributed software applications. In: ICSE, pp. 244–253 (2005)
21. Xu, X., Bandara, H.D., Lu, Q., Weber, I., Bass, L., Zhu, L.: A decision model for choosing patterns in blockchain-based applications. In: ICSA, pp. 47–57: IEEE (2021)

# Architecture Modeling and Design

# Automated Integration of Heteregeneous Architecture Information into a Unified Model

Sven Jordan[1]([✉]), Christoph König[2], Lukas Linsbauer[3], and Ina Schaefer[2][iD]

[1] Group IT Solution and Enterprise Architecture, Volkswagen AG,
Wolfsburg, Germany
`sven.jordan@volkswagen.de`
[2] Institute of Information Security and Dependability,
Karlsruhe Institute of Technology (KIT), Karlsruhe, Germany
`{Christoph.Konig,Ina.Schaefer}@kit.edu`
[3] Institute of Software Engineering and Automotive Informatics,
Technische Universität Braunschweig, Braunschweig, Germany

**Abstract.** As software systems are increasingly complex, architecture documentation becomes more important. Initial documentation of a system's architecture needs to be kept up-to-date as the system evolves. Therefore, automated support for maintaining and evolving architecture information and documentation of interconnected and heterogeneous systems is highly beneficial to engineers, architects, and other stakeholders. To achieve this, we propose to automatically integrate recovered architecture information from heterogeneous data sources and architectural artifacts into a unified data model to create integrated views. Integrated views provide a holistic and up-to-date system representation. In this work, we present an integration approach for architecture information in a unified data model that serves as a digital architecture twin representing the current architecture of a system. We show that the integration approach successfully integrates architecture information by applying adapted metrics.

**Keywords:** Architecture Information · Software Architecture
Recovery · Consolidation · Integration · Unified Model

## 1 Introduction

Software systems have to frequently adapt to different environments, advances in technology, or changing customer requirements. For maintenance and development of a ever-changing software system, it is essential to have up-to-date architecture documentation [3]. However, as a system evolves, the documentation has to keep up with the changes, as otherwise it does not reflect the actual system anymore. Decisions based on out-dated architecture documentation lead to inaccuracies impeding architecture planning and causing higher costs [2].

B. Tekinerdogan et al. (Eds.): ECSA 2023, LNCS 14212, pp. 83–99, 2023.
https://doi.org/10.1007/978-3-031-42592-9_6

However, the creation and continuous maintenance of documentation is linked with high effort, as it is a primarily manual task [16]. Furthermore, different stakeholders require different views on a system at different levels of granularity [4]. Explicitly documenting all these views at any possible level of granularity does not scale, as it adds to the effort to keep the documentation consistent with the system by also keeping its different views consistent with each other [13]. To counter the problem of outdated documentation and decreasing documentation quality, software architecture recovery methods [18] have been proposed.

Software architecture recovery [8] describes methods for retrieving architecture information from an implemented system and associated data sources. Currently, architecture recovery methods are performed in isolation, and none of them represents the system entirely. But a software system has to be described from different related views to fully understand its architecture [13]. Different architecture recovery methods provide architecture information in different output formats and granularity level increasing the complexity to correlate the architecture information with each other. However, by combining results of separate architecture recovery methods to create an integrated view of the recovered architecture information, different aspects can be linked with each other providing a broader overview of the software system. Automating the recovery and integration reduces human effort to have up-to-date architecture documentation.

In this paper, we propose an approach to integrate the different outputs of architecture recovery methods concerned with a static representation of the software system into an unified data model to create integrated views. Integrated views are the basis of a Digital Architecture Twin (DArT) of the software system, which co-evolves with the system and combines different system perspectives. For the integration, we focus on the clustering technique, which is most prominently used, in architecture recovery and its results can be automatically performed and integrated [18]. Our integration approach comprises of five steps, in which different architecture information is integrated while respecting possible conflicting or supplementary architecture information. We evaluate the integration approach by applying it to four open source systems to observe if our approach is able to integrate architecture information without losing any information. We further discuss how to enhance the integration approach to incorporate other architecture information recovery sources.

## 2    Background

Architecture information describes a software system from different views (e.g., structural, behavioral or deployment views). These views include information such as (low- and high-level) system components, interfaces between software systems or design decisions made while designing the software system [7,13].

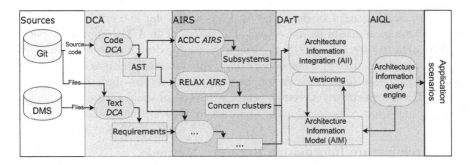

**Fig. 1.** Creation process of Digital Architecture Twin (DArT)

## 2.1  Digital Architecture Twin

The Digital Architecture Twin is an architecture information model that incorporates different architecture information (i.e., different views, different granularity). Figure 1 shows the process to create the DArT. The DArT enables application scenarios like a recommendation system to support future design decisions for software architecture or architecture documentation tailored to the needs of the stakeholder. In the following, we briefly discuss each step of the DArT construction process. The first step of the creation process of the DArT is the extraction of data from heterogeneous data sources using the *Data Collection Agents* (DCAs). They strive to independently extract the raw data from sources like source code repositories, architecture documentation repositories or infrastructure databases and provide it to architecture information recovery services that can make use of the data (e.g., structural information at a certain abstraction such as an abstract syntax tree). During the collection process, preprocessing of the raw data is performed (e.g., parsing of source code into an abstract syntax tree), and the input in the required format for the Architecture Information Recovery Services is generated.

*Architecture Information Recovery Services (AIRSs)* use the preprocessed data and apply architecture recovery methods to recover architecture information. This information is subsequently integrated into the AIM. As the AIRS are supposed to recover the architecture information automatically, the recovery methods need to be automatic and generate results in a reasonable time frame.

The *Architecture Information Model (AIM)* combines different kinds of architectural information (e.g., structural or deployment) at different levels of abstraction (e.g., classes, packages, or components in the case of structural information of a Java system). The AIM includes information about the data sources from which the information was extracted (e.g., source code in a version control system), the AIRS used, and information about the version of the software system. The AIM also contains information from which data sources (e.g., source code in a version control system) and via which recovery service the information was extracted, and version information to track what architectural information corresponds to which system version. The AIM has a modular and extensible design, which allows to generate various views of a system. The AIM comprises aspects such as *architecture rationale* (e.g., design decisions, design patterns), *business* (e.g., domain, capability), *components* (e.g., subsystems, packages, compilation units), *deployment* (e.g., network zone), *interfaces*, and (non-)functional *requirements*. These aspects are chosen as primary drivers for architecture documentation [11] and their consideration for architecture recovery methods.

## 2.2   Architecture Information Recovery Methods

Architecture information can be recovered from different data sources (i.e., artifacts of the system) via architecture recovery methods or from existing documentation [8]. Architecture recovery is the process of extracting architecture information from a system's implementation (e.g., source code or build scripts) or from other architectural artifacts (e.g., textual documentation). Architecture recovery methods range from manual process guidelines to automatic methods.

In the following, we explain four concrete architecture recovery methods, which we use to illustrate integration challenges: ACDC [21], Bunch (NAHC) [19], PKG [15], and RELAX [16]. They automatically produce architectural information describing the system's structure using source code as input and clustering as a technique. We chose ACDC and Bunch because they are state-of-the-art and included PKG and RELAX to have different architecture information.

As an example system, we introduce a simple calculator application implemented in Java. The calculator consists of four classes: `Main` as entry point; `UI` for the user interface; `Calculator` for the calculations; and `BufferedImageCustom` for the insertion of a logo.

*ACDC* [21] is a pattern-driven clustering method, which clusters the structural information of the system based on dependencies and global variables found in the source code. Clusters generated are described as subsystems. ACDC provides comprehensible clusters depicting the structure of the clustered system. Figure 2a displays the shortened results of ACDC revealing a single subsystem (.ss) when applied to a small example system.

*Bunch* [19] uses hierarchical clustering, which generates module dependency graphs based on the source code. The module dependency graph is then partitioned into modules, which are clustered using the Bunch-clustering tools into subsystems producing a high-level overview of the system's structure. Bunch recovers 3 subsystems to reflect the structure of the example system (see Fig. 2b).

*PKG* [15] is a simple method which uses the package structure to recover architecture information. PKG assumes that source code is split into suitable packages. The output generated by PKG (see Fig. 2c) consists of 5 packages.

*RELAX* [16] employs a naive Bayes classifier, in which every Java-class is classified to eight pre-defined categories like security, graphics or database categorizing the functionality. Second, RELAX clusters the classified documents on

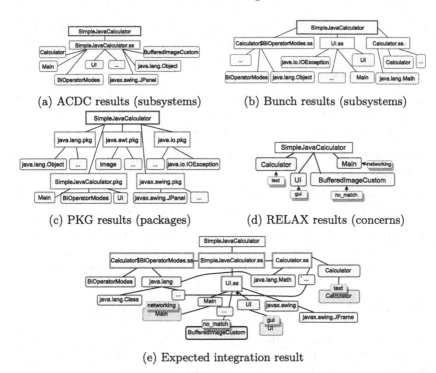

(a) ACDC results (subsystems)  (b) Bunch results (subsystems)

(c) PKG results (packages)  (d) RELAX results (concerns)

(e) Expected integration result

**Fig. 2.** Architecture recovery results depicting the structure of an example system

the basis of the classification results and possible dependencies found within the documents. Figure 2d describes the classified and clustered classes and their relationship among each other of the running example as recovered with RELAX.

The expected results of the integration are depicted in Fig. 2e, it should include every architecture information automatically obtained of the presented architecture recovery methods, unified and connected with each other. Architecture information needs to be transformable into a common format.

## 3  Problem Statement and Challenges for Architecture Information Integration

The main idea of the *DArT* is to employ proven *architecture information recovery* approaches leveraging different *architecture data sources* (e.g., source code, build and deployment scripts) by integrating them into the *AIM* to obtain an updated and linked representation of the software system. Integration of recovered architecture information from different sources into the AIM has to consider different levels of detail of the architecture information results and how results from different perspectives and views can be connected.

While studying architecture information obtained from architecture recovery methods, we identified five challenges for the integration:

**Uniform Data Format.** Architecture recovery methods provide different output formats (e.g., 3-tuple text file, XML-files.) Recovered architecture information needs to be transformed into a uniform representation to automatically integrate this architecture information.

**Automation.** Only automatically obtainable architecture information, not relying on human interpretation can be automatically integrated. Architecture recovery methods like guidelines cannot be automatically integrated.

**Incrementality.** If the architectural information change when system evolves, the information in the unified data model needs to be updated incrementally.

**Computationally intensive.** Architecture information recovery can be computationally intensive (i.e., long computation times or demanding resources).

**Validation.** Integration of recovered architecture information requires a careful validation to assess the correctness of the results, such as presenting stakeholders with either a guideline to assess the integrated architecture information.

## 4    Detailed Architecture Integration Approach

In this section, we describe the *Architecture Information Integration (AII)* process responsible for the integration of recovered architecture information, detailed in Fig. 3. The AII is performed when an AIRS recovers architecture information. The AII is concerned with similar, dissimilar or complementary information recovered from different sources or different layers of architecture information and their integration in the AIM. The AIM unifies different architecture information of different levels and views of the analyzed system.

The recovered architecture information is integrated unaltered, thus providing architecture information of different approaches without redundancies. To support the user assessing the recovered and integrated architecture information in the AIM, we introduce the concept of *confidence*. We assume that architecture information which is recovered more often by AIRSs, is more likely correct in resembling the system. AIRS providing the same results increases the *confidence* in the recovered architecture information.

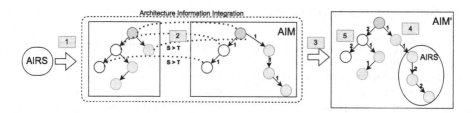

**Fig. 3.** Abstract architecture information integration (AII) example

**Step 1: Transformation of AIRS Output to an Instance of the AIM.** In the first step of the integration approach, the provided architecture information by AIRS is transformed into a directed acyclic graph (DAG) representation, which complies with the underlying AIM. Whether the AIRS is producing cluster information or providing design patterns or requirements, the information is transformed into the directed acyclic graph.

**Step 2: Pairwise Comparison of AIRS Output Model to Contents of AIM.** The transformed architecture information allows a pairwise comparison of the branches and leaves with the architecture information in the AIM. If the comparison happens between two transformed DAGs with only one branch, this is trivial. If the transformed DAG is complex (e.g., more than one branch), the approach compares every leaf of the newly created DAG with leaves in the existing architecture data model. This comparison is passed upwards to the "root" of the DAG. This process is done with every branch in the transformed DAG. Comparing every branch of the new DAG with the existing architecture information identifies possible (dis-)similarities.

For the comparison, we use three different comparators. The first comparator uses the fully qualified identifier. For clustering results of an AIRS, the identification of the similarity and dissimilarity is done by matching the names of the implemented sources (e.g., in Java, this is the combination of package.classname). For other architecture information, this can also span the name of the business capability, requirement, network zone or design pattern.

The second comparator is comparing structures to identify subsets of architecture information, (e.g., subsystem A incorporates classes X, Y Z and new recovered subsystem B incorporates only classes X,Y, so we assume that the new subsystem B is a subset of subsystem A). The subset-comparator, incorporates the type of the compared element. This means that a package cannot be a subset of a class, but vice versa. Therefore it is possible, that architecture information contributes to a subset, when it is of is the same type, but also it has a dependency which does not violate the hierarchies of the types.

The third comparator is based on MojoFM [22]. We calculate *move* and *join* operators performed to transform the new architecture information DAG into the existing architecture information (based on branches). If every leaf of a DAG, and therefore every item in a cluster, has to be allocated to another DAG item (and therefore cluster item), we assume the architecture information to be disjoint, adding a new view of the system. Less transformation steps increase the similarity rating of the compared architecture information.

Every comparator calculates a comparison value and compares it to a threshold. The three comparators are called in sequence, first the name-comparator, second the subset-comparator and last the MoJoComparator. If the name comparator detects a 100% coverage, we evaluate the results of the subset-comparator, which influences how to proceed with the integration. If the name-comparator is not at 100%, we use the MoJoComparator. When all three com-

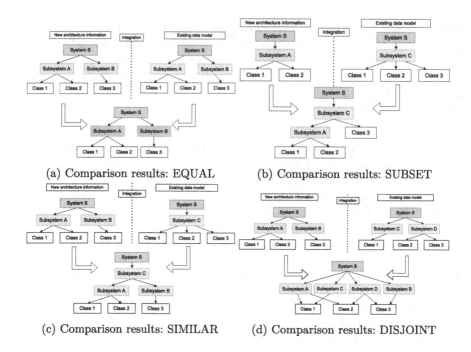

(a) Comparison results: EQUAL    (b) Comparison results: SUBSET

(c) Comparison results: SIMILAR    (d) Comparison results: DISJOINT

**Fig. 4.** Comparison results for the integration

parators do not provide a definitive results, we calculate the arithmetic mean and take this as the result of the integration.

**Step 3: Integration into Updated AIM.** After the comparison step, we differentiate between architecture information (clusters) which are *equal, subsets* of another architecture information (cluster), *disjoint, similar above threshold* and *similar below threshold*. For the integration, we introduced a manual adjustable similarity threshold to differentiate between architecture information, which is not equal or disjoint. Architecture information above the threshold allows to integrate the new architecture information to the existing architecture information. Architecture information below the threshold is stored independently, but linked with the already existing architecture information. Depending on the similarity, the integration is handled as described in the following.

*Equal.* If the compared new branches and leaves and the existing branches and leaves in the AIM are equal, the information will not be stored again as no new information was recovered. The confidence of the architecture information found in the DArT is increased by one (cf. Fig. 4a).

*Subset.* If the compared new architecture information branches and leaves are a subset of the existing architecture information, the subset is added, leading to the integration of a new hierarchy level in the AIM. Furthermore, it increases the confidence of the architecture information found in the DArT (cf. Fig. 4b).

*Similar Above Threshold.* If the new and the existing architecture information is similar above a specific threshold, the architecture information is merged into the AIM. This in turn leads to consolidated clusters as well as integrated architecture information via new connections of the architecture information (cf. Fig. 4c).

*Similar Below Threshold.* If the new and the existing architecture information is similar but below a specific threshold, the new architecture information and the existing architecture information are added as well but the new supplementing information is not merged with the existing architecture information. Merged information as well as new information is stored in the AIM. When possible, new hierarchy levels are added to the AIM.

*Disjoint.* If the new architecture information is disjoint or conflicting to the existing information, we add the new information without integration into the AIM. The new information may be another view on the system's architecture, disjunctive or conflicting to the other existing architecture information (cf. Fig. 4d).

**Step 4: New Structural Levels Are Added Depending on the Consolidated Architecture Information.** When integrating architecture information, different granularity levels must be considered. If lower-level information (e.g., classes) is recovered by one AIRS and higher-level information (e.g., packages) is recovered by another AIRS, we add a hierarchy level in the DArT relating the information with each other. We also add a hierarchy level, when subset or similar above the threshold architecture information is recovered. As different architecture information can be integrated with each other, we also add "hierarchy levels" (e.g., requirements integrated with a subsystem, design patterns with classes) (cf. Fig. 4c). The new hierarchy levels generate new links, which are counted and appropriately increased in terms of confidence.

**Step 5: Compute Confidence in Elements of AIM.** In the last integration step, we calculate the *confidence* of the architecture information. The confidence value helps estimate whether the recovered architecture information is commonly recovered by the AIRSs or if it is recovered by a single approach. We increment the confidence count when two AIRSs recover the same elements and connections, resulting in higher relative confidence in the corresponding cluster and connection. If multiple AIRS are integrated, the confidence value depicts the most reliable architecture information. For example, if an architecture information is recovered by 8 out of 10 AIRSs, we present a confidence of 80% for that information. Confidence also assists in dealing with conflicting information. As different AIRS, which are integrated into the AIM might recover different views, it is possible that contradictory information is recovered. To address this, we store the conflicting architecture information along with the responsible AIRS in the AIM. This, combined with confidence, provides evidence whether the architecture information is often recovered and a valid description of the software system. This is necessary, as the decision, which architecture information is "correct" and which might distort the architecture of the software system cannot be made automatically or even manually decidable, we store the architecture information independently from each other.

*Discussion.* The first challenge (*Uniform data format*) stated in Sect. 3 is addressed by requiring to transform all recovered architecture information into a DAG. Currently, all architecture information provided by the AIRS as well as in the AIM can be transformed into a DAG. Regarding *automation*, we can only select architecture recovery methods which can be automatically integrated [8]. To mitigate the challenge of *validation*, we introduced the concept of confidence such that stakeholders are supported assessing the integrated architecture information. *Incrementality* is addressed within our integration approach, as AIRS can be applied continuously which we will investigate in detail in future work. However, we cannot remedy the challenge of *computationally* intensive architecture recovery methods, but we argue that starting the integration process to recover and integrate the architecture information whenever a data source changes avoids having a computationally bottleneck in case of emergency realtime analysis.

## 5   Implementation

Both the AII and architecture recovery methods are implemented in Java, these are based on the implementation found in Software Architecture INstrument (SAIN)[1]. The unified data model (AIM) is realized and persisted using the Eclipse Modeling Framework[2]. To compare and integrate architecture information, we adapted the *Variability Analysis Toolkit* [20] used to compare program structure and extended it to handle architecture clustering information.

## 6   Evaluation

In this section, we evaluate our architecture information integration approach using a set of four real-world subject systems using metrics published by Guizzardi et al. [6] adapted for our scenario.

### 6.1   Goals and Questions

**Goal.** The goal is to integrate architecture information recovered by independent AIRS and to remove redundancies, relate independently recovered information, and resolve conflicting information.

**Research Questions.** To evaluate our goal, we identified two research questions:

---

[1] https://www.sain.info/.
[2] https://www.eclipse.org/modeling/emf/.

*RQ1.* Can we integrate architecture information from AIRS without losing any recovered information?

*RQ2.* Can we integrate architecture information from AIRS without redundancy and correlate architecture information of different AIRS with each other?

## 6.2 Metrics

For the evaluation, we adapt metrics used to evaluate modeling languages published by Guizzardi et al. [6] and successfully adapted by Ananieva et al. [1] for assessing tool and model variability, showing the metrics adaptability.

**Guizzardi's Metrics.** Guizzardi et al. proposed 4 metrics: laconic, lucid, complete, and sound, which were adapted by Ananieva et al. [1] resulting in metrics of laconicity, lucidity, completeness and soundness. They extended the existing metrics to allow for a range from 0 to 1 indicating the relative property of the examined model and, in their case, tool. Laconicity and lucidity are used to evaluate the granularity and completeness and soundness for the coverage. Adapting the metrics to our case results in the following understanding:

*Laconic.* We understand an AIRS integration to be laconic, iff every entity recovered by the AIRS is mapped to at most one entity in the AIM (rel. *RQ1*).

*Lucid.* We understand the AIM as lucid, iff every entity in the AIM is mapped to at most one entity extracted by an AIRS (rel. *RQ1*).

*Complete.* We understand the AIRS integration to be complete, iff every entity recovered by the AIRS is mapped to at least one entity in the AIM (rel. *RQ1*).

*Sound.* We understand the AIM as sound, iff every entity in the AIM is mapped to at least one entity extracted by an AIRS (rel. *RQ2*).

Following Ananieva et al. [1], we adapted the metrics to AIRSs, to evaluate laconicity, lucidity, completeness and soundness. Entities in our case are both: nodes and edges in the AIM. Whereas nodes are entities like subsystems or classes, edges represent the relation between subsystems and classes. By integrating these information into the AIM, we expect that we do not lose node information (e.g., no classes/subsystems are lost), but we assume that, because of correlating architecture information, an increase of new edges and nodes (e.g., introducing new hierarchy levels) occurs which leads to a decrease in soundness.

## 6.3 Methodology

The dataset used for evaluation includes four open-source systems: JVending, consisting of 1kLOC (8 files and 1 package), fastjson, having 44kLOC (193 files and 73 packages), Apache Hadoop, consisting of 68kLOC (399 files and 82 package), and Apache Struts2, having 70kLOC (568 files and 110 packages).

To evaluate the integration approach, we apply four AIRS (ACDC, Bunch, PKG, RELAX) on our data set and calculate the metrics using the AIRS output. In our studies, we tried different similarity thresholds (50%, 60%, 70%, 80%, 90%). Only clusters with similarity above the specified threshold are merged together. Thresholds above 90% result in minimal integration of architecture information, as they lead to "disjoint" and "similar below threshold" integration results. Thresholds below 50% cause smaller subsystems to be merged into larger ones, resulting in large clusters and a loss of finer granularity in architecture information. In our pre-study, we set the threshold at 80%, as this leads to integrated clusters that were perceived as similar by humans. We further tested if the order of integrating AIRS is significant, but in our pre-study, we could not observe any difference related to the integration order.

## 6.4   Results and Discussion

Table 1 shows the condensed metric results for the subject systems.

**Table 1.** Metric results of integration approach - The range for laconicity, lucidity, completeness and soundness lies between 0 and 1. Values for laconicity, lucidity and completeness closer to 1 are assessed as better, whereas values for soundness closer to 0 are better, as this means we were able to create new connections and hierarchy levels. Values in brackets indicate the elements compared.

| System | | Laconicity | Lucidity | Completeness | Soundness |
|---|---|---|---|---|---|
| JVending | Nodes | 1.00 (122/122) | 1.00 (51/51) | 1.00 (122/122) | 0.86 (44/51) |
| | Edges | 1.00 (110/110) | 1.00 (95/95) | 1.00 (110/110) | 0.77 (73/95) |
| fastjson | Nodes | 1.00 (1951/1951) | 1.00 (669/669) | 1.00 (1951/1951) | 0.94 (627/669) |
| | Edges | 1.00 (1856/1856) | 1.00 (1993/1993) | 1.00 (1856/1856) | 0.93 (1856/1993) |
| Hadoop | Nodes | 1.00 (7558/7558) | 1.00 (1800/1800) | 1.00 (7558/7558) | 0.99 (1777/1800) |
| | Edges | 1.00 (7366/7366) | 1.00 (6169/6169) | 1.00 (7366/7366) | 0.97 (5956/6169) |
| Struts2 | Nodes | 1.00 (7820/7820) | 1.00 (2510/2510) | 1.00 (7820/7820) | 0.99 (2499/2510) |
| | Edges | 1.00 (7577/7577) | 1.00 (7379/7379) | 1.00 (7577/7577) | 0.96 (7105/7379) |

**Results.** Based on our smallest software system (JVending), we discuss the general evaluation concept. We recovered 122 nodes and 110 edges across all AIRSs for JVending. The metrics laconicity and lucidity indicate that there are no duplicate architecture information stored in the AIM (*laconic*) or from the AIRS (*lucid*). Both metrics indicate that we do not store the same architecture information (nodes or edges) recovered by two AIRS twice, which eliminates duplicates. Furthermore, the completeness metric is 1.00 in both cases (nodes: 122/122; edges: 110/110) as well. This indicates that the information recovered by the AIRSs is reliable mapped to at least one entity of the AIM, therefore we can determine that we do not lose any information while integrating. Lastly, we consider the metric of soundness. This metric represents that every information in the AIM can be mapped to a recovered architecture information. We intend to condense the architecture information by creating new hierarchies or expanding the existing architecture information through the introduction of new hierarchy levels resulting in finer architecture information. The soundness metric results for the recovered nodes and edges of JVending show that some edges and nodes are removed by integrating subsystems, which can be mapped to an existing subsystems by being a subset of the latter.

Applied to the other subject systems (see Table 1), the integration strategy shows that the architecture information recovered for all of the subject systems can be integrated in the AIM without losing architecture information and with small gains by linking the architecture information with each other. This aspect, observable by comparing the larger systems like Apache Hadoop with JVending, means that there is no integration of subsets or complete similarity leading to less integration, yet we do not lose any information. This leads to the assumption that the recovered information is supplementing (or contradicting) the existing architecture information. To mitigate this, we introduced the *confidence* of the recovered architecture information, producing similar results by another approach increases the confidence if the recovered architecture information is reliable.

For the integration, we used a Windows Desktop Computer with an Intel(R) Core(TM) i5-3470K CPU @3.20GHz and 32 GB of RAM. The integration times were as follows: JVending (2 s), fastjson (1.11 min), Apache Hadoop (3.67 min), and Apache Struts2 (4.21 min). Bottleneck for the integration for larger systems is the available RAM of the evaluation setup.

**Discussion.** The automatic integration of architecture information into the AIM allows to use different architecture recovery methods and their outputs. Reducing the manual effort for the integration can establish an automated architecture integration process. As different AIRS produce similar yet different architecture information about a system, a general integration, incorporating the different perspectives of the AIRSs, connects perspectives by employing the proposed integration approach. The results indicate that the integrated architecture information does not lose any architecture information and provides a small gain in correlating the architecture information. As indicated by the soundness metric, we can observe integration between output of different AIRSs. The resulting integrated AIM allows to deduce conclusions regarding concerns, subsystems as well as top-level subsystems. Recovered architecture information like subsystems and concern-based clusters can be overlapping and thus assign concerns to subsystems and their contents, which in turn categorizes the system.

Presenting the integrated AIM to experts in a pilot expert interview allowed them to get an idea of architecturally unknown systems (JVending, fastjson). They elaborated that the concept of deferring concerns recovered by RELAX to the integrated subsystems is an interesting insight into the software system. The integration of subsystems and hierarchies enables the specification of key architectural subsystems. To further evaluate our approach, a user study is planned.

Integrating architecture information from AIRS like Bunch and ACDC, shows room for improvements for consolidating the architecture information. We identified that the merging of clusters with a similarity threshold of above 80%, leads to very few consolidated clusters, as clusters are either large yielding a lower chance of similar clusters or quite small, where only small differences lead to the rejection of merging the two clusters. As we applied different thresholds, not much change in the integration results were observed, but introducing a gradual threshold could remedy this challenge. Another insight is that the architecture information recovered by different AIRSs is often supplementary, describing different perspectives of a software system.

The automatic integration of architecture information has room for improvement. It can be enhanced by further integrating heterogeneous architecture information recovered by AIRS from heterogeneous data sources like existing documentation or knowledge data bases. Our current integration strategy is capable of adding architecture information if transformable into a DAG. Introducing a type-aware comparator or high-level comparator could also improve comparing AIRS output and AIM architecture information. Further research is needed by comparing the integrated architecture information of the integration process and the recovered architecture information for test systems and their identified ground truth and if the integration leads to better results.

### 6.5   Threats to Validity

*External Threats.* Known limitations of our research are the limited selection of test systems as well as architecture recovery methods including other systems or methods could yield other results for the integration. We aim to include further AIRS to test if the integration approach is still applicable. We are also limited to AIRS results transformable into a DAG.

*Internal Threats.* A limitation of our research are the borders of the integration process as we compare pair wise on the lowest level, this could have an influence on the respective architecture information and a comparison of higher level outputs (e.g., whole clusters) could improve the integration process. Having a fourth comparator performing a top-down comparison could help integrating architecture information. Lastly, the pairwise comparison leads to an high use of working memory leading to technical limitations when integrating complex and large systems As stated in the results, this is a hardware limitation, which could be mitigated by optimizing the comparison.

## 7   Related Work

The Knowledge Discovery Metamodel [10], designed by the Object Management Group, uses the meta-meta-model (MOF). It was created with the goal to have a common data interchange format for software re-engineering tools. KDM consists of four different layers. KDM incorporates different relevant architecture information. However, it is not focused on automatic integration of architecture information. Yet, the AIM considers similar aspects, but in a concise manner.

Konersmann et al. [12] present a process to explicitly integrate software architecture model information with source code. This approach supports the specific models focused on components and interfaces. It links architecture models using the Intermediate Architecture Description Language (AIDL) with source code to immediately align architecture concepts with the source code. While they state that the focus on a single point of truth for the correlation of architecture information model and source code has its benefits, we argue that integrating different sources is beneficial to get different architecture information.

Kazman et al. [9] propose CORUM II, a framework using a horseshoe-like procedure divided into implementation, component, and business layers. The integrated architecture information allows to use the information for architectural designs, implementations and code generation. Additionally, it aids architects in understanding the analyzed system. While the process is similar to our approach, automating the integration reduces the amount of manual work needed.

Lungu et al. [17] present Softwarenaut, which integrates architecture information as a first step in the architecture recovery process. By aggregating relationships found in software artifacts horizontally, they enhance comprehension of implemented classes and packages. Softwarenaut uses a hierarchical graph to identify where aggregation and consolidation is useful. Their approach focuses on refactoring source code, neglecting important aspects of software architecture.

Farwick et al. [5] propose an approach to automatically integrate cloud architecture information into a enterprise architecture model. They propose a living model tightly coupled to system evolution. The architecture information based on different sources (e.g., CMDB, dev. env.) is integrated into a central data model, however an integration of heterogeneous data sources is not necessary, as specific parts are updated from specific sources. This approach focuses on cloud architecture, whereas our approach can be adapted for different use cases.

Laser et al. [14] propose a architecture workbench named ARCADE, which combines different architecture recovery approaches, but the integration of the architecture information is part of the exploration of the recovered architecture information. They provide valuable architecture information, but integration is done manually and human interaction still needed.

## 8 Conclusion

In this paper, we presented an automated approach for consolidating and integrating architecture information that was obtained from independent architecture information recovery methods into a unified architecture information model. The goal is to remove redundancies in recovered information, relate independently recovered information, and resolve conflicting information as well as estimate confidence in the recovered information. We illustrated the original recovery methods as well as the integration approach using a running example. Finally, we evaluated our approach by applying it to a number of real-world subject systems in order to ensure that no information is lost during integration and to assess how well previously independent information can be related.

# References

1. Ananieva, S., et al.: A conceptual model for unifying variability in space and time. In: SPLC (A), pp. 15:1–15:12. ACM (2020)
2. Behnamghader, P., Le, D.M., Garcia, J., Link, D., Shahbazian, A., Medvidovic, N.: A large-scale study of architectural evolution in open-source software systems. Empir. Softw. Eng. **22**(3), 1146–1193 (2017)
3. van Deursen, A., Hofmeister, C., Koschke, R., Moonen, L., Riva, C.: Symphony: view-driven software architecture reconstruction. In: WICSA, pp. 122–134. IEEE Computer Society (2004)
4. Falessi, D., Babar, M.A., Cantone, G., Kruchten, P.: Applying empirical software engineering to software architecture: challenges and lessons learned. Empir. Softw. Eng. **15**(3), 250–276 (2010)
5. Farwick, M., Agreiter, B., Breu, R., Häring, M., Voges, K., Hanschke, I.: Towards living landscape models: automated integration of infrastructure cloud in enterprise architecture management. In: International Conference on Cloud Computing, CLOUD 2010, Miami, USA, 5–10 July, pp. 35–42. IEEE Computer Society (2010)
6. Guizzardi, G., Ferreira Pires, L., van Sinderen, M.: An ontology-based approach for evaluating the *Domain Appropriateness* and *Comprehensibility Appropriateness* of modeling languages. In: Briand, L., Williams, C. (eds.) MODELS 2005. LNCS, vol. 3713, pp. 691–705. Springer, Heidelberg (2005). https://doi.org/10.1007/11557432_51
7. IEEE/ISO/IEC International Standard for Software: systems and enterprise-Architecture description. Standard International Organization for Standardization (2022)
8. Jordan, S., Linsbauer, L., Kittelmann, A., Schaefer, I.: Software architecture recovery - a systematic literature review. Inf. Softw. Technol. J. Under review
9. Kazman, R., Woods, S.S., Carrière, S.J.: Requirements for integrating software architecture and reengineering models: CORUM II. In: 5th Working Conference on Reverse Engineering, WCRE '98, Honolulu, USA, 12–14 October 1998, pp. 154–163. IEEE Computer Society (1998)
10. Architecture-driven modernization: Knowledge discovery meta-model (KDM). Standard, Object Management Group (2016)
11. Knoll, M.: Handbuch der software-architektur. Wirtschaftsinf. **48**(6), 454 (2006)
12. Konersmann, M.: A process for explicitly integrated software architecture. Softwaretechnik-Trends **36**(2) (2016)
13. Kruchten, P.: The 4+1 view model of architecture. IEEE Softw. **12**(6), 42–50 (1995)
14. Laser, M.S., Medvidovic, N., Le, D.M., Garcia, J.: ARCADE: an extensible workbench for architecture recovery, change, and decay evaluation. In: ESEC/SIGSOFT FSE, pp. 1546–1550. ACM (2020)
15. Le, D.M., Behnamghader, P., Garcia, J., Link, D., Shahbazian, A., Medvidovic, N.: An empirical study of architectural change in open-source software systems. In: MSR, pp. 235–245. IEEE Computer Society (2015)

16. Link, D., Behnamghader, P., Moazeni, R., Boehm, B.W.: Recover and RELAX: concern-oriented software architecture recovery for systems development and maintenance. In: ICSSP, pp. 64–73. IEEE/ACM (2019)
17. Lungu, M., Lanza, M., Nierstrasz, O.: Evolutionary and collaborative software architecture recovery with softwarenaut. Sci. Comput. Program. **79**, 204–223 (2014)
18. Lutellier, T., et al.: Comparing software architecture recovery techniques using accurate dependencies. In: ICSE (2), pp. 69–78. IEEE Computer Society (2015)
19. Mancoridis, S., Mitchell, B.S., Chen, Y., Gansner, E.R.: Bunch: a clustering tool for the recovery and maintenance of software system structures. In: ICSM, p. 50. IEEE Computer Society (1999)
20. Schlie, A., Rosiak, K., Urbaniak, O., Schaefer, I., Vogel-Heuser, B.: Analyzing variability in automation software with the variability analysis toolkit. In: Proceedings of the 23rd International Systems and Software Product Line Conference, SPLC 2019, France, 9–13 September, pp. 89:1–89:8. ACM (2019)
21. Tzerpos, V., Holt, R.C.: ACDC: an algorithm for comprehension-driven clustering. In: WCRE, pp. 258–267. IEEE Computer Society (2000)
22. Wen, Z., Tzerpos, V.: An effectiveness measure for software clustering algorithms. In: 12th International Workshop on Program Comprehension (IWPC 2004), 24–26 June 2004, Bari, Italy, pp. 194–203. IEEE Computer Society (2004)

# An Experience Report on the Design and Implementation of an Ad-hoc Blockchain Platform for Tactical Edge Applications

Nguyen Khoi Tran[1(✉)], Muhammad Ali Babar[1], Julian Thorpe[2], Seth Leslie[2], and Andrew Walters[2]

[1] The University of Adelaide, Adelaide, SA 5005, Australia
{nguyen.tran,ali.babar}@adelaide.edu.au
[2] Defence Science and Technology Group, Adelaide, Australia

**Abstract.** The success of task groups operating in emergency response or military missions largely depends on their ability to access, process, and exchange information, which is enabled by tactical edge software applications. Designing such applications poses challenges for architects due to the need for resilience, trust, and decentralisation of information processing and exchange. Nevertheless, these challenges also present opportunities for exploring new architectural alternatives like blockchain-based decentralised systems. This paper reports the experience from an R&D partnership to architect and implement a decentralised ad-hoc platform for deploying and operating tactical edge software applications, which facilitate information processing and exchange among tactical edge task groups. The platform utilises a peer-to-peer architecture, aided by ad-hoc blockchain networks, to enable secure and decentralised information storage, update, and distribution. By leveraging a kernel-based, service-oriented architecture, the platform can be adapted to different mission contexts and integrated with various task groups' systems and data sources. Additionally, we present a process and heuristics for architecting tactical edge software applications to operate on the platform. We further share our experience in deploying and operating the platform in a government-led field experiment and conclude the report with lessons learned from this case study.

**Keywords:** blockchain · smart contract · platform · information sharing · common operating picture · emergency response

## 1 Introduction

The tactical edge environment of a military or emergency response mission contains various task groups from different organisations. The mission's success depends on the task groups' ability to access, process, and exchange tactical

B. Tekinerdogan et al. (Eds.): ECSA 2023, LNCS 14212, pp. 100–116, 2023.
https://doi.org/10.1007/978-3-031-42592-9_7

information in a timely and secure manner, despite network bandwidth, processor power, data storage, and electrical power constraints [5,17,18]. Secure and resilient information exchange within and across task groups can enable collaborative information processes, such as maintaining a shared library of dynamic reference information (DRI) about environments and objects of interest within a mission to improve situation understanding and facilitate superior decision processes [4]. Within an increasingly digitalised tactical edge environment, collaborative information processes are increasingly aided by software applications, which we denote in this paper as tactical edge software applications.

Tactical edge software applications require an underlying software platform that can support information processing and exchange within and across task groups while ensuring the information's integrity, confidentiality, traceability, and provenance. This paper presents the findings and experiences of a long-standing academia-government partnership focused on architecting and developing a decentralised software platform for information processing and exchange at the tactical edge. The platform functions as an ad-hoc information platform established across computing nodes of task groups prior to or during a mission. It allows for the secure distribution, update, and storage of shared information artefacts without relying on a remote intermediary. One of the platform's key features is its ability to allow task groups to deploy an extensible application suite for facilitating collaborative information processes such as DRI.

The platform is built on ad-hoc blockchain networks [16] and peer-to-peer (P2P) content distribution networks like the Interplanetary File System (IPFS) [1]. We utilise a kernel-based, service-oriented architecture to encapsulate the platform's complexity and enable task groups to adapt the platform to different mission contexts and resource availability by changing the application suite. We have also developed a design process and heuristics for architecting software applications that operate on the platform.

This paper is structured as follows. Section 2 presents the current centralized architecture of a tactical edge environment and proposes an alternative decentralized information platform. Section 3 describes the architecture of the platform that implements the decentralized information platform. Section 4 details a process for creating tactical edge software applications that function on the platform. Sections 5 and 6 describe the experiences and lessons gained from implementing and operating the platform during a government-led field experiment. Section 7 provides an overview of related work. Finally, Sect. 8 summarizes and concludes the paper.

## 2   Context and Architectural Vision

### 2.1   Current Architecture: Centralised Information Platform

Figure 1 depicts the current architecture of a tactical edge environment consisting of two task groups working together. The computing devices used by these

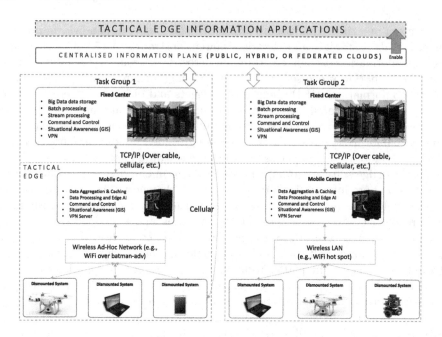

**Fig. 1.** Architecture of an exemplary tactical edge environment and infrastructure

groups are divided into three tiers, named and classified based on MITRE's Tactical Edge Characterisation Framework [5]. The higher a device is in the hierarchy, the more stable its network connectivity, power supply, and computing resources. Devices in the *Dismounted systems* category include wearable devices, smartphones, mobile workstations, and remote-controlled or autonomous vehicles used by first responders during missions. *Mobile centres* are workstations or servers used by field-deployed command and control (C2) to provide situational awareness tools (like Geographic Information System) and C2 facilities to receive updates from first responders, monitor missions, and issue instructions. These centres can also serve as cloudlets [8] for offloading data and AI/ML operations from dismounted systems. *Fixed centres* operate from a remote location away from the tactical edge. They provide commanders with situational awareness and C2 capability over an entire task group. Fixed centres can also serve as a private cloud, providing big data storage and processing capability.

Enabling information exchange and processing among task groups requires connecting their infrastructures. The current cloud-centric solutions leverage intermediary public clouds, hybrid clouds [9], or a federated design to establish a *centralised information platform* to store, distribute, and secure shared information. The exchange of and processing upon shared information can be encapsulated by *tactical edge information applications* operating within the information platform.

**Example: Dynamic Reference Information Management.** DRI is an evolving information library that describes objects of interest, their attributes, and their connection to the observable world, such as the tactical edge environment where a mission occurs [4]. DRI can be maintained by diverse teams to improve their situational understanding and decision-making abilities. Military and emergency service platforms commonly utilize DRI to configure their systems and sensors for a mission. Due to its critical role, ensuring the authenticity, integrity, provenance, and availability of this shared information artefact is essential [18]. The storage and update of DRI serve as an excellent example of a tactical edge information application.

## 2.2 Vision: Decentralised Secure Information Platform

Having presented the current architecture, the remainder of this paper focuses on our effort to architect and engineer an alternative to address the following issues of the current architecture that arose in practice:

**Dependence on Network Uplink.** C2 and first responders might not have access to up-to-date information on a remote cloud due to intermittent connectivity. Moreover, the exchanged information must cross multiple trust boundaries, thus increasing its exposure to cyber threats.

**Single Point of Failure.** The centralised information platform represents an intermediary within the information flow within and across task groups. Even though a defence-in-depth strategy comprising network protection, intrusion detection, authentication and authorisation, encryption, and sandboxing can protect the information platform from external threats, there is still a risk that programming errors, insider threats, or cyber attacks can disrupt the information platform and, thus, deny C2 and responders from accessing and sharing vital information.

**Ownership, Control, and Accountability.** A major issue we faced when architecting tactical edge information exchange and processing services was the ownership and control over the services and the intermediary cloud infrastructure. The task groups might not be willing or able to host the shared data and processes. They might also not trust others or an intermediary enough to hand over the data and processes.

We developed the idea of a *Decentralized Secure Information Platform* after researching the utility of blockchain technology in Internet of Things (IoT) systems [14] and successfully establishing and leveraging an *ad-hoc blockchain network* to collect sensor data during a field experiment [13]. The architecture of this envisioned information platform is shown in Fig. 2. The platform can be deployed in the field and operated directly by tactical edge task groups. Upon the platform, they can deploy *decentralised* tactical edge software applications to facilitate collaborative information processes such as DRI management. The backbone of the platform is a private ad-hoc blockchain network established amongst task groups to provide a decentralised root of trust and synchronisation. Due to the use of an ad-hoc blockchain, we refer to the envisioned decentralised information platform as the *"Ad-hoc Blockchain Platform"* or simply *"platform."*

# 3  Design and Implementation of the Platform

This section presents the platform's architecture and implementation details and elaborates on how the platform achieves the vision described in Sect. 2.2.

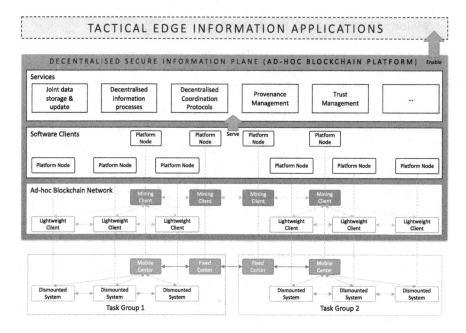

**Fig. 2.** Conceptual view of the Adhoc Blockchain Platform for Tactical Edge

## 3.1  Requirements and Constraints

The platform was architected towards the following requirements, which we derived from the vision described in Sect. 2.2.

**Decentralisation.** The platform should be operable directly by the tactical edge task groups to avoid the issues of ownership, control, accountability, and single point of failure.

**Proximity to the Tactical Edge.** The platform should operate at or close to the tactical edge to improve availability and reduce latency.

**Information Trustworthiness.** We consider information trustworthy if a receiver can ascertain the identity of the sender (authenticity), verify that it has not been modified (integrity), and be sure that the sender cannot falsely deny sending the message (non-repudiation) [10].

**Provenance of Processing Results.** Use cases such as DRI management require updating shared artefacts based on the incoming information. The provenance showing how and by whom the updates were made is vital for both in-situ trust assessment and postmortem analysis. Maintaining such provenance records would lays a foundation and contributes to the trustworthiness of the exchanged information.

**Potentially Large Data Volume.** The platform must support the exchange, processing, and possibly storage of large data payloads captured and exchanged at the tactical edge, such as video and audio recordings.

**Interoperability with Applications and Data Sources.** The platform must support diverse tactical edge information applications. Doing so requires interoperability with various software systems and data sources of task groups.

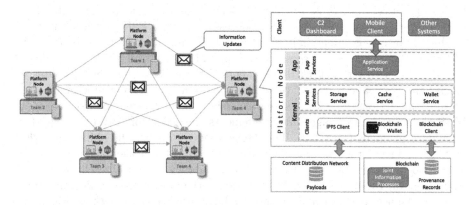

**Fig. 3.** Platform's architecture comprising multiple peer nodes

## 3.2 Platform Architecture

We designed the platform's architecture by leveraging well known architectural styles including peer-to-peer (P2P), service-oriented (SOA), and Microkernel. As a P2P system, the platform is made up of multiple identical software clients called **Platform Nodes** (Fig. 3), which are deployed across the computing devices of task group participants. Each node represents a participant within the platform and retrieves or updates information on their behalf. Participants can interact with the information through decentralised tactical edge applications running locally on their devices. Nodes communicate via pre-established data links like tactical data links, ad-hoc wireless networks, and cellular networks. To ensure the security of the information exchanged, we have adopted a blockchain protocol like Ethereum [19]. Additional capabilities such as data storage and distribution can be enabled by integrating other protocols like IPFS [1]. By adopting a P2P architecture and deploying nodes within the tactical edge, we addressed the first two requirements. We addressed the described requirements regarding trustworthiness of information exchanges by leveraging the built-in security mechanisms of a blockchain protocol.

To facilitate the adaptation of platform nodes to mission contexts and participant devices, we leveraged the microkernel architecture to design platform nodes. The software stack of a node is separated into *kernel space* and *application space*. Both layers comprise software services that abstract the complexity behind predefined service interfaces to simplify the development and integration of applications and data sources. The application space contains *application-specific services*, which are key components of tactical edge information applications running on the platform. This layer's content can be modified based on the application suite of a mission and the information needs and authorisation levels of a participant. We will elaborate on developing and deploying a tactical edge application on the platform later in Sect. 4.

The kernel space contains *clients* and *kernel services* that are vital for platform's operation and, thus, unchanged across missions and participants. The *clients* layer contains software clients necessary for the P2P protocols utilised by the platform (e.g., blockchain client and wallet for blockchain protocol, IPFS client for IPFS). The *kernel services* layer provides a uniform interface for application services to interact with the clients. The *wallet* service encapsulates a blockchain client and a wallet, providing the ability to query a blockchain and submit transactions. The *storage* service encapsulates data payload stores (e.g., IPFS client or local storage) and implements the secure offloading process for large data payloads (Sect. 3.2). The `Cache` service provides the ability to cache on-blockchain records and data payloads. We introduced the cache service to the platform because we found that the read latency from a blockchain, specifically from an Ethereum-based blockchain via the Go-Ethereum, was high and impeded the user experience from the graphical user interface at the application layer.

**Secure Data Offloading.** To save valuable blockchain storage space for critical records, we applied the Off-chain Data Storage pattern [21] to architect a secure mechanism to store data payloads outside the blockchain. In particular, the platform can store incoming audio and video recordings on a node's local storage or a decentralised content network established among platform nodes (e.g., using IPFS). The platform then includes the cryptographic hashes of these data payloads in blockchain transactions to prove their existence. These hashes can be used to identify, locate, and verify the integrity of the data payloads. The storage service can transparently handle this offloading process.

### 3.3   Platform Implementation

Our platform's concept demonstrator uses the Go-Ethereum (Geth) client implementation to support the Ethereum protocol. To handle the creation of Ethereum transactions and interaction with smart contracts, we used the `Ethers.js` for our Wallet service. We implemented the services as NodeJS modules and packaged them as Docker containers. Containerisation helps improve portability across diverse systems that task groups utilize. Additionally, we utilized Docker Compose to provide a programmatic and automated way to deploy the entire stack.

### 3.4   Platform Bootstrapping Process

The platform can be field-deployed by *deployers*, IT operators from participating task groups. Deployers bootstrap the platform on behalf of their task groups and exert no control over the platform after deployment. The process is as follows:

1. *Configure the architecture of the ad-hoc blockchain network.* Platform deployers can tune the network's performance with design decisions such as protocol choice and client deployment. Our preliminary collections of common blockchain network designs provide some templates to aid the design process [16].
2. *Deploy and configure blockchain clients on all computing nodes that participate as platform nodes.* Deployers can leverage an blockchain deployment automation framework such as NVAL [15] to automatically deploy and configure blockchain clients according to the architecture from the previous step.
3. *Deploy and configure the kernel service layer on all platform nodes.*
4. *Deploy tactical edge applications.* This step consists of deploying the smart contract backend of applications and starting application services on platform nodes. Section 4.3 presents more details about the application deployment process.

## 4   Develop and Deploy Applications with the Platform

Tactical edge information applications like DRI management can be developed separately from the platform and deployed upon the platform during the bootstrapping process. This section presents the architecture, development, and deployment processes of tactical edge information applications.

### 4.1   Application Architecture

An application is made up of two parts: on-blockchain and on-platform components. The on-blockchain components are *smart contracts* that store and process information like a DRI library. The on-platform components include *software clients* that users can interact with and an *application service* that connects software clients with smart contracts. These components are installed on the platform node of authorized users.

## 4.2   Application Development Process

After analyzing the project logs, we developed the following process to assist developers in designing and developing applications for the platform.

1. *Determine the suitability of the application.* To determine if an application is suitable for the platform, it is important to identify its information needs. Only shared information artefacts and their updates will benefit from being hosted on the platform.
2. *Identify the data payload and provenance records.* The provenance records benefit from being managed by a blockchain, whilst the payloads represent candidates for offloading to off-chain data stores.
3. *Model the collaborative information processes.* Because blockchains operate like deterministic state machines, it is helpful to model a collaborative information process as a set of actions targeting the shared information artefacts, transitioning them between various states in their life cycle. The artefacts can be represented in a blockchain by smart contracts. Artefacts' stages can be stored within the contracts' variables, and actions can be implemented as smart contract functions. Whenever a user sends a blockchain transaction to a smart contract function to act on the shared information artefact, the transaction becomes part of the provenance record.
4. *Develop an application service.* This service provides an Application Programming Interface (API) that connects external software clients to smart contracts. To make it easier for integration with external software clients, we recommend designing the API at a higher level of abstraction to allow users to retrieve information instead of blockchain transactions.
5. *Develop user-facing software clients (optional).*

## 4.3   Application Deployment Process

Before the platform bootstrap (Sect. 3.4), deployers must acquire and integrate software components of all utilised applications into the deployment package of platform nodes. Each node can possess a different application suite according to its users' information needs and authorisation. Once the ad-hoc blockchain network has been established during platform bootstrapping, deployers can deploy the smart contracts of all applications on the blockchain. They can then use the smart contract identifiers to finish configuring application services. Finally, deployers start the application services and corresponding software clients on platform nodes, completing both application deployment and platform bootstrapping.

# 5   Case Study

We developed and deployed a proof-of-concept demonstration of our platform, along with an application called Decentralised Dynamic Reference Information

(DDRI), as part of a government-led field experiment. Due to the space constraint of this paper, our report in this section will focus on the design and technological decisions of the proof-of-concept platform and the application utilised in the experiment. Detailed quantitative analysis of the platform would be presented in a forthcoming paper.

## 5.1 Context

The case study was part of the Real-time Information Superiority Experimentation (RISE) initiative [17]. RISE was created to test and explore information management, exploitation, and exchange technologies like the platform and DDRI in a field experiment setting. The experiment took place at Port Elliot with Surf Life Saving South Australia and involved three emergency service scenarios. These scenarios included a search and rescue mission for a drifting inflatable, a search and rescue mission for an emergency beacon attached to a boat in distress, and a repeated version of the first scenario with limited communication capabilities. The platform and DDRI application were utilised to maintain a DRI library based on information from three viewpoints, simulating three task groups. Figure 4 presents the map of the experiment area and locations of platform nodes (PESLSC, Commodore's Point, and Lady Bay).

**Fig. 4.** Node locations at Port Elliot Surf Life Saving South Australia (PESLSC), Commodore's Point, and Lady Bay

## 5.2   Implementation

**Background.** We designed the software components of DDRI based on the following DRI formalisation by Consoli and Walters [4]. An reference information library is a set $I_{AP}$, consisting of four subsets: known objects $O$, objects' attributes or features $X_A$, known sensors $S$, and environment's parameters $X_{env}$, such as geographical location.

$$I_{AP} = \{O, X_A, S, X_{env}\}$$

The library is updated due to an observation process $\Theta$. This process generates an observation about a stimulus event $S_e$ at time $t$. The observation is made by a sensor $S$ and describes the attributes $X_A(S)$ of an object of interest $objInt_i$. The observation happens within an environment described by parameters $S_{env}$.

$$\Theta(S_e, t) = \{objInt_i, X_A(S), S, S_{env}\}$$

An observation becomes a reference information update (RI update) if it happens within the mission environment ($S_{env} \in X_{env}$) and either the object of interest is unknown ($objInt_i \notin O$) or attributes of a known object ($X_A(S)$) has changed, the information generated by the observation represents an update to the library. Therefore, a dynamic reference information library can be considered an $I_{AP}$ that can be modified by RI updates during a mission.

**Functional Scope.** DDRI's design began by identifying the elements of DRI management that the platform should host. We decomposed DRI management into four steps: observation, processing, storage, and propagation. While observation and processing can be done manually or with AI-assisted tools, storage and propagation require information exchange among members. Thus, DDRI focused on the storage and propagation steps.

**Smart Contract Design.** Since all observations would come from task groups in the same mission, we assumed they happen in the same observable world. In other words, $S_{env} \in X_{env}$ for all observations, so we omitted $S_{env}$ and $X_{env}$ from our data model without losing information. Therefore, a DRI library comprises the set of available sensors $S$, objects of interest $objInt_i$, and attributes of those objects $X_A(S)$. The set of available sensors, objects, and their attributes describe the *state* of DRI at a time. The DRI transition between states is based on incoming RI updates, reporting observations about changes in attributes of an object of interest. The assessment and appending of RI updates into a DRI form the actions making up the collaborative information process among task groups. The attributes within RI updates represent data payloads. The details regarding the sensor, the observed objects, and attributes' representations (e.g., cryptographic hashes) within RI updates triggering the update of DRI represent the provenance of the shared information artefact.

We designed the smart contract backend of the DDRI application based on the above analysis. The smart contract classes and objects (**struct**) that make up the on-blockchain components of DDRI are presented in the class diagram shown in Fig. 5. We assumed each mission has one DRI and task groups can simultaneously participate in multiple missions. DDRI uses one instance of the `Mission` contract to represent a mission and manage its DRI. The `DDRI` contract maintains a list of registered missions and provides the `createMission` function for deployers to register a new mission. For each mission, the DDRI contract creates a new instance of the `Mission` contract. This contract includes a list of `RIUpdate` objects to capture a DRI's development. Since the latest state of a DRI could be derived from the RI updates, we left the presentation of DRI to off-blockchain software clients and knowledge representation tools. The `addRIUpdate` function handles the processing and appending of RI updates. Future implementations of DDRI could extend the `addRIUpdate` function with collaborative verification and validation protocols.

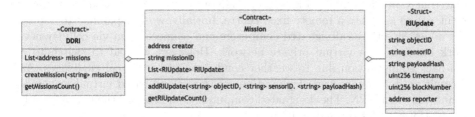

**Fig. 5.** Smart contracts for DRI management

**Services and Clients.** The next step was designing the application service that exposes DDRI smart contracts to external software clients. This service internally calls the storage service to offload the RI update payload and then calls the wallet service to construct and submit the relevant transaction. Additionally, it calls the cache service to check and update the cache before finally returning the sequence result to the upper layer for responding to users. We also developed two types of software clients tailored to different users. The Mobile client is a web-based application accessible via mobile phones for forward-deployed agents to report and record RI updates from the field rapidly. The C2 Dashboard is a web-based dashboard used by team leaders to access and view the status and history of every object of interest in the mission (Fig. 6). The dashboard presents both the RI update list and the latest state of DRI derived from the RI updates.

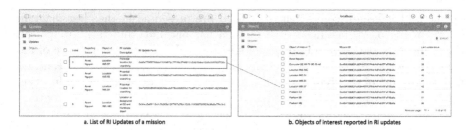

a. List of RI Updates of a mission                    b. Objects of interest reported in RI updates

**Fig. 6.** C2 Dashboard showing an RI update list and a corresponding list of objects of interest

## 5.3   Deployment and Operation

The prototype platform utilised in the experiment comprised three on-site nodes, placed at vantage points in Fig. 4, and a remote located 85 km from the experiment site to simulate a remote fixed centre. Initially, we had planned to deploy the nodes directly on designated computers and connect them via cellular network links using a virtual private network. However, we had to switch to a fall-back configuration due to weather conditions and technical challenges. As a result, all four nodes were deployed on separate cloud-based virtual machines connected via a VPN. The designated computers could control their corresponding platform nodes through a 4G uplink.

During the experiment, the authors took on the responsibility of operating platform nodes to record RI updates. The updates were provided by mission participants who acted as observers and information processors. These updates included verbal instructions and visual observations of the environment and rescue. For instance, an event such as 'Jet Ski 1 pulling the lost inflatable back to the beach to treat the patient' would involve describing the inflatable, patient details, rescue craft and crew status, and the time associated with each action in the situation. Before each experiment, participants were assigned roles as observers and processors, which were also documented in the RI updates.

The entire experiment lasted for 5 h and 45 min. In summary, 361 RI updates were recorded and exchanged through the platform throughout the experiment, with an average time interval of 44 s between updates. The ad-hoc blockchain that supported the platform retained a steady rate of 15 s between blocks, which indicated that the blockchain could keep up with the information. At the end of the mission, the distributed ledger maintained by the platform only grew by 10MB, which suggested that the platform had adequate scalability.

## 6   Lessons Learned

**Blockchain Network Architecture Design as a Means to Achieve Software Requirements.** The quality attributes of blockchain-based software applications depend on the characteristics of their underlying blockchains. The characteristics cannot be modified for public blockchains, so they must be treated as constraints. For private blockchains, architects may be able to swap blockchain implementations or develop new consensus protocols. However, caution should be taken due to these protocols' complexity and adversarial context [2].

We discovered that tweaking the *architecture of a blockchain network* can offer a promising alternative to the approaches mentioned above. For instance, one can reduce the amount of resources consumed by a blockchain network on dismounted systems by disabling the mining feature of their blockchain nodes and tweaking the protocol configurations by switching from Proof-of-Work (PoW) to Proof-of-Authority (PoA). Architects can also embed an organisation's structure into a blockchain network's architecture by controlling the assignment of blockchain nodes and roles (full nodes, archive nodes, miners) to participants. By taking control of such design decisions, architects can optimise the blockchain network's characteristics to ease the constraints at the application design level without developing new blockchain protocols or replacing blockchain implementations altogether. Furthermore, blockchain network architectures provide new research opportunities, such as identifying a design space [13] and patterns (e.g., [16]) that can help practitioners design blockchain networks tailored to their applications.

**Autonomy Versus Control.** Decentralisation implies the autonomy of participants. Such autonomy is realised by bringing the abilities to access, process, and exchange information to the tactical edge and replicating them across participants. While this approach can help strengthen the resilience of information access and processing, it can also create challenges regarding coordinating and controlling a mission. Additionally, participants must take on the responsibility of bootstrapping and managing their software infrastructure to be a part of the platform.

A solution we adopted in the project is introducing a bootstrapping phase to coordinate the platform launch before the mission. During this phase, platform deployers (who are technicians from task groups) can use automation tools like NVAL [15] to deploy and configure platform nodes on task groups' computers according to the mission and their information needs. After deployment, the platform remains decentralised and autonomous. We are also exploring other decentralised monitoring and governance mechanisms so that privileged participants (such as task group commanders) can monitor and take action on the platform, such as disabling platform nodes when compromise is detected.

## 7    Related Work

Blockchain technology has been increasingly leveraged in military and emergency response contexts to prevent cyber attacks, manage complex supply chains, and strengthen the resilience of communication links both within and outside tactical edge environments [3,12]. For instance, Siemon et al. [11] proposed a framework to leverage blockchains as a resilient communication infrastructure among C2 in an emergency response mission. Fend et al. [6] utilised blockchains as a secure mechanism for updating the retransmission policies between military networks (Tactical Data Links or TDL). Rather than focusing on individual use cases, our proposed ad-hoc blockchain platform provides a foundation for developing and operating multiple use-case-specific applications. For instance, task groups can use the platform to secure TDL retransmission policies by deploying a tactical edge information application that manages the policy updates and exposes service endpoints for TDL gateways to retrieve trusted and up-to-date policies.

The platform was designed and developed based on the existing software architecture knowledge about blockchain-based software. Inspired by Xu et al. [20], we leveraged a blockchain as a decentralised software connector for bridging distributed platform nodes. The off-chain data storage pattern [21] and caching tactic [22] were utilised to implement the platform's secure data offloading and caching capabilities. We also leveraged the smart contract registry and factory patterns [21] to design the exemplary application, DDRI. The model-driven approach by Jurgelaitis et al. [7] inspired our proposed heuristics for identifying and modelling the shared information processes for developing smart contracts of tactical edge information applications.

## 8   Conclusions

In this experience report, we discussed a software platform that enables secure information exchange and processing among task groups operating in a tactical edge environment. We provided insights into the platform's analysis, architecture, and implementation. Additionally, we discussed the design process and supporting heuristics for creating tactical edge information applications that can operate on the platform. The platform's applicability was also explored, highlighting its usefulness for further academic-government partnership on research and development of innovative concepts like DRI.

Our platform was designed with decentralisation, adaptability, and integration in mind. Using a peer-to-peer architecture and an ad-hoc blockchain as a software connector, we created a platform that enables task group members to exchange and process information without relying on remote intermediaries. To achieve adaptability, we separated information processing logic from information exchange, storage, and processing services. The Microkernel architecture we chose reinforced this separation. We also ensured ease of integration by adopting a service-oriented architecture for interactions within and outside the platform. Our platform has been evaluated through a field experiment. During platform's development and deployment, we discovered that blockchain network architecture can be leveraged to achieve non-functional requirements at the application level. We also faced the challenge of balancing autonomy and control when operating a decentralised platform. In the future, we plan to investigate decentralised monitoring and governance mechanisms to address this trade-off. We also plan to further the quantitative analysis of the case study to inform the future refinements and optimisations of the platform.

# References

1. Benet, J.: IPFS-content addressed, versioned, P2P file system. arXiv preprint arXiv:1407.3561 (2014)
2. Cachin, C., Vukolić, M.: Blockchain consensus protocols in the wild. arXiv preprint arXiv:1707.01873 (2017)
3. Clementz, G.W.A.Q.R.V.G.: Blockchain in defence: A breakthrough? Tech. rep. (2020). https://finabel.org/blockchain-in-defence-a-breakthrough/
4. Consoli, A., Walters, A.: Dynamic reference information: formalising contextual actionable information for contested environments. In: 2020 14th International Conference on Innovations in Information Technology (IIT), pp. 154–159. IEEE (2020)
5. Dandashi, F., et al.: Tactical edge characterization framework, volume 1: Common vocabulary for tactical environments. Tech. rep. (2007)
6. Feng, W., Li, Y., Yang, X., Yan, Z., Chen, L.: Blockchain-based data transmission control for tactical data link. Digital Commun. Netw. **7**(3), 285–294 (2021). https://doi.org/10.1016/j.dcan.2020.05.007
7. Jurgelaitis, M., Butkienė, R., Vaičiukynas, E., Drungilas, V., Čeponienė, L.: Modelling principles for blockchain-based implementation of business or scientific processes. In: CEUR Workshop Proceedings: IVUS 2019 International Conference on Information Technologies: Proceedings of the International Conference on Information Technologies, Kaunas, Lithuania, April 25, 2019. vol. 2470, pp. 43–47. CEUR-WS (2019)
8. Lewis, G., Echeverria, S., Simanta, S., Bradshaw, B., Root, J.: Tactical cloudlets: moving cloud computing to the edge. In: 2014 IEEE Military Communications Conference. IEEE (oct 2014). https://doi.org/10.1109/milcom.2014.238
9. Mansouri, Y., Prokhorenko, V., Babar, M.A.: An automated implementation of hybrid cloud for performance evaluation of distributed databases. J. Netw. Comput. Appl. **167**, 102740 (2020). https://doi.org/10.1016/j.jnca.2020.102740
10. Schneier, B.: Applied Cryptography Protocols, Algorithms and Source Code in C. Wiley and Sons, Incorporated, John (2015)
11. Siemon, C., Rueckel, D., Krumay, B.: Blockchain technology for emergency response. In: Proceedings of the 53rd Hawaii International Conference on System Sciences (2020)
12. Tosh, D.K., Shetty, S., Foytik, P., Njilla, L., Kamhoua, C.A.: Blockchain-empowered secure internet-of-battlefield things (IoBT) architecture. In: MILCOM 2018–2018 IEEE Military Communications Conference (MILCOM), pp. 593–598. IEEE (2018)
13. Tran, N.K., Babar, M.A.: Anatomy, concept, and design space of blockchain networks. In: 2020 IEEE International Conference on Software Architecture (ICSA). IEEE (mar 2020). https://doi.org/10.1109/icsa47634.2020.00020
14. Tran, N.K., Babar, M.A., Boan, J.: Integrating blockchain and internet of things systems: a systematic review on objectives and designs. J. Netw. Comput. Appl. **173**, 102844 (2021). https://doi.org/10.1016/j.jnca.2020.102844
15. Tran, N.K., Babar, M.A., Walters, A.: A framework for automating deployment and evaluation of blockchain networks. J. Netw. Comput. Appl. **206**, 103460 (2022). https://doi.org/10.1016/j.jnca.2022.103460
16. Tran, N.K., Babar, M.A.: Taxonomy of edge blockchain network designs. In: Biffl, S., Navarro, E., Löwe, W., Sirjani, M., Mirandola, R., Weyns, D. (eds.) ECSA 2021. LNCS, vol. 12857, pp. 172–180. Springer, Cham (2021). https://doi.org/10.1007/978-3-030-86044-8_12

17. Walters, A., et al.: Conducting information superiority research in an unclassified surrogate defence environment. Tech. rep. (Sep 2018)
18. Walters, A., et al.: Building trusted reference information at the tactical edge. Tech. rep. (2019)
19. Wood, G., et al.: Ethereum: a secure decentralised generalised transaction ledger. Ethereum Proj. Yellow Pap. **151**(2014), 1–32 (2014)
20. Xu, X., Pautasso, C., Zhu, L., Gramoli, V., Ponomarev, A., Tran, A.B., Chen, S.: The blockchain as a software connector. In: 2016 13th Working IEEE/IFIP Conference on Software Architecture (WICSA), pp. 182–191. IEEE (2016)
21. Xu, X., Pautasso, C., Zhu, L., Lu, Q., Weber, I.: A pattern collection for blockchain-based applications. In: Proceedings of the 23rd European Conference on Pattern Languages of Programs, pp. 1–20. ACM (jul 2018). https://doi.org/10.1145/3282308.3282312
22. Yánez, W., Bahsoon, R., Zhang, Y., Kazman, R.: Architecting internet of things systems with blockchain: a catalog of tactics. ACM Trans. Softw. Eng. Methodol. (TOSEM) **30**(3), 1–46 (2021)

# Designing a Reference Architecture for the C-ITS Services

Priyanka Karkhanis$^{(\boxtimes)}$ (iD), Yanja Dajsuren, and Mark van den Brand (iD)

Department of Mathematics and Computer Science,
The Eindhoven University of Technology, Eindhoven, The Netherlands
{p.d.karkhanis,y.dajsuren,M.G.J.v.d.Brand}@tue.nl

**Abstract.** Cooperative-Intelligent Transport Systems (C-ITS) services aim to improve road transportation through enhanced cooperative, connected, and automated mobility services. The current reference architectures for C-ITS have different abstractions, with some focusing on technical aspects, while others center on specific traffic issues of particular countries. As a result, they have varying technical details and use ad-hoc notations, which limit their adaptability for cross-border deployment of C-ITS services. This paper presents a method for developing a C-ITS reference architecture, involving three essential parts: abstracting common C-ITS systems, describing them using an architecture framework, and reviewing the reference architecture. Using our method, we developed a C-ITS reference architecture for the C-ITS services for deployment sites across European countries. Our reference architecture offers a clear and easily understandable design of C-ITS systems, eliminates the use of ad-hoc notations, and promotes adaptability. This makes it easier for stakeholders to communicate and collaborate across countries, facilitating the deployment of C-ITS services.

**Keywords:** C-ITS reference architecture · Cooperative Intelligent transport systems · C-ITS

## 1 Introduction

Cooperative Intelligent Transport Systems (C-ITS), also known as connected vehicle technology in the United States, is a group of technologies and applications that enable efficient communication between Vehicle and X, also known as V2X, where X can be any vehicle, piece of infrastructure, or pedestrian [7,24]. The advantages of C-ITS include increased road safety, decreased traffic, improved transportation efficiency, increased mobility, reduced environmental impact, and support for economic development [2].

Since 2008, and even earlier, C-ITS has been at the center of several initiatives [7]. There have been many C-ITS deployment projects in Europe and USA since that time [15]. The C-ITS services are an innovative array of technologies facilitated by digital connectivity between vehicles and between vehicles

B. Tekinerdogan et al. (Eds.): ECSA 2023, LNCS 14212, pp. 117–132, 2023.
https://doi.org/10.1007/978-3-031-42592-9_8

and transport infrastructure to enhance road safety, traffic efficiency, and driving comfort [20]. The primary functions of C-ITS services are to display regulatory boundaries via signs informing road users of specific obligations, restrictions, or prohibitions; to warn road users of impending incidents and the exact nature of those incidents, and to provide information to road users to improve road safety and comfort during a journey [7].

To promote the deployment of C-ITS services, the development of a reference architecture is seen as a crucial first step. In general, reference architecture provides a shared language, reusable structures, and established practices. The ISO 14813-5:2020 Intelligent Transport Systems standard [12] defines a reference architecture as a high-level overview of the systems and connections relevant to C-ITS services and stakeholders. Reference architectures developed in various projects such as CONVERGE [10], DITCM [21], and NordicWay [26] address several challenges, including technical and operational issues. However, their respective reference architectural designs encompass distinct aspects. For example, NordicWay emphasizes communication to gain a deeper technical understanding of interoperability, while DITCM consists of a system architecture and a description of the business aspects within a Dutch context. From these diverse reference architecture designs, three limitations were readily apparent: First, the information contained within the reference architectures is excessively technical, making it difficult for stakeholders in other nations to comprehend and utilize them. Second, using ad-hoc notations to model reference architectures can lead to fragmentation, with each country making its reference architecture that might not work with designs from other countries. Lastly, the majority of reference architectures are designed for specific objectives or countries, which may not be compatible with diverse traffic patterns and geographical conditions. These problems may cause disconnected and disjointed designs, which limit the usefulness of C-ITS as a whole. The widespread implementation of C-ITS services across European Union nations, along with the resolution of road transport issues, necessitates the adoption of a generic reference architecture. By utilizing the generic architecture, the extensive deployment of C-ITS services across nations becomes achievable [16].

Furthermore, it is important to acknowledge that the comprehensive understanding of C-ITS services, regardless of their extent, is limited due to the lack of publications by the academic and research communities. Studies such as [4,18] highlight a lack of emphasis on sharing information that could be crucial and particularly valuable in advancing cooperative transportation. According to our current knowledge, there is no explicitly defined methodology or procedure for developing the C-ITS service reference architecture. Therefore, we define the following research question to develop a reference architecture that can be applied across deployment sites with different C-ITS services.

**RQ: How to develop a reference architecture that can be used to deploy diverse C-ITS services across different deployment sites?**

Our goal is to develop a reference architecture that different deployment sites in the European Union (EU) can use as a model for rolling out C-ITS services. To accomplish this goal, we developed an organized method that aided us in producing an efficient reference architecture. We describe our method, which consists of three phases: the abstraction phase, which involves identifying and separating common C-ITS systems; the description phase, which applies architecture standards; and the architecture review phase, which incorporates the feedback of C-ITS stakeholders to verify the reference architecture. These three phases address the three issues previously mentioned. The abstraction phase eliminates unnecessary technical details and maintains a high-level understanding of the systems that can be readily comprehended by stakeholders from different deployment sites across countries. The challenge of addressing ad-hoc descriptions and constructing a more systematic representation of C-ITS systems is addressed during the description phase. In the final phase of the architecture review, stakeholders from various countries verify the reference architecture's applicability at diverse deployment sites. We demonstrate the usage of the proposed method in the C-MobILE project and developed a C-ITS reference architecture that is applied in eight deployment sites across EU [28]. The C-MobILE (Accelerating C-ITS Mobility Innovation and deployment)[1] is a large-scale C-ITS deployment project with around 37 project partners and took place between 2017 and 2021. The project's objective is to demonstrate C-ITS solutions on a large scale in urban and motorway environments by providing C-ITS services to end-users.

This paper is organized as follows: The Sect. 2 describes the method, which is divided into three phases, i.e., the abstraction, description, and review phases. We present the reference architectural models developed using the proposed method in Sect. 3. We share the lessons learned in Sect. 4. Finally, we conclude our paper and discuss future directions in Sect. 5.

## 2    Method

In this section, we describe the method comprised of three phases-abstraction, description, and architecture review, that were used to create the reference architecture for C-ITS services. The three phases as shown in Fig. 1 address the limitations of excessive technicality of information; ad-hoc notations causing fragmentation and incompatibility between countries' reference architectures; and a lack of adaptability to diverse traffic patterns and geographical conditions.

### 2.1    Abstraction Phase

The process of abstraction in reference architecture includes making decisions concerning the technologies, applications, and vendors involved [1]. It entails extracting important information from a wider amount of data that may include systems, algorithms, implementation methodologies, multiple approaches, or specific domain expertise [11]. The difficulty lies in determining what kinds of high-level information are sufficiently broad to be included in our C-ITS reference architecture. According to Cloutier et al. [5], a reference architecture should

---

[1] https://c-mobile-project.eu/.

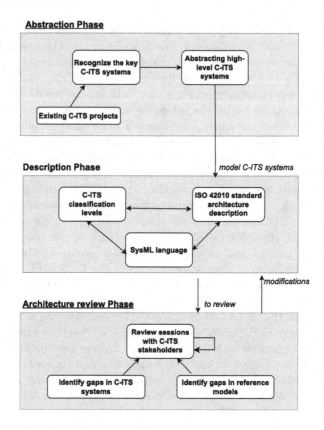

**Fig. 1.** Reference architecture process - three phases

include "business architecture", "customer context", and "technical architecture" in order to demonstrate its completeness and maturity. However, when systems evolve and get more complex, the scope of what should be included in the reference architecture needs to be adjusted [27]. Therefore, it is essential to define the abstraction phase to demarcate what should be included in our reference architecture. In line with the objectives of the C-MobILE project, our reference architecture restricts the incorporation of excessive technical complexities and focuses on eliciting high-level systems of the C-ITS services. This enables subsequent phases to focus on the dedicated attention required to design the technical architecture and business models specific to each individual C-ITS service. By striking this balance, we ensure that our reference architecture provides a solid framework for the development and deployment of C-ITS services while allowing for necessary customization and adaptability in later stages. As shown in Fig. 1, we do the abstraction in two steps: recognizing the key systems of C-ITS and defining the boundary of the abstraction.

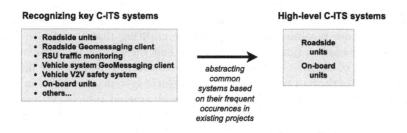

**Fig. 2.** Abstraction phase

**1. Recognizing Key Systems of C-ITS Services.** Understanding the fundamental concepts of systems, interfaces, and their relationships is essential for the efficient operation of C-ITS services. The most reliable method to confirm our understanding of current and ongoing C-ITS services is through an analysis of already-completed C-ITS projects. We considered the projects such as DITCM [21], CONVERGE [10], COMPASS4D [19], NordicWay [26], and US-ITS (ARC-IT) [25] that provide the most recent C-ITS services and relevant technologies, as well as areas for improvement. The projects had already achieved TRL5 and TRL7 milestones. The Technology Readiness Level (TRL) scale, originally developed by NASA in the 1990s s and adopted by EU-funded projects as part of the Horizon 2020 framework program in 2014, is used to measure the maturity of a technology, with levels ranging from TRL 1 to TRL 9[2]. The usefulness of a particular TRL depends on the specific objectives and requirements of the project. TRL 5 is better for analyzing basic technology functionality and feasibility. TRL 7 is better for assessing system performance and readiness for operational deployment. We recognized it is essential to include the existing knowledge from TRL 5 to TRL 7, which provided us with a comprehensive perspective extending from basic functionality to deployment details. From these projects, we gathered information including systems, interfaces, protocols, networks, technology, and terminology, as well as their corresponding C-ITS services, regions, and countries. We maintain such information in an internal repository in a structured way that allows us to organize them based on country- or project-specific details. The repository can be updated to reflect any new information, e.g., country or project. With the aid of this step, we were able to identify C-ITS systems that are widely utilized across all EU countries, as well as any regional systems, and define a glossary for the reference architecture. The next step is to identify which data would be suitable for the reference architecture.

**2. Defining the Abstraction Boundary.** In order to decide what should be a part of a reference architecture, we establish the abstraction phase. Our main objective revolves around the selection of C-ITS systems that exhibit a sufficiently high-level nature. These systems should also be generic, meaning they

---

[2] https://ec.europa.eu/research/participants/data/ref/h2020/wp/2014_2015/
annexes/h2020-wp1415-annex-g-trl_en.pdf.

can be applied to a wide range of scenarios and circumstances. The key criteria we emphasize are flexibility and adaptability, ensuring that the chosen C-ITS systems can be easily adjusted and tailored to suit the specific requirements and characteristics of different deployment sites across various regions. We illustrate our abstraction criterion with roadside and vehicle systems, as shown in Fig. 2. From the collection of key C-ITS systems, we abstracted vehicle systems, such as on-board units (OBUs), as well as their interconnections with other high-level systems, such as roadside units. The C-ITS service uses these terms, "on-board units" and "roadside units", to describe two types of devices. Whatever the specifics of the underlying technology, these systems are always a part of any C-ITS service. The inclusion of this information has been done with the intention of providing a comprehensive overview of C-ITS systems that are common and have been utilized in the past in C-ITS initiatives. Next, we represent them in a structured manner to be understood by interdisciplinary C-ITS stakeholders.

## 2.2  Description Phase

Inconsistent representations of C-ITS systems in the past have been a significant issue, as they can contribute to confusion and misunderstandings among stakeholders [14]. Ad-hoc diagrams, made without a standardized method or notation, can generate confusion since different people will interpret the same system in different ways. In order to address this issue, we introduce a description phase that incorporates well-established standards and practices for describing C-ITS systems. The ISO 14813-5:2020 Intelligent Transport Systems standard [12] recommends using an established method for defining reference architectures within ITS International Standards to ensure seamless integration for deploying C-ITS services internationally. Incorporating well-established standards and practices facilitates the development of a universal and generic reference architecture that can be applied in multiple countries. As shown in Fig. 3 we used the C-ITS architecture framework [28] compatible with the ISO 42010 international stan-

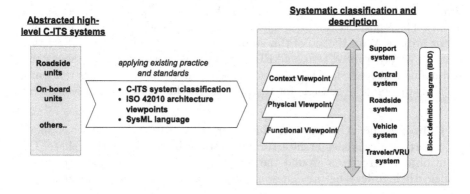

**Fig. 3.** Description phase

dard [13] for describing the architecture. The ISO/IEC/IEEE 42010 architecture framework facilitates a common practice for creating, interpreting, analyzing, and employing architecture descriptions within a specific application domain or stakeholder community [28]. We used C-ITS system classification, which is a common practice utilized in previous projects [10,25] to group C-ITS systems. To model the systems, we used SysML language which is a general-purpose modeling language to represent complex systems, structures, behaviors, and requirements [9,22]. According to a survey conducted by [22], SysML has been adopted in multidisciplinary domains, including automotive, information technology, and transportation. This indicates that SysML has gained recognition as a modeling language appropriate for various domains and system types, supported by a considerable availability of mature tools that facilitate SysML usage [6,22]. Leveraging established practices in the description of C-ITS systems promotes a comprehensive understanding of the system, enhances communication among stakeholders, and provides a structured and unambiguous representation. Next, we discuss the C-ITS system classification and the architecture descriptions.

**C-ITS System Classification** is a well-established practice for categorizing C-ITS systems utilized by numerous initiatives, including DITCM [21], CONVERGE [10], and US-ITS [25]. C-ITS classification facilitates the organization and categorization of various C-ITS system types based on their functionality, making it simpler for various stakeholders, such as vehicle manufacturers, infrastructure operators, and service providers, to communicate and collaborate effectively. Based on the analysis of existing C-ITS projects, we propose a system classification for C-ITS consisting of five levels that categorize various C-ITS system types, and those levels are support system, central system, vehicle system, roadside system, and traveler/VRU system. These levels are consistent with the definitions that were applied during the earlier C-ITS studies, e.g., DITCM [21]. These five levels were used to categorize the high-level C-ITS systems that were analyzed during the abstraction phase.

- **Support System** is comprised of sub-systems performing various tasks like governance, test and certification management, security, and credentials management.
- **Central System** is comprised of subsystems such as traffic monitoring and traffic control, which monitor surveillance cameras to capture and process traffic data, which is then disseminated to drivers through traffic control.
- **Roadside System** is comprised of sub-systems that cover the ITS infrastructure on or along physical road infrastructure, like roadside units or signal control.
- **Vehicle System** is comprised of sub-systems that are integrated within vehicles, such as onboard systems, advanced driver assistance, safety systems, navigation, and remote data collection.
- **Traveler/VRU System** is comprised of personal devices, like mobile devices or navigation devices, and specific systems connected to vehicles of VRUs, like tags.

**C-ITS Architecture Description** is essential for designing, deploying, and managing complex, modern systems that enhance communication and collaboration through coordinated and integrated operations. We used the C-ITS architecture framework that complies with the conceptual model of the international standard ISO/IEC/IEEE 42010 [13]. The international standard provides a comprehensive framework for describing the architecture of a system, ensuring that all stakeholders have a common understanding of the system under development. C-ITS architecture framework consists of five viewpoints that represent the C-ITS systems and their relationships and capture the concerns of various stakeholders [28]. Each viewpoint represents a unique aspect of the system, such as its functionality, structure, behavior, or context. These viewpoints facilitate developers', architects, and end-user's comprehension of the system's architecture. These viewpoints were also utilized in a few C-ITS initiatives, such as COMPASS4D [19] and CVRIA [25]. In this paper, we discuss the context, functional, and physical viewpoints.

- **Context viewpoint** describes how the system interacts with its surroundings (people, systems, and external entities). A context view helps stakeholders comprehend the system's roles and organization.
- **Functional viewpoint** describes the system's runtime functional elements' responsibilities, interfaces, and main interactions. A functional approach helps stakeholders comprehend system structures and affects quality.
- **Physical viewpoint** describes the system's physical deployment and dependencies. A physical view captures the hardware environment, technical environment requirements for each element, and software elements to the runtime environment that will execute them, helping stakeholders deploy, test, and maintain the system.

To effectively model the C-ITS systems in various viewpoints, we employed the SysML Block Definition Diagram (BDD). The BDD allowed us to depict the high-level C-ITS systems, providing stakeholders with essential base-level information about the structure, behavior, and relationships of the C-ITS systems [9,14].

## 2.3   Architecture Review

To determine whether the reference architecture is efficient, an architecture review must be conducted while the project is still in the planning or development phase [17]. The entire project team, including architects, developers, project managers, and business analysts, reviews the system's progress during the development of the reference architecture. We reviewed our reference models, including the structure, components, interfaces, and interactions with the interdisciplinary C-ITS stakeholders. The review phase helped us identify any architectural flaws early on and ensure that the essential C-ITS systems were accurately captured and readily understood by all parties. Overall, the architecture review served as a quality control safeguard to ensure that the reference architecture for C-ITS systems met the project's objectives [3].

The architecture review process is shown in Fig. 4. Main C-ITS systems were initially identified during the abstraction phase. The C-ITS reference architecture consists of a Glossary that details all the concepts and their respective definitions, Reference Architectural Models that are outlined in SysML with the help of the Enterprise Architect tool, and system descriptions that provide more information regarding the C-ITS systems. These were developed during the description phase. The Glossary and System Descriptions are outside the scope of this paper, but can be found in the reference architecture deliverable of C-MobILE project [28]. During the development process, we validated the identified C-ITS systems and models through focused group sessions consisting of 10–15 (depending upon session's goals) architecture experts, use-case experts, deployment site leaders from different countries and regions, and C-ITS application professionals. The C-ITS architects of the C-MobILE project led these focus group sessions, during which the results such as a reference architecture model, a glossary, and a list of open issues and challenges were presented for immediate feedback and discussion. After analyzing the feedback from the focus group, we refined the C-ITS reference architecture. As a result, we updated the repository and models for each session accordingly. This iterative cycle of weekly revisions lasted for about 4–5 months before the final reference architecture was approved by the C-ITS experts of all C-MobILE deployment sites. The outcomes of our C-MobILE reference architecture models are presented below.

## 3   Results

In this section, we present the reference architecture models that were developed using the proposed method for the C-MobILE project. In our deliverable [28], a complete and detailed explanation of outcomes can be found.

### 3.1   C-ITS System Classification

We categorize C-ITS systems into five groups: Support, Central, Roadside, Vehicle, and Traveller/VRU System. We analyzed and reverse architect the systems and subsystems following the steps described in the Sect. 2.1, Abstraction phase. We identified that the DITCM reference architecture covers most of the C-MobILE pre-selected systems. The Fig. 5 shows the high-level systems identified from the abstraction phase.

### 3.2   C-ITS Architecture Description

We describe our C-ITS reference architecture using the C-ITS architecture framework explained in the Description phase in Sect. 2.2. In this paper, we focus on context, functional, and physical viewpoints.

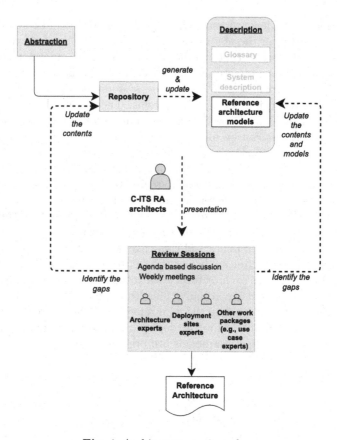

**Fig. 4.** Architecture review phase

**1. Context Viewpoint** defines the system's dependencies and interactions with its surroundings (people, systems, and external things). The context perspective helps stakeholders, such as system/software architects, designers, developers, and users to understand the system context. This viewpoint addresses stakeholders' major concerns by describing the high-level system scope and responsibilities by identifying external entities and their relationships. The notations that we commonly see used for context diagrams are SysML Block Definition Diagram. In Fig. 6, the main C-ITS systems are depicted as black boxes and corresponding actors' connections with those systems [28].

- Vehicle Driver: A actor driving motorized vehicles such as cars, buses, and trucks. The actors in this category interact with the vehicle system using the On-Board unit (OBU), Human Machine Interface (HMI), and other vehicle interfaces.
- Vulnerable Road User (VRU): VRUs are people like pedestrians, cyclists, and motorcyclists. These actors interact with Traveler/VRU systems using HMI, tablet, and mobile.

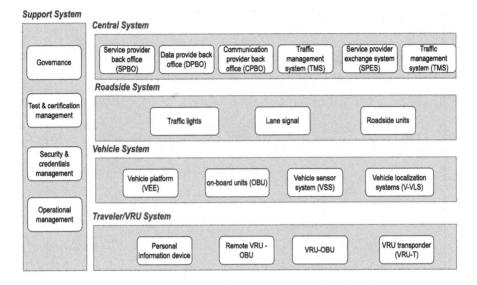

**Fig. 5.** C-ITS system classification [28]

- Road Operator: This actor collects and analyzes roadside data through multiple communication routes.
- Service Provider: This actor directly supports the Central System, which provides numerous functions such as a navigation provider that provides navigation services and a traffic information provider that provides road traffic information such as traffic jams, incidents, and road work warnings to end users or organizations.
- Governance: This actor directly supports the Support System, which includes legal authorities, test and certification management, security, and credentials management.

**2. Functional Viewpoint** describes the system's run-time functional elements' responsibilities, interfaces, and main interactions. The functional view helps stakeholders comprehend system structures and affects quality properties. The functional viewpoint is straightforward to understand and describes the system's functional structure, so stakeholders, especially system architects, developers, and integrators use it. Functional capabilities and external interfaces displaying system interaction are stakeholders' major concerns. In Fig. 7, the dependencies between the C-ITS systems across different levels are shown.

**3. Physical Viewpoint** considers the topology of subsystems and their physical linkages at each domain of interest. Subsystems contain functional components that provide ITS application functionality and interfaces. Users, architects, system maintainers, and OEMs are the major stakeholders in the Physical

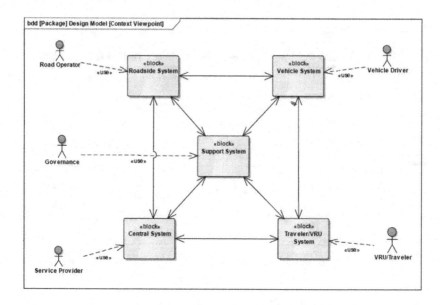

**Fig. 6.** Context model [8, 14, 28]

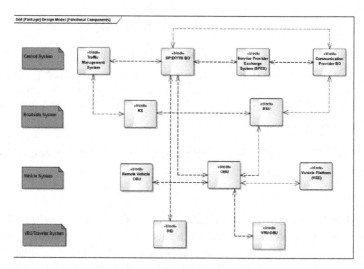

**Fig. 7.** Functional models [8, 14, 28]

Viewpoint. This viewpoint addresses stakeholders' concerns about physical component decomposition and specification. In Fig. 8, the C-ITS systems for each C-ITS system classification level are highlighted.

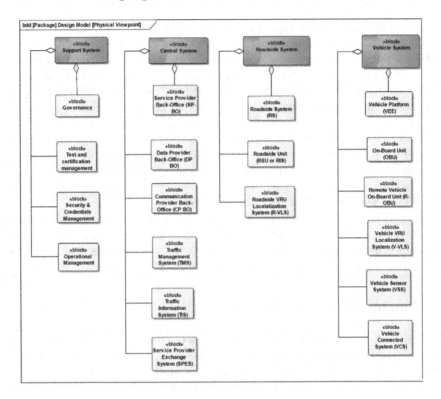

**Fig. 8.** Physical models [8, 14, 28]

## 4    Lessons Learnt

We described the method for developing a reference architecture for C-ITS services and demonstrated its usage in creating a C-ITS reference architecture in the context of C-MobILE project. We share below the lessons learned from both method and their usage in creating a C-ITS reference architecture:

– Dividing the reference architecture design process into distinct phases such as abstraction, description, and review can help in streamlining the process and making it more manageable among interdisciplinary stakeholders from different countries.
– All phases require stakeholders, including architecture specialists from deployment sites and related projects. These phases clarify and improve collaboration. For example, deciding on how to abstract, describe, and assess early on can save time by eliminating redundant discussion on concept definition and description language. It showed that effective participation with clear phases can offer useful expertise and opinions, align concepts, and ensure that the reference design reflects real-world use cases.
– While it was a lengthy process to capture the information in the repository during the abstraction phase of identifying the key C-ITS systems, doing so

served the aim of collecting all data in one place. However, a more efficient technique could be implemented if time and resources are not a constraint.

- As discussed earlier, reference designs are frequently described without a generic language or notations, causing confusion. By selecting the widely utilized modeling language SysML, supported by robust tools like Enterprise Architect and IBM Rational Rhapsody, we successfully minimized unnecessary communication challenges and errors in architecture modeling [22].

- Organizing a meeting with numerous stakeholders can be challenging, which is why we opt for iterative meetings with clear and pre-defined goals during the architecture review phase that concentrates on specific aspects. For example, we prioritize discussions centered around vehicle-to-vehicle C-ITS services and the associated C-ITS systems.

- Given that none of the related projects applied an architecture framework conforming to the ISO 42010 international standard, utilizing an architecture framework was useful in defining the views and perspectives that addressed the concerns of the C-MobILE project's stakeholders [14].

## 5    Conclusion and Future Work

This paper describes the design process for a C-ITS reference architecture. It seeks to address the lack of a method to develop a comprehensive C-ITS reference architecture across different deployment sites. Existing C-ITS reference architectures lack adaptability and are region-specific. We propose therefore a method involving abstraction, description, and architecture review phases. In the abstraction phase, we analyzed existing C-ITS initiatives to identify essential systems and categorize them. In the description phase, these systems were modeled in SysML following the C-ITS architecture framework proposed in [28]. In the review phase, the reference architecture models were evaluated by diverse C-ITS architects and experts, ensuring a high-quality architecture design satisfying the needs of the different deployment sites. The reference architecture models for the C-MobILE project were created using the proposed method. The reference architecture was instantiated by the 8 deployment sites and further helped realize C-ITS services defined in the C-MobILE project.

There are several opportunities for future research in the field of reference architecture for C-ITS. While the method has been developed in the context of European countries, extending its applicability to other countries requires careful consideration of unique factors such as technological infrastructure, industry collaborations, and public acceptance. These factors determine C-ITS service implementation and readiness [23]. Therefore, it is crucial to acknowledge these variations and adapt the method accordingly. Although the reference architecture created using the proposed method was used in the eight deployment sites, there was no feedback after the implementation of the C-ITS services because of the nature of the project plan. Existing evaluation methods for software architecture e.g., ATAM, SAAM may not be suitable for evaluating the reference architecture of C-ITS services. Therefore, further study is needed to develop a more nuanced evaluation approach specifically for reference architectures in this field. Additionally, exploring methods for updating the reference architecture to accommodate future modifications would be valuable.

**Acknowledgment.** The C-MobILE project is funded by the European Union's "Horizon 2020 research and innovation programme" under grant agreement No 723311.

# References

1. Angelov, S., Grefen, P., Greefhorst, D.: A classification of software reference architectures: analyzing their success and effectiveness. In: 2009 Joint Working IEEE/IFIP Conference on Software Architecture and European Conference on Software Architecture, pp. 141–150. IEEE (2009)
2. Asselin-Miller, N., et al.: Study on the deployment of C-ITS in Europe: Final report. Report for DG MOVE MOVE/C 3, 2014-794 (2016)
3. Babar, M.A., Gorton, I.: Software architecture review: the state of practice. Computer **42**(7), 26–32 (2009)
4. Botte, M., Pariota, L., D'Acierno, L., Bifulco, G.N.: An overview of cooperative driving in the European union: policies and practices. Electronics **8**(6), 616 (2019)
5. Cloutier, R., Muller, G., Verma, D., Nilchiani, R., Hole, E., Bone, M.: The concept of reference architectures. Syst. Eng. **13**(1), 14–27 (2010)
6. Dajsuren, Y., van den Brand, M., Serebrenik, A., Huisman, R.: Automotive ADLS: a study on enforcing consistency through multiple architectural levels. In: Proceedings of the 8th international ACM SIGSOFT conference on Quality of Software Architectures, pp. 71–80 (2012)
7. European Union: The c-roads platform an overview of harmonized C-ITS deployment in europe (2020). https://www.c-roads.eu/fileadmin/user_upload/media/Dokumente/C-Roads_Brochure_2021_final_2.pdf
8. Ferrandez, R., Dajsuren, Y., Karkhanis, P., Fünfrocken, M., Pillado, M.: Modeling the C-ITS architectures: C-mobile case study. In: ITS World Congress (2018)
9. Friedenthal, S., Moore, A., Steiner, R.: Omg systems modeling language (omg sysml) tutorial. In: INCOSE International Symposium, vol. 9, pp. 65–67. Citeseer (2006)
10. Fünfrocken, M., Vogt, J., Wieker, H.: The converge project - a systems network for its (2021)
11. Houngbo, H., Mercer, R.E.: Method mention extraction from scientific research papers. In: Proceedings of COLING 2012, pp. 1211–1222 (2012)
12. ISO: Iso 14813–5:2020(en) intelligent transport systems - reference model architecture(s) for the its sector - part 5: Requirements for architecture description in its standards (2020)
13. ISO/IEC/IEEE: Systems and software engineering - architecture description. ISO/IEC/IEEE 42010:2011(E) (Revision of ISO/IEC 42010:2007 and IEEE Std 1471–2000), pp. 1–46 (2011). https://doi.org/10.1109/IEEESTD.2011.6129467
14. Karkhanis, P., van den Brand, M.G., Rajkarnikar, S.: Defining the C-ITS reference architecture. In: 2018 IEEE International Conference on Software Architecture Companion (ICSA-C), pp. 148–151. IEEE (2018)
15. Kotsi, A., Mitsakis, E., Tzanis, D.: Overview of C-ITS deployment projects in Europe and USA. In: 2020 IEEE 23rd International Conference on Intelligent Transportation Systems (ITSC), pp. 1–6. IEEE (2020)

16. Lu, M., et al.: Cooperative and connected intelligent transport systems for sustainable European road transport. In: Proceedings 7th Transport Research Arena, Vienna, Austria (2018)
17. Maranzano, J.F., Rozsypal, S.A., Zimmerman, G.H., Warnken, G.W., Wirth, P.E., Weiss, D.M.: Architecture reviews: practice and experience. IEEE Softw. **22**(2), 34–43 (2005)
18. Marilisa, B., Luigi, P., Nicola, B.G., et al.: C-ITS communication: an insight on the current research activities in the European union. Int. J. Transport. Syst. **3** (2018)
19. Mitsakis, E., et al.: Large scale deployment of cooperative mobility systems in Europe: Compass4d. In: 2014 International Conference on Connected Vehicles and Expo (ICCVE), pp. 469–476. IEEE (2014)
20. Mitsakis, E., Kotsi, A.: Cooperative intelligent transport systems as a policy tool for mitigating the impacts of climate change on road transport. In: Nathanail, E.G., Karakikes, I.D. (eds.) CSUM 2018. AISC, vol. 879, pp. 418–425. Springer, Cham (2019). https://doi.org/10.1007/978-3-030-02305-8_51
21. van Sambeek, M., et al.: Towards an architecture for cooperative-intelligent transport system (C-ITS) applications in the Netherlands. Eindhoven University of Technology, Technical Report Beta Working Paper series (485) (2015)
22. Santos, T.L., Soares, M.S.: A survey on what users think about sysml. Syst. Eng. (2023)
23. Shaaban, K., Elamin, M., Alsoub, M.: Intelligent transportation systems in a developing country: benefits and challenges of implementation. Transport. Res. Procedia **55**, 1373–1380 (2021)
24. Sjoberg, K., Andres, P., Buburuzan, T., Brakemeier, A.: Cooperative intelligent transport systems in Europe: current deployment status and outlook. IEEE Veh. Technol. Mag. **12**(2), 89–97 (2017)
25. USD of Transportation: Architecture reference for cooperative and intelligent transportation. https://www.arc-it.net/
26. Europe Union: Nordicway - architecture, services and interoperability (2017). https://www.nordicway.net/
27. Wang, Q., von Tunzelmann, N.: Complexity and the functions of the firm: breadth and depth. Res. Policy **29**(7–8), 805–818 (2000)
28. Yanja Dajsuren, P.K., Kadiogullari, D., Fünfrocken, M.: C-MobILE d3.1 reference architecture (2017). https://c-mobile-project.eu/wp-content/uploads/sites/19/2018/06/C-MobILE-D3.1-ReferenceArchitecture-v1.1.pdf

# Towards Assessing Spread in Sets of Software Architecture Designs

Vittorio Cortellessa[1] , J. Andres Diaz-Pace[2] , Daniele Di Pompeo[1(✉)] ,
and Michele Tucci[1]

[1] University of L'Aquila, L'Aquila, Italy
{vittorio.cortellessa,daniele.dipompeo,michele.tucci}@univaq.it
[2] ISISTAN, CONICET-UNICEN, Buenos Aires, Argentina
andres.diazpace@isistan.unicen.edu.ar

**Abstract.** Several approaches have recently used automated techniques to generate architecture design alternatives by means of optimization techniques. These approaches aim at improving an initial architecture with respect to quality aspects, such as performance, reliability, or maintainability. In this context, each optimization experiment usually produces a different set of architecture alternatives that is characterized by specific settings. As a consequence, the designer is left with the task of comparing such sets to identify the settings that lead to better solution sets for the problem. To assess the quality of solution sets, multi-objective optimization commonly relies on quality indicators. Among these, the quality indicator for the maximum spread estimates the diversity of the generated alternatives, providing a measure of how much of the solution space has been explored. However, the maximum spread indicator is computed only on the objective space and does not consider architectural information (e.g., components structure, design decisions) from the architectural space. In this paper, we propose a quality indicator for the spread that assesses the diversity of alternatives by taking into account architectural features. To compute the spread, we rely on a notion of distance between alternatives according to the way they were generated during the optimization. We demonstrate how our architectural quality indicator can be applied to a dataset from the literature.

**Keywords:** Architecture alternatives · Multi-objective optimization · Diversity · Quality indicator

## 1 Introduction

When designing or evolving software architectures, the improvement of quality attributes like performance, reliability, or maintainability is a central concern for the designer. This task has recently been the target of an increasing number of automated approaches whose goal is to generate improved versions of an initial architecture [1,6]. The generated architectures are referred to as design alternatives. These alternatives are automatically generated through refactoring,

B. Tekinerdogan et al. (Eds.): ECSA 2023, LNCS 14212, pp. 133–140, 2023.
https://doi.org/10.1007/978-3-031-42592-9_9

which is the application of transformations for improving some quality attributes of interest while keeping the software functionalities unchanged. In practical cases, the designer tackles multiple attributes at the same time. For example, she could aim at improving performance while keeping reliability high and the cost of refactoring low. This context is ideal for multi-objective optimization.

Multi-objective optimization normally needs a series of experiments to determine appropriate configuration parameters. Examples of these parameters can be the choice of the optimization algorithm and its settings, such as the specific genetic algorithm and its population size. A recurring problem is that of deciding which configuration parameters are to be preferred on the basis of the obtained solution sets. In multi-objective optimization, this issue has been traditionally addressed by means of quality indicators for solution sets [5]. These indicators seek to estimate desirable properties of solution sets and, consequently, can help designers to choose parameters that improve such properties. Among these properties, the spread of a solution set plays a fundamental role in assessing how much of the solution space was covered and how diverse the solutions are in the set. The *maximum spread (MS)* [10] is a prominent indicator for such a property. Higher *MS* values indicate that the optimization searched the solution space enough to cover a wide area.

The spread is especially relevant when dealing with architectural alternatives. It highlights that a sizeable number of alternatives were found, and the obtained solution set covers tradeoffs that are dispersed enough to provide a variety of design choices to the designer. Note that quality indicators are computed on the problem objectives, which are the attributes being optimized (*i.e.,* performance, reliability, and cost in the previous example). Although these indicators are valuable for assessing the performance of optimization algorithms, they do not provide insights on the architectural features of the solutions, *i.e.,* the architectural space, which represent more closely the object of the software engineering task we described.

In this paper, we propose an architectural quality indicator, called *MAS (Maximum Architecture Spread)*, for the estimation of the spread in sets of design alternatives. *MAS* is based on the notion of maximum spread by Zitzler et al. [10], but it operates in the architectural space rather than on the objective space. To demonstrate our approach, we show how *MAS* can be applied to a dataset that addresses an architecture optimization problem from the literature. To do this, we calculate the differences among architectural alternatives on the basis of their structure. This is achieved by first encoding the architectures in terms of sequences of refactorings and then using distance metrics on such encodings. Our preliminary results indicate that *MAS* provides an additional architectural view of the optimization, and exhibits a correlation with the *(MS)* indicator.

## 2   Motivating Example

Let us assume that the designer wants to explore design alternatives that improve a performance objective (*e.g.,* minimization of response time) for an initial architecture ($A_0$), while keeping the cost of changes low. For example, this is the case of the $ST+$ system [7], in which architectures are specified in the Palladio Component Model (PCM) notation. An automated optimization tool progressively applies refactorings via a heuristic search and generates a set of design alternatives in the *architectural space* (*i.e.,* the space of PCM architectures). This set can be seen as a tree rooted at $A_0$, in which the nodes correspond to alternatives and the edges correspond to refactorings from one alternative to another, as sketched in Fig. 1 (left). Each alternative is evaluated to provide quantifiable measures for the objectives. Measures for such objectives constitute the *objective space*, in which the designer can analyze tradeoffs between the alternatives, as depicted in Fig. 1 (right). However, the objective space does not reveal details about the structural characteristics or features of the design alternatives. Likewise, the architectural space does not provide insights about tradeoffs between the objectives.

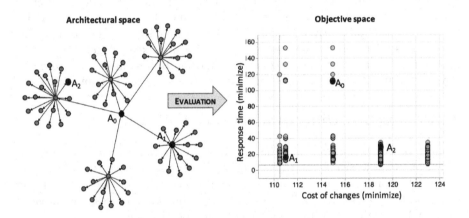

**Fig. 1.** Relationship between the architectural and objective spaces. The architectural space is represented as search tree rooted at the initial architecture ($A_0$).

To assess the quality of solution sets in the objective space, the designer can rely on quality indicators, such as *MS* [10]. However, analyzing only the objective space can be shortsighted, because it does not expose, for example, architectural characteristics of the PCM alternatives in the solution sets.

We argue that insights from the architectural space are crucial for the designer to understand and compare configuration parameters in order to make the optimization process more useful and efficient. Unfortunately, quality indicators for the architectural space have not been reported in the literature, partially because they are not domain independent (as the traditional indicators for the objective space) but depend on the kind of models populating the architectural space. We refer to the quality indicators for this space as *architectural quality indicators*.

## 3   Related Work

We highlight that none of the identified prior studies presented metrics to estimate sets of design alternatives in the architectural space, rather than in the
objective space. Esfahani et al. [2] introduced a quantitative framework to graph-
ically drive architects in selecting design alternatives by means of fuzzy mathematical methods to rank alternatives. Ranking alternatives helps designers to
find the optimal alternative (*i.e.*, the best case) and the most critical one (*i.e.*,
the worst case). Sedaghatbaf and Azgomi [9] proposed a framework for modeling
and evaluating software architectures. They used a multi-criteria decision model
to extract the best and worst alternatives. To this extent, they introduced a distance metric that extracts the maximum and minimum values for the best and
worst alternatives, respectively. In addition, they support the designer in this
complex process by providing a tool named *SQME*. Rahmoun et al. [8] exploited
a genetic algorithm to generate model transformations and obtain design alternatives defined through the Architecture Analysis and Design Language (AADL).
To compare the alternatives generated by their approach and the optimal one,
the authors introduced a distance metric based on Mixed-Integer Linear Programming (MILP). The idea beyond the study by Rahmoun et al. is to find a
way to measure how far the generated alternatives are from the optimal ones.

## 4   Proposed Architectural Quality Indicator

In multi-objective optimization, the spread of a solution set is recognized as the
region of the objective space that is covered by the set. When the solution set
is a Pareto front, the spread is also known as the coverage of the set [5]. Higher
values of the spread are an indication that the optimization process has extended
the search enough to reach a wide area of the objective space.

The *maximum spread (MS)* is a well-known quality indicator [10] that measures the range of a solution set by considering, for any two solutions in the set,
the maximum extent of each objective. It is defined as:

$$MS(S) = \sqrt{\sum_{i=1}^{o} \max_{s,s' \in S}(s_i - s_i')^2}$$

where $S$ is the solution set under consideration, $s$ and $s'$ are solutions in that
set, and $o$ is the number of objectives. Higher values of $MS$ are to be preferred,
as they represent a better coverage of the solution space.

As it is evident, quality indicators like $MS$ are defined on the objective space,
and they are considered a valuable mean to assess the performance of a search
algorithm in producing solution sets coverage. However, when these optimization
techniques are employed in the software architecture context, and specifically
for the generation of design alternatives, the quality of the resulting solution
sets should be assessed also in the architectural space. Indeed, the architectural
features of the solutions represent the final product of the optimization process,

and the designer will make decisions on their basis. Therefore, we provide an estimate of the coverage and diversity of solution sets in the architectural space.

We introduce the *maximum architectural spread (MAS)* by following the same principles behind the original $MS$. It is defined as:

$$MAS(S) = \sqrt{\frac{\sum_{n=1}^{N} \max_{s,s' \in S}(d(s_n, s'_n))^2}{N \max(d)^2}}$$

where $S$ is the considered set, $N$ is its cardinality, while $s$ and $s'$ are solutions in that set. Moreover, $d(s, s')$ is a distance metric that is relevant for the problem, and that can be plugged in the formula to quantify the distance between two architectures. $max(d)$ is the maximum possible value for the distance metric. $MAS$ can be interpreted as the square root of the ratio of two quantities: (i) the sum of the maximum distance of any two solutions in the set, divided by (ii) the maximum achievable spread, that is the maximum value for the distance metric multiplied by the number of solutions in the set. The $MAS$ denominator is used to normalize its value between 0 and 1. When $MAS$ is 0, it represents the limit case in which the set consists of a single solution. Instead, 1 represents the maximum achievable spread, which occurs when every solution is at maximum distance from another. The intent is to provide, numerically, an intuition of how far we are from the maximum diversity of solutions we could theoretically achieve. In addition, the normalization is aimed at enabling the comparison of $MAS$ obtained with different distance metrics.

## 4.1   Architectural Distance as Sequence Distance

The $MAS$ computation depends on having a notion of distance $d(s, s')$ between architecture solutions. Since architectures are usually complex objects, simplifying their representations can help to define intuitive distance metrics. In this work, we rely on the sequences of transformations applied to the initial architecture, and use those sequences as proxies for architectural representations. A sequence is actually a path in the search tree, as illustrated in Fig. 1 (left). More formally, an architecture $A_i$ is modeled by a sequence of transformations $T_i = <t_{1i}, t_{2i}, ..., t_{Li}>$ of length $L$, which comes from the shortest path between the initial node $A_0$ and the node for $A_i$ in the tree. For each $t_{ki}$, the architectural elements targeted by the transformation are parameters in the representation.

Once architectures are encoded as sequences, the distance $d(A_i, A_j)$ is defined in terms of the delta of changes between the elements of their respective sequences. If two transformations $t_{ik}$ and $t_{jk}$ share the same name and parameters, then $d(t_{ik}, t_{jk}) = 0$; and conversely, if they have different names and completely different parameters, then their distance is equal to 1. The problem becomes one of matching sequences, and well-known distances such as *Levenshtein* [4] can be used to compute the sequence distances. To distinguish between the transformation names and their parameters, when matching sequences, we use a separate distance function for each part of the transformation, and combine the results via a weighted sum. For a pair of sequences of length $L$, the distance computation is defined as:

$$d(A_i, A_j) = \sum_{k=1}^{L} simpred(t_{ik}, t_{jk}) * w_{pred} + simargs(t_{ik}, t_{jk}) * w_{args}$$

Functions $simpred()$ and $simargs()$ extract the transformation name and arguments from $t_{ik}$ and $t_{jk}$, respectively, and then calculate the *Levenshtein* formula. We perform a label encoding of the vocabulary of transformation names and arguments used in the architectural space, before evaluating $simpred()$ and $simargs()$. This encoding maps each transformation name or argument to a unique symbol. The maximum possible values of $simpred()$ and $simargs()$ is $L$. The contributions of these functions are weighted by $w_{pred}$ and $w_{args}$, with the constraint $w_{pred} + w_{args} = 1$ to keep $d(A_i, A_j)$ bound to the interval $[0..L]$.

### 4.2   Application of *MAS*

We computed *MAS* on the *ST+* dataset[1], which comprises nine component types for instantiating an architecture alternative, and four quality-attribute scenarios as the optimization objectives. Two objectives (referred to as *p1* and *p2*) involve minimizing response time and CPU utilization [3], while the other two (referred to as *m1* and *m2*) involve minimizing the cost of changes via a complexity metric. The architectural space contains 554 candidate architectures.

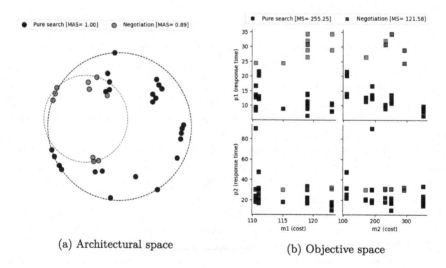

(a) Architectural space

(b) Objective space

**Fig. 2.** Comparison of the architectural and objective spaces for the two search algorithms in *ST+*, along with computed *MAS* and *MS*.

Graphical representations of the architectural and quality-attribute spaces are shown in Fig. 2. The colors refer to the two search strategies (standard search

[1] https://github.com/SQuAT-Team/paper-supplementary.

and negotiation) exercised for $ST+$. The architectural space (Fig. 2a) is visualized using a multi-dimensional scaling (MDS) projection that is derived from the distances $d(A_i, A_j)$ between the PCM architectures. In our MDS chart, each color-coded circle encloses the alternatives returned by an algorithm, and gives a notional view of the spread it achieved.

In the objective space (Fig. 2b), the solutions computed by the standard search lie in the Pareto front, while the negotiated solutions set apart, particularly for $p1$ with respect to $m1$ and $m2$. This would mean that the negotiation algorithm tries to balance the utilities for that tradeoff. The $MS$ values for the two sets show a larger spread in favor of the standard search algorithm.

In the architectural space (Fig. 2a), we observe that the negotiation algorithm achieved a slightly lower $MAS$ than the standard search algorithm, whose spread was maximal. It seems that the space covered by the negotiation algorithm concentrates on a well-defined region. In contrast, the other set is more diverse. Interestingly, some solutions in the negotiation set are at a very close distance of the solutions in the other set. This close distance among the two types of solutions is not evident when looking at the objective space (Fig. 2b).

One of the main findings from this experiment is the relationship between the $MAS$ and $MS$ indicators. Although they operate on different spaces and assess different objects (*i.e.*, architectures and quality values, respectively), there is an apparent correlation between their spreads. The observed correlation, however, might have been influenced by the search algorithms used by $SQuAT$.

If the relationship between $MAS$ and $MS$ proves to hold, it might help the designer to make assumptions about the spread on the objective space while looking at the architectural space, and vice versa. Another observation refers to the architectural distance being used in our evaluation. The assessment of architectural similarities (or dissimilarities) based on their transformation sequences works in the context of an initial architecture and a neighborhood of alternatives that are reachable only via transformation sequences applied to the initial architecture. Therefore, the underlying assumption is that all the sequences have the same starting point. The proposed *Levenshtein* metric, however, is not intended to be a global metric for arbitrary architectures. Furthermore, the metric can be affected by the transformation encoding and by the sequence length.

## 5    Conclusion

In this work, we proposed a quality indicator for estimating the spread in sets of software architectures, namely the *maximum architectural spread (MAS)*. We showed, through a lightweight literature review, that these sets of architectures represent design alternatives and arise in a variety of contexts, especially when multi-objective optimization techniques are employed to generate them. Differently from existing quality indicators in multi-objective optimization, ours aims at computing an estimate of the solutions spread from an architectural point of view. This was achieved by encoding the sequences of modifications being applied to generate each architecture, and then using distance metrics to calculate how far apart the architectures are from each other. Moreover, we showed how our $MAS$ indicator can be applied on practical cases to gain insights on the diversity of architectures and compare optimization settings (*e.g.*, algorithms).

The maximum spread provides an idea of the extent of the solution set, but says nothing about the inner shape of the set or the distribution of its solutions. We intend to overcome this limitation in future work by exploring corner cases in which we obtain similar values of $MAS$ on sets that exhibit contrasting distributions. Furthermore, we will explore complementary indicators to assess properties such as uniformity or convergence within the architectural space.

**Acknowledgments.** Daniele Di Pompeo and Michele Tucci are supported by European Union – NextGenerationEU – National Recovery and Resilience Plan (Piano Nazionale di Ripresa e Resilienza, PNRR) – Project: "SoBigData.it – Strengthening the Italian RI for Social Mining and Big Data Analytics" – Prot. IR0000013 – Avviso n. 3264 del 28/12/2021. J. Andres Diaz-Pace is supported by the PICT-2021-00757 project, Argentina.

# References

1. Cortellessa, V., Di Pompeo, D., Stoico, V., Tucci, M.: Many-objective optimization of non-functional attributes based on refactoring of software models. Inf. Softw. Technol. **157**, 107159 (2023)
2. Esfahani, N., Malek, S., Razavi, K.: Guidearch: guiding the exploration of architectural solution space under uncertainty. In: 35th International Conference on Software Engineering (ICSE), pp. 43–52 (2013)
3. Koziolek, H., Reussner, R.: A model transformation from the palladio component model to layered queueing networks. In: Kounev, S., Gorton, I., Sachs, K. (eds.) SIPEW 2008. LNCS, vol. 5119, pp. 58–78. Springer, Heidelberg (2008). https://doi.org/10.1007/978-3-540-69814-2_6
4. Levenshtein, V.I.: Binary codes capable of correcting deletions, insertions, and reversals. Soviet Phys. Doklady **10**, 707–710 (1965)
5. Li, M., Yao, X.: Quality evaluation of solution sets in multiobjective optimisation: a survey. ACM Comput. Surv. **52**(2), 26:1–26:38 (2019)
6. Ni, Y., et al.: Multi-objective software performance optimisation at the architecture level using randomised search rules. Inf. Softw. Technol. **135**, 106565 (2021)
7. Rago, A., Vidal, S.A., Diaz-Pace, J.A., Frank, S., van Hoorn, A.: Distributed quality-attribute optimization of software architectures. In: 11th Brazilian Symposium on Software Components, Architectures and Reuse, pp. 7:1–7:10 (2017)
8. Rahmoun, S., Mehiaoui-Hamitou, A., Borde, E., Pautet, L., Soubiran, E.: Multi-objective exploration of architectural designs by composition of model transformations. Softw. Syst. Model. **18**(1), 107–127 (2019). ISSN 1619-1366, 1619-1374
9. Sedaghatbaf, A., Azgomi, M.A.: SQME: a framework for modeling and evaluation of software architecture quality attributes. Softw. Syst. Model. **18**(4), 2609–2632 (2019)
10. Zitzler, E., Deb, K., Thiele, L.: Comparison of multiobjective evolutionary algorithms: empirical results. Evol. Comput. **8**(2), 173–195 (2000)

# Continuous Evaluation of Consistency in Software Architecture Models

Priom Biswas[1]([⊠])[iD], Andreas Morgenstern[1][iD], Pablo Oliveira Antonino[1][iD], Rafael Capilla[2][iD], and Elisa Yumi Nakagawa[3][iD]

[1] Fraunhofer IESE, Kaiserslautern, Germany
{priom.biswas,andreas.morgenstern,pablo.antonino}@iese.fraunhofer.de
[2] Rey Juan Carlos University, Madrid, Spain
rafael.capilla@urjc.es
[3] University of São Paulo, São Carlos, Brazil
elisa@icmc.usp.br

**Abstract.** Ensuring consistency between architectural models in software-intensive systems is challenging; hence, this paper presents an industry-oriented solution for the continuous evaluation of the consistency of architecture models aligned with CI/CD pipelines. We evaluated our solution using a concept car to demonstrate its viability and how architectural consistency checking can be automated.

**Keywords:** Software architecture · consistency checking · continuous evaluation · continuous software engineering

## 1 Introduction

The consistency of architecture models has been investigated for years [10]. Some works like [1] discuss the importance of consistency in UML models using a model-driven architecture (MDA) and suggest a validation language to automatically detect and resolve potential inconsistencies. Automatically detecting and tracking inconsistencies in design models is also highlighted in [7]. However, not all the rules for detecting inconsistencies can be evaluated instantly. Nowadays, many development approaches adopt a continuous software engineering (CSE) model to achieve fast deployments. However, checking the conformance between architectures and requirements continuously is still challenging, as stated in [16]. In this approach, the authors suggest a process for detecting inconsistencies using formal specifications, but they do not detail how much they can automate the proposed solution. In [4], the authors describe the application of formal methods in the automotive industry to significantly increase the correctness and reliability of AUTOSAR architectures.

The studies discussed above lack a complete solution to continuously evaluate the consistency between high-level and low-level architecture models. Thus, in this research, we address how to achieve consistency in industrial architecture models and raise the following research questions: (i) **RQ1:** *How to achieve*

B. Tekinerdogan et al. (Eds.): ECSA 2023, LNCS 14212, pp. 141–149, 2023.
https://doi.org/10.1007/978-3-031-42592-9_10

*behavioral interaction consistency between high-level and low-level architecture models?* and (ii) **RQ2:** *To what extent can consistency evaluation be automated in continuous mode?* To answer these research questions, we extend a previous work [2] by enabling model-in-the-loop simulations to be executed using traditional UML sequence and state machine diagrams and integrate them into a CSE approach for continuous consistency checking. The remainder of this paper is organized as follows: Sect. 2 describes related works. Section 3 details the steps of our solution and the tools we developed. Section 4 presents the evaluation of the proposed solution, while Sect. 5 presents our findings answering the RQs and the limitations. Section 6 provides the final remarks of our work.

## 2   Related Work

Some strategies for achieving architectural consistency deal with rules and formal methods aimed to produce an intermediate representation that can be validated [6,13,17]. One recent work [11] discusses architecture consistency checking of security aspects in microservices and cloud-based systems. However, the proposed solution does not discuss how to automatically handle possible deviations of quality. Regarding quality checking in the context of CSE approaches, the authors of [5] suggest a rule-based language to perform structural analysis of software systems in the development cycles, while in [8], the authors suggest an automatic detection mechanism for architectural violations in software artifacts. Another work [12] discusses the validation of architecture in a continuous way and presents four principles for adapting evaluation in continuous settings. In [3], the authors provide an architecture model for checking the quality of architectures under a DevOps approach and based on industrial scenarios. Also, the evaluation of architecture qualities continuously and semi-automatically is discussed in [14]. One complementary but related work [15] suggests a novel runtime architecture evaluation method that can be used to check deviations from performance values in IoT systems to continuously profile architecture decisions. In [11], the authors investigate how to improve consistency checking activities in infrastructure-as-a-code (IaC) deployments, and propose solutions that identify coupling-related patterns to automatically check conformance using technology-independent metrics. In contrast to the works discussed above, we provide means to evaluate architecture consistency with the confidence of simulation in a more automated and integrated manner.

## 3   Approach

Based on our discussions with practitioners from the automotive domain, we propose an automated solution for architecture consistency checking by integrating a simulation-based evaluation tool into a CI/CD pipeline, as depicted in Fig. 1. We extract the relevant information of the UML diagrams, simulate the structural and behavioral models, and evaluate the consistency. Our solution automates consistency checking using simulation without formal methods

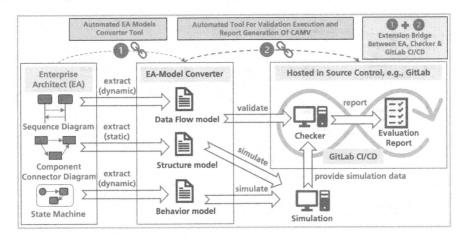

**Fig. 1.** Continuous evaluation process for architecture model consistency checking

or petri nets. The results are reported continuously through a GitLab CI loop. We use a custom-built bridge that connects the Enterprise Architect (EA) modeling tool with a simulator and checker tools for automated model extraction and evaluation, and integrate this solution into a GitLab CI/CD pipeline.

### 3.1 Supporting Tools

The tools supporting our process are:

**Model Converter:** This is an EA plugin that converts sequence and state machine diagrams into semantically predefined textual representations in YAML.

**FERAL Simulator:** We adopted the FERAL[1] [9] simulation framework to simulate the behavior models according to discrete event simulation semantics.

**Checker:** We refer to the checker as CAMV (Continuous Architecture Model Validator), whose workflow is shown in Fig. 2.

At first, UML sequence, component connector and state machine models have been created in EA (**Step 1**). Next, manual creation (**Step 2**) and placement (**Step 3**) of YAML files for events and components (structure model) from component connector diagram is required due to the lack of support in the model converter. However, sequence (data flow model) and state machine YAMLs (behavior models) can be converted using models converter, but still they need to be placed manually within CAMV. For architecture evaluation, evaluation scenarios are specified manually within CAMV. They detail which state machine YAMLs to compare with the sequence YAML. CAMV automatically generates executable models from YAML files using FERAL. Afterwards, CAMV verifies the structural conformity according to the events and components YAML,

---

[1] https://www.iese.fraunhofer.de/en/services/digital-twin/feral.html.

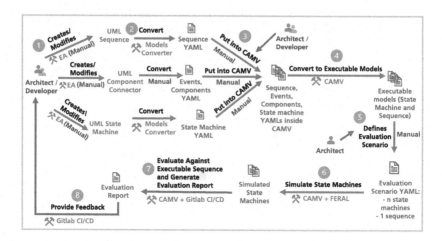

**Fig. 2.** CAMV workflow

simulates the state machines, checks for consistency between state machine and sequence models, and reports inconsistencies. Through a GitLab CI/CD pipeline, CAMV performs continuous consistency checks, where each model modification results in a commit that triggers the pipeline and produces reports. In the following, we detail the major technical steps performed by CAMV.

**Executable Model Creation:** CAMV first turns the YAML representation of a state machine into a Java object, which is subsequently converted into an executable simulation model based on FERAL discrete event semantics (**Step 4**). CAMV also transforms sequences into executable representations, derived from deserialized sequence YAMLs, where the sequence messages are sorted in the order they appear in the sequence. Lastly, CAMV crafts a FERAL simulation scenario according to the specified evaluation scenario (**Step 5**).

**Consistency Checking Procedure:** The evaluation starts after executable models have been created. A simulation end time is set for the FERAL simulation. Each executable state machine is initialized, with the transition from the initial state being performed automatically as an initial step. The executable sequence is initialized by setting all sequence messages to a non-taken state and sequence elements to inactive. The evaluation process begins by initiating the first sequence message as an event and making the corresponding source sequence element active. This initiation triggers a simulation of the state machine connected to the source sequence element (**Step 6**). Using the data from this state machine simulation, CAMV subsequently assesses whether the state machine transition prompted by the sequence message is in alignment with the sequence message itself (**Step 7**). In this way, CAMV iterates over all the sequence messages, triggers state machine simulations for each message, and evaluates the consistency. In case there are no active sequence elements, CAMV checks whether there are any waiting messages from an environment sequence element and triggers that message for simulation. *Environment* sequence elements are special elements for which we do not detail the behavior. After iterations over all sequence messages are completed, CAMV logs the inconsistencies (*incidents*) in a textual report, which is then provided as feedback (**Step 8**). Supported incident types are: (i) *UnexpectedEventIncident:* an event was produced but not expected; (ii) *UnsatisfiedStateChangeIncident:* a component does not reach an expected state while an event is being consumed by the sequence; and (iii) *MissingEventIncident:* a sequence failed to be executed due to the missing event.

**Bridge:** The Bridge, integrated into a GitLab CI/CD pipeline, streamlines interactions among EA, the model converter, and the checker, thereby enabling continuous architecture evaluation. It employs two automated tools, as depicted in Fig. 1: *Automated EA Model Converter Tool* and *Automated Tool for Validation Execution and Report Generation of CAMV*. The former automatically extracts YAMLs and places them into the CAMV tool, while the latter automates CAMV's consistency evaluation process, integrating it into the GitLab CI/CD pipeline. These tools allow for scheduled continuous evaluations according to the needs of CSE solutions.

## 4  Evaluation

This section shows the evaluation of our solution in the context of a consulting project with a German Tier 1 supplier of automotive parts. A proof of concept was first performed in a concept car developed by Fraunhofer IESE. After several iteration cycles, it was delivered to the Tier 1 supplier.

**Concept Car Architecture:** The concept car is a 1:5 scale remote-controlled car that emulates some real-world use cases of a car system. It incorporates *SensorBoards* and an *ActuatorBoard*, as well as a *ControlBoard* that manages complex tasks. In this paper, we focus solely on the *initialization of the concept car's actuator at power-up*, presuming the sensors are ready and there are no issues with the electronic boards. For evaluation purposes, we considered that in each development cycle, the models must be checked for consistency. Hence, Figs. 3a and 3b present the high-level architecture, while Figs. 3c and 3d present the low-level detailed designs. More specifically, Fig. 3a shows the *static architecture view* (component connector) that defines the decomposition and communication channels of the *ControlBoard* and *ActuatorBoard* components. Figure 3b offers the *dynamic architecture view* (sequence) that represents the dynamic interactions between components. The illustrated sequence switches the actuator up and down by performing interactions between *SystemController* and *ActuatorController*, which are detailed in Figs. 3c and 3d using state machines. All these models were manually designed in EA.

**Evaluation Result:** For the evaluation, we followed the CAMV workflow described in Sect. 3.1. We first generated the events and components YAML from the static view. Next, in the evaluation scenario, we specified that the state machines in Figs. 3c and 3d are to be evaluated against the sequence in

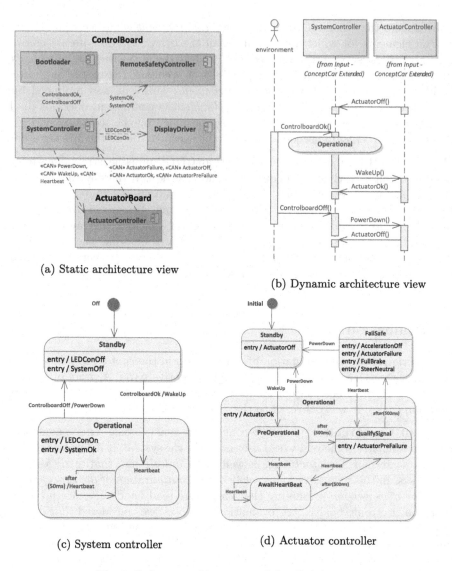

**Fig. 3.** Software architecture and detailed design

Fig. 3b. The first run of the evaluation using the bridge tool generated a report indicating seven inconsistencies (incidents). Two were related to *UnexpectedEventIncidents*, such as *SystemOff* and *LEDConOff*, which were not modeled in the sequence, but present in the state machine (Fig. 3c). The third inconsistency was an *UnsatisfiedStateChangeIncident*, where the expected state after signal transmission *ControlboardOk* was incorrect (correct would be Operational/ Heartbeat). The other four inconsistencies were *UnexpectedEventIncidents*, such as *LEDConOn* and *SystemOk* events after *ControlboardOk* event. Considering these inconsistencies, we modified the sequence in EA manually by introducing the missing events and executed the pipeline for a second time, which reported *No Incidents* in the evaluation report.

## 5   Discussion

Regarding **RQ1** (*How to achieve behavioral interaction consistency between high-level and low-level architecture models?*), we improved consistency checking by transforming non-executable architecture models into executable ones. Those models can be integrated within a feedback loop to simulate the behavior of a system. Furthermore, these models enable evaluation of the system's functionality and interactions in a simulated environment before deploying it in the real world. Concerning **RQ2** (*To what extent can consistency evaluation be automated?*), we observed that our evaluation can be achieved semi-automatically; in particular, the conversion from non-executable architecture models to executable ones is still challenging considering the lack of supporting tools. Our simulation-based approach reduces the cumbersome task of manual model transformation processes. Furthermore, the conversion is a semi-automated process that encapsulates the complex interactions among the tools developed. Additionally, we traced the execution of the process, reporting incidents about possible inconsistencies in the different combinations of UML diagrams. Moreover, continuous evaluation was possible by incorporating architecture consistency analysis into a configurable CI/CD pipeline that can be scheduled at any time.

**Limitations:** Although we considered the architecture's dynamic view (represented by a sequence diagram), the static view (represented by a component diagram), and the detailed behavior of components (represented by state machines), there might be other aspects that cannot be covered by these three diagrams. Moreover, the architectural models need to conform to a set of rules. Currently, there are no mechanisms for checking the conformity of these rules during the manual modeling activity. However, we believe this task could be partially automated using a domain-specific language (DSL). In addition, manual creation of YAML files for static architecture models can be error-prone and inconvenient, which can lead to incorrect specifications. Therefore, we need ways to facilitate the conversion of the static architecture models into YAML or similar formats.

## 6   Final Remarks

Our approach advances previous architecture model checking approaches as we provide an integrated simulation-based solution using CI/CD pipelines to automatically evaluate the consistency of models that we applied in one industrial project. As future work, we plan to increase the number of architectural views and modeling techniques addressed by our solution, with particular attention to the UML activity diagram, which is commonly used in industry projects. We also intend to reduce some manual tasks like model conversion by extending the EA model converter plugin. Adding facilities for visualizing the evaluation results through the EA modeling environment is another feature we plan to implement, with a mechanism to enforce the modeling rules during design time. Lastly, we also intend to tackle the difficult problem of automatic model correction based on the evaluation report in the future.

# References

1. Allaki, D., Dahchour, M., En-nouaary, A.: Building consistent UML models for better model driven engineering. J. Digit. Inf. Manag. **15**, 289–300 (2017)
2. Antonino, P., et al.: Enabling continuous software engineering for embedded systems architectures with virtual prototypes. In: 12th European Conference on Software Architecture (ECSA), pp. 115–130 (2018)
3. Antonino, P.O., et al.: A quality 4.0 model for architecting industry 4.0 systems. Adv. Eng. Inform. **54**, 101801 (2022)
4. Beringer, S., Wehrheim, H.: Consistency analysis of AUTOSAR timing requirements. In: 15th International Conference on Software Technologies (ICSOFT), pp. 15–26 (2020)
5. Buchgeher, G., Weinreich, R.: Continuous software architecture analysis. In: Agile Software Architecture, pp. 161–188 (2014)
6. Chen, X., Liu, Q., Mallet, F., Li, Q., Cai, S., Jin, Z.: Formally verifying consistency of sequence diagrams for safety critical systems. Sci. Comput. Program. **216** (2022)
7. Egyed, A.: Automatically detecting and tracking inconsistencies in software design models. IEEE Trans. Softw. Eng. **37**(2), 188–204 (2011)
8. Goldstein, M., Segall, I.: Automatic and continuous software architecture validation. In: 37th IEEE International Conference on Software Engineering (ICSE), pp. 59–68 (2015)
9. Kuhn, T., Forster, T., Braun, T., Gotzhein, R.: FERAL - framework for simulator coupling on requirements and architecture level. In: 11th ACM/IEEE International Conference on Formal Methods and Models for Codesign, pp. 11–22 (2013)
10. Lucas, F.J., Molina, F., Álvarez, J.A.T.: A systematic review of UML model consistency management. Inf. Softw. Technol. **51**(12), 1631–1645 (2009)
11. Ntentos, E., Zdun, U., Soldani, J., Brogi, A.: Assessing architecture conformance to coupling-related infrastructure-as-code best practices: metrics and case studies. In: 16th European Conference on Software Architecture (ECSA), pp. 101–116 (2022)
12. Ågren, S.M., et al.: Architecture evaluation in continuous development. J. Syst. Softw. **184**, 1–12 (2021)
13. Schroder, S., Buchgeher, G.: Formalizing architectural rules with ontologies-an industrial evaluation. In: 2019 26th Asia-Pacific Software Engineering Conference (APSEC), pp. 55–62 (2019)
14. Soares, R., Capilla, R., Santos, V., Nakagawa, E.: Trends in continuous evaluation of software architectures. Computing, pp. 1–24 (2023)
15. Sobhy, D., Minku, L., Bahsoon, R., Chen, T., Kazman, R.: Run-time evaluation of architectures: a case study of diversification in IoT. J. Syst. Softw. **159**, 110428 (2020)
16. Vogelsang, A., Eder, S., Hackenberg, G., Junker, M., Teufl, S.: Supporting concurrent development of requirements and architecture: A model-based approach. In: 2nd International Conference on Model-Driven Engineering and Software Development (MODELSWARD), pp. 587–595 (2014)

17. Yao, Q., Cui, X.: Approach to check the consistency between the uml2.0 dynamic diagrams. In: 5th Intetnational Conference on Instrumentation and Measurement, Computer, Communication and Control (IMCCC), pp. 1115–1119 (2015)

# Artificial Intelligence and Autonomous Systems

# Architecting Explainable Service Robots

Marcello M. Bersani[1], Matteo Camilli[1], Livia Lestingi[1(✉)],
Raffaela Mirandola[1], Matteo Rossi[1], and Patrizia Scandurra[2]

[1] Politecnico di Milano, Milan, Italy
{marcellomaria.bersani,matteo.camilli,livia.lestingi,raffaela.mirandola,
matteo.rossi}@polimi.it
[2] University of Bergamo, Bergamo, Italy
patrizia.scandurra@unibg.it

**Abstract.** Service robots entailing a tight collaboration with humans are increasingly widespread in critical domains, such as healthcare and domestic assistance. However, the so-called Human-Machine-Teaming paradigm can be hindered by the black-box nature of service robots, whose autonomous decisions may be confusing or even dangerous for humans. Thus, the explainability for these systems emerges as a crucial property for their acceptance in our society. This paper introduces the concept of explainable service robots and proposes a software architecture to support the engineering of the self-explainability requirements in these collaborating systems by combining formal analysis and interpretable machine learning. We evaluate the proposed architecture using an illustrative example in healthcare. Results show that our proposal supports the explainability of multi-agent Human-Machine-Teaming missions featuring an infinite (dense) space of human-machine uncertain factors, such as diverse physical and physiological characteristics of the agents involved in the teamwork.

**Keywords:** Human-Machine Teaming · Explainability · Software architecture · Statistical model checking · Interpretable ML

## 1 Introduction

Service robots are being used for a wide range of applications such as telepresence, education, personal care, and assistive medicine [10]. In these applications, humans and robots become "peers" as they share the environment and collaborate to achieve a common goal through coordinated actions. This paradigmatic collaboration is referred to as Human-Machine Teaming [28] (HMT).

Effective teaming results from the ability of team members to coordinate their actions based on mutual *trust*. The level of trust depends on several factors, including dependability aspects and mutual understanding among agents. However, the adoption of complex control policies including Machine learning (ML) techniques often makes robotic agents "opaque", hence difficult for humans to understand [13]. According to Bersani et al., [2,3], to achieve better trust, robotic agents must exhibit behavior that offers strong assurances, along with human

B. Tekinerdogan et al. (Eds.): ECSA 2023, LNCS 14212, pp. 153–169, 2023.
https://doi.org/10.1007/978-3-031-42592-9_11

interpretable *explanations* of the expected collaboration outcome. In particular, human stakeholders need to know the main reasons for phenomena of interest occurring during the teaming, such as dependability issues or excessive fatigue of human agents. The phenomena (or *explananda*) must be understood in terms of interpretable and measurable (changing) factors [2,3].

Recent studies focus on particular facets of explainability related to the decision-making strategies of the robotic agents [12,29], while other teaming aspects such as those mentioned above are often neglected. Ultimately, there is still a limited understanding of systematic engineering methods that can generate useful explanations to human stakeholders. Indeed, there exist frameworks that help designers build adaptive HMT-based systems [24] by extending the MAPE-K control loop architectural style with human-related tasks and runtime models to support online teaming monitoring [6]. To the best of our knowledge, there is a lack of design guidelines for service robots realizing *explainable* HMT.

In line with M.A. Köhl et al. [18], we consider explainability as a pivotal requirement. We introduce six different levels of explainability that service robots may achieve during the realization of an HMT. We then propose a software architecture for explainable service robots that supports the (offline) specification and analysis of multi-agent HMT and the (online) generation of explanations for the phenomena of interest. Our solution combines our experience in the domain of service robots, formal verification through Statistical Model Checking [7] (SMC), and interpretable ML [27]. Explanations are generated in a collective manner— i.e., they are produced by multiple cooperating agents that collectively achieve the HMT goals. We evaluate the proposed architecture considering different explainability scenarios occurring in an existing HMT in the healthcare domain. Results show that our proposal supports explainable service robots running HMT missions with infinite (dense) space of factors, such as diverse physical and physiological characteristics of the agents involved in the teamwork.

This paper is organized as follows. In Sect. 2, we provide preliminary concepts and then we introduce an illustrative example in Sect. 3. In Sect. 4, we characterize the notion of explainability and levels of explainability in HMT. In Sect. 5, we describe our architectural solution, while we discuss a scenario-based evaluation in Sect. 6. We discuss related work in Sect. 7 and then draw conclusions in Sect. 8.

## 2   Preliminaries

Predictive ML models are built by using supervised learning techniques [26] to create a concise representation of the distribution of an outcome $y$ in terms of quantifiable properties, known as *features* (or *explanatory variables*). A data point $x$ is a vector that contains a value $x_j$ for each feature $j$. A supervised learning algorithm that implements classification or regression is referred to as *classifier* and *regressor*, respectively (more in general, *predictor*). Supervised learning uses a *training set* that includes pre-labeled data points $\langle x, y \rangle$ to "learn" the desired prediction function $\hat{f}$. There exist several popular predictors (either classifiers or regressors) in supervised ML including, for instance, Decision Trees, Random Forests, and Neural Networks.

Interpretable ML [27] refers to the extraction of relevant knowledge from an ML model concerning existing relations contained in the data or learned by the predictive function. In this context, we refer to *interpretability* (or explainability as introduced by Miller [25]) as the ability of a model to be understood and explained by humans. Some predictive models are designed to have a clear and simple structure, and their predictions are inherently explained (e.g., Linear Regression, Decision Trees). More complex techniques (e.g., Neural Networks, Random Forests) do not explain their predictions and are referred to as *black box* (or *non-interpretable*) models.

The scope of interpretability is either *global* (i.e., holistic model interpretability) or *local* (i.e., interpretability for a single prediction). Global explanations describe the average behavior of a given model. They give a holistic view of the distribution of the target outcome (e.g., class labels) based on the features. Partial Dependence Plot [27] (PDP) is a global model-agnostic method that shows the marginal effect that selected features have on the predicted outcome of a model. Local explanations, such as those produced by Local Interpretable Model-agnostic Explanation [27] (LIME), take into account an individual data point of interest $x$ and examine the prediction $\hat{f}(x)$ to explain possible reasons based on an interpretable surrogate model. The model so built has the local fidelity property, that is, it represents a good approximation of local predictions, but it does not have to be a good global approximation.

## 3   Towards Explainable HMT

To illustrate our approach, we adopt an example of HMT *mission* in the healthcare domain introduced by Lestingi et al. [22]. The mission features a hospital ward with an analysis room, a waiting room for patients, and a storage room with medical equipment. A service robot assists the patients and the hospital's personnel during daily operations. The robot executes the following sequence of *services* to complete the mission: (*i*) the robot *escorts* a patient from the entrance to the waiting room; (*ii*) the doctor *leads* the robot to a storage room to retrieve the equipment required for the visit; (*iii*) the robot *follows* the doctor to the analysis room while carrying the equipment; and (*iv*) the robot *escorts* the patient from the waiting room to the analysis room set up for the visit.

The example yields a highly dynamic setting in which human agents may indeed behave differently based on their own characteristics. These dynamics can be formally modeled as a Stochastic Hybrid Automata (SHA) network, an automata-based formalism that allows the specification of stochastic behavior and time-dependent physical phenomena through generalized differential equations [8]. The SHA network of our illustrative example includes five automata, together modeling the mission, the behavior of human agents (i.e., the patient and the doctor), the service robot, the physical dynamics of the battery, and the robot controller[1]. Given the SHA network, Statistical Model Checking [7]

---

[1] We let the reader refer to [22] for a comprehensive treatment of the model and its accuracy w.r.t. a real-world deployment.

**Table 1.** HMT factors of our illustrative example.

| Factor | Agent | Type | Domain |
|---|---|---|---|
| Free will profile | Patient/Doctor | Categorical | {*focused, nominal, inattentive*} |
| Health status | Patient/Doctor | Categorical | {*healthy, sick, unsteady*} |
| Age group | Patient/Doctor | Categorical | {*young, elderly*} |
| Walking Speed | Patient/Doctor | Continuous | [30.0, 100.0] cm/s |
| Initial position $x$ | Doctor | Continuous | [0.0, 50.0] m |
| Initial position $y$ | Doctor | Continuous | [0.0, 8.0] m |
| Translational Speed | Robotic Device | Continuous | [30.0, 100.0] cm/s |
| Battery charge | Robotic Device | Continuous | [11.1, 12.4] V |
| Maximum Distance | Robot Controller | Continuous | [5.0, 7.5] m |
| Minimum Distance | Robot Controller | Continuous | [2.0, 4.5] m |
| Maximum Fatigue | Robot Controller | Continuous | [0.5, 0.8] |
| Minimum Fatigue | Robot Controller | Continuous | [0.1, 0.4] |
| Time Bound ($\tau$) | - | Continuous | [250, 700] |

(SMC) can be used to analyze the HMT mission. For instance, the robot *succeeds* in escorting a human when both are sufficiently close to the destination. This kind of property can be expressed through a logical condition expressed in terms of network elements modeling the successful completion of a certain service provided by the robot. Hence, given a sequence of services, the mission is *complete* when all services in the sequence have been provided. In this case, the robot is *dependable* if it completes the mission within a given time bound, that is, the mission is successful. This is formalized through the Metric Temporal Logic (MTL) property $\psi = \Diamond_{\leq \tau} \bigwedge_i^{N_s} \gamma_{i,\text{scs}}$, where $\gamma_{i,\text{scs}}$ models the completion of the service $i$ in the sequence $N_s \in \mathbb{N}$, $\Diamond$ is the "eventually" operator and $\tau \in \mathbb{N}$ is the time bound for the completion of the mission. UPPAAL SMC [7] can be used to estimate the probability of $\psi$ holding. In addition, UPPAAL can quantify other properties, such as the fatigue of the patients. This quantity can be estimated as the maximum expected value $\mathbb{E}[\leq \tau](\max : F_j)$, where $F_j$ is a real-valued variable modeling the physical fatigue of a human subject $j$ in the SHA network.

Achieving explainability in this context is typically challenging since there is a huge (dense) space of uncertain characteristics that can change and collectively affect the mission—hence the phenomena we want to explain. Table 1 lists a number of selected characteristics, hereafter referred to as HMT *factors*, with their intuitive meaning and ranges of values specific to this work. Some factors apply to the agents participating in the mission (e.g., robots or humans), while others apply to software components (e.g., the robot controller). For instance, humans may pay more or less attention to the robot's instructions according to different *free will profiles* representing their inherent attitude. People may walk at different *speed*. Each robot is managed by a controller, which decides when the robot must move or stop based on the fatigue of the patients (*min/max fatigue*) and on protective human-robot distance (*min/max distance*). Ultimately, the HMT factors yield a possibly dense space $\mathcal{V}$ of elements $\bar{v}$ and, therefore, an infinite set of SHA networks $\mathcal{M}[\bar{v}]$, one for each $\bar{v}$. Hence, explainability by exhaustive exploration of the factor space is unfeasible.

Table 2. Levels of HMT explainability.

| Level | Description |
|-------|-------------|
| L1 | **No explanability**: The system ignores any possible explanandum $X$. |
| L2 | **Recognition of explainability needs**: The system is aware that an explanandum $X$ for stakeholders $G$ exists. Thus, it collects knowledge about the context $C$ either passively or actively, by means that are deliberately designed to increase explainability through exploration. |
| L3 | **Local explainability**: The system provides an explanation $E$ for an explanandum $X$ by considering a specific (punctual) operating context $C$ to make $G$ able to understand how the relevant individual elements of $C$ influence $X$. |
| L4 | **Global explainability**: The system provides an explanation $E$ for an explanandum $X$ by considering a varying operating context $C$ to make $G$ able to understand the extent to which changes of relevant elements of $C$ influence $X$ on average. |
| L5 | **Collective local explainaibility**: The process of local explainability (L3) is realized by multiple cooperating agents that collectively achieve the mission objectives. Each agent has a partial view of the operating context $C$ whose relevant elements are collected (and possibly analyzed) in a decentralized manner. |
| L6 | **Collective global explainaibility**: The process of global explainability (L4) is realized by multiple cooperating agents that collectively achieve the mission objectives. Each agent has only a partial view of the operating context $C$ whose relevant elements are collected (and possibly analyzed) in a decentralized manner. |

## 4    Explainability Levels

We define explainability concerns in HMT, building upon the conceptual analysis proposed by M.A. Köhl et al. [18]. In particular, we hereby refer to an explanation $E$ with respect to an explanandum $X$, a group of stakeholders $G$, and a context $C$, as the ability to make any representative of $G$ understand $X$. Thus, a system is *explainable* if and only if it is able by a means $M$ to produce an explanation $E$ of an explanandum $X$ for a target group $G$ in a certain operating context $C$. In other words, the system satisfies a given explainability requirement, defined as a tuple $R := \langle X, G, C \rangle$. The means $M$ that produces an explanation $E$ to satisfy $R$ may be part of the system responsible for $X$ or not. When a means $M$ is directly integrated into the system, we consider the system *self-explainable*.

In our view, the context is a composite element that contains factors characterizing relevant phenomena that may affect $X$ according to domain knowledge. Since explanations are directed to $G$ and constructed according to $C$, it is important that selected factors in $C$ can be interpreted by representatives of $G$.

The notion of explainability, and in particular the characterization of context $C$ and means $M$, can be given according to different (increasing) *levels*. We take inspiration from the classification introduced by Camilli et al. [5] that identifies levels of explainability of self-adaptive systems based, in turn, on the guidelines introduced by the roadmap for robotics in Europe [9]. In Table 2, we identify and describe different levels of explainability in the HMT domain. *Collective* levels L5 and L6 (highlighted in Table 2) are the focus of this work.

To instantiate the abstract notions introduced in Table 2, we exemplify here L5 and L6 with two scenarios occurring in our illustrative HMT mission. The scenarios include multiple mission agents, stakeholders, and different explainability requirements, i.e., explananda (aspects related to mission dependability and patient fatigue), as well as contexts composed of various HMT factors listed in Table 1. We assume that this list captures domain knowledge, and therefore, contains relevant factors of the agents involved in the HMT as described in [21].

**SL 5 (Patient Fatigue).** The doctor $(G)$ wants to understand the main characteristics of all agents—including the robot(s), the patient, and the doctor himself/herself—that currently affect the fatigue of the patient $(X)$. Understanding the positive/negative impact $(E)$ of these characteristics can suggest to the doctor how to reduce the level of stress of the patient. The context $C$ consists of the HMT factors characterizing the agents involved in the HMT. Furthermore, $C$ does not include factors that cannot be interpreted by the doctor (e.g., controller configuration) who is the main stakeholder in this scenario. An explanation $E$ here may reveal that joint high doctor and high robot speed have a strong negative effect on fatigue only when the patient has unsteady health. It is worth noting that reasoning on the joint effect of factors of multiple agents is possible here because the scenario yields a collective explainability level. A non-collective level (e.g., L3, L4) would lead to short-sighted explanations based on factors of individual agents only (e.g., speed of the doctor without taking into consideration the health status of the patient), ultimately leading to reduced business impact of stakeholder decisions.

**SL 6 (Mission Dependability).** The system administrator $(G)$ wants to understand what are the important configuration options of the software components (e.g., min and max distance) and how the interactions between them and the other characteristics of the agents affect the likelihood $(E)$ of satisfying the dependability requirements of the mission $(X)$. In this case, context $C$ is composed of all HMT factors, including those concerning the controller configuration that can be interpreted by the system administrator. As an example, the explanation $E$ may suggest to the administrator that the max distance configuration has almost no impact. At the same time, on average there is a linear dependency between max fatigue and the likelihood of mission success.

## 5  Architectural Solution

Figure 1 illustrates the key components of our architectural solution to realize collective explainability (i.e., L5 and L6) for service robots. The main building

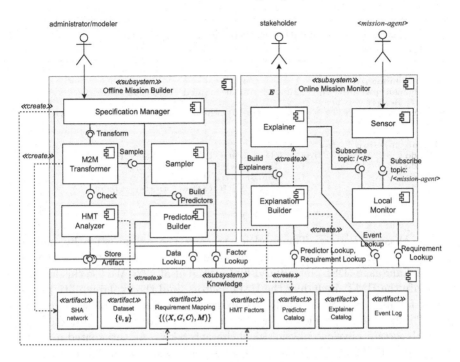

**Fig. 1.** Component diagram of our software architecture.

blocks are subsystems `Offline Mission Builder`, `Online Mission Monitor`, and the shared `Knowledge` repository.

The component `Specification Manager` assists the modeler in capturing the domain knowledge by creating all necessary artifacts to produce the explanations at runtime. These artifacts are stored in the `Knowledge` subsystem and include the `SHA network` and `HMT factors` modeling the target mission, and then `Requirement Mapping` that contains a set of tuples $\langle X, G, C \rangle$ mapping to the corresponding means $M$ used to produce explanations for $X$ to stakeholder $G$, according to the context $C$. In our current solution, $X$ is an MTL property that can be automatically estimated on SHA networks using statistical model checking, $G$ is a unique identifier associated with the stakeholder, $C$ is a nonempty subset of the HMT factors, while $M$ is a categorical variable that identifies a particular interpretable ML technique (either global or local).

`Offline Mission Builder` uses these artifacts to build a number of alternative predictors in charge of forecasting the explanandum $X$ under changing operating context. Then, `Online Mission Monitor` supervises an ongoing mission taking into account the information in `Requirement Mapping`. In particular, for each tuple $\langle X, G, C \rangle$, it monitors the context $C$ and provides the stakeholder $G$ with explanations for the predicted quantity $X$ using the selected technique $M$. In the following, we describe the main subsystems in more detail.

**Listing 1.1.** Specification excerpt defining our illustrative HMT.

```
1  define robots:
2      robot Tbot in (2300.0,400.0) type turtlebot3_wafflepi charge 90.0
3
4  define humans:
5      human patient in (2300.0, 600.0) speed 40.0  is young_sick
          freewill inattentive
6      human doctor in (4400.0, 700.0) speed 100.0 is elderly_healthy
          freewill focused
7
8  define mission m for Tbot:
9      do robot_leader for patient with target waiting_room
10     do robot_follower for doctor with target storage_room
11     do robot_follower for doctor with target analysis_room
12     do robot_leader for patient with target analysis_room
```

*Offline Mission Builder.* The modeler triggers the offline stage by interact-ing with **Specification Manager**, a modeling workbench featuring a Domain-Specific Language (DSL) introduced by Lestingi et al. [22]. We use this language to specify the HMT, including the HMT factors, and the explainability require-ments. Listing 1.1 shows a small DSL extract describing our illustrative exam-ple[2]. The fragment specifies the agents: a robot, a patient, and a doctor, each one with certain physical/physiological characteristics. As anticipated in Sect. 3, the mission is defined by a sequence of services carried out by the robot(s) and defined leveraging pre-defined templates (e.g., "robot leader", or "robot fol-lower") instantiated for the desired agent(s) and for a target location, such as "waiting room"—that is, an alias for a location in the physical space shared by all agents.

The modeler also defines the HMT factors as a set of variables with type and domain (Table 1) and the **Requirement Mapping** by defining all tuples of interest $\langle X, G, C \rangle$ and the corresponding means $M$. An explanandum $X$ is a quantitative MTL property that can be computed or estimated given the specification of the mission and an assignment to the HMT factors. For instance, in SL5, $X$ is the maximum expected value of the fatigue of the patient. In SL6, $X$ is an MTL property $\psi$ whose probability $P(\psi)$ is the likelihood of mission success. The com-ponent in charge of estimating the explananda is the **HMT Analyzer**. Our current solution makes use of UPPAAL SMC given that the HMT is formally specified as an SHA network. To this end, **M2M Transformer** processes the DSL sources to generate an SHA $\mathcal{M}[\bar{v}]$, with $\bar{v}$ a valid value assignment to HMT factors accord-ing to their definition. This is carried out by a fully automated model-to-model transformation in which a set of UPPAAL templates corresponding to the ele-ments of the SHA network are customized based on the DSL specification [22]. Our illustrative example reduces to a SHA network with structural complexity equal to $\sim 176 \times 10^3$ (calculated as the product of the number of locations, edges, and the cardinality of state variables' domains).

---

[2] A package with full mission specification, data and sources to replicate our results is available at https://doi.org/10.5281/zenodo.8110691.

The objective of the `Sampler` component is to mitigate the uncertainty due to changing HMT factors by enriching `Knowledge` through a stochastic exploration[3] of the factor space rather than exhaustive enumeration (generally unfeasible). `Sampler` produces many assignments $\bar{v}$ to HMT factors. Then, the corresponding SHA network $\mathcal{M}[\bar{v}]$ is generated and analyzed through `HMT Analyzer`. This latter component estimates the explanandum $X$ for each tuple $\langle X, G, C \rangle$.

The analysis, executed for all $\bar{v}$ and all requirements, produces the artifact `Dataset`, which is a set $\{\langle \bar{v}, y \rangle\}$, where $y$ is the value of $X$ for model $\mathcal{M}[\bar{v}]$. For instance, value $y$ in SL5 is the patient fatigue represented as a percentage (i.e., a real value in $[0, 1]$). In SL6, instead, the outcome is the mission success represented by a Boolean value (i.e., a categorical variable in $\{0, 1\}^4$). When `Dataset` is available, `Predictor Builder` creates a `Predictor` component by training/testing a predictive model (e.g., neural network regressor/classifier) to forecast the explanandum given new HMT value assignments. A predictor is created for each explainability requirement in `Requirement Mapping`, according to the nature of $X$ and context $C$. In our scenarios, we create regressors for real-value variables and classifiers for categorical variables. Context $C$ determines the subset of HMT factors used for training. Note that we define $C$ based on domain knowledge. Nonetheless, our solution does not prevent engineers from complementing this practice through automated techniques to feature selection.

*Online Mission Monitor.* This subsystem is invoked by `Mission Builder` once `Predictor Catalog` is complete and available in `Knowledge`. The `Explainer Builder` component uses each available predictor to create an `Explainer` component according to $M$ for each tuple in textttRequirement Mapping. An `Explainer` embeds a global/local model-agnostic interpretable ML technique to make the predicted explananda interpretable by stakeholders. Our current implementation adopts PDP for global explanations and LIME for local explanations (see Sect. 2). Once `Explainer Catalog` is ready, the subsystem initializes a publish-subscribe mechanism to realize the *collective* explainability levels introduced in Sect. 4. In particular, for every requirement $R$, the corresponding requirement topic `/<R>` is instantiated. Then, the corresponding `Explainer` component subscribes to topic `/<R>`. Finally, for each HMT agent, there is a `Local Monitor` component subscribed to one or more `/<mission-agent>` topics to receive sensor data. Our solution adopts the *Event Sourcing* pattern[5], whereby explanations are determined and possibly reconstructed on demand by storing all messages exchanged over topics `/<R>`. Persisting the messages enables the `Explainer` components to have a complete chronicle of past context changes.

Once the HMT application is deployed, the explanations $E$ are realized at runtime using the publish-subscribe mechanism. Each sensor periodically samples an HMT factor and the associated `Sensor` component publishes the data to the corresponding `/<mission-agent>` topic. The subscriber `Local Monitor` can clean or aggregate raw data received by sensors. Since a `Local Monitor`

---

[3] Our current implementation relies on uniform random sampling.

[4] Mission success occurs if $P(\psi)$ is greater than a user-defined probability threshold.

[5] https://martinfowler.com/eaaDev/EventSourcing.html.

belongs to an individual agent, collected data represents a subset of the HMT factors, namely a portion $C'$ of one or more contexts. The outcomes of a `Local Monitor` are published to the identified topics `/<R>` and, therefore, received by all `Explainers` subscribed to them. This mechanism allows each `Explainer` to run a continuous collection of the relevant HMT factors used to build the explanations $E$ to the stakeholders based on the latest context available. A stakeholder initiates a direct interaction with an `Explainer` component solely at times when an explanation is required. Through Event Sourcing, the `Explainer` components can reconstruct the temporal sequence of explanations over a specific time window by using historical data of the context retrieved from `Event Log`.

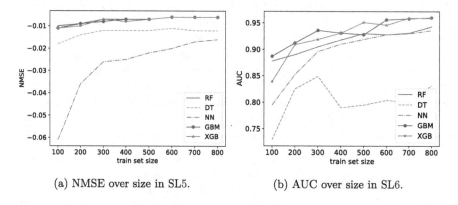

(a) NMSE over size in SL5.          (b) AUC over size in SL6.

**Fig. 2.** Model score over training set size.

## 6    Evaluation

The evaluation of our approach aims to answer the following research questions:

**RQ1:** What is the cost of producing accurate predictors in our solution?
**RQ2:** Is our solution able to support explainability up to level 6?

*Design of the Evaluation.* To answer RQ1 and RQ2, we conducted an experimental campaign using our illustrative example. As reported in Sect. 5, the resulting SHA network specifying the mission is not trivial (i.e., structural complexity $10^3$). To check the satisfaction of explainability requirements, we adopt a scenario-based assessment considering two selected scenarios: SL5 and SL6 (local and global collective explainability, respectively).

For each scenario, we controlled the HMT factors of interest (see Table 1) collectively composing the context $C$, and we generated $1k$ unique assignments $\{\bar{v}\}$ using uniform random sampling. For all $\mathcal{M}[\bar{v}]$ with $\bar{v} \in \mathcal{V}$, we used UPPAAL to estimate the explanandum $X$ in each scenario Concerning human fatigue, parametrization of the formal model has been carried out considering experiments with real human subjects [15]. Estimates of the explananda are obtained through SMC. The results have been used to create a mapping between $\bar{v}$ and the corresponding real-valued outcome $y \in [0, 1]$ (i.e., patient fatigue) as well as Boolean outcome $y' \in \{0, 1\}$ (i.e., mission failure/success). The two datasets $\{\langle \bar{v}, y \rangle\}$ and $\{\langle \bar{v}, y' \rangle\}$ have been used to feed the offline stage and study the cost of building accurate predictors. Finally, for each scenario and corresponding context $C$, we collected and analyzed the output $E$ of the Explainer components to assess the achievement of the target explainability requirements, that is, whether $E$ is interpretable by $G$ and can help in understanding the explanandum $X$.

The experimental campaign has been conducted using a commodity hardware machine running UBUNTU OS v22.04 with 64GB RAM and a quad-core Intel x86_64 CPU at 2.1 GHz.

*Results RQ1 (Cost of Producing Accurate Predictors).* To study the cost in terms of execution time, we conducted multiple runs of the offline stage using $\{\langle \bar{v}, y \rangle\}$ and $\{\langle \bar{v}, y' \rangle\}$ for SL5 and SL6, respectively. For both scenarios, we considered five state-of-the-art predictors commonly adopted to address classification and regression problems: Random Forests (RF), Decision Tree (DT), Neural Network (NN), Gradient Boosting Machine (GBM), and eXtreme Gradient Boosting Tree (XGB). We refer the reader to [26] for further details about these techniques.

**Table 3.** Cost of verification and predictor train/test.

| size | SMC (sec.) | train/test regressors (sec.) | | | | | train/test classifiers (sec.) | | | | |
|---|---|---|---|---|---|---|---|---|---|---|---|
| | | RF | DT | NN | GBM | XGB | RF | DT | NN | GBM | XGB |
| 100 | 107805.50 | 0.33 | **0.01** | 0.30 | 0.23 | 1.91 | 0.16 | **0.01** | 0.56 | 0.45 | 1.62 |
| 200 | 177798.85 | 0.35 | **0.02** | 0.75 | 0.33 | 1.88 | 0.48 | **0.02** | 0.78 | 0.50 | 1.71 |
| 300 | 282922.82 | 0.46 | **0.03** | 0.63 | 0.49 | 1.94 | 0.50 | **0.03** | 1.17 | 0.81 | 1.78 |
| 400 | 373003.94 | 0.47 | **0.02** | 0.83 | 0.59 | 2.02 | 0.52 | **0.04** | 1.40 | 1.02 | 1.47 |
| 500 | 479403.91 | 0.51 | **0.02** | 0.81 | 0.72 | 2.09 | 1.86 | **0.19** | 1.73 | 1.14 | 1.52 |
| 600 | 563768.23 | 0.56 | **0.02** | 0.88 | 0.86 | 2.21 | 2.03 | **0.05** | 2.05 | 1.40 | 1.37 |
| 700 | 652054.33 | 0.54 | **0.03** | 0.97 | 0.97 | 2.15 | 2.07 | **0.01** | 2.65 | 1.47 | 1.37 |
| 800 | 756494.90 | 0.62 | **0.03** | 1.08 | 1.15 | 2.08 | 2.03 | **0.02** | 2.47 | 1.60 | 1.34 |

For each scenario, multiple predictors have been created by varying the size of the training set from 100 to 800 data points to determine the cost of achieving a relatively high and steady accuracy level. Once trained, each predictor has been tested using the same test set composed of 200 data points that do not belong to the training set. To measure the accuracy of regressors, in SL5, we adopt the Negative Mean Squared Error (NMSE), which is a negative value that increases to zero as the error decreases. In SL6, we adopt the Area Under the receiver operator characteristic Curve (AUC) to measure the accuracy as the discriminatory power of the classifiers [11]. The AUC ranges between 0 (worst), 0.5 (no better than random guessing), and 1 (best).

Figure 2 shows the accuracy of the predictors obtained in SL5 (Fig. 2a) and SL6 (Fig. 2b) using training sets of increasing size. We can observe that the accuracy generally increases as the size of the training set does. In both scenarios, the best predictors, stabilizes around size 600. Table 3 shows the cost considering verification and creation of predictors. Each row shows the cost of generating the dataset of a certain size as well as the train/test cost per each individual model. The most time-consuming part of the offline stage is due to the SMC being repeatedly executed for each data point. Around 6.5 days are necessary to collect 600 data points ($\sim$ 10 mins per run) and produce the predictors with the highest accuracy. The time required to train and test the predictors is always negligible compared to SMC. DT yields the lowest execution time (boldface).

To further assess the accuracy of predicting the target explanandum $X$, we adopt 10-fold cross-validation using 600 points for the training set (as discussed above) and the remaining 400 points as the test set. After cross-validation, we created a rank of the predictive models using the non-parametric Scott-Knott Effect Size Difference (ESD) test [30]. Namely, we partitioned the set of AUC/NMSE values into distinct groups with a non-negligible difference. Consistently with the data in Fig. 2, RF is one of the first-rank regressors, and in particular it is the one that predicts the fatigue of the patient (SL5) with the highest median NMSE, equal to $-0.01$. Also, GBM is the first-rank classifier that predicts (un)successful missions (SL6) with the highest median AUC, equal to 0.96.

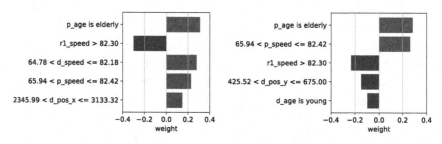

(a) 79% patient fatigue explanation.          (b) 43% patient fatigue explanation.

**Fig. 3.** Explanations for SL5 using a LIME `Explainer` component.

---

**RQ1 Summary.** The most expensive part of the process is offline SMC. In our scenarios around 6.5 days are necessary to collect 600 data points and achieve high and steady accuracy. The time required by training/testing is negligible (less than 3 s). RF is the best regressor in SL5 (median NMSE $-0.01$). GBM is the best classifier in SL6 (median AUC 0.96).

*Results RQ2 (Satisfaction of Explainability Requirements).* To answer this question we executed the online stage and we collected the results produced by the Explainer components in our two selected scenarios. Then, we carried out a qualitative assessment of the explanations to determine the extent to which the target explanandum can be understood by stakeholders.

Concerning SL5, all the HMT factors that can be interpreted by the doctor (i.e., all factors except for those affecting the robot controller) are collected and then dispatched to the local Explainer component paired with the best Predictor trained to forecast the patient fatigue (i.e., RF regressor according to RQ1). Then, we adopt a LIME Explainer to build an on-the-fly (interpretable) local surrogate model that, given a snapshot of the context, predicts the fatigue and explains the contribution of the factors. Figure 3a shows a LIME explanation for a mission run where the patient fatigue is relatively high (79%). The plot shows the relative importance of the top 5 HMT factors and illustrates whether each value contributes to an increase or decrease in the expected fatigue level. For instance, the *elderly* age group has the highest positive weight (0.31) and, therefore, represents the main root cause of high fatigue levels. The robot speed being greater than 82.3 cm/s has the lowest negative weight (−0.29). According to Fig. 3a, the doctor can see there are some factors under his/her own control that have a high positive contribution: a relatively high walking speed (between 65.9 and 82.4 cm/s) and the initial position $x$ (between 2345.9 and 3133.3). The doctor can indeed inspect these values and change them to understand the extent to which these changes impact the target explanandum. Figure 3b shows the LIME explanation for a new assignment where these two latter factors have been changed to decrease the expected fatigue. We can see that the new assignment of doctor speed and position reduces their overall impact since they are not in the top 5 factors anymore. Under the new assignment, the doctor can see that the expected fatigue level in SL5 decreases from 79% to 43%.

Concerning SL6, all HMT factors (including those affecting the robot controller) are collected and dispatched to the global Explainer component paired

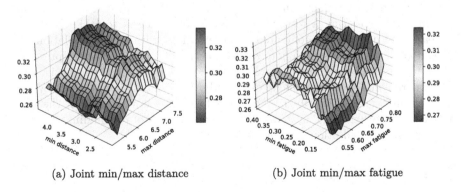

(a) Joint min/max distance            (b) Joint min/max fatigue

**Fig. 4.** Explanations for SL6 using a PDP Explainer component.

with the best `Predictor` trained to forecast the mission success (i.e., GBM classifier according to RQ1). In this scenario, we adopt a PDP `Explainer` that builds explanations to understand the marginal effect of selected HMT factors on the expected probability of success. Figure 4 shows two selected PDP explanations illustrating the joint effect of *min/max* distance (Fig. 4a) and *min/max* fatigue (Fig. 4b). These factors represent system configuration options that affect the decisions of the robot (e.g., the robot stops and waits for the human when the distance is higher than the *max* value). The administrator can inspect the plots using a causal interpretation since, in this case, we explicitly model the probability of success as a function of the HMT factors. As an example, Fig. 4b shows an almost linear dependency between max fatigue and probability of success, while min fatigue affects the success with a concave function. The administrator can thus (re)configure the robot controller by selecting the ranges that maximize the expected success: max fatigue 80% and min fatigue between 25% and 35%.

> **RQ2 Summary.** Considering our two selected scenarios, HMT factors have been collected from multiple mission agents and dispatched to the corresponding local/global `Explainer` components. In both scenarios, we illustrate the achievement of the desired explainability level by showing how the stakeholders can interpret the explanations and take decisions to influence the explanandum by changing relevant aspects of the operating context.

*Threats to Validity.* We limited *construct validity* threats by assessing the metrics adopted in our experiments before using them. Both AUC and NMSE are widely suggested to evaluate predictive models [20]. We also use a mainstream measure of the cost in terms of execution time required by the main stages of our approach. *Conclusion validity* threats have been mitigated by reducing the possibility of overfitting on the test set by applying 10-fold cross-validation [31]. Conclusions are partially based on a qualitative assessment carried out by the authors rather than the stakeholders involved in SL5 and SL6. Comprehensive understanding of the quality of the explanations from the point of view of real stakeholders requires further investigation. We addressed *internal validity* threats by creating a testbed with fine-grained access to HMT factors to increase internal validity compared to observations without manipulation. We also adopted stratified sampling to reduce the risk of obtaining underrepresented HMT factors while building the predictors. *External validity* threats exist since our experiments consider a single case study. We limited these threats by considering an example described by existing literature as indicative of the characteristics of other HMT systems. The generalization of our findings to other domains requires additional experiments.

## 7   Related Work

In recent years, explainability—i.e., the ability to provide a human with understandable explanations of the results produced by AI and ML algorithms—has become a key aspect of designing tools based on these techniques [1], especially in critical areas such as healthcare [33]. As such, it is attracting a growing interest in the Software Engineering community [32], as witnessed by explainable analytical models for predictions and decision-making [32], explainable counterexamples [14], and explainable quality attribute trade-offs in software architecture selection [4]. In the area of self-adaptive systems, there are preliminary approaches that aim at embedding explainability in software applications [16,17] and providing a more general approach to the construction of human-understandable explanations for successful adaptation in robotic scenarios [5]. The role of humans in self-adaptive systems has been mainly classified into "humans-out-of-the-loop" (if humans cannot change the system's behavior/outcome), and "humans-on/in-the-loop" (if they act as external controllers and supervisors [19,24], or as input providers for the system [23]). To facilitate the understanding of the system operation through explanations, humans-on/in-the-loop have been modeled using stochastic models, which undergo model checking [4,23]. Stochastic models have been applied to develop service robotic applications for which formal guarantees on the feasibility of the collaborative scenarios are obtained through SMC [22]. In such applications, the integration of explainability techniques allows both the designers of robotic scenarios and the humans involved in the interaction with robots to understand the reasons why collaboration can fail or successfully complete [2,3]. Although these works show an effective combination of ML, explainability techniques, and formal methods, they lack a detailed investigation of the architectural aspects involved.

## 8    Conclusion and Future Work

We addressed the problem of providing meaningful explanations in multi-agent HMT applications to foster trust by introducing six levels of explainability and presenting an architectural solution capable of providing stakeholders with human interpretable explanations based on user-specified explainability requirements. Our evaluation shows that the proposed architectural solution supports explainability up to level six. We plan to extend our solution with other factor sampling strategies based on metaheuristic optimization, in order to push the exploration of the factor space toward specific conditions of interest. We also plan to validate the approach with human participants by presenting real stakeholders with the produced explanations and having them assess their quality.

## References

1. Angelov, P.P., Soares, E.A., Jiang, R., Arnold, N.I., Atkinson, P.M.: Explainable artificial intelligence: an analytical review. WIREs Data Min. Knowl. Discov. **11**(5), e1424 (2021)
2. Bersani, M.M., Camilli, M., Lestingi, L., Mirandola, R., Rossi, M.: Explainable human-machine teaming using model checking and interpretable machine learning. In: International Conference on Formal Methods in Software Engineering, pp. 18–28. IEEE (2023)

3. Bersani, M.M., Camilli, M., Lestingi, L., Mirandola, R., Rossi, M., Scandurra, P.: Towards better trust in human-machine teaming through explainable dependability. In: ICSA Companion, pp. 86–90. IEEE (2023)

4. Cámara, J., Silva, M., Garlan, D., Schmerl, B.: Explaining architectural design tradeoff spaces: a machine learning approach. In: Biffl, S., Navarro, E., Löwe, W., Sirjani, M., Mirandola, R., Weyns, D. (eds.) ECSA 2021. LNCS, vol. 12857, pp. 49–65. Springer, Cham (2021). https://doi.org/10.1007/978-3-030-86044-8_4

5. Camilli, M., Mirandola, R., Scandurra, P.: XSA: Explainable self-adaptation. In: International Conference on Automated Software Engineering. ASE'22. ACM (2023)

6. Cleland-Huang, J., Agrawal, A., Vierhauser, M., Murphy, M., Prieto, M.: Extending MAPE-K to support human-machine teaming. In: SEAMS, pp. 120–131. ACM (2022)

7. David, A., Larsen, K.G., Legay, A., Mikučionis, M., Poulsen, D.B.: UPPAAL SMC tutorial. STTT 17(4), 397–415 (2015)

8. David, A., et al.: Statistical model checking for networks of priced timed automata. In: Fahrenberg, U., Tripakis, S. (eds.) FORMATS 2011. LNCS, vol. 6919, pp. 80–96. Springer, Heidelberg (2011). https://doi.org/10.1007/978-3-642-24310-3_7

9. EU: Robotics 2020 Multi-Annual Roadmap For Robotic in Europe (2016). https://www.eu-robotics.net/sparc/upload/about/files/H2020-Robotics-Multi-Annual-Roadmap-ICT-2016.pdf

10. García, S., Strüber, D., Brugali, D., Berger, T., Pelliccione, P.: Robotics software engineering: a perspective from the service robotics domain, pp. 593–604. ESEC/FSE 2020. ACM (2020)

11. Hanley, J.A., McNeil, B.J.: The meaning and use of the area under a receiver operating characteristic (ROC) curve. Radiology 143(1), 29–36 (1982)

12. Hayes, B., Shah, J.A.: Improving robot controller transparency through autonomous policy explanation. In: HRI, pp. 303–312. IEEE (2017)

13. Jovanović, M., Schmitz, M.: Explainability as a user requirement for artificial intelligence systems. Computer 55(2), 90–94 (2022)

14. Kaleeswaran, A.P., Nordmann, A., Vogel, T., Grunske, L.: A systematic literature review on counterexample explanation. Inf. Softw. Technol. 145, 106800 (2022)

15. Kang, H.G., Dingwell, J.B.: Differential changes with age in multiscale entropy of electromyography signals from leg muscles during treadmill walking. PLoS ONE 11(8), e0162034 (2016)

16. Khalid, N., Qureshi, N.A.: Towards self-explainable adaptive systems (SEAS): a requirements driven approach. In: Joint Proceedings of REFSQ. CEUR Workshop Proceedings, vol. 2857. CEUR-WS.org (2021)

17. Kordts, B., Kopetz, J.P., Schrader, A.: A framework for self-explaining systems in the context of intensive care. In: ACSOS, pp. 138–144. IEEE (2021)

18. Köhl, M.A., Baum, K., Langer, M., Oster, D., Speith, T., Bohlender, D.: Explainability as a non-functional requirement. In: RE, pp. 363–368. IEEE (2019)

19. de Lemos, R.: Human in the loop: what is the point of no return? In: SEAMS, pp. 165–166. ACM (2020)

20. Lessmann, S., Baesens, B., Mues, C., Pietsch, S.: Benchmarking classification models for software defect prediction: a proposed framework and novel findings. IEEE Trans. Softw. Eng. 34(4), 485–496 (2008)

21. Lestingi, L., Askarpour, M., Bersani, M.M., Rossi, M.: A deployment framework for formally verified human-robot interactions. IEEE Access 9, 136616–136635 (2021)

22. Lestingi, L., Zerla, D., Bersani, M.M., Rossi, M.: Specification, stochastic modeling and analysis of interactive service robotic applications. Robot. Autonom. Syst. **163** (2023)

23. Li, N., Cámara, J., Garlan, D., Schmerl, B.R., Jin, Z.: Hey! Preparing humans to do tasks in self-adaptive systems. In: SEAMS, pp. 48–58. IEEE (2021)

24. Madni, A.M., Madni, C.C.: Architectural framework for exploring adaptive human-machine teaming options in simulated dynamic environments. Systems **6**(4) (2018)

25. Miller, T.: Explanation in artificial intelligence: insights from the social sciences. Artif. Intell. **267**, 1–38 (2019)

26. Mitchell, T.M.: Machine Learning, 1st edn. McGraw-Hill Inc., New York (1997)

27. Molnar, C.: Interpretable Machine Learning. 2 edn (2022). https://christophm. github.io/interpretable-ml-book

28. Ozkaya, I.: The behavioral science of software engineering and human-machine teaming. IEEE Softw. **37**(6), 3–6 (2020)

29. Paleja, R., Ghuy, M., Ranawaka Arachchige, N., Jensen, R., Gombolay, M.: The utility of explainable AI in ad hoc human-machine teaming. In: NEURIPS, vol. 34, pp. 610–623. Curran Associates, Inc. (2021)

30. Scott, A.J., Knott, M.: A cluster analysis method for grouping means in the analysis of variance. Biometrics **30**(3), 507–512 (1974)

31. Stone, M.: Cross-validatory choice and assessment of statistical predictions. J. Roy. Stat. Soc.: Ser. B (Methodol.) **36**(2), 111–133 (1974)

32. Tantithamthavorn, C.K., Jiarpakdee, J.: Explainable AI for software engineering. In: ASE, pp. 1–2. ACM (2021)

33. Tjoa, E., Guan, C.: A survey on explainable artificial intelligence (XAI): toward medical XAI. IEEE Trans. Neural Netw. Learn. Syst. **32**(11), 4793–4813 (2021)

# Analysing Interoperability in Digital Twin Software Architectures for Manufacturing

Enxhi Ferko[1(✉)], Alessio Bucaioni[1], Patrizio Pelliccione[2], and Moris Behnam[1]

[1] Mälardalen University, Västerås, Sweden
{enxhi.ferko,alessio.bucaioni,moris.behnam}@mdu.se
[2] Gran Sasso Science Institute, L'Aquila, Italy
patrizio.pelliccione@gssi.it

**Abstract.** Digital twins involve the integration of advanced information technologies to create software replicas that control and monitor physical assets. Interoperability is an essential requirement in the engineering of digital twins. This paper is the first study analysing interoperability in digital twin software architectures in the manufacturing industry. We began with an initial set of 2403 peer-reviewed publications and after a screening process, we selected a final set of 21 primary studies. We identified the set of technologies used for data exchange and the level of interoperability achieved during such an exchange. We organised the results according to the ISO 23247 standard and the level of conceptual interoperability model.

**Keywords:** Software Architecture · Interoperability · Digital twin · ISO 23247 · LCIM

## 1 Introduction

A Digital Twin (DT) is a virtual representation of a physical component, system, or process (i.e., the physical twin) that functions as a digital equivalent for the remote monitoring and controlling of the physical twin [23]. The functional suitability of DTs is heavily dependent on interoperable subsystems that are able to seamlessly and effectively exchange data [29]. Interoperability goes beyond the mere data transmission and is defined as *"the degree to which two or more systems, products or components can exchange information and use the information that has been exchanged"* [20]. Achieving interoperability for DTs can be challenging [14,22,27]. DTs include a high diversity of subsystems responsible for different functionalities. These subsystems may use different communication technologies for data exchange that are developed without considering the need to operate with each other causing interoperability issues [P5]. This is the case of the ISO 23247 - digital twin framework for manufacturing - standard that provides a functional reference architecture for DTs comprising entities and sub-entities without explicitly discussing how to support interoperability [19]. The observable manufacturing elements (OME) entity and the data collection sub-entity may communicate using a proprietary network with a specialised configuration, while the application service, operation and management sub-entities may use a wired network running IP-based protocols [19]. This diversity in communication technologies makes it challenging to establish interoperability between subsystems, especially when they are developed by different vendors or organisations. Moreover, as the demand for DT federations increases, achieving interoperability between DTs becomes an upcoming requirement [15]. To the best of our knowledge, we are still missing a comprehensive analysis and assessment of the interoperability requirements and support for DTs.

Therefore, *the research goal (RG) of this paper is to analyse interoperability in DT software architectures for manufacturing.* We analyse how data is exchanged and which level of interoperability is reached during such an exchange in proposed architectures for DTs in manufacturing. We focus on the manufacturing domain for two primary reasons. Firstly, the widespread adoption of DTs in this domain has made it a significant area of interest, with more than 70% of the research on DTs specifically targeting manufacturing [11]. Additionally, the manufacturing domain is only domain that has a dedicated standard for DTs, namely the ISO 23247 standard [19]. We use the ISO 23247 standard together with the Level of Conceptual Interoperability Model (LCIM) [33]. We use LCIM due to its recognition as one of the most effective models for addressing interoperability at early stages of software development, particularly in architectural design [33]. Moreover, LCIM has been successfully applied in several domains, including manufacturing [32]. It is worth noting that adhering to the ISO 23247 standard ensures the broader applicability of our research outcomes [15, 26]. We tackled the above goal using a research method built on the guidelines for systematic studies [21]. We analysed 21 DT architectures resulting from a systematic literature review of 2403 peer-reviewed studies. We analysed the final set of 21 DT architectures following a data extraction, analysis, and synthesis process. We identified the technologies employed for data exchange and clustered them according to the network view of the ISO 23247 reference architecture. To indicate the interoperability levels that existed for each of the networks in the proposed DT architectures, we used the descriptive view of the LCIM. In addition, we used the prescriptive view to discuss the requirements necessary to achieve higher interoperability levels.

The remainder of this paper is structured as follows. Section 2 presents an overview of background information. Section 3 describes the adopted research methodology. Section 4 and Sect. 5 present and discuss the results of this work. Section 6 gives an overview of the related works and Sect. 7 concludes the paper with final remarks and future works.

## 2  Background

This section provides an overview of the ISO 23247 standard (part four) and LCIM [33].

## 2.1    ISO 23247 and Information Exchange

The ISO 23247 standard comprises four parts [19]. Part four defines the technical requirements for the information exchange between the entities of the reference architecture. In ISO 23247, a network can be seen as a communication point between functional or sub-functional entities of the reference architecture. The standard identifies four types of networks (identified with the numbers 1–4 in Fig. 1): user, service, access, and proximity.

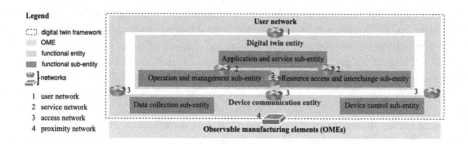

**Fig. 1.** ISO 23247 networking view of digital twin reference models [19].

The proximity network (4 in Fig. 1) connects the device communication entity with the OMEs, e.g., resources like equipment. Hence, the device communication entity uses the proximity network, for transmitting commands to and receiving results from OMEs. The access network (3 in Fig. 1) connects the device communication entity with the digital twin and the user entity. The digital twin entity synchronises OMEs with their DTs by hosting applications and services such as simulation, analysis, etc. The digital twin entity hosts applications and services using the DT models for humans and other systems. Hence, the device communication entity transmits data collected from the OMEs to the digital twin entity through the data collection sub-entity. Similarly, the device control sub-entity transmits commands from the user entity or the digital twin entity to control the OMEs. The service network (2 in Fig. 1) connects digital twin sub-entities among them. Finally, the user network (1 in Fig. 1) connects the user entity with the digital twin entity to enable the use of the DT instances managed by the digital twin entity.

## 2.2    The Conceptual Interoperability Model

A precise understanding of shared data is essential to achieve interoperability between different systems. According to Carney et al., the assessment of interoperability is crucial and must be measurable to attain success [7]. Several models for evaluating interoperability have been proposed to date. Leal et al. have conducted a thorough review and comparison of 22 such models [24]. In this paper, we refer to the Level of Conceptual Interoperability Model (LCIM) [33].

LCIM identifies 7 levels of interoperability, spanning from no interoperability to conceptual interoperability. At level zero, systems function independently and do not share data. At level one, systems can technically exchange data in the form of raw bits and bytes. At level two, systems use a common data format to achieve syntactic interoperability. However, the meaning of the exchanged data remains undefined at this stage. Semantic interoperability, level three, requires the data meaning to be explicitly specified. At level four, interoperating systems understand the context, system states, and processes, as well as the meaning of the exchanged data, which results in pragmatic interoperability. At level five, dynamic interoperability is achieved as systems can comprehend state changes over time. Lastly, at level six, conceptual interoperability is attained, where interoperating systems fully comprehend each other's information, processes, contexts, and modelling assumptions.

## 3    Research Methodology

We performed this research using the guidelines for systematic and empirical studies in software engineering [21,30]. Our methodology consists of three phases: planning, conducting, and documenting. In the planning phase, we identified the needs for this study, defined the research goal and questions, and described the research protocol that we followed for carrying out the study. In the conducting phase, we executed all the steps defined in the research protocol, which were search and selection, definition of the classification framework, data extraction and data analysis. In the search and selection step, we exercised the selected scientific databases and indexing systems using the defined search string. We followed a rigorous selection process and filtered the candidate studies to get the final set of primary studies. We complemented the automatic search with fully recursive forward and backward snowballing activities [35]. Using the key-wording process [28], we defined a classification framework, and compared and evaluated the primary studies. We used the classification framework to analyse each primary study and extract relevant information through an iterative process. Finally, we analysed the extracted data to answer the elicited research questions. We conducted both quantitative and qualitative analyses. In the documenting phase, we reported on possible threats to validity and related mitigation strategies. To enable independent verification and replication of this study, we provide a complete and public replication package[1] containing the data from the search and selection, data extraction, the complete list of primary studies, and summary of the findings.

### 3.1    Research Goal and Questions

Using the Goal-Question-Metric perspectives [4], we defined the RG of this study, that is *(Purpose) Identify, classify, and analyse (Issue) needs, solutions, and*

---

[1] The replication package is available at https://anonymous.4open.science/r/ analysing-interoperability-replication-package-ECSA2023/README.md.

*challenges of (Object) interoperability in DTs in manufacturing from (Viewpoint) the point of view of researchers.* We broke down the RG in the following research questions (RQs).

*RQ1 – How is the data exchanged within a DT and among DTs?* We determine which technologies are employed for data exchange. This information is needed for assessing interoperability, identifying its limitations, and assessing potential trade-offs.

*RQ2 – Which interoperability levels do current DT implementations reach?* We determine the extent of interoperability attained by existing DT implementations according to LCIM [33], together with the identification of challenges that may hinder seamless integration within and across DTs.

## 3.2   Search and Selection Process

Following the steps described in Fig. 2, we identified the set of primary studies. We started with the search string (*"Digital Twin" AND Architect\**) and queried four of the largest and most reputable scientific databases and indexing systems in software engineering [5,21]: *IEEE Xplore Digital Library, ACM Digital Library, SCOPUS*, and *Web of Science*. We opted for a concise search string that could help gathering as many relevant studies as possible that we filtered through the application of selection criteria, mitigating potential threats to construct validity.

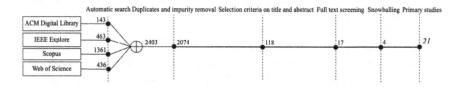

**Fig. 2.** Overview of the search and selection process

The automatic search on title, abstract and keywords provided an initial set of 2403 studies, from which we removed impurities and duplicates, and obtained a new set of 2074 studies. Following the recommendations in [1], we applied the following selection criteria to the title, abstract, and keywords, and selected only those studies that satisfied all the Inclusion criteria (IC) and Exclusion criteria (EC). The IC are: (i) studies proposing a DT architecture in the manufacturing domain, (ii) studies proposing DT architectures with well-identified and documented components, (iii) studies providing implementation details on how comprised components of the architecture exchange data, (iv) peer-reviewed studies [34], (v) studies written in English, and (vi) studies available as full-text. The EC are: (i) secondary or tertiary studies, (ii) studies published as tutorial papers, short papers (less than 5 pages), poster papers, editorials and manuals. We obtained a new set of 118 studies, and, by analysing the full text, we

**Table 1.** Classification framework

| Facet | Category | Description | Value |
|-------|----------|-------------|-------|
| RQ1 | Technologies | Technologies (e.g., protocols, standards, data models) enabling interoperability | String |
| RQ2 | Levels of interoperability | Levels of conceptual interoperability [33] reached | No interoperability, technical, syntactic, semantic, pragmatic, dynamic, conceptual |

selected 17 primary studies. To reduce possible threats to construct validity we performed closed recursive snowballing activities [35]. As a result, we obtained the final set of 21 primary studies that are shown at the end of the paper.

### 3.3 Classification Framework and Data Extraction

We built a classification framework for extracting and classifying information from the primary studies (Table 1). The framework comprises two facets, one for each RQ.

For RQ1, we collected the list of technologies like protocols, standards, data models, models, etc. used for enabling interoperability. For RQ2, we collected the levels of conceptual interoperability [33] reached by the solution described in the study. For both RQs, we grouped the collected information according to the network defined in the ISO 23247 standard [19]. We arranged the collected information into groups similar to the sorting phase of the grounded theory methodology [9]. During the data extraction, we refined the classification framework with additional information. Hence, we analysed again the primary studies according to the refined framework and extracted data.

### 3.4 Data Analysis and Synthesis

We used the recommendations by Cruzes et al. [10] for analysing and synthesising the extracted data according. We performed vertical analysis for discovering information on each category of the classification framework. In particular, we analysed each study individually and categorised its features using the classification framework. Later, using the line of argument synthesis [34], we reasoned on the entire set of primary studies for uncovering potential patterns.

### 3.5 Threats to Validity

To ensure the *internal validity* of our research, we defined a research protocol using well-established guidelines [21]. Moreover, we employed rigorous descriptive statistical methods for data analysis [31,36] to further mitigate internal validity threats related to data analysis and synthesis. We are confident that the selected primary studies are representative of the population defined by the research questions, as we followed a well-defined and validated protocol. To mitigate threats to *construct validity* associated with data extraction, we developed a framework for extracting data from the studies. Each author independently repeated the process of extracting data from the studies. In case of doubts, the authors added annotations to the respective primary studies and discussed them until reaching a consensus. The ensure *external validity* of our research, we conducted a comprehensive search of four different electronic databases in software engineering and complemented the automatic search with a fully recursive snowballing process. Further, we filtered the studies using selection criteria [1]. We mitigated potential threats to *conclusion validity* by meticulously documenting every step of our research and providing a public replication package to ensure transparency and replicability. In addition, we reduced potential bias during the data extraction process by using well-established models, such as LCIM. All authors participated in data extraction, analysis, and synthesis steps. The conclusions drawn on the interoperability needs and open challenges originated from the primary studies. However, any hypotheses and conjectures were clearly identified as such.

## 4 Results

We analysed the primary studies and classified their features according to the classification framework in Table 1.

### 4.1 How Is Data Exchanged? (RQ1)

For each network identified in the ISO 23247 standard, we investigated the primary technologies utilised for data exchange. We focused on two critical aspects of data exchange: data transmission (see Table 2), and data representation and management (see Table 3).

Using the grounded theory methodology [9], we clustered the technologies for data transmission into four groups: protocols, standards, architectural patterns, and open-source platforms. We clustered the technologies for data representation and management in six groups: information models, data formats, graphic APIs, open-source platforms, query language, and standards. This helped us to identify the most commonly utilised technologies and their relationships with one another per each network.

The proximity network enables communication between the device communication entity and OMEs, allowing the device communication entity to receive sensor data from OMEs and send commands to them. In the proximity network, data transmission relies on communication protocols like Profinet and Modbus each of which defines a specific syntax and format. However, there is no apparent consideration for data representation and management within this network. Modbus is the most commonly cited communication protocol in our analysis, appearing in 28% of the primary studies. It is often used to collect data from OME such as sensors, Programmable Logic Controllers (PLCs), and Internet of

**Table 2.** Technologies used for data transmission.

| Network | Technology | | Primary study |
|---|---|---|---|
| Proximity | Protocol | Profinet | [P4], [P17] |
| | | Modbus | [P8], [P11], [P13], [P16], [P17], [P19] |
| | | MQTT | [P10] |
| | | LoRaWAN | [P21] |
| Access | Protocol | OPC UA | [P2], [P3], [P4], [P7], [P8], [P12], [P14], [P15], [P16], [P17], [P18], [P20], [P21] |
| | | MTConnect | [P4] |
| | | MQTT | [P4], [P9], [P11], [P16] |
| | | AMQP1.0 | [P6] |
| | | WebSocket | [P10] |
| | | NC-link | [P14] |
| | Standard | IEC 61499 | [P5] |
| | | IEEE 1451 | [P5] |
| | Architectural pattern | IDS | [P2] |
| | Open-source platform | Eclipse Hono | [P6] |
| Service | Protocol | OPC UA | [P3], [P18] |
| | | MQTT | [P18] |
| | Open-source platform | Apache StreamPipes | [P21] |
| | | Solace | [P10] |
| User | Protocol | OPC UA | [P3] |
| | | HTTP | [P4], [P6], [P7], [P8], [P9], [P11], [P13], [P15], [P16], [P18], [P19], [P21] |
| | | SMTP | [P10] |
| | | WebSocket | [P6], [P17], [P20] |
| | Architectural pattern | IDS | [P9], [P15] |
| | | REST | [P4], [P6], [P7], [P8], [P9], [P11], [P13], [P15], [P16], [P18], [P19], [P21] |

Things (IoT) devices. In over 50% (11/21) of the primary studies, OME was integrated with the device communication entity within a single system, and then, a proximity network was not necessary. As an example, a modern computer numerical control machine may support direct numerical control for data input and use MTConnect for reporting results [19].

The access network serves as a means to transmit the collected data from the data collection sub-entity to the digital twin entity, and to transmit commands from the user entity to the device control sub-entity within the device communication entity. The most commonly used protocol for transmitting data in this network is Open Platform Communication Unified Architecture (OPC UA), which was utilised in more than 60% of the primary studies. Kim et al. motivate the adoption of OPC UA over other protocols due to its ability to facilitate integration across different platforms, timely detection of anomalies, and data security through user authorisation and authentication [P3]. Other primary studies aim to support publish/subscribe method for data exchange to enhance scalability utilised Message Queue Telemetry Transport (MQTT) [P4].

**Table 3.** Technology used for data representation and management.

| Network | Technology | | Primary study |
|---|---|---|---|
| Access | Information model | AAS with eCl@ss dictionary | [P2] |
| | | AutomationML | [P7], [P11], [P14] |
| | Data format | JSON-LD | [P5] |
| Service | Open-source platform | Eclipse Ditto | [P6] |
| | | Eclipse rdf4j | [P13] |
| | Data format | PMML | [P3] |
| | | JSON | [P10] |
| User | Information model | AAS | [P1],[P7],[P8], [P9],[P15],[P18],[P21] |
| | | AutomationML | [P1] |
| | | DTDL | [P1] |
| | Standard | ISO 10303 (STEP) | [P4] |
| | | ISO 23952 (QIF) | [P4] |
| | Data format | JSON | [P6], [P11], [P18] |
| | Graphic API | WebGL | [P4], [P17] |
| | | OpenGL | [P4], [P11] |
| | Query language | JSONata | [P8] |
| | | SPARQL | [P13] |

MQTT is a messaging protocol for IoT that defines a publish/subscribe messaging method [19]. Moreno et al. have advocated for the adoption of the International Data Space (IDS) architectural pattern, which is responsible for ensuring a secure and reliable channel of communication [P2]. In a similar vein, Rocha et al. have utilised standardised approaches such as IEEE 1451 and IEC 61499 to build an interoperable digital twin for monitoring water levels [P5]. The IEEE 1451 family of standards manage sensors and actuators of industrial systems, providing communication protocols for data acquisition and exchange that meet Industry 4.0 requirements. When combined with the IEC 61499 standard for data control and visualisation, it becomes a powerful tool for enhancing interoperability. Kherbache et al. propose the use of open-source platforms like Eclipse Hono for implementing the access network, which can eliminate protocol silos in the different OMEs [P6]. Eclipse Hono uses micro-services, called protocol adaptors, that map the supported protocols (e.g., HTTP, MQTT, or CoaP) to its API. This approach enables seamless integration and communication across multiple devices and protocols, facilitating interoperability and scalability in digital twin systems [P6]. When it comes to data representation in the access network, only a few primary studies (4/21) make use of an additional information model or data format on top of the protocol or standards used for data transmission. The most commonly used information model is AutomationML (AML). For instance, Fan et al. use AML to model all the components of a flexible manufacturing system [P14].

The service network is responsible for connecting sub-entities that offer different services within the digital twin core entity, such as operation and management, application and service sub-entity, and resource access and interchange. However, some current implementations of DT systems are designed as single private systems, in which services can communicate directly within the system without the need for a separate service network. Consequently, only a few papers (6/21) have implemented the service network in their digital twin systems. In such cases, data transmission protocols such as OPC UA and MQTT are used. Other primary studies have utilized open-source platforms to manage data transmission for different services within the digital twin, such as Apache StreamPipes [P21] and Solace [P10]. For example, Jacoby et al. utilized Apache StreamPipes to implement and manage multiple DT models. The primary motivation behind using Apache StreamPipes was its support for commonly used protocols, as well as the abundance of readily available implementations that can easily be customized with specific deep learning models, statistical analysis, or complex event processing [P21]. Open-source platforms are also preferred for data representation and management in the service network. Kherbache et al. utilized Eclipse Ditto to model and manage data in the service network, motivated by its easy access to data [P6]. Similarly, Bamunuarachchi et al. utilized Eclipse rdf4j to support ontology models and RDF data [P13].

The user network connects the DT entity with third-party systems such as Enterprise Resource Planning (ERP) or Manufacturing Execution System (MES), allowing them to use the services provided by the DT [19]. Data transmission in the user network typically relies on protocols such as HTTP, WebSocket, SMTP, and OPC-UA. HTTP is the most commonly used protocol, cited in 57% (12/21) of primary studies. The WebSocket protocol is instead recommended in [P17] to support bidirectional communication for real-time data exchange. Some papers also suggest using the IDS architectural pattern in the user network to enable secure data exchange among different organisations [P9,P15]. The primary studies place significant emphasis on the technologies used for data representation and management within the user network. Information models, standards, graphical APIs, and query languages are some of the approaches identified. Asset Administration Shell (AAS) is favoured by around 30% (7/21) of the primary studies. AAS is employed to represent information related to physical assets and share it as a common information model with other stakeholders [P1]. Standards, e.g., ISO 10303 (STEP) and ISO 23952 (QIF) are used to represent CAD/CAM information [P4]. Assad et al. utilised WebGL, a JavaScript API, to render 2D/3D graphics [P17].

## 4.2   Interoperability Level (RQ2)

To answer this RQ, we investigated the LCIM levels of interoperability achieved for each network identified in the ISO 23247 standard. We used the LCIM descriptive view and our analysis involved examining the technologies utilised for data exchange and the requirements for achieving a particular level [33]. Table 4 presents a comprehensive summary of the LCIM level accomplished for

**Table 4.** Levels of interoperability reached

| Network | LCIM level | Technology |
|---|---|---|
| Proximity | Syntactic | Profinet [P4], [P17], Modbus [P8], [P11], [P13], [P16], [P17], [P19], MQTT [P10], LoRaWAN [P21] |
| Access | Syntactic | MTConnect [P4], MQTT [P9], [P16], AMQP 1.0 [P6], Web-socket [P10], Eclipse Hono [P6] |
| | Semantic | OPC UA [P2], [P3], [P4], [P8], [P12], [P15], [P16], [P17], [P18], [P20], [P21], OPC UA + AutomationML [P7],[P14], MQTT + AutomationML [P11], AAS with dictionaries eCl@ss [P2], IEC 61499 and IEEE 1451 [P4], JSON-LD [P5] |
| Service | Semantic | OPC UA [P3], [P18], ApacheStreamPipes [P21], Eclipse Ditto [P6], Eclipse rdf4j [P13], PMML [P3], Solace [P10], JSON [P10] |
| User | Syntactic | HTTP [P6], [P11], [P16], [P19], SMTP [P10], WebSocket [P6], [P17], [P20] |
| | Semantic | AAS [P1], HTTP + AAS [P7], [P8], [P9], [P15], [P18], [P21], AutomationML [P1], DTDL [P1], ISO 10303 [P4], ISO 23952 [P4], HTTP + SPARQL [P13] |

each network, as well as the specific technology employed to achieve it. It is worth remarking that the LCIM levels are hierarchical, with each level encompassing all the capabilities of the lower levels. Consequently, we have reported in the table the highest level of interoperability was achieved and noted the lower levels for the same network only if different technologies were employed. In addition, the same primary study might be encountered in different levels of interoperability for the same network if there were different options suggested to implement certain networks.

The proximity network uses a communication protocol, such as Profinet or Modbus for data transmission. These protocols define a specific syntax and format for the exchanged data, thereby fulfilling the requirements of syntax interoperability level. However, there is no evidence of using data models to define the meaning of the exchanged data in the proximity network, which would be the requirement to reach semantic interoperability level. Therefore, the highest interoperability level reached in the proximity network is syntax interoperability.

In the access network, 28% (6/21) of the primary studies reached syntactic interoperability using a communication protocol (such as MTConnect, and AMPQ 1.0). However, the majority of the implementations for the access network 66% (14/21) achieved semantic interoperability, where systems exchange data that can be semantically parsed. This was accomplished by employing OPC UA and information models such as AAS and AutomationML or standards such as IEC 61499 and IEEE 1451. In the manufacturing and automation domain, OPC UA is emerging as a universal standard protocol for achieving semantic interoperability among connected systems [P12]. OPC UA offers extendable information models for a range of application domains, enabling semantic interpretation of encoded information. It goes beyond being just a transport protocol for industrial applications and provides a comprehensive set of services and functionalities to support secure and reliable communication between different components of a distributed system [16]. However, to achieve full semantic interoperability, the information models should be well-defined and consistent. Moreno et al. used AAS in combination with eCl@ss dictionary to standardise information models and achieve semantic interoperability in the access network [P2]. The Reference Architecture Model for Industry 4.0 presents the concept of AAS as the foundation for interoperability, which is defined as a digital representation of an asset [P7]. The use of standardised dictionaries such as eCl@ss can simplify the task of assigning semantic descriptions to the information models [P2].

In the service network, semantic interoperability is achieved through all the reported approaches by the use of open-source platforms and the OPC UA protocol. Kim et al. proposed a DT architecture based on the ISO 23247 RA for anomaly detection, with the main services that communicate through the service network being the data presentation and anomaly detection and prediction services [P3]. Communication is based on OPC UA, which gathers data in information models. The pre-processed OPC UA data is then used to generate convolutional neural network (CNN)-based real-time anomaly detection and prediction DTs. Finally, the model is converted to Predictive Model Markup Language (PMML). All technologies used in the service network support semantic interoperability [P3]. Jakoby et al. use the ApacheStreamPipes platform to manage services, which also supports a semantic description level [P21]. Other open-source platforms that support semantic interoperability used in the service network are Eclipse Ditto [P6] and Eclipse rdf4j [P13]. Eclipse Ditto and Eclipse rdf4j both utilize semantic technologies such as JSON-LD, RDF, and SPARQL to enable devices and systems to achieve semantic interoperability. By using a shared data representation, they facilitate communication and integration regardless of underlying technologies or protocols.

Our analysis showed that 43% (7/16) of the studies addressing the user network used a protocol for data transmission such as HTTP [P16,P19], SMTP [P10]. Alternatively, they used WebSocket [P17,P20] and JSON [P6,P11] as a data format. In these cases, syntactic interoperability is reached. Conversely, other primary studies (57% or 9/16) reached semantic interoperability by leveraging various information models, standards, and semantic technologies. The most used information model is AAS, commonly implemented over HTTP APIs. However, we found no evidence of methods or taxonomies employed to enable interoperating systems to anticipate the context of exchanged data, a prerequisite for achieving a higher level of interoperability such as pragmatic interoperability.

## 5    Summary, Discussion and Future Directions

In this section, we summarise and discuss our findings on the technologies used for data exchange and the level of interoperability achieved. Table 5 gives an overview of our findings and serves as a prescriptive tool for each network.

In particular, the table points out the levels of interoperability reached along with the most commonly used technology. The technologies corresponding to each level of interoperability, except for the technical level, are documented in the primary studies. For the technical level, specifications from the ISO 23247 standard are included since this information was not available in the primary studies. The interested reader can check the detailed findings in the replication package (See footnote 3). In addition, Table 5 highlights levels of interoperability that may be desirable to achieve along with possible technologies for achieving them (marked with the blue italic text). We have determined these based on motivating examples found in the primary studies as well as our consolidated experience in collaborative research projects on DTs. For the empty cells of Table 5, we did not find evidence regarding the technologies employed to attain specific levels of interoperability or motivation for their necessity. For the cells highlighted in grey, we reason that there is no need for reaching higher interoperability levels. Using these findings and LCIM requirements as a basis, we discuss the needs and trade-offs involved in attaining higher levels of interoperability.

Our analysis has shown that the highest level of interoperability reached in the proximity network is syntactic interoperability. This is in line with the primary purpose of this network, which is to collect data from physical entities and transmit it to the data collection entity, without significant processing of the data occurring at this stage. The Modbus protocol is commonly employed in the proximity network to achieve syntactic interoperability, typically over industrial Ethernet or proprietary networks. Although it is possible to achieve semantic interoperability in the proximity network, we believe that it may not be necessary or desirable given the network's primary purposes. Achieving higher levels of interoperability would require some form of reasoning and language, which could potentially impact the timeliness of communication. In this case, achieving higher levels of interoperability at the expense of performance and efficiency may not be worthwhile, even if possible (grey cells in Table 5).

**Table 5.** Various LCIM levels achieved per ISO 23247 network along with the most used technology.

| | Technical | Syntactic | Semantic | Pragmatic | Dynamic | Conceptual |
|---|---|---|---|---|---|---|
| Proximity | Industrial Ethernet or proprietary network | Modbus | | | | |
| Access | LAN/ WLAN or cellular network | MQTT | OPC UA | | | |
| Service | Wired IP-based protocols | OPC UA | OPC UA | *SOA & microservices* | | |
| User | Internet or private intranet | HTTP | AAS | *Linked data and ontologies* | *Linked data and ontologies* | *Linked data and ontologies* |

Our analysis has shown that the highest level of interoperability achieved for all other networks (including access, service, and user) is semantic interoperability. While OPC UA is used to achieve semantic interoperability in the access and service networks, AAS is the most common technology used in the user network. Although our analysis did not identify any studies that explicitly discussed the need for achieving higher interoperability levels in the access and service networks, we believe that pragmatic interoperability is needed in the service network. Pragmatic interoperability requires that the systems can exchange information describing the services along with their availability. The service network provides means of communication for sharing DT applications and services including simulation, analysis of data captured from OMEs, and reporting production status [19]. Hence, pragmatic interoperability in the service network seems to be not only desirable but needed for ensuring the functional suitability of DTs. Several studies have explored the use of Service-Oriented Architecture (SOA) and micro-service patterns as promising solutions for achieving pragmatic interoperability [13]. At these networks, achieving dynamic or conceptual interoperability may negatively impact other DTs' qualities namely security and privacy as we discuss in the following paragraph [3].

In the user network, our analysis has revealed the need for higher levels of interoperability than semantic in situations where data is exposed to external systems or other DTs. A use case provided by Kuruppuarachchi et al. in the additive manufacturing domain highlights this need [P1]. In this scenario, a product owner has contracted several manufacturers to produce parts for their product, and each manufacturer has their own DT for their product part. The manufacturers share product-related information with a collaborative DT system. The goal is to optimise the production line, avoid downtime, and reduce costs by modifying individual manufacturing capabilities based on the states of other manufacturers. However, achieving this requires at least dynamic interoperability. One example of achieving dynamic interoperability using linked data and ontologies in the domain of System of System has been proposed by Axelsson [3], which could be applicable in this case. To achieve higher levels of interoperability beyond semantic, it is necessary for DTs exchanging data to have access to each other information regarding properties and functions, and to interpret data in light of this information. While this can be a challenging task for many software-intensive systems, it is even more daunting for DTs due to several reasons. To begin with, it can be difficult to determine which data from DT sub-systems or other DTs should be shared and for how long it needs to be stored. As a result, this can lead to gathering an excessive amount of data, ultimately resulting in decreased performance [17]. In situations when interoperating DTs are owned by different organisations, granting access to other DTs' internal data may be difficult due to confidentiality, accuracy and trust, and security [3]. This is particularly true when internal data holds significant value (e.g., commercial competitive situations) and its manufacturer may be hesitant to share it with external organisations [3]. Moreover, even if the data is shared, it may be difficult for an external organisation to verify its accuracy and reliability [3]. Ensuring safe and secure storage of such data is also essential [3]. Eventually, there may be situations in which data can not be shared due to privacy regulations. Web Ontology Language (OWL) and Resource Description Framework (RDF) can help mitigate some of the above-mentioned challenges associated with high levels of interoperability [18]. Hence, further research is needed to develop and refine existing standards to meet the evolving needs of complex and diverse DTs taking into account OWL and RDF for enhancing interoperability. Low-code development is another emerging paradigm that enhances interoperability by simplifying data source integration [6].

## 6   Related Work

Numerous studies have explored ways to improve interoperability both within and between DT systems. Nonetheless, to the best of our knowledge, current research appears to lack a comprehensive analysis and assessment of the interoperability requirements and support for DTs. Li et al. presented a framework for achieving seamless interaction between the physical and virtual spaces of a single DT system [25]. To uniformly model all manufacturing units, they proposed a semantic modelling methodology. Damjanovic-Behrendt and Behrendt have stressed the importance of utilizing open-source technologies to facilitate interoperability in DTs [12]. To this end, they have introduced a collection of the most significant open-source tools and technologies for designing and building DTs in the context of smart manufacturing [12]. In addition, the authors have discussed the use of a micro-service architecture for the DT demonstrator to support semantic data interoperability. Park et al. made a significant contribution to enhancing the interoperability of DTs with external systems in smart manufacturing [27]. They proposed a new data schema to incorporate existing standards for smart manufacturing, ensuring interoperability. The authors also developed a cloud-based DT that uses the proposed schema, which is interoperable with existing legacy systems. Ariansynah and Pardamean have highlighted the importance of integrating asset prognostic and health monitoring DTs with other software systems that manage business operations such as CMMS and ERP to minimise asset downtime [2]. To address this issue, they proposed using rule-based ontology modelling and reasoning to improve the interoperability of DTs with CMMS and ERP systems. Cavalieri and Gambadoro presented a novel approach for enhancing the semantic interoperability of digital twins (DTs) with external systems [8]. The primary objective of their research was to establish communication between DTs based on Digital Twins Definition Language (DTDL) and any applications that conform to the Open Platform Communications Unified Architecture (OPC UA).

## 7   Conclusion and Future Work

This paper investigates interoperability in digital twin software architectures for manufacturing. We analysed 21 primary studies selected from an initial pool of 2403 peer-reviewed publications. Through an examination of the data extracted from these primary studies, we identified the specific technologies employed for data exchange in DTs, as well as the degree of interoperability that was achieved during such exchanges. Our analysis has revealed that current DT architectures are successful in achieving semantic interoperability. However pragmatic and dynamic interoperability levels are desirable, particularly in federated DTs. Achieving higher levels of interoperability in federated DTs presents challenges related to accuracy, trust, security, and privacy. To overcome these challenges, standards and standardised semantic mapping frameworks hold promise.

Concerning future works, one area of interest involves exploring the potential of linked data and ontologies for achieving pragmatic, dynamic and conceptual interoperability. Also, we aim to focus on defining a standards-based architectural framework for digital twins in manufacturing that facilitates data interoperability. This framework will consist of several views, including the functional view, technical adaptation and implementation view, and interoperability view.

## Primary Studies

P1. P. M. Kuruppuarachchi et al. "Trusted and secure composite digital twin architecture for collaborative ecosystems," *IET Collab. Intell. Manufacturing*, v 5, n. 1, 2023.

P2. T. Moreno et al. "Scalable digital twins for industry 4.0 digital services: a dataspaces approach," *Production & Manufacturing Research*, vol. 11, no. 1, p. 2173680, 2023.

P3. D. B. Kim et al. "A digital twin implementation architecture for wire+ arc additive manufacturing based on iso 23247," *Manufacturing Letters*, vol. 34, pp. 1–5, 2022.

P4. A. Farhadi et al. "The development of a digital twin framework for an industrial robotic drilling process," *Sensors*, v.22, n.9, 2022.

P5. H. da Rocha et al. "An interoperable digital twin with the ieee 1451 standards," *Sensors*, vol. 22, no. 19, p. 7590, 2022.

P6. M. Kherbache et al. "Digital twin network for the iiot using eclipse ditto and hono," *IFAC-PapersOnLine*, vol. 55, no. 8, pp. 37–42, 2022.

P7. K. Ding et al. "Aml-based web-twin visualization integration framework for dt-enabled and iiot-driven manufacturing system under i4. 0 workshop," *Journal of Manufacturing Systems*, vol. 64, pp. 479–496, 2022.

P8. F. Schnicke et al. "Architecture blueprints to enable scalable vertical integration of assets with digital twins," in *IEEE 27th Int. Conference ETFA*. IEEE, 2022, pp. 1–8.

P9. F. Yallıç et al. "Asset administration shell generation and usage for digital twins: A case study for non-destructive testing by x-ray."

P10. V. Leiras et al. "Iso23247 digital twin approach for industrial grade radio frequency testing station," in *IEEE 27th Int. Conference ETFA*. IEEE, 2022, pp. 1–8.

P11. G. N. Schroeder et al. "A methodology for digital twin modeling and deployment for industry 4.0," *Proceedings of the IEEE*, vol. 109, no. 4, pp. 556–567, 2020.

P12. A. Redelinghuys et al. "A six-layer architecture for the digital twin: a manufacturing case study implementation," *Journal of Intelligent Manufacturing*, vol. 31, pp. 1383–1402, 2020.

P13. D. Bamunuarachchi et al. "Cyber twins supporting industry 4.0 application development," in *Proceedings of the 18th International Conference on Advances in Mobile Computing & Multimedia*, 2020, pp. 64–73.

P14. Y. Fan et al. "A digital-twin visualized architecture for flexible manufacturing system," *Journal of Manufacturing Systems*, vol. 60, pp. 176–201, 2021.

P15. M. Jacoby et al., "An approach for industrie 4.0-compliant and data-sovereign digital twins," *at-Automatisierungstechnik*, vol. 69, no. 12, pp. 1051–1061, 2021.

P16. F. Pires et al. "Decision support based on digital twin simulation: a case study," in *Service Oriented, Holonic and Multi-Agent Manufacturing Systems for Industry of the Future: Proceedings of SOHOMA 2020*. Springer, 2021, pp. 99–110.

P17. F. Assad et al. "Utilising web-based digital twin to promote assembly line sustainability," in *2021 4th IEEE International Conference on Industrial Cyber-Physical Systems (ICPS)*. IEEE, 2021, pp. 381–386.

P18. M. Redeker et al. "A digital twin platform for industrie 4.0," in *Data Spaces: Design, Deployment and Future Directions*. Springer International Publishing Cham, 2022, pp. 173–200.

P19. E. Russo et al. "Lidite: a full-fledged and featherweight digital twin framework," *IEEE Trans. on Dependable and Secure Computing*, 2023.

P20. K. Židek et al. "Digital twin of experimental smart manufacturing assembly system for industry 4.0 concept," *Sustainability*, v.12, n.9, 2020.

P21. M. Jacoby et al. "An approach for realizing hybrid digital twins using asset administration shells and apache streampipes," *Information*, vol. 12, no. 6, p. 217, 2021.

**Acknowledgements.** The work in this paper has been supported by the Swedish Knowledge Foundation (KKS) through the ACICS and Modev projects, by the Excellence in Production Research (XPRES) Framework, by the EU - NextGenerationEU under the Italian MUR National Innovation Ecosystem grants ECS00000041 - VITALITY, and PE0000020 - CHANGES. The authors also acknowledge the support of the MUR (Italy) Department of Excellence 2023 - 2027 for GSSI.

# References

1. Ali, N.B., Petersen, K.: Evaluating strategies for study selection in systematic literature studies. In: Proceedings of ESEM (2014)
2. Ariansyah, D., Pardamean, B.: Enhancing interoperability of digital twin in the maintenance phase of lifecycle. In: Proceedings of ICITISEE. IEEE (2022)
3. Axelsson, J.: Achieving system-of-systems interoperability levels using linked data and ontologies. In: INCOSE International Symposium, vol. 30, pp. 651–665. Wiley Online Library (2020)
4. Basili, V.R., Caldiera, G., Rombach, H.D.: The goal question metric approach. In: Encyclopedia of Software Engineering (1994)
5. Brereton, P., Kitchenham, B.A., Budgen, D., Turner, M., Khalil, M.: Lessons from applying the systematic literature review process within the software engineering domain. J. Syst. Softw. **80**, 571–583 (2007)
6. Bucaioni, A., Cicchetti, A., Ciccozzi, F.: Modelling in low-code development: a multi-vocal systematic review. Softw. Syst. Model. **21**(5), 1959–1981 (2022)

7. Carney, D., Oberndorf, P.: Integration and interoperability models for systems of systems. Technical report, Carneige-Mellon Univ Pittsburgh PA Software engineering Inst (2004)
8. Cavalieri, S., Gambadoro, S.: Proposal of mapping digital twins definition language to open platform communications unified architecture. Sensors **23**(4), 2349 (2023)
9. Charmaz, K., Belgrave, L.L.: Grounded theory. The Blackwell encyclopedia of sociology (2007)
10. Cruzes, D.S., Dyba, T.: Recommended steps for thematic synthesis in software engineering. In: Proceedings of ESEM (2011)
11. Dalibor, M., et al.: A cross-domain systematic mapping study on software engineering for digital twins. J. Syst. Softw. **139**, 111361 (2022)
12. Damjanovic-Behrendt, V., Behrendt, W.: An open source approach to the design and implementation of digital twins for smart manufacturing. Int. J. Comput. Integr. Manuf. **32**(4–5), 366–384 (2019)
13. Ferko, E., Bucaioni, A., Behnam, M.: Architecting digital twins. IEEE Access **10**, 50335–50350 (2022)
14. Ferko, E., Bucaioni, A., Behnam, M.: Supporting technical adaptation and implementation of digital twins in manufacturing. In: International Conference on Information Technology-New Generations, pp. 181–189. Springer, Heidelberg (2023). https://doi.org/10.1007/978-3-031-28332-1_21
15. Ferko, E., Bucaioni, A., Pelliccione, P., Behnam, M.: Standardisation in digital twin architectures in manufacturing. In: 2023 IEEE 20th International Conference on Software Architecture (ICSA), pp. 70–81 (2023)
16. Graube, M., Hensel, S., Iatrou, C., Urbas, L.: Information models in opc ua and their advantages and disadvantages. In: 2017 22nd IEEE International Conference on Emerging Technologies and Factory Automation (ETFA), pp. 1–8. IEEE (2017)
17. Henningsson, K., Wohlin, C.: Understanding the relations between software quality attributes-a survey approach. In: Proceedings 12th International Conference for Software Quality (2002)
18. Herzog, R., Jacoby, M., Podnar Žarko, I.: Semantic interoperability in iot-based automation infrastructures: how reference architectures address semantic interoperability. at-Automatisierungstechnik **64**(9), 742–749 (2016)
19. International Organization for Standardization: ISO 23247–1:2021. https://www.iso.org/standard/75066.html
20. ISO: ISO/IEC 25010. https://iso25000.com/index.php/en/iso-25000-standards/iso-25010
21. Kitchenham, B., Brereton, P.: A systematic review of systematic review process research in software engineering. Inf. Softw. Technol. **55**, 2049–2075 (2013)
22. Kuruppuarachchi, P., Rea, S., McGibney, A.: An architecture for composite digital twin enabling collaborative digital ecosystems. In: Proceedings of CSCWD, pp. 980–985. IEEE (2022)
23. Lattanzi, L., Raffaeli, R., Peruzzini, M., Pellicciari, M.: Digital twin for smart manufacturing: a review of concepts towards a practical industrial implementation. Int. J. Comput. Integr. Manuf. **34**(6), 567–597 (2021)
24. Leal, G.D.S.S., Guédria, W., Panetto, H.: Interoperability assessment: a systematic literature review. Comput. Ind. **106**, 111–132 (2019)
25. Li, J., Zhang, Y., Qian, C.: The enhanced resource modeling and real-time transmission technologies for digital twin based on qos considerations. Rob. Comput.-Integr. Manuf. **75**, 102284 (2022)

26. Lidell, A., Ericson, S., Ng, A.H.: The current and future challenges for virtual commissioning and digital twins of production lines. In: Proceedings of SPS2022 (2022)
27. Park, Y., Woo, J., Choi, S.: A cloud-based digital twin manufacturing system based on an interoperable data schema for smart manufacturing. Int. J. Comput. Integr. Manuf. **33**(12), 1259–1276 (2020)
28. Petersen, K., Feldt, R., Mujtaba, S., Mattsson, M.: Systematic mapping studies in software engineering. In: Proceedingss of EASE (2008)
29. Qi, Q., Tao, F.: Digital twin and big data towards smart manufacturing and industry 4.0: 360 degree comparison. IEEE Access **6**, 3585–3593 (2018)
30. Shull, F., Singer, J., Sjøberg, D.I.: Guide to Advanced Empirical Software Engineering. Springer, Heidelberg (2007). https://doi.org/10.1007/978-1-84800-044-5
31. Stol, K.J., Ralph, P., Fitzgerald, B.: Grounded theory in software engineering research: a critical review and guidelines. In: Proceedings of the 38th International conference on software engineering (2016)
32. Tolk, A.: The elusiveness of simulation interoperability - what is different from other interoperability domains? In: 2018 Winter Simulation Conference (WSC), pp. 679–690 (2018)
33. Wang, W., Tolk, A., Wang, W.: The levels of conceptual interoperability model: applying systems engineering principles to m&s (2009). arXiv preprint arXiv:0908.0191
34. Wohlin, C., Runeson, P., Höst, M., Ohlsson, M., Regnell, B., Wesslén, A.: Experimentation in Software Engineering. Springer, Heidelberg (2012). https://doi.org/10.1007/978-3-642-29044-2
35. Wohlin, C.: Guidelines for snowballing in systematic literature studies and a replication in software engineering. In: Proceedings of EASE (2014)
36. Wohlin, C., Höst, M., Henningsson, K.: Empirical research methods in software engineering. In: Conradi, R., Wang, A.I. (eds.) Empirical Methods and Studies in Software Engineering. LNCS, vol. 2765, pp. 7–23. Springer, Heidelberg (2003). https://doi.org/10.1007/978-3-540-45143-3_2

# Architecting Artificial Intelligence for Autonomous Cars: The OpenPilot Framework

Luciano Baresi[1] and Damian A. Tamburri[1,2(✉)]

[1] Politecnico di Milano, Milan, Italy
luciano.baresi@polimi.it
[2] Eindhoven University of Technology, JADS, Eindhoven, The Netherlands
d.a.tamburri@tue.nl

**Abstract.** Openpilot is a vast open-source semi-automated driving system developed by comma.ai, with 200+ contributors and 750K lines of code according to the OpenHub open-source community-tracking portal. On the one hand, the documentation available gives insights on what Openpilot is capable of doing, how to install it and how people can contribute to it, while the development team posts periodically update on the company's blog on the state of the project and implementation of new features. On the other hand, this material does little in helping newcomers to embrace the technology with near-zero knowledge over its intended programming model. What is more, not having access to closed-source autonomous-driving framworks does not warrant an appropriate architectural analysis of the framework, the decisions to be made, and the concerns typically emerging in such a decision-making process. This study addresses this gap by exploiting mixed-methods research, featuring (a) an ethnographical study of the community's operations and (b) a reverse engineering of the OpenPilot codebase both from a structure and operations perspective. This paper is intended as an early-stage adopter study for those software designers, operators, policy-makers and other practitioners aiming at embracing the aforementioned framework and programming model for their own professional endeavours.

**Keywords:** Automotive Software Architecting · Smart Autonomous Vehicles · Smart Cars · autonomous-driving

## 1 Introduction

Recent reports[1] forecast that roughly 33 million autonomous vehicles (AVs for short) are going to hit the road by 2040. At the same time, 55% of small businesses—in the US alone—remark that they are going to have a fully autonomous fleet in the next two decades. This implies that while people are expected to get used to driverless cars, so is the software industry that controls

---

[1] https://policyadvice.net/insurance/insights/self-driving-car-statistics/.

everything else around such cars. For example, The German brand Audi plans on
spending $16 billion on self-driving cars by 2023, not only to make autonomous
driving a better, safer, and more sustainable reality, but also to adapt its software and industrial systems to cope with the new model of vehicular engineering
implied. At the same time, the rapid development of the Internet economy and
Artificial Intelligence (AI) has promoted the progress of all onboard systems
inside self-driving cars, into a software realm fusing both AI and smart software
engineering often called *autonomous-driving* [8]. Unlike what many would think,
self-driving a car is not a hardware problem, instead is almost completely related
to software, specifically, AI software engineering [5]. For example, modern cars
are built in such a way that all the relevant information about the status of the
car is exchanged over standardized channels; when accessed, these 'levers' allow
controlling the car in 100% of all its functions, electric, mechanical or otherwise
[1]. All cars support (to some extent) automated driving, e.g., they use a set of
sensors that aid the operation of the vehicle via the interoperation of cameras
and sensors; this allows the car driver, its internal systems, or its autonomous-
driving AI to be aware of its surroundings and make instrumented decisions.
These data are typically elaborated through AI and machine-learning architectures. And this is exactly where the OpenPilot framework steps in. The research
problem we address around OpenPilot is that of providing a solid foundational
introduction to the framework, its architecture and intended operations to allow
practitioners and researchers to address the framework more easily and with an
expedient approach as driven by our results and insight. Specifically, this article
offers such a study over the OpenPilot technical space and an analysis of its
operational model, namely, how applications developed through it are intended
to work and what are the limitations that come with the solution, providing a
complete overview of all of its components. In addition, we perform a quality
assessment of the framework in an attempt to establish its technical maturity
and practical feasibility, with a focus on the community structure and operations. We conclude that the OpenPilot framework offers a mature and stable
basis to approach simple to complex automotive programming tasks, including
the design and implementation of complex-scale AI software including multiple machine-learning models as well as sensorial equipment. At the same time,
we observe a relative lack of autonomous-driving guidelines, especially in the
realm of AI software design and interoperation, which is bound to incite further
research and practical work in this direction. The rest of this paper is structured as follows. Section 2 offers a motivational and methodological perspective
over the work. Section 3 provides an overview of the OpenPilot framework, its
architecture and general characteristics. Section 4 elaborates further into the
aforementioned architecture and offers an in-depth view over its essential components. Section 6 discusses our results, and Sect. 7 concludes the manuscript.

## 2   Research Materials and Methods

As previously introduced, what presented in this paper was obtained through
a mixed-methods approach, tailored from [12], that features ethnomethodologi-

cal research following the same process introduced by Zhou et al. [13]. Figure 1 reports an overview of the overall research method. A 9-month ethnography study of (a) the community environment, (b) the community workflows and (c) the OpenPilot codebase evolution was enacted to follow any code-relevant activities such as: (a) git commit actions; (b) pull request actions; (c) issue-closing actions; (d) releases; (e) forks. Such actions were logged into a live-doc in the form of a csv file for later quantitative and qualitative analysis. Subsequently, the aforementioned actions were analysed through a combination of content analysis [6] and card-sorting [14] to determine: (a) methodological steps intended in the community workflows; (b) the intended programming model behind the OpenPilot use and operations (see Sect. 1). Finally, from the perspective of the software reverse engineering is *"the practice of analyzing a software system, either in whole or in part, to extract design and implementation information"* [4]. To provide for the expected results in this study we combined the use of the Architexa architectural reconstruction suite[2] and the VisualParadigm

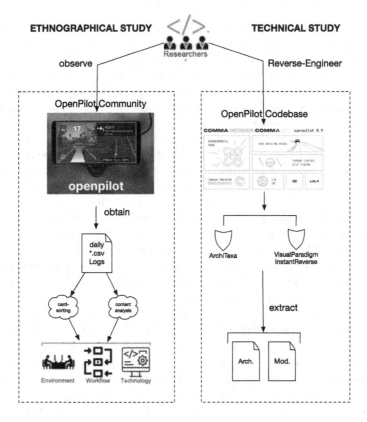

**Fig. 1.** An overview of the research methods adopted in this study.

---

[2] https://www.architexa.com/.

deepParse automodeller[3]. For what concerns the data involved in our study, its synthesis and reliability assessment, all available data was loaded into tables formatted to be analysed with the R data analytics toolkit in parallel by the two authors of the paper; the purpose of analysis was to produce the statistics, plots and representations currently showcased in the rest of this paper. At this point, for all analyses which involved inter-coder reliability such as card-sorting, we assessed observer reliability evaluating the agreement across analyses over the data tables we produced. Subsequently, we computed the Krippendorff's $\alpha$ coefficient for observation agreement [6] - the $\alpha$ score essentially measures a confidence interval score stemming from the agreement of values across two distinctly-reported observations about the same event or phenomenon. In our case the value was applied to measure the agreement between coding and card-sorting results of our analysis. The value was calculated initially to be 0.86, hence $\alpha > .800$, which is a standard reference value for highly-confident observations.

## 3    Framework Architecture

Comma.ai is an AI startup founded by George Hotz (@geohot) in September 2015. The mission of the company is to "solve self-driving cars while delivering shippable intermediaries". To achieve this mission, in 2016 Comma.ai launched Openpilot, an open-source, semi-automated driving system. It is a comprehensive system of driver assistance features supporting a wide range of car models. Today, Comma.ai sold more than 7.000 devices and has more than 3500 active users.

The Society of Automotive Engineers (SAE) defines 6 levels of driving automation ranging from 0 (fully manual) to 5 (fully autonomous). These levels have been adopted by the U.S. Department of Transportation. OpenPilot allows reaching a level 2 driving automation level, meaning that the vehicle on which the device is installed can control both steering and accelerating/decelerating. At a level 2 automation, the human still monitors all the (autonomous-)driving tasks and can take control at any time. It is substantially different from other automated driving systems since it can be installed by anyone that buys the Comma Two or Comma Three development kit available in their online shop and flashes the Openpilot software available on the public GitHub repository. Openpilot offers many functionalities based on machine learning and computer vision, such as Automated lane-centering, Adaptive cruise control and more. The Openpilot repository is available online[4] and it counts more than 5.000 forks and is starred by more than 25.000 users. Developers that want to contribute to the project push their changes on the master branch, which is stripped and minified by CI (GitLab Continuous Integration) and pushed to master-ci automatically if the tests pass. When the version on the master branch is ready to be published on the release branch, master-ci is pushed to devel-staging, opening a pull request into devel. This pull request is the spot for comments on the new release,

---

[3] https://circle.visual-paradigm.com/docs/code-engineering/instant-reverse/how-to-generate-uml-from-cpp/.

[4] https://github.com/commaai/Openpilot.git.

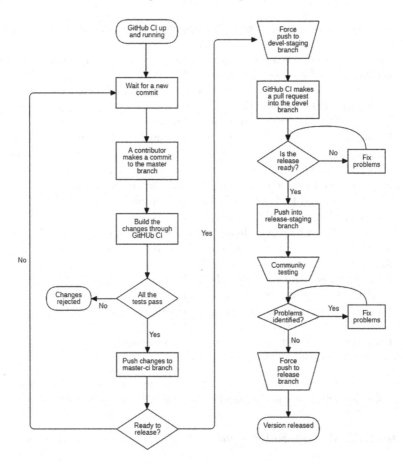

**Fig. 2.** Flowchart diagram of the development process of OpenPilot, supported by GitHub CI actions as of Feb. 2021.

and hotfixes at this point is cherry-picked from master into devel-staging. Devel is built by CI and pushes the built versions to release-staging and dashcam-staging signed with the official comma release key. After the -staging branches are tested by the community for a 1-3 days, then changes are pushed to release and dashcam. For the sake of completeness, we report that the release branch is structured as follows:

1. cereal: the messaging spec and libs used for all logs;
2. common: library like functionality and utility functions;
3. installer/updater: manages updates of NEOS, that is, the operating system for the comma.two and EON Gold Dashcam Development Kits;
4. opendbc: files showing how to interpret data from cars;
5. panda: code used to communicate on CAN;
6. phonelibs: external libraries;

7. pyextra: extra python packages not shipped in the standard NEOS distribution;
8. selfdrive: code needed to bootstrap and drive the car or change the operational behavior of any of its components;
   - assets: fonts, images, and sounds for User Interfacing (UI) as well as extension of the actual UI;
   - athena: allows communication with the app;
   - board: daemon to talk to the motherboard of the autonomous-driving vehicle;
   - camerad: driver to capture images from the camera sensors;
   - car: car specific code to read states and control actuators;
   - common: shared C/C++ code for the daemons;
   - controls: planning and controls;
   - debug: tools to help you debug and do car ports;
   - location: precise localization and vehicle parameter estimation;
   - logcatd: Android logcat as a service;
   - loggerd: logger and uploader of car data;
   - modeld: driving and monitoring model runners;
   - proclogd: Logs information from processes;
   - sensord: IMU interface code;
   - test: unit tests, system tests, and a car simulator;
   - ui: all assets related to the UI;

Conversely, for the sake of simplicity, we focus on the biggest and most important portion of this technical space, namely, the *selfdrive* sub-structure.

# 4   OpenPilot and SelfDrive

Openpilot needs many components that allow the software to interface with the car and exchange messages with it. These components, after the open-sourcing of the software, are organized in different repositories, allowing to better manage them and have a clear distinction of what role each component plays. This section offers an excursus of the package structure that is available in the main Openpilot component—namely the selfDrive technical space—and focuses on summaryzing the functionalities that are provided. Subsequently, the section closes by illustrating the critical *ModelD* artificial intelligence module, that is, the key module with which all artificial intelligence components stemming from the OpenPilot framework are to be defined.

## 4.1   Package Structure

To describe the architecture of Openpilot the rest of the exposition takes advantage of the 4+1 architectural view model proposed by Kruchten [7], which provides four software architecture essential viewpoints [11] as a systematic way to describe a system architecture according to different views, namely, logical, process, development, physical, and use-case views. In the following, we offer details on the first four, given that the scope and focus of this study is that of a study over the OpenPilot framework, with a focus on the selfdrive technical space, intended as the packages contained in the root of the framework architecture, i.e., the selfDrive directory. The selfdrive directory is the largest repository of Openpilot and contains the definition of the Python and C++ processes executed on the Comma device. Table 1 shows an overview of the programming languages (Col. 1) present in the key technical space of selfdrive, including #files, #blank lines, comments and actual source Lines of Code (SLOC), defined and counted by means of the IntelliJ idea IDE[5]. At the same time, the reader should note that the selfdrive technical space is less than 20% of the total amount of lines of code for the entire framework. On the one hand our study focuses on selfdrive, but on the other hand, the rest of the software code deserves future work and experimentation, perhaps in the scope of a feasibility study or a code quality analysis.

> **Reflection.** The structure offers an overview which is well-modularised and is expected to reflect the necessities for contextualisation, customisation, and extensibility clearly ascribed to the target context.

**Table 1.** Lines of code in the selfdrive critical technical space, arranged by programming language.

| Language | Files | Blanks | Comments | SLOC |
|---|---|---|---|---|
| **Python** | 164 | 3.935 | 1.630 | 19.587 |
| **C++** | 103 | 3.458 | 1.444 | 16.736 |
| **C** | 11 | 958 | 212 | 10.275 |
| **C/C++ Header** | 121 | 2.244 | 3.056 | 9.736 |
| **OpenCL** | 7 | 88 | 60 | 556 |
| **SVG** | 15 | 0 | 0 | 242 |
| **JSON** | 2 | 0 | 0 | 104 |
| **HTML** | 2 | 11 | 0 | 89 |
| **Bourne Shell** | 8 | 17 | 3 | 83 |
| **QML** | 1 | 5 | 0 | 42 |
| **Cython** | 1 | 4 | 2 | 22 |
| **Tot.** | **435** | **10.720** | **6.407** | **57.472** |

*Logical View.* Quoting from Kruchten's original definitions, "The logical view focuses on representing the functionality that the system provides to its intended end-users". As for this view of the Openpilot architecture, the only tasks that

---

[5] https://plugins.jetbrains.com/plugin/4509-statistic.

middleware explicitly aims at supporting are to (a) drive a car effectively and (b) offering AI-driven capabilities to instrument any component in the driving process. From version 0.8.7 onwards, the system also supports the use of a navigator.

---

**Reflection.** As previously mentioned, the extensibility of the framework is high, as confirmed by the rapid release of versions in which further extensions are offered.

---

*Process View.* Looking at the process view, selfdrive is characterized by the parallel execution of different processes, which take care of the different aspects that need to be controlled during the software execution. OpenPilot processes include both Python and C++ processes. Generally, the C++ processes are those which require a high level of performance and that can be executed natively on the Comma device. These include the processes taking care of the prediction and elaboration of the acquired frames of the camera, the processes directly controlling or showing content on the device, and logging functionalities.

---

**Reflection.** Again the process view itself reflects a business logic which is rigged for extensibility and customisability, as reflected by the native compatibility of the Comm device with multiple externals.

---

*Development View.* Again, quoting the original definitions of the framework, "the development view illustrates a software system from a programmer's perspective and is concerned primarily with software management". Looking at the development view, Openpilot is made of different packages which allow communication with the car and run the predictive models necessary for its AI-driven operations. Figure 3 offers an overview of the packages and their interdependencies, using a coloring schema—decreasing in intensity from red (for the Debug package) to dark magenta (for Modeld, UI, Assets, etc.)—to weigh the criticality of the packages measured by the unwighted quantity of SLOC in each package[6].

Each package contains the source necessary to enact different processes of Openpilot. From a runtime perspective, the processes and operations communicate by using the Cereal messaging specifications, but they also provide common functionalities and Application Programmers' Interfaces (APIs) that can be used by other processes to retrieve various details, such as the hardware version, the car model on which the device is mounted, and so on.

---

[6] a larger and browsable version of this same figure is available online: https://tinyurl.com/ECSA-openpilot.

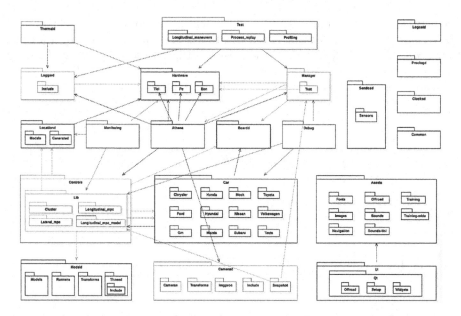

**Fig. 3.** Interdependencies of the `selfdrive` packages within their respective namespace.

**Reflection.** From a development perspective, it is in fact the granularity of the components which aids AI architectures' developers in their own contextualisation work. In fact such granularity offers an approachable technical space, which blends well with the necessities of practice.

*Physical View.* From the original definitions: "The physical view (aka the deployment view) depicts the system from a system engineer's point of view. It is concerned with the topology of software components on the physical layer as well as the physical connections between these components". The physical components that are involved are essentially three: the Comma device (Comma Two or Comma Three), a Comma Pedal to communicate with the car, and the supported car itself. The car provides the raw data that is given to the AI model to generate an output that is then transformed into actions by the car actuators. Raw data come from the car camera, radar, and sensors. Data are then transmitted over the CAN bus, and the Panda device interfaces with the car and intercepts the data over the CAN bus. These data are then transmitted, over USB, to the Comma device. The Openpilot software running on the device, comes with different process daemons that manage the acquired data, give them to the AI model, and generate a message that is sent to the car over the same CAN bus. Specifically, the camera daemon, (*camerad*), sends the frames acquired by the car and device's camera to the model daemon (*modeld*), which generates the predictions based on AI algorithms, and the sensor daemon (*sensord*) elaborates the output of the car's sensors. All of these data are input into the control daemon (*controlsd*), which generates the messages that are sent to the car through Panda and over the CAN bus. A high-level representation of the physical view is recapped in Fig. 4, represented as a standard UML deployment diagram.

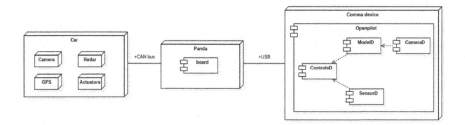

**Fig. 4.** The standard deployment overview of OpenPilot-oriented software.

> **Reflection.** From a phisical perspective, the Openpilot technical space offers an easily understandable deployment, which addresses well the necessities and granularities typical of the IoT technology entailed by automotive computing.

### 4.2   The ModelD Artificial Intelligence Module

The main model takes in a picture from the road camera and answers the question "Where should I drive the car?" It also takes in a desire input, which can command the model to act, such as turning or changing lanes. The full ModelD data-flow representation is available on the full technical report for this work[7].

The input of the model is retrieved by a thread that takes the data from the socket *liveCalibration* containing the calibrated frames elaborated by the process *calibrationd*. The representation of the camera frames is built by considering both the intrinsic parameters, that are the camera parameters that are internal and fixed to a particular camera/digitization setup, and the extrinsic parameters, that are the camera parameters that are external to the camera and may change concerning the world frame. If the intrinsic parameters define the location and orientation of the camera concerning the world frame, the intrinsic Parameters allow a mapping between camera coordinates and pixel coordinates in the image.

The processed calibrated frames are then used by the model to make the predictions. The actual frames are sent using VisionIPC and can be corrected by using the calibrated frame information computed by the thread managing the

---

[7] https://www.politesi.polimi.it/bitstream/10589/181889/2/2021_12_Fontana_02.
pdf.

calibration. The VisionIPC client connects to the socket camerad and the model is initialized. The model which runs the neural network to make the predictions is called Supercombo and as the default setting it is uses the Snapdragon Neural Processing Engine (SNPE), which is a Qualcomm Snapdragon software accelerated runtime for the execution of deep neural networks.

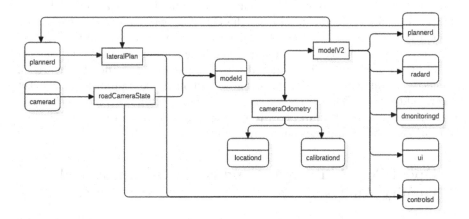

**Fig. 5.** The ModelD data-flow representation.

To make the model faster and more efficient, the framework also introduced Thneed, an SNPE accelerator. The Thneed model runs on the local device, caching a single model run and replaying it at a higher speed. Apart from the caching functionalities, the Thneed module does not change any aspect of the default SNMP. The specifics of the model and the definition of its inputs and outputs are defined in the official Openpilot wiki[8]. The model is trained using the comma2k19 dataset, a dataset of over 33 h of drive. The dataset contains 10.000 camera acquisitions, which were manually labeled to the different elements of the frames. The features vectors are then fed to the Recurrent Neural Networks that generate the driving policy. Subsequently, for feature extraction from frames, Comma uses a lot of skip connections and converts a $12 \times 128 \times 256$ (two YUV format consecutive frames with 3 extra alpha channels). The model learns to encode all the relevant information required for planning into a compressed form. This vision encoding is later forked into several branches which are processed independently to output lanes, paths, etc. When the model receives the YUV frames from the VisionIPC server, they are first prepared and transformed using the transformation matrix obtained after processing the calibrated frame. This preparation step initializes the ModelFrame, which is a virtual camera frame with even width and height frame that can be used by the model. Subsequently, after the ModelFrame relative to the acquired YUV frames are

---

[8] https://opwiki.readthedocs.io/en/latest/user_manual/gcs_install_op.html.

ready, the model execution starts[9]. The model, through the directory `ioctl()` (input/output control), can communicate with the Qualcomm Kernel Graphic Support Layer (KGSL). It also leverages the OpenCL functionalities supported by the Qualcomm platform to increase the performance and efficiency of the computation of the predictions. When the execution of the model is triggered, the command `clEnqueueNDRangeKernel()` enqueues a command to execute the OpenCL kernel on the device. The cached commands are elaborated by the KGSL and the result is retrieved from the OpenCL read buffer. The instruction on what type of predictions the model has to make are contained in the `desire`, which is computed by the lateral planner and indicates on what direction the car should proceed. Finally, The model also runs `posenet`[10] to generate the visual odometry parameters, estimated from the model output and published on socket cameraOdometry. With posenet we generally refer to computer vision techniques that estimate the position of an object, in the specific case of the rotation and translations of the frame estimated by the model.

## 5   OpenPilot: A Technical and Socio-Organizational Quality Analysis

Assessing the quality of the contributions in an open-source software (OSS) is not an easy task: unlike industrial software, OSS is often developed under a non-traditional structure and, as a result, is seen as the product of teams composed almost exclusively of developers. This picture is of course incomplete at best, as is well known by those involved with OSS. While young projects can thrive under the guidance of lone developers or small unsupported teams, more mature projects usually benefit from contributions to the project that transcend code. These non-code contributions may include, for example: moderating communication channels associated with the project or its issue tracker(s), fielding questions, outreach, infrastructure, governance, funding acquisition, documentation, or even mere attention, these contributions are all crucial determinants of a project's continued success [10]. To have a complete picture of the community contributions made to openpilot over time, in the following analysis is considered both code contributions and non-code contributions. To simplify the process of data mining, the analysis is supported by an ad-hoc tool developed for this purpose, that from now on is referenced as contributors-profiler. The tool collect the data leveraging the GitHub APIs and for each contributor it compute the key performance indicators (KPIs). For the code contributions, we consider the number of commits, and the ratio between the successful GitHub actions executed after the commits and the total amount of actions triggered by the contributor's commits, as a proxy of the errors introduced with each commit. The non-code data include the amount of issues made by each contributor and

---

[9] Note that if Thneed is used, a full execution is required only the first time since then the outputs are recorded and can be used to make faster predictions.

[10] https://iq.opengenus.org/posenet-model/.

their activity on the Discord server, since it is the main place where the community interact. For the code contribution, the granularity is of a week, both to speed up the execution and because a finer granularity is not meaningful for this analysis' purpose. To understand the extent to which top-level core contributors of the project perform within the development community we computed a trend of their community contribution success and failure rates (see Fig. 6). The trend clearly reflects a coherently positive success rate of contributions overall.

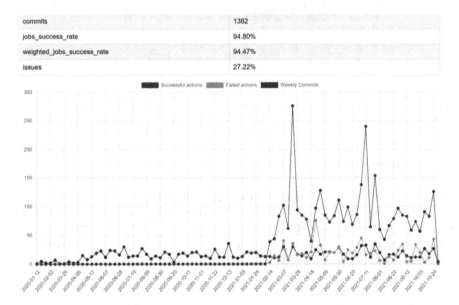

**Fig. 6.** An overview of contribution success and failure rates for key community developers.

In addition, another performance indicator typically used to assess the quality of the contribution is the entropy of commits [9]. The software entropy takes its name from the entropy in real world, that can be defined as a measure of chaos that either stays the same or increases over time. In the case of software entropy, this indicator is a proxy of the chaos of a software, and measures of how specific each commit was in relation to the entire code base. Very specific commits only affect a small set of files, and thus have a low entropy. Commits that touch a large number of files are much less specific and have a higher entropy as a result. Software entropy impacts the overall quality of software systems. High entropy hinders developers from understanding the purpose of a piece of code and can cause developers to make sub-optimal changes and introduce bugs. The overall software entropy of Openpilot can be measured using the tool commit-entropy, which allows to compute the average entropy per day and a 30-day rolling average. The result of this analysis is shown in Fig. 7.

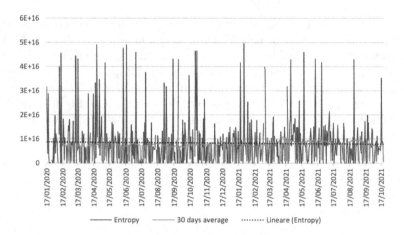

**Fig. 7.** Overall software entropy computed on a 30-day rolling average for the Open-Pilot community.

# 6  Discussions

In the course of the experimentation recapped in this article, we made several key observations and reflections on our results. On the one hand, some of such observations effectively constitute design principles—according to the definition of Bass et al. [3]—to aid the (re-)application of the OpenPilot framework. On the other hand, the observations lead to further work to refine or expand on the materials proposed in this work. The rest of this section reports on these observations and reflections.

**OpenPilot Intends to be used as part of a more Coherent Component Model.** Although the OpenPilot framwork is thought as a software engineering framework, namely, a set of guidelines, standards, and best practices that are used to develop and maintain autonomous-driving software systems, the framework actually focuses on providing a structured approach to the AI software development process intended in autonomous-driving by defining the tasks, roles, and responsibilities of the AI development team, as well as the ML tools/libraries and modelling techniques they should use to achieve their objectives within the intended scope of autonomous-driving. This focus however makes the use of the framework rather narrow and purely dedicated to the AI components in an automotive software component array; this essentially precludes the use of OpenPilot as an independent middleware but rather *promotes the use of the framework within a larger series of components intended to operate together in a service-like orchestration.* This design principle reflects on the need to use the framework in combination with other design-time counterparts, such as the AutoSAR framework [2].

**OpenPilot Supports Federated Learning and Onboard Data-Processing Model.** While the main focus of this study was rotating around a study over the core components of the OpenPilot framework—and from the perspective of the ML components, we primarily focused on the ModelD modelling classes and abstractions—the rest of the framework offers multi-sensor and multi-vocal data fusion support and furhter processing. This extended and multidiverse support *promotes the use of the framework as part of onboard embedded data-processing pipelines consistent with edge-computing and therefore with a private-by-design data processing model.* This design principle therefore dictates the way in which the typical processing needs to take place within the intended scope of the OpenPilot framework. This not withstanding, the community itself is considerably active in offering interactive context-awareness support to the framework's own possibilities, such that, for example, the aforementioned pipelines might also interact with sensors available in the context of automotive operation and connectable via Over-The-Air (OTA).

**Community Structure Changes Quality** . Finally, from a community perspective, it should be noted that the community structure and operations were seriously changed when the community around the framework decided to adopt a more continuous CI/CD pipeline structure featuring GitHub actions, specifically, as of Feb. 2021. After such date, the community contributions are subject to rigorous evaluation, scoring, and merging procedures which themselves are, on the one hand a guarantee of the quality behind the framework's code but on the other hand constitute a serious hampering of the community's commit procedures and contribution policy. *This limitation should be taken into account for any study interested not only in using the framework in action but also contributing to or otherwise augmenting the framework itself.*

## 7   Conclusions

Openpilot turned out to be a truly vast and complex software. The aim of this work was to clearly define its framework, by focusing on the relationships that all the different components of which are made work and interact with each other.

The analysis of the packages gives insights on the main classes defined, describing their methods and the relationship with the other classes of the packages, and focusing on the theoretical basis behind the main design choices. Trying to see the big picture of the framework is not an easy task, given its size and the number of modules of which is made, and that is the reason why a bottom-up approach was adopted for what concerns the analysis of the overall structure: analyzing the submodules first allows to have the necessary knowledge to better understand how openpilot leverages them to run its key processes.

We conclude that this work is a first rudimentary stepping stone to approach the problem of Autonomous-Driving Car onboard software engineering.[11]

---

[11] The authors would like to thank Mr. Francesco Fontana for his invaluable help in preparing the materials conveyed in this manuscript.

# References

1. Dajsuren, Y., van den Brand, M.: Automotive software engineering: past, present, and future. In: Automotive Systems and Software Engineering, pp. 3–8. Springer, Cham (2019). https://doi.org/10.1007/978-3-030-12157-0_1
2. AUTOSAR: Guidelines for the use of the C++14 Language in Critical and Safety-related Systems. AUTOSAR, 839 edn. (2017)
3. Bass, L., Clements, P., Kazman, R.: Software Architecture in Practice. SEI series in software engineering, Addison-Wesley (2003)
4. Cipresso, T., Stamp, M.: Software Reverse Engineering. In: Stavroulakis, P., Stamp, M. (eds.) Handbook of Information and Communication Security, pp. 659–696. Springer, Berlin, Heidelberg (2010). https://doi.org/10.1007/978-3-642-04117-4_31
5. Djuric, D., Devedzic, V., Gasevic, D.: Adopting software engineering trends in AI. IEEE Intell. Syst. **22**(1), 59–66 (2007)
6. Krippendorff, K.: Content Analysis: An Introduction to Its Methodology (second edition). Sage Publications (2004)
7. Kruchten, P.: The 4+1 view model of architecture. IEEE Softw. **12**(6), 42–50 (1995)
8. Lee, H.H.S., Clemons, J.: Automotive computing. IEEE Micro. **38**(1), 29–30 (2018), http://dblp.uni-trier.de/db/journals/micro/micro38.html#LeeC18
9. Roca, J.L.: Microelectron. Reliab. **36**(5), 609–620 (1996)
10. Tamburri, D.A., Palomba, F., Kazman, R.: Success and failure in software engineering: a followup systematic literature review. IEEE Trans. Eng. Manage. **68**(2), 599–611 (2021). https://doi.org/10.1109/TEM.2020.2976642
11. Tamburri, D.A., Lago, P., Muccini, H.: Leveraging software architectures through the ISO/IEC 42010 standard: a feasibility study. In: Proper, E., Lankhorst, M.M., Schönherr, M., Barjis, J., Overbeek, S. (eds.) TEAR 2010. LNBIP, vol. 70, pp. 71–85. Springer, Heidelberg (2010). https://doi.org/10.1007/978-3-642-16819-2_6
12. Teddlie, C., Tashakkori, A.: Foundations of Mixed Methods Research?: Integrating Quantitative and Qualitative Approaches in the Social and Behavioral Sciences. SAGE, Los Angeles (2009)
13. Zhou, X., Huang, H., Zhang, H., Huang, X., Shao, D., Zhong, C.: A cross-company ethnographic study on software teams for DevOps and microservices: organization, benefits, and issues. In: 2022 IEEE/ACM 44th International Conference on Software Engineering: Software Engineering in Practice (ICSE-SEIP), pp. 1–10. Association for Computing Machinery, New York (2022)
14. Zimmermann, T.: Card-sorting. In: Menzies, T., Williams, L.A., Zimmermann, T. (eds.) Perspectives on Data Science for Software Engineering, pp. 137–141. Academic Press (2016), http://dblp.uni-trier.de/db/books/collections/MWZ2016.html#000116

# Designing and Evaluating Interoperable Industry 4.0 Middleware Software Architecture: Reconfiguration of Robotic System

Sune Chung Jepsen$^{(\boxtimes)}$ and Torben Worm

University of Southern Denmark, The Mærsk-McKinney Møller Institute,
SDU Software Engineering, Odense, Denmark
{sune,tow}@mmmi.sdu.dk
https://www.sdu.dk/en/forskning/sdusoftwareengineering

**Abstract.** Interoperable middleware is a step towards fulfilling the Industry 4.0 (I4.0) vision to support the reconfiguration of production systems. Therefore examining interoperable middleware software architectures supports the development of flexible I4.0 production systems. This paper aims to design and evaluate an I4.0 middleware software architecture based on a developed interoperability quality attribute scenario (QAS). An industry use case for production reconfiguration is described and used as input to develop a quantifiable interoperability QAS. Production concepts are clarified as background to specify an interoperability QAS. An interoperable middleware software architecture is designed using architectural tactics to meet the QAS. An experiment evaluates the proposed middleware software architecture on actual production equipment. The results show a promising middleware software architecture design that fulfills the specified interoperability QAS.

**Keywords:** Interoperability · Industry 4.0 Middleware Software Architecture · Reconfiguration · Cyber-Physical System

## 1 Introduction and Motivation

Flexible production is a central topic in realizing the Industry 4.0 (I4.0) vision to achieve a more efficient production system supporting, e.g. rapid changeovers between production scenarios [14]. A flexible production system is characterized by possessing the ability to change or react to changes with a low penalty in time, effort, cost, or performance [17]. A change in a production system, e.g. producing a new product or introducing new production equipment, often involves changing the functionality of assets/components [6,15] of the production system, e.g. reprogramming a robot. Changing production functionality requires communication between the components of the production system and therefore also interoperability of the production components. The components of production systems are heterogeneous and reside on different levels (from sensors to

B. Tekinerdogan et al. (Eds.): ECSA 2023, LNCS 14212, pp. 205–220, 2023.
https://doi.org/10.1007/978-3-031-42592-9_14

Enterprise resource planning (ERP)), and therefore middleware is introduced to facilitate the connectivity and interoperability. Connectivity and interoperability requirements are specified with quality attributes (QA). The architecture of the middleware must furthermore support reconfigurability to support the changes in the production functionality.

In this paper, we design and evaluate middleware software architecture to support production reconfiguration in a manufacturing company that produces stainless steel components for the food industry. The work has been part of an industrial collaboration project [5] investigating connectivity and reconfiguration for smart manufacturing in a small and medium-sized enterprise (SME). The manufacturing company has 25 production cells that process many small-batch production orders which involve software reconfiguration.

A production cell typically contains a robotic arm and a computerized numerical control (CNC) machine. The robotic arms can perform different tasks depending on the tools equipped to them, e.g. take a metal item from a pallet and place it inside CNC machine. Furthermore the robot needs a program containing the instructions to perform the task. The programs for the robots and CNC machines are typically stored in a folder on a computer from which it is manually uploaded to the machine or robot via a USB stick, proprietary protocols (e.g. over RS232), or through the robot arm's native embedded interface (teach pendant). Especially the software part is influenced by error-prone, time-consuming, and manual tasks, e.g. finding the correct program in a folder structure on a computer and transferring the program from the computer to the machine. The company is thus a representative candidate to establish a real-world production use case to investigate interoperability requirements for the middleware.

Figure 1 shows the high-level middleware software architecture designed at the university [8]. The middleware provides an infrastructure that supports the connection of production components, e.g. warehouses, autonomous mobile robots, magnetic transport tracks, and production cells, to each other and to high-level business components, e.g. an ERP system, in an I4.0 context.

The work has been part of building up an infrastructure at the university's I4.0 Laboratory (I4.0 Lab) to establish an ecosystem around flexible production in an interdisciplinary collaboration between researchers and industry partners. The I4.0 Lab contains state-of-the-art robotics and automated solutions, and the design and development of the lab and the software has been described and documented in various papers [7,9–13]. The middleware software architecture is designed to facilitate information exchange between production components and to examine QAs such as interoperability [2].

This paper uses an industry use case as a background to establish more knowledge and experience with interoperability requirements for middleware software architectures. The use case is reproduced in the I4.0 Lab to provide a stable environment for experimentation that does not interrupt the actual production. Based on the use case and the setup in the lab this paper evaluates the proposed middleware software architecture design based on a stated QA requirement.

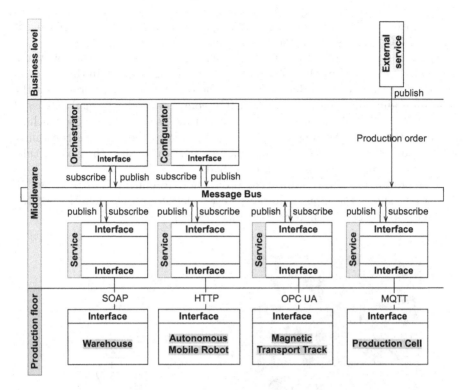

**Fig. 1.** A high-level overview of the designed Industry 4.0 middleware software architecture.

The structure of the paper is as follows. Section 2 outlines the production use case followed by the research question and approach. Section 3 specifies the interoperability quality attribute scenario (QAS) based on the presented use case. Section 4 introduces the middleware software architecture design. Section 5 evaluates the middleware software architecture through an experiment.

## 2   Problem and Approach

In this Section the use case from the company is presented, and based on this the research question is stated followed by the approach taken to answer the research question.

### 2.1   Use Case: Upload Program

The production cell in the use case is an instance of the production cells described earlier containing a robotic arm and a CNC machine. The robotic arm is capable of performing different tasks depending on the tools equipped to it and the program executed by the robot, e.g. taking a metal item pallet and placing it inside a CNC machine for further processing.

When the item produced in the cell is changed, the tools on the robot and the program executed by the robot often need to change as well. In this use case, only the program needs to change because the tools are general purpose for the range of productions handled by the cell. The company produces small batches of items in the cell, and therefore the amount of time used to change the machine setup (in this case, the program) is essential to keep the machine constantly working and the cost at a minimum. In this particular case, the upload time should be low and ideally below three seconds.

The production setup subject to production reconfiguration is shown in Fig. 2a and shows the input material (the wooden crate), the robot, the CNC machine and the output material (the metal rings).

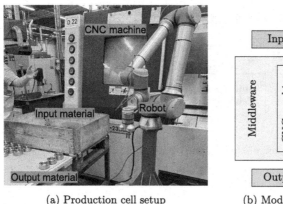
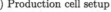
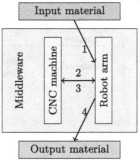

(a) Production cell setup                    (b) Model used in the lab

**Fig. 2.** Production use case.

The machines in the setup are connected through the proposed middleware to support the production. To evaluate the middleware, the company setup is replicated in the I4.0 Lab as illustrated in Fig. 2b where the (re)programming of the robot is the central item being investigated. The numbers indicate the flow of material, and the middleware underlies the CNC machine and the robot and communicates with both. The middleware is deployed on proprietary hardware developed to provide a research setup for the I4.0 demonstrator in the I4.0 Lab. The hardware is a self-contained unit called I4.0-In-A-Box, containing the necessary components to run an I4.0 experiment [10].

## 2.2   Problem

Based on the use case and the identified interoperablity QA, the following research question is stated:

*Is the developed middleware software architecture design able to support the stated production use case and fulfill the QA requirement?*

## 2.3   Approach

A QAS is a general approach [2] to specify architectural requirements for software architectures originally proposed by the Carnegie Mellon Software Engineering Institute (SEI) [3]. The QAS approach has also been applied in the I4.0 domain [1,8].

To answer the research question we therefore use a QAS to specify the architectural requirements to the middleware. Following the specification of the architectural requirements, they serve as input to the design of the architecture for the middleware using suitable tactics for the QAs [2]. The designed middleware is then evaluated in an experiment in the I4.0 Lab. The middleware is evaluated in the lab rather than in the company in order to provide a stable testing environment and to aviod interrupting the production.

# 3   Quality Attribute Scenario

This Section describe the needed concepts to provide a context to understand the specified interoperability QAS.

An asset will be used throughout the description of the QAS. In this context, an asset is referred to anything that needs to be connected to create an I4.0 solution, e.g. machines, sensors, or software [15]. The asset includes an assembly production cell; mobile transportation; in our context, the robot arm is the asset. The robot arm contains a program to execute tasks, e.g. moving a rounded object from one location to another. A program in this context is referred to as capability. We define capability as:

**Definition 1. (Capability).** A capability is a set of functions invoked in a particular order.

As an example for the robot arm, a program (e.g. robot script) with functions is made available through an interface to invoke externally and execute the capability. Therefore, uploading a new program means changing the capability, e.g. moving a rounded object to moving a squared object. Likewise, if the upload functionality can be invoked in a particular sequence, then it also classifies as a capability offered by the robot arm, which is the case in this context. The upload communication to an asset is an important step in a reconfiguration process [11] where the middleware needs to handle communication between production components to handle changes efficiently, e.g. a new production order.

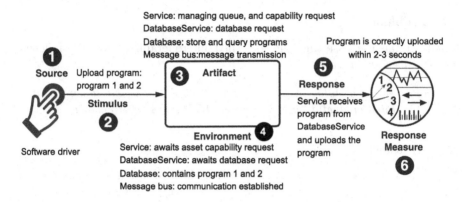

**Fig. 3.** Excerpt of the interoperability quality attribute scenario.

The QAS contains six parts to specify the interoperability requirement, i.e. source, artifact, environment, response, and response measure [2], as seen in Fig. 3. The source initiates the stimulus to the artifact under some environmental conditions. The response is the activity that occurs to handle the stimulus, and the response measure is the measurable part of the scenario such that the requirement can be tested to determine whether the requirement is achieved. Figure 3 gives a short overview of the QAS, and Table 1 provides full details of the scenario. The software driver initiates that a new program needs to be uploaded to the robot arm. The source is a business application such as an ERP system that initiates stimulus, which is the change of program. The stimulus will alternate between two programs to demonstrate the interoperability, i.e. the upload of the program and acknowledgment of successful upload. The programs represent a small, realistic robotic script of size 971 bytes, which moves the robot arm from one location to another. The artifact represents the Service, DatabaseService, Database, and Message bus components in the middleware, which need to interoperate to accomplish the upload. The Service is responsible for managing the capability request queue and invoking capability requests on the asset, whereas the DatabaseService handles requests to the Database. The environment specifies the conditions for the interoperating components. The conditions are that the Service and Database await request, the Database contains the two programs, and the communication between the components is established. The response details how the stimulus is handled. The Service requests the DatabaseService, which queries the Database and returns the program to the Service, which uploads the program to the asset. The response measure is the measurable goal for the requirement. In this case, the interaction process should take less than 2–3 s before the program is correctly uploaded. Correctly in this context, means acknowledging whether the program is uploaded at the correct location on the robot arm system.

**Table 1.** Interoperability quality attribute scenario.

| Portion of scenario | Values |
|---|---|
| Source | A software driver, i.e. an application that mimics the part of a business system responsible for issuing capability change of the asset. |
| Stimulus | The software driver switches between program 1 and program 2 of size 971 bytes each, which must be uploaded to the asset. |
| Artifact | Integrating components<br>– *Service*<br>  • Responsible for handling capability requests, managing queue in terms of adding or removing capability requests, and responding to information requests<br>  • Responsible for requesting a program from a database via the message bus, deserializing the program and uploading the program to the asset.<br>– *DatabaseService*   : Responsible for handling requests for files, i.e. interacting with a database, extracting the requested file and returning the requested file via the message bus.<br>– *Database*  : Responsible for storing and querying data, e.g. programs.<br>Coordinating component:<br>– *Message bus*   : Responsible for message transmission between the Service and DatabaseService. |
| Environment | – *Service*  : Awaits capability requests<br>– *DatabaseService*    : Awaits request for querying database<br>– *Database*  : Contains program 1 and 2<br>– *Message bus*   : The communication between components is established, and messages are transmitted. |
| Response | Service:<br>– The Service receives a capability request from the message bus, stating that a program must be uploaded to the asset<br>– The Service sends a message to the message bus, requesting the required file defining the program<br>DatabaseService:<br>– The DatabaseService receives the file request, stating the requested file.<br>– The DatabaseService extracts the requested file from a connected database<br>– The DatabaseService sends a message to the message bus, containing the file in a serialized format.<br>Service:<br>– The Service receives the file from the message bus, containing the file in a serialized format<br>– The Service deserializes the file into the format required by the asset and thus converts it to a program.<br>– The Service uploads the program to the asset<br>– The Service ensures that the program has been uploaded by checking the existence of the program in the requested file listing |
| Response Measure | Success criteria uploading a program<br>– It should take less than 2-3 seconds for the process (response) to upload the required program to the asset correctly. |

# 4   Middleware Software Architecture Design

This Section describes the Service and DatabaseService design using module views [4] and used tactics that aims to archieve the stated QAS.

## 4.1   Design

The Service contains three primary responsibilities: 1) communication with the Message bus, 2) handling the queue for incoming requests, and 3) communication with an asset. Figure 4 shows the Service module view containing the abovementioned responsibilities through the abstractions IBusClient, IExecutionHandler, and the IAssetClient. Abstractions are generally favored to accomplish a modifiable and scalable architecture to support new messages busses, assets, databases etc.

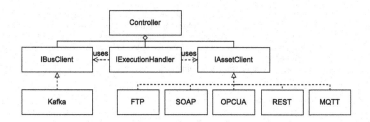

**Fig. 4.** Module view of the Service architecture.

The IBusClient provides the communication layer between middleware components. The concrete Message bus implementation is a Kafka message bus [18] which, among others, provides publish-subscribe functionality through topics. The IBusClient implementation is used on all components that need communication with Kafka making it easy to manage changes across components.

The IAssetClient provides a client communcation with the concrete asset. In this case, the FTP client will provide upload functionality to the robot arm. The Service supports communication protocols with different assets, as seen in Fig. 1, which includes SOAP, OPC UA, REST, and MQTT protocols. The IExecutionHandler is the glue between the IBusClient and IAssetClient that handles incoming requests from the IBusClient and requests to the IAssetClient. The IExecutionHandler contains a queue from which it manages the requests to the IAssetClient. The Controller has two main responsibilities: 1) initialization of IBusClient, IExecutionHandler, IAssetClient dependencies based on configurations, and 2) handling incoming messages. The incoming messages from Kafka are sent to the IExecutionHandler.

The DatabaseService contains three main responsibilities: 1) communication with Kafka, 2) database creation, and 3) database client. Figure 5 shows the DatabaseService module view containing the abovementioned responsibilities through the abstractions IBusClient (contains the same responsibility as explained above), IDatabaseClientCreator, and the IDatabaseClient.

The IDatabaseClientCreator is responsible for creating a concrete database instance based on provided configurations (e.g. username, password, port). The database will be returned to the Controller as an IDatabaseClient. The IDatabaseClient contains responsibilities for querying and inserting into the

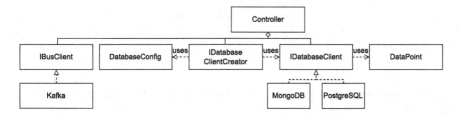

**Fig. 5.** Module view of the DatabaseService architecture.

database. The IDatabaseClient uses DataPoint as an abstraction to return data and insert data into the database uniformly across different database technologies. All messages sent between components internally in the middleware use a JSON structure. Data values like configurations and programs are part of the JSON structure. MongoDB is one example of a document database with good support for saving JSON structures, making it a reasonable choice for saving needed JSON data. The PostgreSQL database is an example of a relational database instance used in another context for time series data. The Controller has two primary responsibilities: 1) initialization of IBusClient, IDatabaseClientCreator, and IDatabaseClient dependencies based on configurations, and 2) handling incoming messages. The incoming messages from Kafka are sent to the IDatabaseClient.

## 4.2 Tactics

The tactics employed in the design are chosen based on handling communication with the robot arm and efficient communication between the Service and DatabaseService to impact the total time for the uploading process stated in the response measure in the QAS.

The encapsulation tactic [2], i.e. define an explicit interface, is used to vary between 1) communication upload, e.g. to change functionality on the robot, and 2) communication to invoke a physical task on the robot. The defined interface allows for different implementations to support the two mentioned types of communications. The encapsulation is realized through the IAssetClient interface shown in Fig. 6.

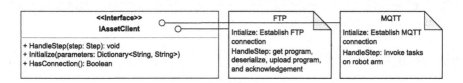

**Fig. 6.** Encapsulation tactic.

The interface's purpose is to handle different states, i.e. change functionality (e.g. upload a new program) and invoke a physical task (e.g. assembly task) on the robot arm. The FTP class is an implementation of the change functionality, which gets the program from the database, and handles the deserialization of the program to a file format that the robot arm can interpret. Next, the file is uploaded, and confirmed that it resides on the robot. In contrast, the MQTT class implements the execution communication of tasks on the robot arm.

The communication (i.e. upload process) between the Service and the robot arm is a step in a reconfiguration process [11] where each step must be efficiently handled by the middleware. Consequently, it does not matter whether the necessary reconfiguration functionality is achieved if the reconfiguration does not occur at the right time. Therefore the second tactic employed is the increase efficiency [2] tactic focusing on "tuning up" how components communicate. The focus is to achieve efficient communication between the Service and DatabaseService to lower the uploading process time to reduce the total reconfiguration time. The increase efficiency is realized through the publish-subscribe pattern [2] shown in Fig. 7.

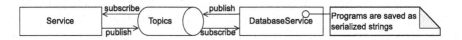

**Fig. 7.** Increase efficiency tactic.

The Service and DatabaseService communicate through a publish-subscribe pattern through topics [18]. The Service publishes a request for a program through a topic to which the DatabaseService subscribes, and DatabaseService publishes the program back through a topic to which the Service subscribes. The publish-subscribe pattern increases efficiency by providing instant event notifications that reduce potential Service idle time between fetching the program from the DatabaseService and upload functionality.

## 5   Evaluation

This Section describes the evaluation of the middleware based on the stated QAS. It includes the experiment design, measurements of the QAS response measures, pilot testing, and an analysis of the result.

### 5.1   Design

The middleware is deployed to the I4.0-In-A-Box, which contains four Raspberry Pi's and a router. Figure 8 shows the allocation view of the middleware mapped to the hardware in the I4.0-In-A-Box.

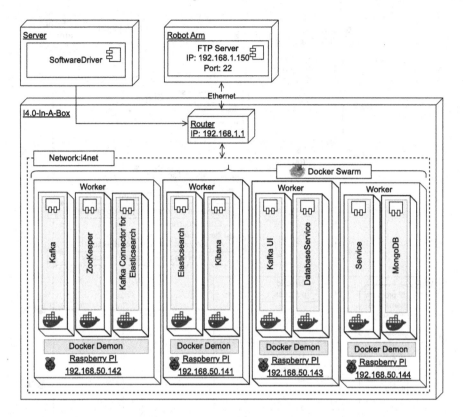

**Fig. 8.** Allocation view of the middleware software.

The box contains its own network to support separations of networks in a production environment, e.g. information technologies and operation technologies [16]. The software is deployed using Docker container technology to package and deploy the software and its dependencies easily. Docker Swarm is used as a lightweight orchestration software tool to distribute the load of the deployed components between the Raspberry Pi's. Elasticsearch and Kibana are technologies used to save and visualize logs from the middleware components. The ZooKeeper software is used to maintain and configure Kafka, whereas Kafka UI is used to monitor Kafka. The middleware communicates with the FTP server to the robot arm connected with Ethernet to the router. The SoftwareDriver is deployed on an external server and is responsible for initiating upload requests to the middleware for uploading a program, i.e. alternate between uploading program 1 and program 2. The idea of alternating between two programs is to demonstrate that a new program is uploaded. Running multiple repetitions also means the same program filename is uploaded. Therefore, a unique file name (representing program 1 or program 2) is used for each repetition to ensure acknowledgment that a new program is uploaded rather than being overridden or not uploaded due to an error.

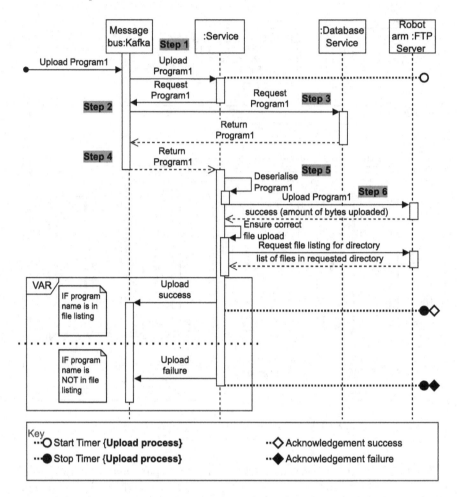

**Fig. 9.** Measurements for the uploading process.

## 5.2 Measurements, Pilot Test, and Analysis

*Measurements.* Measurements are taken to log that programs are correctly uploaded according to the stated QAS in Table reftab:qas. The sequence diagram in Fig. 9 illustrates the interacting components from Sect. 4 and the measurements indicated by the open circle/filled circle and open diamond/filled diamond. The red steps are used as a referable part of the sequence, which will be used later in the analysis. An upload program message is initially sent to the Service through Kafka. The Service requests the DatabaseService for the program, which it receives in a serialized format. The Service deserializes the program and uploads the program to the FTP Server, and checks whether the program is located in the correct folder on the FTP server by doing a filename lookup in the FTP server directory. The first measure is the upload process time (open and closed circle), and the second measure checks that the program is uploaded correctly (open and closed diamond). All the measurements are saved in Elasticsearch.

***Pilot Test.*** A pilot test of 10 replication was conducted to get familiar with running the middleware software on the physical equipment. The pilot test also determined the number of replications in the evaluation, establishing the validity of the results, i.e. how close the parameter is to the true parameter. Therefore a hypothesis t-test was performed to compute the validity of the number of replications in the evaluation. In the pilot test, the standard deviation was computed to 494.817 milliseconds (ms). For the scope of this experiment, it is fair to have a precision of +-300 ms (one order of magnitude) where the uploading process goal is 2-3 s.

**Listing 1.1.** R code for computing sample size

```
1  power.t.test(delta = 300, type = "one.sample",
2  alternative = "one.sided", sd= 494.817, sig.level = 0.05,
3  power=0.9)
```

**Table 2.** Acknowledgement of program exchange, timeformat hh.mm.ss.ms.

| ID | Start time | End time | Ack. | ID | Start time | End time | Ack. |
|---|---|---|---|---|---|---|---|
| 1 | 16.50.03.296 | 16.50.03.850 | Success | 14 | 16.50.10.708 | 16.50.11.259 | Success |
| 2 | 16.50.03.852 | 16.50.04.412 | Success | 15 | 16.50.11.259 | 16.50.11.804 | Success |
| 3 | 16.50.04.414 | 16.50.04.978 | Success | 16 | 16.50.11.805 | 16.50.12.346 | Success |
| 4 | 16.50.04.979 | 16.50.05.539 | Success | 17 | 16.50.12.348 | 16.50.12.893 | Success |
| 5 | 16.50.05.540 | 16.50.06.101 | Success | 18 | 16.50.12.894 | 16.50.13.457 | Success |
| 6 | 16.50.06.102 | 16.50.06.655 | Success | 19 | 16.50.13.458 | 16.50.14.024 | Success |
| 7 | 16.50.06.656 | 16.50.07.194 | Success | 20 | 16.50.14.025 | 16.50.14.569 | Success |
| 8 | 16.50.07.195 | 16.50.07.740 | Success | 21 | 16.50.14.569 | 16.50.15.102 | Success |
| 9 | 16.50.07.741 | 16.50.08.284 | Success | 22 | 16.50.15.103 | 16.50.15.637 | Success |
| 10 | 16.50.08.285 | 16.50.09.069 | Success | 23 | 16.50.15.637 | 16.50.16.182 | Success |
| 11 | 16.50.09.070 | 16.50.09.611 | Success | 24 | 16.50.16.183 | 16.50.16.728 | Success |
| 12 | 16.50.09.612 | 16.50.10.157 | Success | 25 | 16.50.16.728 | 16.50.17.277 | Success |
| 13 | 16.50.10.157 | 16.50.10.708 | Success | | | | |

The standard deviation of 494.817 ms and the delta of 300 ms is inserted into the formula shown in Listing 1.1, resulting in 25 replications. The result means running 25 replications gives a precision of +-300 ms of the true uploading process time.

***Analysis.*** After the experiment was conducted and the measurements were collected, the results could be analyzed, i.e. data supporting the correct upload in Table 2 and the uploading process time in Fig. 10.

Table 2 shows the 25 program uploads, i.e. program1, program2, program3 etc.; start and end time; and the acknowledgement of the program upload. As the Table 2 shows all programs are uploaded successfully and no errors where discovered during the experiment.

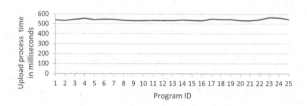

**Fig. 10.** Upload process time.

Figure 10 shows the upload program process time for the 25 uploads. There is a stable tendency, which was expected because, in principle, the two same programs get uploaded, and no complex computation is involved. The average upload process time is 542 ms, where approximately 504 ms are caused by Kafka batching messages. A pattern found in the data logs shows that Kafka uses 504 ms before the message are transferred from the DatabaseService and retrieved by the Service (step 4 in Fig. 9).

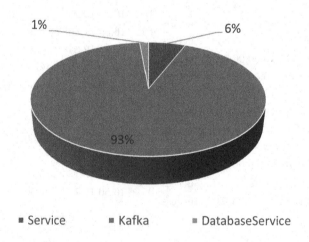

**Fig. 11.** Upload process distribution time.

Figure 11 shows a pie chart of the upload process time distributed on the Service, Kafka, and DatabaseService. The DatabaseService takes 1% of the time to query the database (step 3 in Fig. 9). The Service takes 6% of the time, where approximately 4% is used to prepare program upload (step 1 + 5 in Fig. 9), and

2% is used on FTP upload and acknowledgment (step 6 in Fig. 9). The encapsulation tactic has supported increased interoperability by having different implementations of an interface to support different interactions and exchange types of information. The increase efficiency tactic has been beneficial in minimizing potentially unsuccessful pull requests from the Service to the DatabaseService, thereby lowering wasted processing time.

From the results, the configuration and batching of messages in Kafka could be further optimized to improve the transmission of messages. However, the overall requirement of 2-3 s to upload programs correctly is successfully acknowledged and achieved with an average of 542 ms.

## 6  Conclusion

In this experience paper, a middleware software architecture has been designed and evaluated according to the stated interoperability QAS. The middleware components and component interactions have been examined and documented through architectural views, diagrams, and tactics to unfold the design of a middleware architectural structure. The results show that the middleware software architecture design meets the QAS requirements, and therefore we conclude that the middleware software architecture is one solution that contains the architectural structures to support production reconfiguration. It also means that the middleware is a starting point for analyzing reconfigurable middleware software architectures as well as reconfiguring the physical equipment in a production system. The scope of this middleware evaluation has been limited to the needs described in the use case. However, the setup supports that experiments can be conducted involving many more dimensions, e.g. varying the size of pay-loads (programs), the bandwidth of communication protocols, and physical limitations such as cables etc.

**Acknowledgements.** We would like to thank the SDU Industry 4.0 Initiative and DigitalLead [5] for financial support, and SDU Robotics, and SDU Industry 4.0 Laboratory for valuable discussions.

## References

1. Antonino, P.O., Schnicke, F., Zhang, Z., Kuhn, T.: Blueprints for architecture drivers and architecture solutions for industry 4.0 shopfloor applications. In: Proceedings of the 13th European Conference on Software Architecture - Volume 2, pp. 261–268. ECSA 2019, Association for Computing Machinery, New York, NY, USA (2019). https://doi.org/10.1145/3344948.3344971
2. Bass, L., Clements, P., Kazman, R.: Software Architecture in Practice. Addison-Wesley Professional, Boston, Massachusetts, USA (2012)
3. Bass, L., Klein, M., Bachmann, F.: Quality attribute design primitives. Tech. rep., CMU/SEI-2000-TN-017, Software Engineering Institute, Carnegie Mellon University, Pittsburgh, PA (2000). http://resources.sei.cmu.edu/library/asset-view.cfm?AssetID=5139

4. Clements, P., et al.: Documenting Software Architectures: Views and Beyond. Addison-Wesley (2002)
5. DigitalLead: Connectivity og rekonfiguration i industri 4.0 (2022). https://digitallead.dk/innovation/projekter/connectivity-og-rekonfiguration-i-industri-4-0/. Accessed 23 Jan 2023
6. Groover, M.P.: Automation, Production Systems, and Computer-Integrated Manufacturing, Fourth edn. Pearson (2015)
7. Jepsen, S.C., Mørk, T.I., Hviid, J., Worm, T.: A pilot study of industry 4.0 asset interoperability challenges in an industry 4.0 laboratory. In: 2020 IEEE International Conference on Industrial Engineering and Engineering Management (IEEM), pp. 571–575. IEEE, Singapore (2020). https://doi.org/10.1109/IEEM45057.2020.9309952
8. Jepsen, S.C., Siewertsen, B., Worm, T.: A reconfigurable industry 4.0 middleware software architecture. In: 2023 IEEE 20th International Conference on Software Architecture Companion (ICSA-C), pp. 1–11 (2023). https://doi.org/10.1109/ICSA-C57050.2023.00023
9. Jepsen, S.C., Worm, T., Christensen, H.B., Hviid, J., Sandig, L.M.: Experience report: a systematic process for gathering quality attribute requirements for industry 4.0 middleware. In: 2021 IEEE 25th International Enterprise Distributed Object Computing Workshop (EDOCW), pp. 166–175. IEEE, Gold Coast (2021). https://doi.org/10.1109/EDOCW52865.2021.00046
10. Jepsen, S.C., et al.: A research setup demonstrating flexible industry 4.0 production. In: 2021 International Symposium ELMAR, pp. 143–150. IEEE, Zadar (2021). https://doi.org/10.1109/ELMAR52657.2021.9550961
11. Jepsen, S.C., Worm, T., Kang, E.: Reconfigurability for industry 4.0 middleware software architectures. In: 2022 International Conference on Omni-layer Intelligent Systems (COINS) (2022)
12. Jepsen, S.C., Worm, T., Mørk, T.I., Hviid, J.: An analysis of asset interoperability for i4.0 middleware. In: Proceedings of the 36th Annual ACM Symposium on Applied Computing, pp. 707–710. SAC 2021, Association for Computing Machinery, New York (2021). https://doi.org/10.1145/3412841.3442094
13. Jepsen, S.C., Worm, T., Mørk, T.I., Hviid, J.: Industry 4.0 middleware software architecture interoperability analysis. In: 2021 IEEE/ACM 3rd International Workshop on Software Engineering Research and Practices for the IoT (SERP4IoT), pp. 32–35. IEEE, Madrid (2021). https://doi.org/10.1109/SERP4IoT52556.2021.00012
14. Plattform industrie 4.0: the asset administration shell: implementing digital twins for use in industrie 4.0 (2019). https://www.plattform-i40.de/IP/Redaktion/EN/Downloads/Publikation/VWSiD%20V2.0.html. Accessed 23 Dec 2020
15. Plattform industrie 4.0: the asset administration shell: implementing digital twins for use in industrie 4.0 (2019). https://www.plattform-i40.de/PI40/Redaktion/EN/Downloads/Publikation/VWSiD%20V2.0.html. Accessed 23 Dec 2020
16. Saturno, M., Pertel, V.M., Deschamps, F., Loures, E.F.R.: Proposal for new automation architecture solutions for industry 4.0. Logforum 14(2), 185–195 (2018). https://doi.org/10.17270/J.LOG.266
17. Terkaj, W., Tolio, T., Valente, A.: A review on manufacturing flexibility. In: Tolio, T. (eds.) Design of Flexible Production Systems. Springer, Berlin, Heidelberg (2009). https://doi.org/10.1007/978-3-540-85414-2_3
18. Thein, K.M.M.: Apache kafka: next generation distributed messaging system. Int. J. Sci. Eng. Technol. Res. 3(47), 9478–9483 (2014)

# Shaping *IoT* Systems *Together*: The User-System Mixed-Initiative Paradigm and Its Challenges

Romina Spalazzese[1,2](✉) ⓘ, Martina De Sanctis[3] ⓘ, Fahed Alkhabbas[1,2] ⓘ, and Paul Davidsson[1,2] ⓘ

[1] Department of Computer Science and Media Technology, Malmö University, Malmö, Sweden
{romina.spalazzese,fahed.alkhabbas,paul.davidsson}@mau.se
[2] Internet of Things and People Research Centre, Malmö University, Malmö, Sweden
[3] Gran Sasso Science Institute (GSSI), L'Aquila, Italy
martina.desanctis@gssi.it

**Abstract.** Internet of Things (IoT) systems are often complex and have to deal with many challenges at the same time, both from a human and technical perspective. In this vision paper, we (i) describe *IoT-Together*, the Mixed-initiative Paradigm that we devise for IoT user-system collaboration and (ii) critically analyze related architectural challenges.

**Keywords:** Mixed-initiative paradigm · User-System Collaboration · Intelligent IoT Systems · Novel Experiences · Goal-driven IoT Systems

## 1 Introduction

Internet of Things (IoT) systems are complex and this implies dealing with many challenges at the same time. For instance, the IoT ecosystem of a Smart City is characterized by IoT, automation, connectivity, and comprises people and multiple application areas, e.g., Smart Environment, Smart Health, Smart Mobility, Smart Living. The IoT is a cross-cutting dimension and, if exploited at the best, can enable novel and powerful experiences for users. Indoor and outdoor city spaces are equipped with IoT sensors, actuators, and devices. Examples are points of interests, like monuments and museums, equipped with, e.g., presence sensors, cameras, Augmented Reality headsets, displays, supporting interactive exhibitions [1], green houses and botanical gardens equipped with IoT technologies for planting and monitoring, supporting participation and learning. Some IoT devices in the smart city are spread all around, e.g., weather, pollution and presence sensors, while others are only in main locations, e.g., interactive screens in main stations. In this settings, an example of *novel experience* is "create and visit your botanical garden through mixed-reality", where the user interacts with the IoT devices and system at the city botanical garden.

From a technical perspective, IoT systems include different dimensions of heterogeneity, quality, and dynamicity, may show diverse faults and errors, and

B. Tekinerdogan et al. (Eds.): ECSA 2023, LNCS 14212, pp. 221–229, 2023.
https://doi.org/10.1007/978-3-031-42592-9_15

often involve humans. From a human perspective (e.g., users and software architects), IoT systems may range from known to unknown, from fully specified to underspecified [2]. In the case of more unknown, underspecified, and dynamic IoT systems as well as user needs and preferences, users should be able to find out in easy ways, in conversation with intelligent IoT systems, what are suitable possibilities for them to achieve their current needs according to their preferences. At the same time, intelligent IoT systems should be able to gain more knowledge about the users to better support them in this process of serving them with novel experiences. To address this in the best way possible, i.e., without overwhelming the user or proposing low relevant possibilities, IoT user and system should shape together the most suitable intelligent IoT system.

This is in line with the *Mixed-Initiative Interaction* (MII), identified as a key missing link between Artificial Intelligence (AI) and Human-Computer Interaction (HCI) [3,4]. MII refers to a flexible interaction strategy among both humans or computer agents, each contributing what they do best to solve problems or perform tasks. Nevertheless, the MII idea was described around two decades ago, it has been mainly investigated in the HCI area with a major focus on user interfaces, and in the AI area, e.g., to inform the design of human-robot systems [5]. Existing solutions (technologies and research) within Recommender Systems, AI Planning and Goal-driven are not sufficient as they are, since the (intelligent) IoT systems we focus on are at their overlap and require additional efforts and different solutions to provide the expected novel enhanced experiences.

In this vision paper, we (i) describe *IoT-Together*, a Mixed-initiative Paradigm for IoT user-system collaboration (Sect. 3), and (ii) critically analyze related architectural challenges (Sect. 4). The mixed-initiative paradigm aims at filling the gap between intelligent IoT systems and users that need, and are willing, to work in partnership to shape suitable shared (intelligent) IoT systems. With **intelligent IoT systems** we mean that, through the collaboration, they try to: understand and learn user goals and preferences; present the most suitable interfaces and experiences to the users; adjust where needed. As a contribution example, we provide a Smart City Scenario (Sect. 3) to support illustrating the type of targeted systems, the paradigm, and challenges.

## 2    Related Works

To engineer *goal-driven self-adaptive IoT systems*, several approaches have been developed to support users to achieve their goals seamlessly in arbitrary, dynamic, and uncertain IoT environments. Mayer et al. [6] make use of a user interface to configure ambient settings. Rahimi et al. [7] proposed an agent-based approach exploiting reinforcement learning to learn users' behaviours. Alkhabbas et al. [8] exploited Emergent Configurations to dynamically form, enact, adapt goal-driven IoT systems. De Sanctis et al. [9] proposed a multi-level self-adaptive approach supporting users to define run-time goals. Abughazala et al. [10] use agent-based social simulation. To cope with dynamic and unknown IoT settings and to avoid overwhelming users, IoT systems' interfaces should be intelligent [11,12]. *Intelligent User Interfaces* (IUI) provide the ability to perform adaptations to improve users' Quality of Experience (QoE). Existing approaches consider multiple factors e.g., user goals, context, emotions, behaviours, and accessibility needs [13]. To this aim, different techniques can be exploited, e.g., machine learning [14], model-driven engineering [15], and digital twins [16]. Shim et al. [17] identified the categories of concerns to consider when engineering *human-centered IoT systems* for interaction. Geetha et al. [18] surveyed Human-centered IoT applications and demonstrated multiple scenarios. In [19], authors proposed an architectural approach for automating users' environments based on the context (e.g., users' activities) and users' preferences. Users get recommendations about the services achievable in their environments. Mäkitalo et al. [20] proposed collaborative co-located interactions through social devices, where both people and (mobile) devices with physical proximity can start interactions proactively.

To summarize, the majority of existing approaches do not fully support users to benefit from the IoT in *uncertain* situations, e.g., where the user needs are underspecified and IoT environments are dynamic and possibly not fully known.

## 3   Smart City Scenario and *IoT-Together* Paradigm

**Scenario.** Consider a tourist that arrives in a city with no precise plans. At the central station, she starts interacting with a totem. The totem has access and can interact with any public IoT device and service in the city (e.g., to get info about crowdedness and queues at public places, hospitals, museums, timetables and current position of buses, air quality), to provide users with novel enhanced experiences through (intelligent) systems based on their needs and preferences. The system software (on the totem -possibly other devices and the Cloud) can run in any smart city's application domain. The user may find herself in an *unplanned, volatile situation*, and she might not have fully clear activities and objective in mind. The *system* needs to know something about the user (e.g., interests, preferences), for finding a subset of appropriate options to show her. A *user-system collaboration* is required, so that both user and system start disclosing something about their *needs* and *knowledge*, respectively.

To support the user identifying interesting activities, the system can ask input to the user or take it from the shared user data through her devices. This allows the system to *prune/build* the solution space, to understand the user's goal that would be very difficult if not impossible otherwise -given the enormous amount of possible options in a smart city. Exchanged information can be how much time she has, by which means she is willing to move, her current interests and preferences. If her interests include, e.g., gardening, art, and food, and she wants to walk, prefers quite places, and has 3 h of time, multiple options of *enhanced experiences* are possible, e.g.: "IoT gardening: grow a flower with IoT tech at the botanical garden", "Interactive exhibition: the music, lights, and art installations experience". Table 1 lists some examples of IoT settings. However, the system excludes (x) the park in the suburbs, the cathedral and the city green house, according to the sensors data. The food truck area, quite at the

**Table 1.** Some places, installed sensors, and their provided data related to enhanced experiences.

| Place | Installed Sensors (current data) | System's selection | User's selection |
|---|---|---|---|
| Park in the suburbs | weather sensors (a storm is coming) | x | |
| Botanical garden | presence sensor (normal), IoT tech for plantation e.g., smart soil, moisture, nutrient sensors (normal) | | ✓ |
| City green house | presence sensor (crowded) | x | |
| Cathedral | presence sensor (queue), smart-screens | x | |
| Modern art museum | presence sensor (normal), hololens, smart-screens, eye-tracking | | ✓ |
| Food trucks area | cameras (lively in a while), noise sensor (good) | ~ | ~ |

moment, it seems will become lively. It can be checked again later on ($\sim$). Only the most feasible alternatives (and combinations of them) are suggested based on their estimated duration, i.e., the remaining ones. The user selects the botanical garden and the modern art museum ($\checkmark$), and she books them on the totem's screen. At the garden, the user attends an interactive workshop experiencing the planting and growing of flowers, by leveraging IoT devices e.g., to check the terrain status, water temperature, presence of nutrients, and cameras to monitor her flowers on her smartphone in the next days. At the modern art museum she decides for an interactive exhibition with the given devices. When the visit to the museum is going to finish, the suitability to go to the food trucks area is computed by verifying if the user's preferences (e.g., quietness of the place) are still accomplished.

**The *IoT-Together* Paradigm.** Fig. 1 provides a logical view of the mixed-initiative paradigm. *IoT Environment* includes (intelligent) things, i.e., IoT devices, sensors, and actuators, that expose their atomic and more complex capabilities, *IoT Environment Capabilities*, e.g., turn on the light, set up interactive exhibition. *Users* use IoT environment capabilities to accomplish their *User Goals* that can be not fully specified (e.g., find interesting smart city activities for three hours) and considering their preferences (e.g., the user wishes to walk). The *IoT-Together core platform* is key (software) to realize the mixed-initiative paradigm. It supports the synergistic collaboration between IoT Environments and Users to shape/co-generate (intelligent) IoT systems, including both hardware and software, that support users to reach their goals, given the available capabilities in the IoT environments. Within the paradigm, there is an *Initial Interaction Point* (e.g., the totem or the user's smartphone) where at least the initial user-system interaction takes place. The shown options could be based

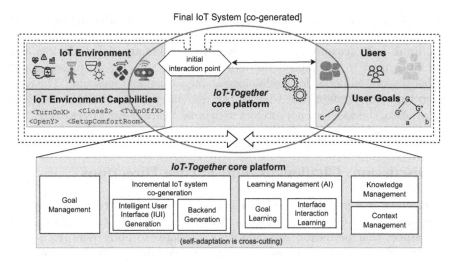

**Fig. 1.** Logical view of the mixed-initiative paradigm.

e.g., on past learned interactions, goals, preferences/profile from both her and others. The *IoT-Together* core platform has the following responsibilities.

(i) *Goal Management* that concerns reasoning about users' goals (e.g., find interesting smart city activities for three hours) and their sub-goals (e.g., the interactive exhibition experience at the museum) that need to be achieved in order to achieve the goals. Ontologies, natural language processing, and goal models can be used to achieve this responsibility; (ii) *Incremental IoT system co-generation* for enabling the interaction-driven co-generation of IoT systems. This involves the incremental and dynamic generation and adaptation of systems' backends and intelligent user interfaces considering multiple aspects, including the degree of knowledge of users' goals and preferences, context (e.g., users' activities), and the capabilities of the systems (i.e., devices and applications). Multi-Agent Systems, AI planning, feedback loops, low-code platforms, and machine learning could be exploited to realize this responsibility; (iii) *Learning Management* including *Goal Learning (GL)* and *Interface Interaction Learning (IIL)*. The GL concerns learning the goals in the interest of users within specific context (e.g., time, user activity, location). Transfer learning could be applied between the user's smartphone and totem to support the platform recommending relevant activities to the user. The IIL revolves around learning users' interaction style (e.g., their ability to use technology) e.g., through reinforcement learning; (iv) *Context Management* concerns collecting and analyzing contextual information (that may be uncertain) about the environment (e.g., the estimated number of people in the cathedral), the proposed IoT systems, and the user. To achieve this, micro-services technologies could be used; (v) *Knowledge Management* concerns maintaining the knowledge retrieved by analyzing the collected contextual information (e.g., the current quietness level of the food trucks area) through technologies such as (non-)relational databases or ontologies. Lastly,

*Self-adaptation* is a cross-cutting aspect w.r.t. (i), ... (v) and is included in all of them.

A **final IoT system** will be co-generated, including all IoT devices and capabilities used to accomplish the user's goal (e.g., the totem, presence and weather sensors, cameras, IoT technology at the garden and museum). The final system can evolve/adapt, e.g., due to the user interaction, evolving goal and context. Also, the user may not interact with or be aware of every device (e.g., the presence sensor at the cathedral).

## 4    Discussion, Challenges, and Future Directions

*IoT-Together* is a paradigm characterized by a *human perspective* (e.g., users and software architects) and a *system perspective*. The *degree of (un)known* is a key aspect that permeates the paradigm: it relates to both users (e.g., they move around, their goals and preferences may not be fully specified) and systems (e.g., they may be brand new market products or users may be unfamiliar with their capabilities). Another dimension is the *size of physical* or *logical boundaries*, that can range from *small*, e.g., a hotel room or an open space office, to *big* like a whole smart city. This is shown in Fig. 2, where we also highlight four main challenge areas (discussed below) in relation to *IoT-Together*. The four areas are in addition to the well-known IoT challenges, e.g., interoperability, scalability, security, privacy, trust, energy efficiency. The Y-axis in Fig. 2 shows that the challenges can be looked upon from either the user or the IoT system perspectives.

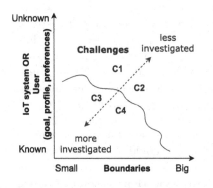

**Fig. 2.** *IoT-Together* Core Challenges.

**C1 - User Interface, Goal, and Preferences.** By critically reflecting upon *IoT-Together*, we identify *correlations* between boundaries, user/IoT system (un)known, and challenges. In smaller and more known IoT settings, the IoT devices and their capabilities are more known to users. Consequently, their goals are often more known too. An example is when a researcher arrives into a shared work-space she has never visited before and needs to set up a meeting on-the-fly. This setting, among all, seems the one with more manageable challenges, i.e., the user goal is clear, and is reasonable to assume that preferences about configurations setting are known or easy to be known, e.g., through an explicit request. Thus, it should be possible to build and show to the user intelligent user interfaces with a reasonable technical effort, by using e.g., goal-driven and IUI approaches mentioned in Sect. 2.

In a setting where boundaries are bigger, instead, and IoT devices and their capabilities are more unknown to users, also their needs and preferences are usually more open/underspecified. An example is the whole smart city scenario where the researcher has not been before and there are potentially nearly infinite devices, capabilities and opportunities for new enhaced experiences. (However, users' needs and preferences can be more open/underspecified also in more known and smaller IoT settings. An example could be if the researcher needs to do a check and use smart health services at the unknown city hospital.)

In the bigger and more unknown setting, the challenges for the generation of intelligent IoT systems revolve around both user goal, preferences and interface; and both the user and the IoT system should interact and incrementally co-generate intelligent IoT systems. From an *architectural perspective*, the paradigm should be engineered to meet both Quality of Service (QoS) (e.g., security, interoperability, scalability) and user's QoE. If either of the qualities decreases (e.g., the systems' performance degrades or the UI feels not easy to a user), the architecture of the running (final) IoT system needs to self-adapt to improve the qualities. For instance, more computational resources could be dynamically allocated to improve the IoT system's performance, or the final IoT system could be adapted by changing the interaction mode to voice.

**C2 - Explainability.** To identify a meaningful and useful IoT system, explainability is a core challenge to be addressed as part of the mixed-initiative interactions. During the user-system collaboration, the system needs to *understand* to some extent (part of) the user goal and preferences. While supporting users to better identify how to satisfy their current needs and preferences, the system should also constantly *explain* in an understandable way to different users (with different abilities) the meaning of/reasons for its proposed options, without overwhelming users with too many requests and/or irrelevant proposals. From an *architectural perspective*, architects should design IoT systems to execute suitable explanation algorithms, monitor users' QoE, and adapt the explanation algorithms in the IoT systems components for a better user experience.

**C3 - Deployment.** In the paradigm, user and system start interacting through an initial interaction point to identify a final IoT system. The identification/co-generation process is usually heavily based on run-time situations and their related run-time data. For this, another key challenge to be addressed is the effective and efficient continuous run-time deployment of such intelligent IoT systems. From an *architectural perspective*, due to the dynamicity of IoT environments and the incremental co-generation of final systems, the deployment topologies (nodes and their interconnections) of the systems need to be generated incrementally and dynamically across the Cloud-Edge continuum. For instance, the system supporting the planting is deployed when the user is at the garden and based on available sensors and devices.

**C4 - Tradeoffs and Quality, Self-adaptation.** Within *IoT-Together*, self-adaptation as well as tradeoffs w.r.t. *quality* are cross-cutting challenges that need to be continuously dealt with while addressing the above discussed challenges. IoT systems' *architects* should be supported to understand how design decisions may impact the satisfaction of requirements.

To conclude, when IoT systems or/and user needs and preferences are mainly unknown, underspecified, and volatile a good way to identify an intelligent IoT system offering interesting enhanced experiences is through the *IoT-Together* mixed-initiative paradigm. We described the elements of the paradigm and highlighted related challenges. Much research is still needed within the IoT, especially under more unknown and bigger boundaries settings. As future work, we plan to investigate solutions realising *IoT-Together* and validate them in practice.

**Acknowledgments.** This work was partially funded by the Knowledge Foundation (KK-Stiftelsen) via the project Intelligent and Trustworthy IoT Systems (Grant 20220087), and by the PON Cultural Heritage (AIM1880573), Italian National Project at GSSI. The author De Sanctis acknowledges the support of the MUR (Italy) Department of Excellence 2023–2027 for GSSI.

# References

1. Bröring, A., et al.: IntellIoT: intelligent IoT environments. In: Internet of Things - 5th The Global IoT Summit, GIoTS 2022. Revised Selected Papers, vol. 13533, pp. 55–68 (2022)
2. Weyns, D., Andersson, J., Caporuscio, M., Flammini, F., Kerren, A., Löwe, W.: A research agenda for smarter cyber-physical systems. J. Integr. Des. Process. Sci. **25**(2), 27–47 (2021)
3. Hearst, M.A.: Trends & controversies: mixed-initiative interaction. IEEE Intell. Syst. **14**(5), 14–23 (1999)
4. Horvitz, E.: Principles of mixed-initiative user interfaces. In: Williams, M.G., Altom, M.W. (eds.) Proceeding of the CHI 1999 Conference on Human Factors in Computing Systems: The CHI is the Limit, 1999, pp. 159–166. ACM (1999)
5. Jiang, S., Arkin, R.C.: Mixed-initiative human-robot interaction: definition, taxonomy, and survey. In: 2015 IEEE International Conference on Systems, Man, and Cybernetics, 2015, pp. 954–961. IEEE (2015)
6. Mayer, S., Verborgh, R., Kovatsch, M., Mattern, F.: Smart configuration of smart environments. IEEE Trans. Autom. Sci. Eng. **13**(3), 1247–1255 (2016)
7. Rahimi, H., Trentin, I.F., Ramparany, F., Boissier, O.: Q-smash: Q-learning-based self-adaptation of human-centered internet of things. In: IEEE/WIC/ACM International Conference on Web Intelligence and Intelligent Agent Technology, pp. 694–698 (2021)
8. Alkhabbas, F., Spalazzese, R., Davidsson, P.: ECo-IoT: an architectural approach for realizing emergent configurations in the internet of things. In: Software Architecture: 12th Europoean Conference on Software Architect, ECSA 2018, pp. 86–102 (2018)
9. De Sanctis, M., Muccini, H., Vaidhyanathan, K.: A user-driven adaptation approach for microservice-based IoT applications. In: IoT 2021: 11th International Conference on the Internet of Things, 2021, pp. 48–56. ACM (2021)

10. Abughazala, M.B., Moghaddam, M.T., Muccini, H., Vaidhyanathan, K.: Human behavior-oriented architectural design. In: Biffl, S., Navarro, E., Löwe, W., Sirjani, M., Mirandola, R., Weyns, D. (eds.) ECSA 2021. LNCS, vol. 12857, pp. 134–143. Springer, Cham (2021). https://doi.org/10.1007/978-3-030-86044-8_9

11. Alkhabbas, F., Spalazzese, R., Davidsson, P.: Human-centric emergent configurations: supporting the user through self-configuring IoT systems. In: Ayaz, H., Asgher, U., Paletta, L. (eds.) AHFE 2021. LNNS, vol. 259, pp. 411–418. Springer, Cham (2021). https://doi.org/10.1007/978-3-030-80285-1_48

12. Brdnik, S., Heričko, T., Šumak, B.: Intelligent user interfaces and their evaluation: a systematic mapping study. Sensors **22**(15), 5830 (2022)

13. Yigitbas, E., Jovanovikj, I., Biermeier, K., Sauer, S., Engels, G.: Integrated model-driven development of self-adaptive user interfaces. Softw. Syst. Model. **19**, 1057–1081 (2020)

14. Moghaddam, M.T., Alipour, M., Kjærgaard, M. B.: User interface and architecture adaption based on emotions and behaviors. In: IEEE 20th International Conference on Software Architecture Companion (ICSA-C), pp. 101–105 (2023)

15. Zouhaier, L., BenDalyHlaoui, Y., Ayed, L.B.: Adaptive user interface based on accessibility context. Multimedia Tools Appl., 1–30 (2023)

16. Madni, A.M., Madni, C.C., Lucero, S.D.: Leveraging digital twin technology in model-based systems engineering. Systems **7**(1), 7 (2019)

17. Shim, J.P., Sharda, R., French, A.M., Syler, R.A., Patten, K.P.: The internet of things: multi-faceted research perspectives. Commun. Assoc. Inf. Syst. **46**(1), 21 (2020)

18. Geetha, A., Kalaiselvi Geetha, M.: An appraisal on human-centered internet of things. In: Acharjya, D.P., Geetha, M.K. (eds.) Internet of Things: Novel Advances and Envisioned Applications. SBD, vol. 25, pp. 263–280. Springer, Cham (2017). https://doi.org/10.1007/978-3-319-53472-5_13

19. Alkhabbas, F., Alawadi, S., Spalazzese, R., Davidsson, P.: Activity recognition and user preference learning for automated configuration of IoT environments. In: Proceedings of the 10th International Conference on the Internet of Things, pp. 1–8 (2020)

20. Mäkitalo, N., et al.: Social devices: collaborative co-located interactions in a mobile cloud. In: Proceedings of the 11th International Conference on Mobile and Ubiquitous Multimedia (MUM 2012), pp. 1–10 (2012)

# Software Architecture Implementation and Deployment

# Analyzing the Evolution of Inter-package Dependencies in Operating Systems: A Case Study of Ubuntu

Victor Prokhorenko[1,2]([✉]), Chadni Islam[3], and Muhammad Ali Babar[1,2]

[1] CREST - The Centre for Research on Engineering Software Technologies,
The University of Adelaide, Adelaide, Australia
{victor.prokhorenko,ali.babar}@adelaide.edu.au
[2] Cyber Security Cooperative Research Centre (CSCRC), Joondalup, Australia
[3] Queensland University of Technology, Brisbane, Australia
chadni.islam@qut.edu.au

**Abstract.** An Operating System (OS) combines multiple interdependent software packages, which usually have their own independently developed architectures. When a multitude of independent packages are placed together in an OS, an implicit inter-package architecture is formed. For an evolutionary effort, designers/developers of OS can greatly benefit from fully understanding the system-wide dependency focused on individual files, specifically executable files, and dynamically loadable libraries. We propose a framework, DepEx, aimed at discovering the detailed package relations at the level of individual binary files and their associated evolutionary changes. We demonstrate the utility of DepEx by systematically investigating the evolution of a large-scale Open Source OS, Ubuntu. DepEx enabled us to systematically acquire and analyze the dependencies in different versions of Ubuntu released between 2005 (5.04) to 2023 (23.04). Our analysis revealed various evolutionary trends in package management and their implications based on the analysis of the 84 consecutive versions available for download (these include beta versions). This study has enabled us to assert that DepEx can provide researchers and practitioners with a better understanding of the implicit software dependencies in order to improve the stability, performance, and functionality of their software as well as to reduce the risk of issues arising during maintenance, updating, or migration.

**Keywords:** Dependency extraction · Package architecture ·
Binary-to-library dependencies · Package relation · Software coupling

## 1 Introduction

Combining multiple independent software packages together is commonly used to form complex inter-connected ecosystems. A typical example of such large software ecosystems is various Linux distributions. Such ecosystems tend to consist

B. Tekinerdogan et al. (Eds.): ECSA 2023, LNCS 14212, pp. 233–249, 2023.
https://doi.org/10.1007/978-3-031-42592-9_16

of hundreds or thousands of packages, libraries, binaries, and configuration files with an order of magnitude more dependencies among them [12,13].

Developers and researchers have expressed interest in software complexity measurement in an attempt to reason about characteristics of large code bases [29]. Software complexity is viewed as a result of different design decisions and implementation specifics and is a crucial component of long-term effects like the maintainability of software [14]. Although software complexity is a crucial consideration for package managers, Linux distributors, and maintainers, we currently have limited knowledge about the evolution of this complexity over the software lifespan. While the complexity of individual packages is tamed by their corresponding developers, combining thousands of packages materializes a new emergent layer of complexity. It is also uncertain whether different metrics for measuring software complexity exhibit similar or varying patterns of evolution.

A significant amount of research has extensively explored source-level software complexity [2]. As a result, various complexity metrics have been defined, such as cyclomatic, branching, or data flow complexity [1,15]. These metrics are primarily used for software design, debugging, and optimization purposes [14].

These metrics are, however, not applicable when analyzing closed-source software distributed only in binary form without access to the source code. In such cases, binary dependency analysis is required to understand the interactions and dependencies between compiled binary executables. Additionally, even when source code is available, there may be situations where the compiled binary may behave differently from what is expected due to specific environment configurations. Thus, binary dependency analysis can provide a more accurate and complete understanding of run-time software behavior, which can be crucial for identifying potential issues or vulnerabilities.

This work considers an OS as a whole rather than focusing on analyzing individual software binaries. Considering an OS enables the identification of cross-application relations, which make up an emergent **inter-package relation architecture** instead of just the intra-package software complexity. We propose a framework that enables the extraction of binary-to-library dependencies and constructs a full OS dependency graph to obtain insights on overall OS complexity which we determine through inter-package dependency coupling. By coupling we mean any type of dependency of one code fragment on another (library inclusion, function call, etc.).

Our study focused on Ubuntu as a case study to examine the evolution of large software ecosystems over almost two decades. Through empirical research and evidence-based findings, we aimed to assess the current state of package, library, and binary dependencies and identify areas for improvement in management tools, policies, and ecosystem analysis platforms. We believe that a deep understanding of emergent inter-package architecture resulting from combining a multitude of independently developed software subsystems would benefit software developers and OS maintainers. The proposed techniques and tools are expected to minimize manual labor associated with multi-package maintenance.

Following are the key contributions of our work

- We have introduced a framework for dependency coupling analysis for multi-package software to extract the inter-package relations architecture that is applicable to a broader range of OS due to the binary-level analysis.
- We have defined four techniques to quantitatively measure software coupling in terms of executable and dynamically loadable library dependencies at different granularities.
- We have investigated the evolution of Ubuntu OS in terms of the proposed library presence dependency type, which revealed the changes in OS-wide inter-package relations over time.

## 2    Background and Motivation

### 2.1    Software Complexity

Throughout the lifetime of any software system, various code modifications must be implemented in order to adapt to ever-changing user requirements and environmental conditions. An intuitive expectation is that large and complex software systems may be more difficult to update and maintain. Thus, in efforts to gain a stricter definition of complexity, multiple code complexity measurement techniques, such as straightforward line count or cyclomatic complexity, have been proposed so far [1]. However, analyzing multiple diverse software systems as a whole is not trivial due to (i) lack of access to the source code of all third-party components, (ii) lack of formal interoperability specification and (iii) highly dynamic state of execution environment at run time.

Several techniques are typically employed to handle the growing complexity of large software systems (such as a full OS). For instance, the system package manager may track package dependency information at the OS level. This tracking enables detecting incompatibilities between separate software subsystems and repairing them if possible. Unfortunately, manual labor is commonly used in determining and maintaining information on such version-level incompatibilities [4]. Due to the large number of files in a typical OS, manual efforts typically target only high-level dependency definitions, such as package level only [6]. As each package may consist of multiple files containing executable code (i.e., executable binaries and libraries), such package dependency understanding may not represent the dependencies precisely.

Further challenges arise due to modern complex software systems commonly developed in various programming languages. For instance, purely-binary compiled languages are intertwined with interpreted script languages leading to execution flow frequently being transferred between them. The dependency chains within such complex systems may propagate through a significant portion of files in the file system through the indirect reliance of different code fragments on each other. A typical example includes PHP web pages relying on the PHP interpreter, web server, and third-party PHP libraries. Such immediately obvious (direct) dependencies, in their turn, recursively rely on other system-provided and third-party libraries. Therefore we argue that automated and precise dependency tracking would benefit software system maintainers and administrators and may provide useful insight to software developers.

## 2.2  Code Dependency Types

One piece of code can depend on another in numerous ways. For instance, within the source code analysis context, a function may call other functions. Similarly, class methods may work by invoking other class methods. These types of dependencies present in the same code base are well understood and routinely used in modern IDEs (Integrated Development Environments) to aid software developers. In contrast, cross-language code dependencies spanning across multiple independently developed software systems are less formal and challenging to identify. For instance, a PHP-oriented IDE would not detect incompatible changes in the libc library which is required by the PHP interpreter itself.

Focusing solely on software running within the same OS while not taking network-based dependencies into consideration, we propose the following four conceptual types of dependencies suitable in the executable code analysis context. These four types include (i) the presence of third-party libraries, (ii) the extent of library coverage, (iii) library function call occurrences, and (iv) the run-time usage of functions (Fig. 1).

| Presence | Coverage | Occurrence | Usage |
|---|---|---|---|
| Header section | Header section | Header section | Header section |
| Library 1<br>Library 2<br>Library 3 | Library 1<br>  Function A<br>  Function B<br>Library 2<br>  Function C | ... | ... |
|  |  | Code section | Code section |
| Code section | Code section | FunctionA()<br>...<br>FunctionC()<br>FunctionC()<br>FunctionC()<br>...<br>FunctionB() | Loop X times:<br>  FunctionA()<br>...<br>If condition:<br>  FunctionC()<br>...<br>FunctionB() |
| ... | ... |  |  |

**Fig. 1.** Executable code dependency measurement approaches.

The **third-party library presence dependency** relates to file-level granularity. This type of dependency indicates a requirement for a dynamically loadable library to be *present* in the system for an executable binary to be able to load and start. In Windows-based systems, libraries and executables are denoted by .dll and .exe file extensions, while on Linux-based these are .so and typically extension-less ELF (Executable and Linkable File) correspondingly. While high-level, this file granularity is crucial as a missing library file typically causes the executable file loader to indicate an error and prevents any further file execution.

**Coverage dependency** focuses on the library fragments (e.g., functions or class methods) that a developer explicitly uses or relies on. This type of dependency refers to specific *function existence requirements*. Thus, the library coverage aspect reflects the degree of reliance on a given library by the executable. Depending on the OS, programming language, and execution environment, individual function-level requirements can be implemented in various ways. For instance, in the context of the Windows PE executable, the list of required functions is tied to a specific library. In contrast, the lists of required libraries and functions are independent in the Linux ELF executable [28]. These implementation specific differences complicate coverage analysis in the general case.

**Function occurrence** dependency type attempts to provide further insight into the code dependency by observing that a single external function can be *referred* to multiple times in the original code. For instance, some heavily used functions can be mentioned all over the code, while some rarely used functions may only appear once. Extracting this type of dependency is extremely complicated and involves computationally-heavy disassembling of compiled code or parsing of interpreted languages. Initial unoptimized attempts revealed a significant time overhead for extracting such occurrence-level dependencies. While certain optimizations can be taken for production-ready usage, it can be concluded that this type of analysis is currently unsuitable for real-time applications.

Lastly, **dependency usage** refers to the actual run-time external code flow control transfers (i.e., the actual function *calls*). This level of detail may, for example, reveal that one function call is contained within a high-count loop while other function calls may be a part of a condition rarely satisfied at run time. Run-time observation would reveal a deeper understanding of the level of reliance on third-party libraries in both cases. Despite seemingly most accurate and closest to reality, relying on this type of dependency suffers from a major drawback. Different executions or instances of the same executable may exhibit different behavior due to different run-time conditions. In other words, observing a single execution does not guarantee to reveal all external code usage cases.

Note that a purposefully crafted executable may incorporate external dependencies that would not be reflected using the proposed dependency measurement techniques. For instance, if an executable downloads code over the network and executes it in place, no third-party library references, function names, or function calls related to the downloaded code may be present in the original executable. Moreover, the downloaded code downloaded can be different on each program invocation, making any dependency analysis futile in such a context. Based on the identified dependency types, we propose an extensible plugin-based framework suitable to extract code dependencies for various types of executable code.

## 3   Our Approach and Implementation

Analyzing the full file system enables a more complete and consistent understanding of the dependencies. Software developers only *express a requirement* for dynamically loadable library *presence*, but do not have actual guarantees of the library's *existence* in a given system. We implement a Python-based proof of concept solution to analyze system-wide dependencies.

On a conceptual level, our proposed approach for **Dependency Extraction** (**DepEx** consists of a file system scanner, a plugin dispatcher, multiple user-definable file-type-specific plugins, and the resulting database. The following steps provide an overview of the DepEx operation:

- The existing dependency extraction plugins (also Python-based) are queried to prepare the list of all supported file types
- The specified file system is iterated over and each file of a supported type is passed to a corresponding plugin for dependency extraction
- The dependencies extracted by the plugin are stored in an SQLite database

Having the knowledge of individual file type structures, each plugin is responsible for external dependency detection and extraction. Note that while the current implementation assumes one-to-one relation between file types and plugins, it is possible for multiple plugins to process the same files to extract different types of dependencies. While we have implemented a proof of concept plugins for PHP, Bash, and, to a lesser degree, Python scripts, in this research we primarily focus on ELF executables and .so libraries with the library presence dependency.

Once the unattended phase of the dependency extraction is complete, several interactive analysis and usage scenarios become accessible. These include visualization, statistical reporting, and forward and reverse update impact estimation. For instance, various system health characteristics, such as "number of missing libraries" or "number of executables with unfulfilled dependencies" can be queried and plotted if necessary. Similarly, update impact calculation enables obtaining the list of executables and libraries that would be potentially affected in case a given library is updated.

In order to aid comprehension of the large amounts of data collected, we developed a visualization subsystem. Using DOT language for graph representation enables rendering the resulting graphs using existing tools as well (such as GraphViz or Gephi). While the individual executable file graphs were readable, the full-system dependency graph was too cluttered for human comprehension. At this stage, interactive filtering was implemented to allow the hiding of popular libraries responsible for most of the visual noise (as shown in Fig. 2b). We are also planning to implement automated filtering based on various features, such as node type, sub-string matching, and popularity.

Other auxiliary scripts for dependency graphs exploration include querying all binaries and libraries that depend on a given library (`who-uses`) and individual binary/library dependency graph generation (`get-deps` and `get-all-deps`). Individual library dependencies can also be visualized in a more detailed view.

## 4    Studying the Architectural Aspects of Ubuntu

We focus on the following Research Questions (RQs) to investigate the file-level package relation architecture in Ubuntu systems using DepEx. We considered the *presence* dependency in this case study. We collected and analyzed the dependencies of 84 consecutive live Ubuntu Linux images that span over 18 years of development and evolution. The research questions we primarily focus on revolve around the emergent inter-package OS-wide architecture implicitly *forming as a result of combining* multiple independent software packages as well as the related *architectural changes observed* throughout longer time periods. In addition, we investigate the *complexity perception* from the perspectives of individual software package developers and whole system maintainers.

- RQ1. How do binary-to-library dependencies manifest in the Ubuntu OS in terms of a system-wide dependency graph?
- RQ2. What is the difference between individual library complexity directly exposed to developers vs. overall internal system complexity that emerges as a result of combining multiple subsystems together (direct vs. recursive dependencies)?
- RQ3. How does the whole Ubuntu OS binary-to-library dependency graph evolve over a longer period?

Having high popularity, rich history, and open-source nature, Ubuntu serves as a comprehensive data source. Despite other Linux distributions, such as Alpine, gaining popularity, we were unable to find another dataset comparable in size and quality. Specifically, older Alpine versions were unavailable for download and Debian produced fewer live images.

Throughout the development of our DepEx framework, we relied on well-established existing open-source software, such as squashfs-tools[1], binutils[2] and ldd[3]. SquashFS-related tools were used to expose compressed live Ubuntu images for analysis. Note that different versions of SquashFS had to be used depending on the age of the Ubuntu image. Binutils package, particularly the GNU nm tool, was used to extract ELF-specific data such as imported library names. Lastly, ldd was used to extract library search locations. Special precautions had to be taken to lookup for the library paths inside the mounted image rather than resolving paths within the host system that conducted the analysis. For this purpose, we relied on standard Linux chroot functionality.

Solely mounting the Ubuntu ISO files directly does not provide access to the live file system, as another layer of compression is typically present for disk space optimization purposes. Thus, we implemented a two-step unpacking process to gain visibility of the inner live file system.

Interestingly, extracting the images generated over 18 years revealed how *live image preparation* changed over time. We noticed different compression techniques used throughout the time period analyzed that ranged from compressed *loop files* (*cloop*) to SquashFS versions 2.1–4.0. We also observed that modern SquashFS kernel modules could not transparently mount images compressed by older versions. Thus, we developed a supporting script to provide access to all of the downloaded images in a uniform manner.

---

[1] https://github.com/plougher/squashfs-tools.

[2] https://www.gnu.org/software/binutils/.

[3] https://man7.org/linux/man-pages/man1/ldd.1.html.

Using our DepEx framework, we recursively built the full library dependency graph for each identified executable using `readelf`, `nm` and `ldconfig` tools. Extracting library dependencies requires analyzing `RPATH` and `RUNPATH` variables, system library cache as well as the binary executable file path. Finally, we used an SQLite database to store the collected dependency data for all the scanned Ubuntu images. This data can be queried for further analysis and visualization.

# 5   Findings and Results

The dependency data extracted from a typical OS is a rich source of information on the high-level system architecture. In contrast to *planned layer* of architecture, this layer refers to the *unwritten* architectural aspects that emerge as a result of combining a multitude of independently-developed software packages. Coupled with temporal updates, this data can serve as a basis for a deeper system evolution trends analysis. For instance, long-term trends such as libraries gaining or losing popularity or executable complexity inflation may be detected. Predicting potential OS library or executable removal may help developers adjust the development plans. In addition, determining and removing unused libraries could be useful in optimizing disk space usage and reducing the attack surface.

Throughout the data collection conducted, we focused on three key aspects. Firstly, we investigated the OS-level dependency graph as a whole (RQ1). Secondly, we examined various aspects of complexity in binary dependencies determined through coupling analysis (RQ2). Lastly, we analyzed evolutionary trends in the OS dependency graph (RQ3).

## 5.1   OS-Wide Dependency Graph

Analyzing the resulting SQLite database, which covers 84 Ubuntu images, revealed the following number of binaries, libraries and dependencies per image. We found that from Ubuntu 5.04 to 23.04 the number of binary executables ranged from 1519 to 2753 and the number of libraries ranged from 1683 to 3673. In terms of dependencies detected, the numbers ranged from 18 165 to 37 641 in the images scanned. A total of 408 364 binary and library files were processed to extract the dependencies, which returned almost 2 million dependencies. The total SQLite database size generated is over 83MB of raw dependency data.

We noticed that highly popular libraries such as (`libc`) make the graphs unreadable. Thus we implemented filtering out libraries from the sorted (by popularity) list of all the involved libraries. We observe that hiding the top 10–15 libraries increases the readability of the whole system graph. Notably, loosely coupled subsystems, such as the networking subsystem, become apparent. The libraries presented alongside the diagram also provide insight into the relative popularity of individual libraries within a system.

We have observed that number of libraries imported but not present in the system varied from 20 (v5.04) to 8 (v23.04) with the highest number being 92

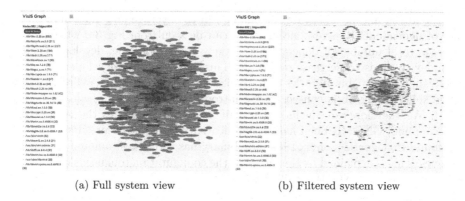

(a) Full system view                    (b) Filtered system view

**Fig. 2.** Dependency visualization filtering effects.

(v21.10b). As a consequence, the number of other libraries directly impacted by the missing dependencies varied from 4 (v17.10 and v17.10.1) to 27 (v13.04 and v9.04). Similarly, we see that the number of unused libraries (i.e., not imported by any other library or executable) ranged from 1301 (v5.04) to 1666 (v23.04). These numbers constitute a significant proportion of the total number of libraries included (around 77% and 62% respectively). Potential explanations for such a high number of unused libraries could be a) plugin-based applications that do not import libraries directly, b) "forgotten" legacy libraries and c) libraries shipped "just in case" for use by applications commonly installed at a later stage.

## 5.2 Dependencies Coupling Aspects

Software dependencies represent the reliance of a given piece of code on external code. In practice, software developers only deal with a subset of the code required for an application to run. A graphics-oriented library may expose a simpler set of functions to developers, while relying on a multitude of other complex hardware-specific libraries to implement the advertised functionality. Thus, a complex and large code base is made to look simple from the developer's perspective.

This perception difference opens the possibility of measuring code coupling in direct and recursive ways. The direct coupling of an application reflects how many specific libraries a developer deals with explicitly. In contrast, recursive coupling takes all the underlying dependencies into consideration as well.

In addition, there is an inherent asymmetry in dependency tracking. Forward tracking from a given binary to all the required libraries is trivial, as this information is contained within the binary. Reverse tracking from a given library to determine all the binaries and libraries that require the specified library is complicated, as this information is not stored explicitly. Reverse tracking essentially reflects the popularity of a given library and requires scanning the whole file system to be calculated. Thus we developed functionality to measure the (i) direct coupling, (ii) total (recursive) coupling, and (iii) library popularity.

Figures 3a and 3b illustrate the changes in the average and maximum number of dependencies correspondingly. As can be seen from Fig. 3a, whereas the average total number of dependencies largely stays the same, developer-facing complexity tends to decrease over time. This indicates that developers tend to re-arrange code within libraries to minimize the coupling they face directly. The large spike in Fig. 3b is caused by the introduction of Gnome Shell in Ubuntu 17.10. We, therefore can conclude that while maintaining roughly the same external coupling, GNOME Shell has a complicated internal structure. Particularly, we found that `gnome-control-center` binary has the largest amount of dependencies. This is explained by the fact that the configuration tool needs to interact with most of the GNOME Shell subsystems.

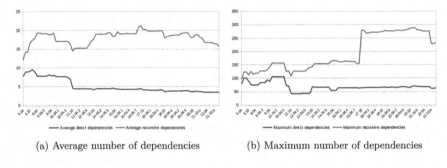

(a) Average number of dependencies          (b) Maximum number of dependencies

**Fig. 3.** Direct and recursive dependencies.

A complementary aspect of dependency coupling is popularity. We define library popularity through the number of other libraries or executables that depend on it. In other words, damaging or removing more popular libraries would impact a larger number of executables in a system. In terms of popularity, the top 10 most used libraries (i.e. imported from other libraries and executables) in Ubuntu are: `libc` (4397), `libpthread` (1438), `libglib` (1037), `libgobject` (945), `libm` (836), `librt` (719), `libgthread` (660), `libgmodule` (658), `libgtk-x11` (656), `libdl` (601). The numbers alongside the libraries refer to the number of uses (i.e., library importing) averaged across all Ubuntu versions the library was present in.

We notice that 7 out of the top 10 directly-coupled libraries relate to various GNOME subsystems while the other 3 relate to the Evolution mail client. Interestingly, the most compl `ximian-connector-setup` executable with 100 direct dependencies was only present in two Ubuntu versions. This likely indicates that such high coupling was not tolerated, leading to the application removal.

Lastly, analyzing total coupling by taking recursive dependencies into account, we found the top 10 complex libraries and binaries: `empathy-call` (154), `evolution-alarm-notify` (156), `gnome-control-center` (273), `gnome-todo` (155), `libvclplug_gtk3lo` (154), `smbd.x86_64-linux-gnu` (155), `libiradio` (158), `gnome-initial-setup` (169), `libgrilo` (158), `shotwell-publishing` (164).

## 5.3  Dependency Graphs Evolutionary Trends

Running a large-scale analysis on a set of Linux distributions developed and released over 18 years revealed a number of shifts occurring in the domain. In constant efforts to attract users, Ubuntu is known for conducting experiments, such as introducing new large software packages as a replacement for existing ones. For instance, the significant dip in the number of dependencies on Fig. 4b is explained by the replacement of GNOME 2 with Unity. On a longer scale it is also visible that despite limited local successes of such experiments, the overall trend indicates a slow growth of the number of files and dependencies.

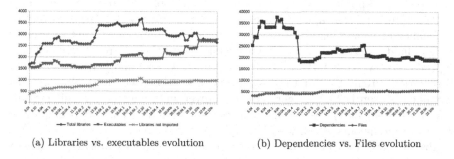

(a) Libraries vs. executables evolution        (b) Dependencies vs. Files evolution

**Fig. 4.** Overview of file-level evolutionary trends.

Interestingly, we also observed a significant amount of not explicitly required .so files are present in the system (Fig. 4a). In other words, up to 37% of libraries physically located in the file systems were not mentioned in the import tables of any of the binaries or libraries. This likely indicates that such libraries are primarily used as plugins and could be loaded at run-time through dynamic directory scanning if necessary. Note that these conditional dependencies may be impossible to detect in advance due to the unpredictable nature of external factors. For instance, a user controlled application configuration can determine whether a given plugin library should be loaded at run time. The overall trend also hints that such a dynamic plugin-based approach gains popularity as the proportion of libraries not imported keeps steadily growing.

Another observation discovered throughout our analysis relate to the longevity of the libraries and binaries in Ubuntu. Namely, while complex binaries are periodically removed in search of better alternatives, highly popular libraries tend to stay around. Once a popular library is introduced in a particular Ubuntu version, it is unlikely to be removed as such removal would impact all libraries and executables that rely on the library's existence. Even internal code reorganizations affecting highly popular libraries require extra care to maintain compatibility[4].

---

[4]  https://developers.redhat.com/articles/2021/12/17/why-glibc-234-removed-libpthread.

# 6  Discussion

## 6.1  Threats to Validity

While we primarily focused on dependency-centric package management in Linux OS, other factors may explain some of the observations. Despite high popularity, packages might get removed from the system due to licensing, compatibility, security, or maintainability issues. Dependency analysis should, therefore, be coupled with change log analysis to verify and confirm the findings.

To enhance the external validity of our dependency analysis, we selected a highly popular Linux distribution. By including all of the available versions we expect our approach to be generalizable and applicable to a broader range of OSs. Widening the input data set on the time axis enabled the discovery of uncommon cases and long-term trends. Being well-maintained, Ubuntu served as a high-quality dataset. Legacy Ubuntu versions and their corresponding change logs were still available for download[5] In contrast, Alpine (another popular Linux distribution) archives did not go far back in time. Moreover, the Alpine archives contained broken links for older versions, preventing image downloading. Similarly, while considering Debian systems, we discovered different and incompatible system image layouts which would complicate the analysis.

Primary threats to external validity are abrupt changes causing significant paradigm shifts, lower granularities skewing the results, and implicit dependencies. *Abrupt changes* may be introduced throughout evolution. Such changes introduce incompatibilities, forcing to amend the scanning process accordingly. Notable examples we observed include compression algorithm changes, folder hierarchy alterations, and transition from RPATH to RUNPATH. We noticed a different layout of binary files in the file system that required consideration due to the changes introduced in Ubuntu 19.04. Specifically, /bin and /sbin directories were converted to symbolic links to /usr/bin and /usr/sbin correspondingly[6]. Depending on whether 19.04 is being installed from scratch or on top of the previously installed version, the number of binaries may look like being suddenly doubled in version 19.04. We alleviated this problem by resolving symbolic links.

In addition to library dependencies stored in executable binary file import tables, other types of coupling occur in practice. For instance, network communication, special files like Unix domain sockets, Inter-Process Communication (IPC) calls, message-oriented buses, and pipes provide various means of code interactions. Discovering such code coupling instances may not be possible in practice (e.g., new code fragments might be downloaded over a network). Taking into account these code coupling types may significantly skew our findings.

---

[5] Ubuntu wiki: Releases - https://wiki.ubuntu.com/Releases.

[6] https://lists.ubuntu.com/archives/ubuntu-devel-announce/2018-November/001253.html.

## 6.2   Challenges and Limitations

The two primary technical challenges we encountered throughout our data collection and analysis are the large data set sizes and performance issues related to extracting dependencies at lower granularities.

As the distributed Ubuntu images are growing in size, so do the number of executable files and their individual sizes. This steady growth is observed over all Ubuntu versions analyzed. For example, within 18 years analyzed, the live Ubuntu image size grew from 600 MB (version 5.04) to 3.7 GB (version 23.04). Likewise, the number of executable files experienced a 70% increase in size (1605 in 5.04, 2753 in 23.04).

Through practical experiments, we established that restricting the dependency granularity is crucial to achieving acceptable processing speed as lower granularity dependency extraction incurs large overheads. Disassembling executable binaries to identify individual third-party library function calls slows the dependency extraction and incurs significant memory overheads. For instance, we have observed cases of over-disassembly and analysis of a single executable taking 40 min on an average laptop-class CPU. Thus, while technically possible and potentially interesting to gain further insights, lower-level granularity analysis is out of reach for real-time applications we initially aimed for. At this stage, we restricted the analysis to the file level only.

## 7   Related Work

The prior work primarily revolves around two aspects, (i) diverse conceptual complexity metrics definitions and (ii) dependency extraction and analysis.

Various types of software complexity metrics have been widely studied in the literature [19]. Some studies have focused on metrics that are useful in source code analysis but are not easily applicable in binary code analysis [1,2,16]. Others have discussed the deficiency of methods to obtain global dependency knowledge and the difficulty in visualizing the resulting graphs [10]. The use of software complexity metrics to detect vulnerabilities has also been investigated, with some studies proposing dependency-oriented and execution-time complexities [3]. Dependency extraction aspects and challenges have also been explored, with some studies focusing on specific languages or ecosystems [17,26].

Package management and dependency validation have been popular research topics, with a set of studies proposing methods to address issues arising from package evolution (e.g., splitting into multiple different packages) [4–6]. User questions related to package management, such as calculating the consequences of removing or modifying a package, have also been explored [7,23]. Efficient package management tools and query languages have been proposed, including tools for efficient package management and relations lookup [8]. However, similar to software complexity metrics research efforts, multiple studies have focused only on source-level rather than binary dependencies [9,20].

In efforts to resolve binary compatibility issues, some works have investigated relying on version ranges rather than minimum version requirements [11].

Unfortunately, the large downside of the proposed approach is the requirement of debug symbols availability, which is rare in commercial software. An interesting use of dependency extraction has been proposed for Windows executables for malware detection [24,27]. Taking the notion of the extent of a dependency into account enables detecting and eliminating insignificant dependencies [18].

Overall, it should be noted that dependency related studies primarily focus on source code dependency analysis and package-level relations [22,25] and do not typically examine software package evolution over time. We, therefore, conclude that a more precise file-based dependency extraction is an under researched area that might benefit from providing better structural visibility for large-scale systems comprising multiple independently developed packages. We also see that understanding software evolution is essential for maintaining software, ensuring compatibility, and improving security. Having this understanding aids developers in making informed decisions about updates and maintenance, ensures software remains compatible with other systems, and reduces the risk of security issues. Additionally, understanding software evolution can lead to new innovations and improvements in software design and development.

## 8    Conclusion and Future Work

In this study, we introduce automated extraction of dependency graphs for a whole system at the executable files level (as opposed to manually maintained traditional package-level dependency graphs). The resulting system-wide dependency graph provides a high-level view of the OS architecture emerging from interactions between the different subsystems and user packages. In addition, this study enabled the discovery of general high-level trends/common patterns in Ubuntu Linux architecture evolution over time.

We also differentiate between developer-facing complexity (defined through direct dependency coupling) and overall system complexity (defined through recursive dependency coupling). The motivation behind such a separation is that developers typically deal with third-party libraries without having full visibility of the back-end side of the libraries. In other words, a developer may include one library, while the library itself can have a complicated graph of dependencies not directly visible to the developer. These invisible dependencies may cause software bloating and increase the attack surface. We believe the findings of this study will provide useful insights for software developers and OS maintainers in terms of gaining a holistic quantitative understanding of inter-package architecture management that would be useful, for example, in optimizing disk space and improving system maintainability.

We have identified two main directions for future research lines. Specifically, expanding the dependency extraction approach to a *wider set of platforms* to support and *more types of dependencies* to extract. For future research, we aim to perform Windows-based analysis and implement support for other levels of granularity, such as individual function dependencies. Also, in contrast to the convenient, holistic file system structure used in live editions, non-live distribution variants are composed of multiple compressed packages, complicating the dependency extraction and analysis. Implementing analysis for such non-live distributions could be a potential future research line.

As opposed to fixed library imports, code fragments interacting through various communication channels are loosely coupled. Such non-obvious dependencies are not trivial to detect. For instance, changing code on one side of a UNIX pipe may negatively affect the results of the next program in the pipeline. Furthermore, such dependencies may not be predefined in advance and are only required intermittently while being completely unnoticeable most of the time. We believe that comprehensive and accurate detection of such concealed dependencies would greatly enhance the overall system architecture, evolution, and run-time operation understanding and visibility and enable early detection of potential compatibility breaks caused by code modifications.

**Acknowledgment.** The work has been partially supported by the Cyber Security Research Centre Limited whose activities are partially funded by the Australian Government's Cooperative Research Centres Programme.

**Data Availability Statement.** As the current project is funded by industry partners, we are unable to publish the source code at this stage. However, aiming to increase transparency and reproducibility in research, we have made the obtained dataset available for public access [21]. Researchers and interested parties can access the dataset and utilize it to replicate or build upon our findings.

# References

1. Honglei, T., Wei, S., Yanan, Z.: The research on software metrics and software complexity metrics. In: International Forum on Computer Science-Technology and Applications, Chongqing, China 2009, pp. 131–136 (2009). https://doi.org/10.1109/IFCSTA.2009.39
2. Yu, S., Zhou, S.: A survey on metric of software complexity. In: 2010 2nd IEEE International Conference on Information Management and Engineering, Chengdu, China, pp. 352–356 (2010). https://doi.org/10.1109/ICIME.2010.5477581
3. Shin, Y., Williams, L.: An initial study on the use of execution complexity metrics as indicators of software vulnerabilities. In: Proceedings of the 7th International Workshop on Software Engineering for Secure Systems (SESS 2011), pp. 1–7. Association for Computing Machinery, New York. https://doi.org/10.1145/1988630.1988632
4. Artho, C., Di Cosmo, R., Suzaki, K., Zacchiroli, S.: Sources of inter-package conflicts in debian (2011). arXiv preprint arXiv:1110.1354
5. de Sousa, O.F., de Menezes, M.A., Penna, T.J.: Analysis of the package dependency on debian gnu/linux. J. Comput. Interdisc. Sci. 1(2), 127–133 (2009)
6. Lan, Y.-Q., et al.: Extraction methods on Linux package dependency relations. In: 2009 International Conference on Information Engineering and Computer Science. IEEE (2009)
7. Mithun, X.L.E., van de Wetering, H.M.M.: Linux Package Dependency Visualization. Master's Thesis at Department of Mathematics and Computer Science, pp. 1–64 (2009)

8. Boender, J., Di Cosmo, R., Vouillon, J., Durak, B., Mancinelli, F.: Improving the quality of GNU/Linux distributions. In: 2008 32nd Annual IEEE International Computer Software and Applications Conference, pp. 1240–1246. IEEE (2008)
9. Lungu, M., Robbes, R., Lanza, M.: Recovering inter-project dependencies in software ecosystems. In: Proceedings of the IEEE/ACM International Conference on Automated Software Engineering, pp. 309–312 (2010)
10. Wang, J., Wu, Q., Tan, Y., Xu, J., Sun, X.: A graph method of package dependency analysis on Linux Operating system. In: 2015 4th International Conference on Computer Science and Network Technology (ICCSNT), Harbin, pp. 412–415 (2015). https://doi.org/10.1109/ICCSNT.2015.7490780
11. Jia, Z., Li, S., Yu, T., Zeng, C., Xu, E., Liu, et al.: DepOwl: detecting dependency bugs to prevent compatibility failures. In: 2021 IEEE/ACM 43rd International Conference on Software Engineering (ICSE), pp. 86–98. IEEE (2021)
12. Spinellis, D., Avgeriou, P.: Evolution of the unix system architecture: an exploratory case study. IEEE Trans. Softw. Eng. 47(6), 1134–1163 (2021). https://doi.org/10.1109/TSE.2019.2892149
13. Spinellis, D.: A repository with 44 years of unix evolution. In: 2015 IEEE/ACM 12th Working Conference on Mining Software Repositories, Florence, Italy, pp. 462–465 (2015). https://doi.org/10.1109/MSR.2015.64
14. Weyuker, E.J.: Evaluating software complexity measures. IEEE Trans. Softw. Eng. 14(9), 1357–1365 (1988). https://doi.org/10.1109/32.6178
15. Ebert, C., Cain, J., Antoniol, G., Counsell, S., Laplante, P.: Cyclomatic complexity. IEEE Softw. 33(6), 27–29 (2016). https://doi.org/10.1109/MS.2016.147
16. Zhang, M., Baddoo, N.: Performance comparison of software complexity metrics in an open source project. In: Abrahamsson, P., Baddoo, N., Margaria, T., Messnarz, R. (eds.) EuroSPI 2007. LNCS, vol. 4764, pp. 160–174. Springer, Heidelberg (2007). https://doi.org/10.1007/978-3-540-75381-0_15
17. Robillard, M.P.: Topology analysis of software dependencies. ACM Trans. Softw. Eng. Methodol. 17(4), 36 (2008). Article 18. https://doi.org/10.1145/13487689.13487691
18. Cox, R.: Surviving software dependencies. Commun. ACM 62(9), 36–43 (2019)
19. Jász, J., et al.: Static execute after/before as a replacement of traditional software dependencies. In: 2008 IEEE International Conference on Software Maintenance. IEEE (2008)
20. Ossher, J., Bajracharya, S., Lopes, C.: Automated dependency resolution for open source software. In: 2010 7th IEEE Working Conference on Mining Software Repositories (MSR 2010). IEEE (2010)
21. DepEx Dataset. https://figshare.com/s/ce3247b81fac82528495
22. LaBelle, N., Wallingford, E.: Inter-package dependency networks in open-source software. arXiv preprint cs/0411096 (2004)
23. Kikas, R., et al.: Structure and evolution of package dependency networks. In: 2017 IEEE/ACM 14th International Conference on Mining Software Repositories (MSR). IEEE (2017)
24. Narouei, M., et al.: DLLMiner: structural mining for malware detection. Secur. Commun. Netw. 8(18), 3311–3322 (2015)
25. Horváth, Á.: The software package dependency networks of some Linux distributions. In: 2012 IEEE 4th International Conference on Nonlinear Science and Complexity (NSC). IEEE (2012)
26. Decan, A., Mens, T., Grosjean, P.: An empirical comparison of dependency network evolution in seven software packaging ecosystems. Empir. Softw. Eng. 24, 381–416 (2019)

27. Xie, X., Wang, W.: Lightweight examination of dll environments in virtual machines to detect malware. In: Proceedings of the 4th ACM International Workshop on Security in Cloud Computing (2016)
28. TIS Committee. Tool interface standard (TIS) executable and linking format (ELF) specification version 1.2 (1995)
29. Alakus, T.B., Das, R., Turkoglu, I.: An overview of quality metrics used in estimating software faults. In: 2019 International Artificial Intelligence and Data Processing Symposium (IDAP), pp. 1–6. IEEE (2019)

# A Graph-Based Java Projects Representation for Antipatterns Detection

Roberta Capuano[(⊠)] [iD] and Henry Muccini[iD]

University of L'Aquila, L'Aquila, Italy
{roberta.capuano,henry.muccini}@univaq.it

**Abstract.** The identification and resolution of antipatterns in legacy Java code is a crucial process that can enhance the overall quality of software. However, detecting these antipatterns is often challenging, especially in large-scale projects where the codebase is complex and extensive. Relying solely on developers' knowledge and expertise to identify antipatterns can be time-consuming, labor-intensive, and may result in missed opportunities to improve code quality.

To address this challenge, this paper proposes a semi-automatic approach to antipattern detection in Java code-based systems. The approach involves the use of a graph-based representation of the software system, which captures the structural aspects of the code, such as classes, methods and their relations. The approach also employs mathematical rules to identify three common antipatterns: *God Class*, *Circuitous Treasure Hunt*, and *Empty Semi-Truck*. The proposed semi-automatic approach can support developers in identifying and resolving antipatterns that affect legacy code. By detecting these antipatterns, developers can improve software quality, maintainability, and reduce technical debt. Overall, this research offers a promising solution for detecting antipatterns in Java code through a semi-automatic approach, which can aid in the refactoring of legacy code.

**Keywords:** Refactoring · Antipatterns · Java code analysis

## 1 Introduction

Software maintenance and evolution are crucial stages in the software development life cycle, aimed at improving code quality, enhancing extensibility, and ensuring maintainability [1,2]. As software systems increase in size and complexity, addressing issues becomes progressively challenging. These issues leading to poor software quality, are commonly addressed through software refactoring, which involves improving the code structure while preserving its behavior [3].

To facilitate the refactoring process, design patterns and antipatterns are commonly used as guiding principles [4]. Design patterns offer established and experience-based solutions to common software development problems, providing

B. Tekinerdogan et al. (Eds.): ECSA 2023, LNCS 14212, pp. 250–265, 2023.
https://doi.org/10.1007/978-3-031-42592-9_17

adaptable solutions that can be tailored to specific contexts. They serve as a basis for best practices in software system design and enable knowledge reuse across different software systems. Conversely, antipatterns document recurring suboptimal solutions to common design problems that lead to negative consequences. They identify "bad practices" in software development and offer potential solutions to rectify them. Antipatterns can be used in software development to tackle architectural, design, and development problems. Identifying antipatterns early on can prevent issues and improve software quality [5].

During refactoring, understanding the software is crucial. Techniques like static and dynamic analysis are commonly employed. Different graphs, such as the Data Flow Graph (DFG) and Control Flow Graph (CFG), capture data and control flow between program elements [6]. The Program Dependence Graph (PDG) combines data and control dependencies in a unified graph for a procedure. The System Dependence Graph (SDG) represents inter-procedural dependencies, including program dependencies and procedural calls across procedures [7]. SDGs, also known as call graphs, are widely used in program analysis and software testing [8,9]. For the best of our knowledge, there exist a lack in the literature, in addressesing the antipatterns detection problem analysing a graph representation of the system.

In this paper, we propose a semi-automatic approach for detecting three antipatterns in Java projects: *God Class, Circuitous Treasure Hunt,* and *Empty Semi-Truck.* Our approach leverages a graph representation of the software projects, constructed through static code analysis. By formulating the selected antipatterns as mathematical problems on the constructed graph representation, we identify their potential instances within the software project. The resulting detection mechanism provides developers with actionable insights for refactoring efforts. The main contributions of this paper can be summarized as follows:

- Introduction of a graph representation tailored to Java software projects, providing a comprehensive view of the codebase and enhancing understanding of its underlying structure. To that purpose, we developed a Java parser that, based on the Java 9 grammar, automatically generates the graph-based representation of the system.
- Presentation of a mathematical formulation for the detection of potential instances of the *God Classes, Circuitous Treasure Hunts,* and *Empty Semi-Truck* antipatterns within the constructed graph representation. To help the reader in the understanding of the formulations, we provide an example of application on an open-source Java projects called PetClinic.

The paper is organized as follows: Sect. 2 presents the proposed approach for constructing the graph-based representation of Java projects, capturing the codebase relationships. It also includes the implementation of the automatic approach to graph generation. Section 3 introduces the mathematical formulation used to detect the three mentioned performance antipatterns. The PetClinic application is analyzed as an example of antipattern detection. Section 4 presents related work on software representation through graphs and antipattern detection, highlighting the advantages of our approach and its limitations. Finally, Sect. 5 concludes the paper.

## 2 Proposed Approach for Graph Construction

The graph-based representation of the system presented in this paper is generated automatically through static code analysis. The system is modeled as a directed graph denoted as $G = (V, E)$, where the set of nodes is denoted as $V$, while the set of edges is referred to as $E$. We establish the core elements to be represented as a node in the graph to facilitate the antipatterns detection. Thus, we define the set of nodes $V$ as a combination of two distinct sets: $V = M \cup C$. The initial set $M$ consists of nodes that represent methods, whereas the set $C$ comprises nodes that represent classes. The definitions of these sets are as follows:

$$M = \{m_1, m_2, ..., m_k \mid m_j \quad is \ a \ Method \quad \forall \quad j \in 1, ..., k\} \qquad (1)$$

$$C = \{c_1, c_2, ..., c_n \mid c_i \quad is \ a \ Class \quad \forall \quad i \in 1, ...n\} \qquad (2)$$

The relationships between classes and methods are represented through a comprehensive set of edges denoted as $E$. In the following subsections, we introduce and categorize the relationships based on the nodes involved.

### 2.1 Relations Between Classes

Our investigation primarily focuses on analyzing class relationships to uncover the intricate structure and dependencies inherent in the system, thereby providing valuable insights into its underlying architecture. In this study, we consider two general classes, referred to as $c_1$ and $c_2$, both belonging to the set of classes $C$. We have identified four types of relationships between these classes: implements, imports, and composed_by. However, the exist relationship will not be discussed further in this paper due to limited space constraints and its exclusion from the antipatterns detection process.

*implements.* The implements relationship provides insights into the interdependencies and interactions within a software system. When class $c_1$ implements class $i_1$, the implements relationship is established as $(c_1, i_1) \in E$. Please note that interfaces and abstract classes are nodes in the class relationship graph. By establishing the implements relationship, class $c_1$ realizes the specified methods and behaviors encapsulated by class $i_1$. Figure 1a depicts a scenario where class $c_1$ effectively implements the methods and behaviors specified by interface $i_1$. The relation is represented by the directed arrow from class $c_1$ to interface $i_1$.

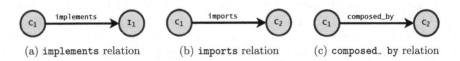

(a) implements relation      (b) imports relation      (c) composed_ by relation

**Fig. 1.** Relations between classes.

*imports.* The `imports` relationship represents a dependency between classes, where one class relies on another for specific functionality. If class $c_1$ imports class $c_2$, it establishes the `imports` relationship $(c_1, c_2) \in E$ and is represented in Fig. 1b by the directed arrow from $c_1$ to $c_2$. This relationship highlights the dependency of class $c_1$ on class $c_2$ for the necessary functionality.

*composed_by.* The `composed_by` relationship signifies the composition and aggregation of classes in a system. Note that, if the class $c_1$ is composed_by the class $c_2$, than $c_1$ has an attribute of type $c_2$. Thus, if class $c_1$ is composed or aggregated by class $c_2$, then the edge $(c_1, c_2) \in E$ is created. Figure 1c provides an example of the `composed_by` relationship where class $c_1$ is composed or aggregated by class $c_2$. The relationship is represented by the directed arrow from $c_1$ to $c_2$. Understanding the `composed_by` relationship provides insights into the structural organization of classes in the system, showcasing how they are composed or aggregated to create more complex entities.

## 2.2 Relations Between Classes and Methods

Another type of relationships that we analyze are those that exist between classes and methods. These relationships play a crucial role in understanding the interactions and dependencies within a software system. Specifically, we consider four types of relationships: `owns`, `uses_as_var`, `uses_as_arg`, and `returns`. For the sake of space, we do not deal with `uses_as_var`, `uses_as_arg`, and `returns` relationship which definition can be found in the *readme* file of the GitHub repository[1]. For the sake of exemplification, in the following we consider two classes, $c_1, c_2 \in C \subset V$ and a method $m_1 \in M \subset V$.

*owns.* The `owns` relationship is essential for organizing and defining software systems. It allows classes to manage and manipulate methods efficiently, leading to coherent designs. When a class owns a method, denoted as $(c_1, m_1) \in E$, it takes responsibility for its implementation and accessibility within its scope. This relationship enables encapsulation, with the class gaining authority over the owned method. Class $c_1$ owning method $m_1$ is visually represented in Fig. 2 as a directed edge outgoing from $c_1$. and incoming in $m_1$.

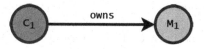

**Fig. 2.** `Owns` relation between classes and methods.

---

[1] https://github.com/conferenceRepoSubmission/ECSA23.

## 2.3   Relations Between Methods

In the scope of graph representation for Java systems outlined in this paper, we have specifically focused on the `calls` relationship as the sole relationship between methods that is crucial for our objectives. The `calls` relationship denotes the invocation of one method by another method within the system. The `calls` relationship as the primary connection that adequately represents the method-level dependencies essential to achieving our objectives. By leveraging this relationship, we can establish a comprehensive understanding of how methods interact and rely on one another within the Java system. If we have two methods, $m_1, m_2 \in M$, where $m_1$ calls $m_2$, we represent this relationship as $(m_1, m_2) \in E$. This relationship captures the fundamental dependencies and interactions between methods, allowing us to analyze the control flow and data flow within the system. Figure 3 depicts an example of the `calls` relationship. Thus, if the method $m_1$ calls method $m_2$, then a direct edge is created.

**Fig. 3.** `calls` relation between methods.

## 2.4   Automatic Graph Generation: Tool Implementation

The system's graph representation tool was developed to capture the relationships between classes and methods in a Java project. To accomplish this, the Java source code files are parsed using a customized parser implemented on top of *ANTLR*[2] and the *Java 9 grammar definition*[3]. *ANTLR* is configured to generate a *Python3*-based *Java lexer* and *Java parser skeleton*. This parser skeleton is then utilized in a custom *Python3* script, which extracts class and method definitions, along with the relationships specified in the previous section, to create a structured representation. The script can handle data from multiple Java source files and complete codebases, consolidating them into a unified data structure that does not consider the native Java classes as for example the class *"Class"*. The resulting graph is constructed using the *Neo4j*[4] graph-based database management system (DBMS) and its official *Python3* library. The tool, described in this paper, is available on a GitHub repository[5]. To test the implemented tool and provide examples on how to apply the mathematical formulations for antipattern detection presented in Sect. 3, the *spring-petclinic*[6] open source Java project has been used. We decided to analyse this project since it has been largely

---

[2] https://www.antlr.org/.

[3] https://github.com/antlr/grammars\discretionary-v4.

[4] https://neo4j.com/.

[5] https://github.com/conferenceRepoSubmission/ECSA23.

[6] https://github.com/spring-projects/spring-petclinic.

stuided in the literature for different purposes such as architectural refactoring of monoliths [30], architectural performance models extraction [31], and performance optimization using genetics algorithms [32].

# 3   Antipatterns Mathematical Formulation

In the forthcoming subsections, we will introduce the mathematical formulations of three specific antipatterns: *God Class, Circuitous Treasure Hunt,* and *Empty Semi-Truck.* We decided to analyse those three antipatterns since they are largely discussed in the litterature, giving us the opportunity to evaluate the results of the application of our approach. Each mathematical formulation will be applied on the PetClinic project to exemplify their application. Using the mathematical models, we aim to identify potential instances of these antipatterns to be considered in the refactoring process.

## 3.1   *God Class* Antipattern: Mathematical Formulation

The *God Class* antipattern occurs when a class takes on excessive responsibilities and violates the *Single Responsibility Principle* [24,26,27]. The problem arises when a class performs all of the application's work or holds all of its data, leading to increased message traffic and degraded performance. The recommended solution involves redistributing intelligence across top-level classes, achieving a balanced distribution of data and behavior throughout the system.

To identify instances of the *God Class* antipattern within the graph representation, a metric $C$ has been devised based on the class nodes' incoming and outgoing edges. The metric, denoted as $C(c)$, quantifies the complexity of a class node $c \in C \subset V$ relative to the total number of nodes $N = |V|$ in the graph. A high number of connections indicates a *God Class* burdened with numerous relationships and functionality. The metric is calculated using the formula:

$$C(c) = \frac{I(c) + O(c)}{N} \tag{3}$$

In the given formula, $I(c)$ represents incoming edges, $O(c)$ represents outgoing edges, and $N$ represents the total number of nodes in the graph (including classes and methods).

In the context of the modeled graph, the calculation of the metric $C(c)$ considers the following edges:

- **owns**: given a class $c \in C \subset V$, we analyse all its outgoing edges labeled as **owns**. As already described, the **owns** relation connect the class with each of its methods. Thus, we can recognize the number of method in the class. Indeed, a class that contains to many methods have an high probability to expose to many functionalities having high responsibility.
- **import**: given a class $c \in C \subset V$, we count both the incoming and outgoing edges of this type. On one hand, if the class $c$ imports a lot of classes, there is an high probability that it will be used for many funtionalities violating

the principle of *single responsibility*. On the other hand, if $c$ is imported into many classes, this means that it is required to performs different operations. This situation may represent a high degree of coupling.

- implements: given a class $c \in C \subset V$, that implements interfaces, we consider all the outgoing edges of this type. If a class implements a lot of interfaces, there is an high probability that the class has to many responsibility.

By comparing the calculated values across class nodes, excessively connected classes, known as *God Classes*, can be identified. This metric helps detect and assess *God Classes*, allowing developers to address design issues and improve software quality and maintainability.

To identify instances of *God Classes*, a threshold value $T$ is established. If the calculated metric $C(c)$ for a class node $c \in C \subset V$ exceeds the threshold value ($C(c) > T$), the corresponding class node is classified as a *God Class*. Thus, the presence of the *God Class* antipattern within the graph can be evaluated using the mathematical expression:

$$\forall c \in C, \ if \ C(c) > T, \ thenc is \ aGod \ Class. \qquad (4)$$

The threshold value $T$ is specific to the domain and may vary across different projects. By applying this mathematical expression software developers and analysts can effectively detect potential *God Classes* within the graph representation of the system.

***Example.*** In the following we provide an example of the detection of this antipatterns into the PetClinic application. o this purpose, we generated the following Cypher code running on the Neo4j Graph to retreive all the information needed to evaluate the metric $C(c)$. Table 1 reports the first six results of the Cypher query.

```
MATCH (c:Class)
RETURN c.name,
    size([o=(c)-[:OWNS]-()|o]) AS ownsOutgoing,
    size([i1=(c)-[:IMPORTS]-()|i1]) AS imports,
    size([i2=(c)-[:IMPLEMENTS]-()|i2]) AS implements,
(size([o=(c)-[:OWNS]-()|o])
    +size([i1=(c)-[:IMPORTS]-()|i1])
    +size([i2=(c)-[:IMPLEMENTS]-()|i2])) AS totalEdges,
(size([o=(c)-[:OWNS]-()|o])
    +size([i1=(c)-[:IMPORTS]-()|i1])
    +size([i2=(c)-[:IMPLEMENTS]-()|i2]))/187.0 AS complexity,
ORDER BY (complexity) DESC
```

If we consider the threashold $T > 0.9$, the classes *Owner* and *Pet* reveal the possible *God Class* antipattern. Figure 4 highlights all the relationship of type owns, implements, and import in which the class *Owner* is involved.

**Table 1.** Results of the Cypher Query for the God Class Antipattern.

| c.name | ownsOutgoing | imports | implements | totalEdges | complexity |
|---|---|---|---|---|---|
| "Owner" | 11 | 10 | 0 | 21 | 0.11229946 |
| "Pet" | 7 | 13 | 0 | 20 | 0.10695187 |
| "Vet" | 6 | 10 | 0 | 16 | 0.08556149 |
| "OwnerController" | 12 | 2 | 0 | 14 | 0.07486631 |
| "PetController" | 10 | 2 | 0 | 12 | 0.06417112 |
| "Visit" | 4 | 5 | 0 | 9 | 0.04812834 |

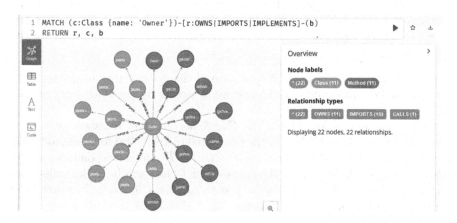

**Fig. 4.** *God Class* - Example: Class *Owner*.

## 3.2 *Circuitous Treasure Hunt* Antipattern: Mathematical Formulation

The *Circuitous Treasure Hunt* antipattern is distinguished by an extended sequence of method invocations or attribute accesses spanning across multiple classes degrading the software performance [24,25,27].

To detect the *Circuitous Treasure Hunt* antipattern in the graph representation, we use a metric that measures the length and complexity of method call chains. The metric is based on the idea that a long and convoluted call chain indicates participation in the antipattern. To this end, we introduce the metric $C(m)$ for a method node $m \in M \subset V$, defined as follows:

$$C(m) = L(m) \times W(m) \tag{5}$$

In the above formula:

- $L(m)$ denotes the length of the method call chain originating from the method node $m$. The recursive definition of $L(m)$ is as follows:

$$L(m) = \begin{cases} 0 & \forall\, m \in M \text{ s.t. } \nexists\, m' \in M \text{ s.t. } (m, m') \in E \\ 1 + \max(L(m')) & \forall\, m' \in M \text{ s.t. } (m, m') \in E \end{cases} \tag{6}$$

Thus, the value $L(m)$ is equal to 0 if $m$ lacks outgoing edges representing method call. Otherwise, the value is set to $1 + \max(L(m'))$ for all $m'$ such that $m$ calls $m'$.

- $W(m)$ signifies the weight of the method node $m$, reflecting its complexity. We define $W(m)$ as follows:

$$W(m) = N(m) + 1 \qquad (7)$$

Note that $N(m)$ represents the count of outgoing edges from $m$ that pertain to method calls, incremented by one to avoid multiplication by zero in formula (5) when $m$ lacks outgoing edges representing method calls. Note that $W(m)$ is necessary to avoid that wrapper and helper function are wrongly detected as *Circuitous Threasure Hunt*. Thus, the parameter is used to improve the trustability of the formula.

Considering the graph-based representation of the system, this antipattern can be recognized on a method $m \in M \subset V$ by analysing its outgoing edges of type `calls`.

For the purpose of identifying the *Circuitous Treasure Hunt* antipattern, a threshold value $T$ is established. If the calculated metric $C(m)$ for a method node $m$ exceeds the predefined threshold value ($C(m) > T$), the corresponding method node is considered to be part of the antipattern. Consequently, we formulate the mathematical expression to assess the presence of the *Circuitous Treasure Hunt* antipattern within the graph as follows:

$$\forall m \in M, \; if \; C(m) > T, \; then \; m \, is \; part \; of \; the \, Circuitous \; Treasure \; Hunt. \qquad (8)$$

Note that the threshold value $T$ is context-dependent and may vary based on the specific characteristics of the project. The utilization of this mathematical expression empowers software developers and analysts to effectively detect instances of the *Circuitous Treasure Hunt* antipattern within the system's graph representation.

***Example.*** In the following we provide an example of the detection of this antipatterns into the PetClinic application. To this purpose we created the Cypher query shown in Fig. 5. The query is performed to evaluate the parameter $L(m) = 4$. Considering, the number of outgoing edges of type `calls` of the method $m$ *processNewVisitForm*, its weight results to be $W(m) = 3$. Thus, in this case the metric is equal to $C(m) = 4 \times 3 = 12$.

On the other hand, the same metric for the length of the method $m'$ *loadPetWithVisit* is $W(m') = 2$. Thus, in this case the metric results to be $C(m') = 4 \times 2 = 8$. If we consider the threashold $T = 8$, then we can consider the method $m$ named *processNewVisitForm* as a part of a potential *Circuitous Threasure Hunt*.

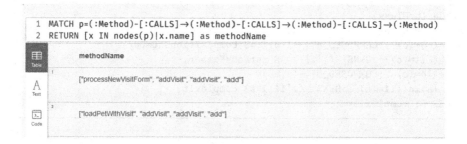

**Fig. 5.** *Circuitous Treasure Hunt* - Example.

### 3.3  *Empty Semi Truck* Antipattern: Mathematical Formulation

The *Empty Semi-Truck* antipattern occurs when a class lacks attributes or methods and serves solely as a namespace or grouping mechanism [24, 26]. It represents a situation where the class lacks functionality and is used only for organizing or categorizing elements.

To identify this antipattern within the graph-based representation of the system, we introduce a metric that gauges the emptiness of a class node. The emptiness metric $E(c)$ for a class node $c$ is defined as follows:

$$E(c) = F(c) + M(c) \tag{9}$$

In the provided formula, $F(c)$ denotes the number of attributes associated with the class node, whereas $M(c)$ signifies the number of methods associated with the class node $c$.

To evaluate if a class $c$ represent this antipattern, we evaluate two types of edges:

- composed_by: the sum of the outgoing edges of this type, represents the number of field of the class $c \in C \subset V$.
- owns: the number of outgoing edges of this type, represents the number of methods associated to the node class $c \in C \subset V$.

To detect the *Empty Semi-Truck* antipattern, a threshold value $T$ is established. If the calculated emptiness metric $E(c)$ for a class node $c$ falls below the predefined threshold $(E(c) < T)$, the class node $c$ is identified as part of the potential antipattern. Thus, the related mathematical expression is formulated as follows:

$$\forall c \in C, \text{ if } E(c) < T, \text{ then } c \text{ is part of the Empty Semi-Truk.} \tag{10}$$

***Example.*** In the following we provide an example of the detection of this antipatterns into the PetClinic application. To this purpose we created the following Cypher query to extract all the composed_by and owns relationship in wich the class $c$ is involved. Thus, the metric $E(c)$ has been evaluated by following the proposed formula. Table 2 shows the first six results of the created query.

```
MATCH (c:Class)
RETURN c.name,
size([o=(c)-[:COMPOSED_BY]-()|o]) AS compositionsNumber,
size([i1=(c)-[:OWNS]-()|i1]) AS methodsNumber,
size([o=(c)-[:COMPOSED_BY]-()|o])
    +size([i1=(c)-[:OWNS]-()|i1]) AS complexity
ORDER BY complexity
```

**Table 2.** Results of the Cypher Query for the Empty-Semy Truck Antipattern.

| c.name | compositionsNumber | methodsNumber | complexity |
|---|---|---|---|
| "Visit" | 1 | 0 | 1 |
| "OwnerController" | 1 | 0 | 1 |
| "PetType" | 1 | 0 | 1 |
| "SetVisit" | 1 | 0 | 1 |
| "PetController" | 1 | 0 | 1 |
| "PetTypeFormatter" | 1 | 0 | 1 |

## 4   Related Work

In recent years, there has been a growing interest in the field of software engineering to develop effective techniques for refactoring and improving the quality of software systems. In this context two types of studies can be identified. On one hand there are scientific works addressing the challenge of software comprehension through graph-based representation of the software. On the other hand, researchers have explored various approaches to address common code smells and antipatterns in software projects. In this section we will present the main contributions in the field, comparing them to our work.

### 4.1   Graph-Based Representation of Object-Oriented Projects

In the realm of representing dependency relationships, various language-specific graph variations have been proposed for C++ [14–17] and Java programs. These variations aim to capture the interdependencies among elements within the program. One such representation is the call-based object-oriented system dependence graph (COSDG), which incorporates additional annotations to account for calling context and method visibility details. Several studies have employed and advocated for the use of COSDG in their research [18,19]. Another notable representation is the Java software dependence graph (JSDG), which comprises multiple dependence graphs that depict control, data, and call dependencies among different program elements. JSDG has gained extensive usage within the Java context [20]. In order to enhance the capabilities of JSDG, Zhao proposed an augmented version known as the Java system dependence graph (JSDG+), which includes a specialized mechanism to handle polymorphism and interfaces, thereby improving the representation of dependencies in Java programs [21]. Building upon JSDG, JavaPDG provides a static analyzer for Java bytecode as well as a browser for visualizing various graphical representations, such as the procedure dependence graph, system dependence graph, control flow graph, and call graph [20,22]. Additionally, an improved version of JavaPDG called jpdg focuses specifically on enhancing the representation of program dependence graphs (PDGs) for code mining purposes [22,23].

Our proposed tool for graph-based representation carefully analyzes the relationships between classes and methods. In contrast to the existing works, our approach utilizes a simpler notation and focuses solely on capturing the essential elements required for detecting antipatterns. As a result, our approach achieves easier graph generation and, unlike other tools, it has been specifically designed for the purpose of antipattern detection.

## 4.2 Antipatterns Detection

Authors in [10] introduce MicroART, an Architecture Recovery Tool systems based on microservices. Utilizing Model-Driven Engineering principles, this tool generates software architecture models for microservice-based systems. These models can be managed by software architects to support system maintenance and evolvability. In [11] the PADRE tool is presented, which detects performance antipatterns in UML models. The tool also applies refactoring techniques to eliminate identified antipatterns from the UML models. Similarly, in [12], the authors propose a technique for enhancing the quality of use case models, demonstrated using a real-world system. This method detects antipattern defects in use case models and automatically refactors them through appropriate model transformations. Authors in [13] propose an algorithm that analyzes multiple architectural antipatterns representing the modularization problems to identify refactoring opportunities. The recommendations aim to minimize changes that have a significant impact on the overall system quality. In the study presented in [28], authors provide a systematic process, to identify and resolve performance issues with runtime data by using load testing and and data profiling. Similarly, authors in [29], presents a tool for antipatterns detection that uses Java profilers allowing to perform the dinamic analysis of the system. It is noticeable to present two industrial project: *Arcan*[7] and *Designate*[8]. The first, helps discovering the architectural debt to prevent its accumulation. The second, identifies architecture smells and visualize them. Each detected smell is presented with its definition and its cause.

Our work differs from the presented because of the following advantages:

- Our approach does not require the use of UML models, which can be limiting. Nowadays, with the increasing adoption of agile development processes, there

---

[7] https://www.arcan.tech/.
[8] https://www.designite-tools.com/.

is a lack of documentation. This often results in the absence of pre-existing UML models, which need to be regenerated. Even though automatic generation of such models is possible, it still requires the intervention of a software architect to ensure their correctness. In contrast, our system relies solely on the code, reducing the need for software architect intervention.

- The dynamic analysis of the system facilitates the detection of antipatterns as the system is simulated, producing more accurate results. However, with the advent of cloud architectures, dynamic system analysis becomes more complicated. Simulating the behavior of the system becomes challenging because a single application can be executed simultaneously on multiple cloud nodes. This makes the analysis of results more difficult, as they are influenced by uncontrollable external factors. Our approach, on the other hand, focuses solely on the internal structure of the system, bringing to light the most common antipatterns that have been deemed significant and impactful on performance within the scientific and industrial community.

### 4.3   Open Challenges of the Approach

This section highlights potential limitations that affect our study.

- Limited coverage of antipatterns: although the graph representation presented in this study is sufficiently general to detect various antipatterns, its coverage is still limited. Additionally, not all antipatterns can be identified solely through static analysis; dynamic analysis is required. To overcome these limitations, we plan to expand the range of antipatterns that our tool can detect by i) carefully analyzing new antipatterns to create a valuable mathematical formulation, ii) incorporate dynamic analysis capabilities to annotate the graph, thereby potentially increasing the number of detectable antipatterns.
- Manual intervention for antipattern detection: while we employed static analysis techniques to automatically construct the graph representation, our approach does not include an automated antipattern detection mechanism. As a result, the architect's assistance is necessary to identify the antipatterns by manually creating Cypher queries. By highlighting this limitation, we emphasize the need for developing an automated tool based on our methodology. This would not only validate its effectiveness but also enhance its practical usage, as it would eliminate the reliance on manual intervention and make the detection process more efficient.
- Lack of comparative tools for validation: as discussed in Sect. 4, various tools have been proposed in both academic and industrial contexts. However, we were unable to directly compare our work with these tools for a significant reason: unlike other existing approaches, our methodology relies solely on static analysis. Consequently, we cannot evaluate the accuracy of our results through a comparative analysis.
- Specificity to Java projects: Although the methods for representing software using graphs and detecting antipatterns mathematically are universally applicable to Object Oriented languages, the tool designed for automatic graph

generation is limited to Java projects. This restriction arises from the tool's reliance on a parser developed specifically for the Java 9 grammar. Therefore, while the general approaches and mathematical formulations are transferable, the tool's functionality is confined to Java-based systems.

## 5    Conclusion

In this paper, we presented a semi-automatic approach for detecting three antipatterns, namely the *God Class, Circuitous Treasure Hunt,* and *Empty Semi-Truck,* in Java projects. To achieve this goal, we developed a Java code parser based on the Java grammar that helps for the automatic generation of a graph representation of the system, providing a comprehensive view of the codebase and enhancing understanding of its underlying structure. By formulating the selected antipatterns as mathematical problems on this graph representation, we effectively identified potential instances of the antipatterns within the software projects. We exemplified the application of these formulations on the open-source Java project, PetClinic, to illustrate the efficacy of our approach.

As future work, we plan to explore and analyze new antipatterns, providing them with appropriate mathematical formulations. Furthermore, we aim to annotate the graph with parameters obtained through dynamic analysis of the system. Currently absent in our tool, this enhancement will allow for the detection of those antipatterns requiring consideration of the system's behavior. This improvement will enable a more accurate assessment of the tool's precision in detecting antipatterns by comparing our results with existing market solutions.

**Acknowledgment.** This work was supported by the project *"Modernization of Legacy Systems: Microservices Architecture and Non-Functional Requirements"* funded within *Programma Operativo Nazionale Ricerca e Innovazione 2014–2020.*

## References

1. Al-Saiyd, N.A.: Source code comprehension analysis in software maintenance. In: 2017 2nd International Conference on Computer and Communication Systems (ICCCS), Krakow, Poland, pp. 1–5 (2017). https://doi.org/10.1109/CCOMS.2017.8075175
2. Alshayeb, M.: Empirical investigation of refactoring effect on software quality. Inf. Softw. Technol. **51**(9), 1319–1326 (2009)
3. Beck, K., Fowler, M., Beck, G.: Bad smells in code. Refactoring: Improv. Des. Existing Code **1**(1999), 75–88 (1999)
4. William, H.B., et al.: AntiPatterns: Refactoring Software, Architectures, and Projects in Crisis. Wiley, Hoboken (1998)
5. Avritzer, A., et al.: A multivariate characterization and detection of software performance antipatterns. In: Proceedings of the ACM/SPEC International Conference on Performance Engineering (ICPE 2021). Association for Computing Machinery, New York, NY, USA, pp. 61–72 (2021). https://doi.org/10.1145/3427921.3450246

6. Ferrante, J., Ottenstein, K.J., Warren, J.D.: The program dependence graph and its use in optimization. ACM Trans. Program. Lang. Syst. **9**(3), 319–349 (1987). https://doi.org/10.1145/24039.24041
7. Horwitz, S., Reps, T., Binkley, D.: Interprocedural slicing using dependence graphs. ACM Trans. Program. Lang. Syst. **12**(1), 26–60 (1990). https://doi.org/10.1145/77606.77608
8. Eichinger, F., Krogmann, K., Klug, R., Böhm, K.: Software-defect localisation by mining dataflow-enabled call graphs. In: Machine Learning and Knowledge Discovery in Databases: European Conference, ECML PKDD 2010, Barcelona, Spain, 20–24 September 2010, Proceedings, Part I 21, pp. 425–441. Springer, Berlin (2010). https://doi.org/10.1007/978-3-642-15880-3_33
9. Law, J., Rothermel, G.: Whole program path-based dynamic impact analysis. In: Proceedings of the 25th International Conference on Software Engineering (ICSE 2003). IEEE Computer Society, USA, pp. 308–318 (2003)
10. Granchelli, G., Cardarelli, M., Di Francesco, P., Malavolta, I., Iovino, L., Di Salle, A.: MicroART: a software architecture recovery tool for maintaining microservice-based systems. In: 2017 IEEE International Conference on Software Architecture Workshops (ICSAW), pp. 298–302. IEEE (2017)
11. Cortellessa, V., Di Pompeo, D., Stoico, V., Tucci, M.: Software model refactoring driven by performance antipattern detection. ACM SIGMETRICS Perform. Eval. Rev. **49**(4), 53–58 (2022)
12. Khan, Y.A., El-Attar, M.: Using model transformation to refactor use case models based on antipatterns. Inf. Syst. Front. **18**, 171–204 (2016)
13. Dietrich, J., McCartin, C., Tempero, E., Shah, S.M.A.: On the existence of high-impact refactoring opportunities in programs. In: Proceedings of the Thirty-fifth Australasian Computer Science Conference-Volume 122, pp. 37–48 (2012)
14. Harrold, M.J., Rothermel, G.: A coherent family of analyzable graphical representations for object-oriented software. Department of Computer and Information Science, The Ohio State University, Technical Report OSU-CISRC-11/96-TR60 (1996)
15. Larsen, L., Harrold, M.J.: Slicing object-oriented software. In: Proceedings of IEEE 18th International Conference on Software Engineering, pp. 495–505. IEEE (1996)
16. Mallo, B., McGregor, J.D., Krishnaswamy, A., Medikonda, M.: An extensible program representation for object-oriented software. ACM Sigplan Not. **29**(12), 38–47 (1994)
17. Rothermel, G., Harrold, M.J.: Selecting Regression Tests for Object-Oriented Software. In: ICSM, vol. 94, pp. 14–25 (1994)
18. Najumudheen, E.S.F., Mall, R., Samanta, D.: A dependence graph-based representation for test coverage analysis of object-oriented programs. ACM SIGSOFT Softw. Eng. Notes **34**(2), 1–8 (2009)
19. Najumudheen, E.S.F., Mall, R., Samanta, D.: A dependence representation for coverage testing of object-oriented programs. J. Object Technol. **9**(4), 1–23 (2010)
20. Zhao, J.: Applying program dependence analysis to Java software. In: Proceedings of Workshop on Software Engineering and Database Systems, 1998 International Computer Symposium, pp. 162–169 (1998)
21. Walkinshaw, N., Roper, M., Wood, M.: The Java system dependence graph. In: Proceedings Third IEEE International Workshop on Source Code Analysis and Manipulation, pp. 55–64. IEEE (2003)
22. Shu, G., Sun, B., Henderson, T.A., Podgurski, A.: JavaPDG: a new platform for program dependence analysis. In: 2013 IEEE Sixth International Conference on Software Testing, Verification and Validation, pp. 408–415. IEEE (2013)

23. Henderson, T.A., Podgurski, A.: Sampling code clones from program dependence graphs with GRAPLE. In: Proceedings of the 2nd International Workshop on Software Analytics, pp. 47–53 (2016)
24. Trubiani, C.: Automated generation of architectural feedback from software performance analysis results. Unpublished PhD thesis). Universita di L'Aquila (2011). http://www.di.univaq.it/catia.trubiani/phDthesis/PhDThesis-CatiaTrubiani.pdf
25. Smith, C.U., Williams, L.G.: Software performance antipatterns; common performance problems and their solutions. In: International CMG Conference, pp. 797–806 (2001)
26. Smith, C.U., Williams, L.G.: Software performance antipatterns. In: Proceedings of the 2nd International Workshop on Software and Performance, pp. 127–136 (2000)
27. Smith, C.U., Williams, L.G.: New software performance antipatterns: more ways to shoot yourself in the foot. In: International CMG Conference, pp. 667–674 (2002)
28. Trubiani, C., Bran, A., van Hoorn, A., Avritzer, A., Knoche, H.: Exploiting load testing and profiling for performance antipattern detection. Inf. Softw. Technol. **95**, 329–345 (2018)
29. Trubiani, C., Pinciroli, R., Biaggi, A., Fontana, F.A.: Automated detection of software performance antipatterns in Java-based applications. IEEE Trans. Softw. Eng. (2023)
30. Sellami, K., Saied, M.A., Ouni, A.: A hierarchical DBSCAN method for extracting microservices from monolithic applications. In: Proceedings of the 26th International Conference on Evaluation and Assessment in Software Engineering, pp. 201–210 (2022)
31. Walter, J., Stier, C., Koziolek, H., Kounev, S.: An expandable extraction framework for architectural performance models. In: Proceedings of the 8th ACM/SPEC on International Conference on Performance Engineering Companion, pp. 165–170 (2017)
32. Singh, R., Bezemer, C.P., Shang, W., Hassan, A.E.: Optimizing the performance related configurations of object relational mapping frameworks using a multi objective genetic algorithm. In: Proceedings of the 7th ACM/SPEC on International Conference on Performance Engineering, pp. 309–320 (2016)

# Scalable Cloud-Native Pipeline for Efficient 3D Model Reconstruction from Monocular Smartphone Images

Potito Aghilar[1]($\boxtimes$), Vito Walter Anelli[2], Michelantonio Trizio[1], and Tommaso Di Noia[2]

[1] Wideverse, Via Orabona 4, 70125 Bari, Italy
{potito.aghilar,michelantonio.trizio}@wideverse.com
[2] Politecnico di Bari, Via Amendola 126/b, 70126 Bari, Italy
{vitowalter.anelli,tommaso.dinoia}@poliba.it

**Abstract.** In recent years, 3D models have gained popularity in various fields, including entertainment, manufacturing, and simulation. However, manually creating these models can be a time-consuming and resource-intensive process, making it impractical for large-scale industrial applications. To address this issue, researchers are exploiting Artificial Intelligence and Machine Learning algorithms to automatically generate 3D models effortlessly. In this paper, we present a novel cloud-native pipeline that can automatically reconstruct 3D models from monocular 2D images captured using a smartphone camera. Our goal is to provide an efficient and easily-adoptable solution that meets the Industry 4.0 standards for creating a Digital Twin model, which could enhance personnel expertise through accelerated training. We leverage machine learning models developed by NVIDIA Research Labs alongside a custom-designed pose recorder with a unique pose compensation component based on the ARCore framework by Google. Our solution produces a reusable 3D model, with embedded materials and textures, exportable and customizable in any external 3D modelling software or 3D engine. Furthermore, the whole workflow is implemented by adopting the microservices architecture standard, enabling each component of the pipeline to operate as a standalone replaceable module.

**Keywords:** 3D Model Reconstruction · Microservices architecture · Augmented Reality · Computer Vision

## 1 Introduction

In contemporary times, 3D models and complete 3D environments have become ubiquitous across different sectors, including art, entertainment, simulation, augmented reality, virtual reality, video games, 3D printing, marketing, TV and manufacturing. The attraction of having a digital version of any physical object as a 3D model lies in its versatility and adaptability for varied purposes. This digital replica, known as a *Digital Twin (DT)*, is a virtual model that accurately reflects and maps physical goods in a digital space [1]. DTs can be utilized to replicate physical objects in a virtual environment, thereby enabling specific tasks on the simulated model and observing their effects on the real-world counterpart. The integration of Industrial Augmented Reality (IAR) in Industry 4.0 can significantly enhance worker productivity and task effectiveness by providing real-time data and information. IAR is beneficial in manufacturing, where it assists workers in making informed decisions in realistic situations [2], streamlines engineering workflows throughout the design and manufacturing stages [3], and increases productivity by equipping workers with the necessary information to perform tasks more efficiently and safely. IAR is also effective in marketing and sales, where it can provide interactive information about products, dispel uncertainty, and influence client perceptions [4,6–8]. Furthermore, IAR can facilitate training by offering detailed instructions and reducing the time required to train new personnel while minimizing their skill requirements [9]. Over the years, modeling techniques have undergone significant evolution, leading to the development of more intuitive and less time-consuming tools for creating or generating 3D models. These models can be created from a set of primitive shapes, mathematical equations, or even a 2D image. The most commonly used techniques for creating 3D models are manual modeling, photogrammetry, and Light Detection and Ranging (LIDAR). Manual modeling, while effective, can be expensive in terms of time and resources since it involves a significant amount of manual labor and is unsuitable for large-scale applications. Alternatively, photogrammetry involves the use of photographs taken from different angles by a camera to make measurements. Finally, specialized hardware-based techniques such as LIDAR technology are also utilized. In addition, the industrial research sector is actively exploring this research domain. In the last decade, Artificial Intelligence and Machine Learning techniques [5,13] have gained significant attention and NVIDIA is currently developing novel algorithms to enhance the quality of generated 3D models. Two of the approaches analyzed in this paper are based on recent research publications from 2022: *Instant NeRF* - a set of instant neural graphics primitives for NeRF [10] - and *nvdiffrec* - which leverages differential rendering and Deep Marching Tetrahedra (DMTet) [11].

The aim of this paper is to present a distributed, cloud-native, and scalable pipeline capable of solving the 3D model reconstruction problem using a set of monocular two-dimensional images. The proposed pipeline is designed to reduce time and resources, providing a cost-effective solution for large-scale industrial applications by leveraging microservices architecture standards. Furthermore, the pipeline is enhanced by Augmented Reality (AR) capabilities to improve the data acquisition workflow. The main contributions of this paper are:

- definition of a scalable cloud-native pipeline for the automatic generation of 3D models from monocular two-dimensional images with respect to the microservices architecture standard;
- design and implementation of a custom pose recorder component based on ARCore to acquire both images of the object and poses of the camera.

## 2   Background and Technology

This section provides a list of conventional and standard techniques alongside AI-based ones. It focuses on main drawbacks and how to overcome them.

### 2.1   Standard and Conventional Techniques

Manual modeling involves creating a 3D model using specialized software by an experienced 3D artist or modeler. This technique can be time-consuming and not suitable for large-scale applications due to the time involved for the design process for a single 3D model. The 3D artist is responsible for addressing various issues during the modeling process, such as mesh creation, material definition, texture generation, model rigging, environment, and lighting. Commonly used software for manual modeling includes techniques such as *polygonal modeling*, *surface modeling*, and *digital sculpting*[1].

Photogrammetry is a technique for generating 3D models from two-dimensional images. It involves using a collection of photos taken from different angles with a standard 2D camera and extracting material properties using methods from optics and projective geometry. This technique is useful in achieving a realistic feeling during Physically-Based Rendering (PBR)[2].

Lastly, LIDAR is a remote sensing technology that uses pulsed laser light to measure variable distances from a source point to a hit point, thereby collecting data about the shape and elevation of the scanned object's surface. LIDAR is commonly used in 3D model reconstruction of real-world objects and is also known as a 3D laser scanner. The output of a LIDAR scan is a point cloud, which comprises a set of geo-located colored data points in a 3D space and provides additional information about the object's material properties[3].

### 2.2   AI-Based Techniques

This paragraph discusses about how AI-based techniques can be used to overcome the aforementioned standard techniques' drawbacks. In particular, *Instant NeRF* and *nvdiffrec* from NVIDIA Research Labs [10, 11].

**Instant NeRF.** It is a more advanced and efficient implementation of the NeRF technique, which enables the creation of 3D models from 2D images using neural networks and a multi-resolution hash encoding grid. The technique involves reconstructing a volumetric radiance-and-density field from 2D images and their corresponding camera poses, which can then be visualized through ray marching. The encoding phase is task-agnostic and only the hash

---

[1] https://en.wikipedia.org/wiki/3D_modeling, 2022.
[2] https://en.wikipedia.org/wiki/Photogrammetry.
[3] https://en.wikipedia.org/wiki/Lidar.

table size is adjusted, which affects the trade-off between quality and performance. The multi-resolution structure enables the network to resolve hash collisions more effectively. The implementation heavily relies on parallelism, utilizing fully-fused CUDA kernels with *FullyFusedMLP* [12,14]. If this is not available, the algorithm falls back to *CutlassMLP* - CUDA Templates for Linear Algebra Subroutines[4] [15], with a focus on minimizing unnecessary bandwidth and computational operations. The primary limitation of this methodology is its dependence on the NeRF technique, which produces a point cloud as its output. Consequently, the authors had to devise a method to extract the mesh of the scene from the encoded data within the neural networks. To accomplish this, they employed the Marching Cubes (MC) algorithm, a mesh extraction technique that is dependent on a point cloud as its initial input. However, the resulting mesh presents surface irregularities in the form of various holes, lacks UV coordinates, and does not possess any materials. As a result, it is essentially an unusable gray mesh for any 3D modeling software.

**nvdiffrec.** It is a tool that enables the creation of 3D models from 2D images. What sets nvdiffrec apart from Instant NeRF is its ability to reconstruct a 3D model surface, complete with texture and materials. The authors approached this task as an "inverse rendering" problem, using a 2D image loss function to optimize as many steps as possible jointly. The goal is to ensure that the reconstructed model's rendered images are of high quality compared to the input imagery. The approach used in nvdiffrec enables the learning of topology and vertex positions for a surface mesh without the need for any initial guesses about the 3D geometry. The tool's *differentiable surface model* relies on a *deformable tetrahedral mesh* that has been extended to support spatially varying materials and high dynamic range (HDR) environment lighting through a novel differentiable split sum approximation. The resulting 3D model can be deployed on any device capable of triangle rendering, including smartphones and web browsers, without the need for further conversion and can render at interactive rates [11]. The paper tackles the challenge of 3D reconstruction from multi-view images of an object, with known camera poses and background segmentation masks, producing triangle meshes, spatially-varying materials (stored in 2D textures), and HDR environment probe lighting. Specifically, the authors adapt *Deep Marching Tetrahedra (DMTet)* to work in the setting of 2D supervision and jointly optimize shape, materials, and lighting. Unlike Instant NeRF, the mesh in this approach is UV-mapped with customizable materials and multiple textures linked to it, allowing for the reuse of the mesh in any 3D engine, such as Blender[5], Maya[6], 3DS Max[7], and Unity[8] [11].

---

[4] https://developer.nvidia.com/blog/cutlass-linear-algebra-cuda/.
[5] https://www.blender.org/.
[6] https://www.autodesk.it/products/maya/overview.
[7] https://www.autodesk.it/products/3ds-max/overview.
[8] https://unity.com/.

# 3  Proposed Pipeline

Skilled service professionals are capable of maintaining and repairing complex machinery and industrial facilities. These professionals utilize their knowledge in industrial maintenance and assembly tasks by employing a combination of simulation, capturing techniques, multimodal interaction, and 3D-interactive graphics to achieve distributed training [16]. The acquired competencies are then adapted to realistic training situations that are utilized in industrial training facilities. In [16], the authors refer to this as *immersive training*, which involves *"Real-time simulations of object behavior and multimodal interaction that support the development of complex training simulators that address cognitive skills [...] and sensorimotor skills."*. Industrial Augmented Reality (IAR) is a combination of computer vision and computer graphics that utilizes camera-based interaction. IAR can be exploited to facilitate the data acquisition process for the proposed scalable cloud-native pipeline. The adoption of a powerful container orchestration platform is crucial for achieving scalable DTs: Kubernetes facilitates the deployment, scaling, and management of containerized applications across distributed systems.[9]. In our proposed architecture, we leverage Kubernetes clustering to facilitate the deployment of the different phases of the pipeline as Jobs to worker nodes. This approach enables us to achieve scalability while reducing operational overhead and infrastructure costs. Worker nodes require an NVIDIA GPU to handle the high-end capabilities needed for dataset preprocessing and reconstruction jobs. Therefore, the complete reconstruction pipeline consists of various phases that can be executed either on an embedded device or in the cloud, depending on the different resource requirements. The approach of using schedulable Jobs to fulfill resource-intensive tasks, instead of standard Kubernetes Deployment resources, allows to dynamically scale up the approach and reduces resources. Actually, GPUs allocation is impactful for the overall infrastructure cost, which needs to be addressed in an industrial perspective.

## 3.1  Pipeline Definition

We defined a reconstruction pipeline (Fig. 1) by identifying a set of phases that are executed progressively, each performing specific operations on the dataset. The pipeline phases are described below:

- *Data acquisition*, a custom written *pose recorder* with a *poses compensation algorithm* is implemented;
- *Preprocessing*, the images and poses are preprocessed and the relative alpha masks are generated (silhouettes);
- *Reconstruction*, the 3D model is generated alongside a preview of the current pipeline status in order to provide feedback to the end user.

---

[9] https://kubernetes.io/.

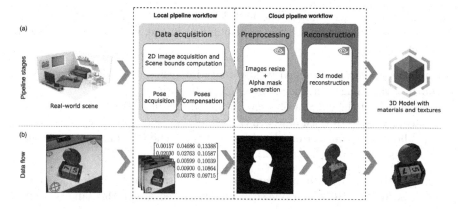

**Fig. 1.** A graphical representation of the proposed pipeline. In (a), the sequence of operations required to achieve the expected result is described. In (b), the data flow between the intermediate stages of the pipeline is illustrated.

The pipeline is constituted by two sub-workflows: a local workflow and a cloud workflow. The former is implemented in a mobile Android native app and comprises the data acquisition phase. The latter is deployed in the cloud and includes both Preprocessing and Reconstruction phases (see Sect. 3.5). Upon completion of the entire process, the end user can interact with the generated 3D model and visualize it from different angles directly on his smartphone. We have adopted a distributed storage solution that caches both final model and each intermediate output for the entire pipeline's flow in MinIO: an high-performance, S3 compatible, Kubernetes-native object storage solution[10].

## 3.2 Data Acquisition

The initial step in the reconstruction pipeline is the generation of the dataset through data acquisition. The dataset comprises a collection of images and corresponding poses. These crucial components are obtained through a native Android application that implements the ARCore framework[11]. The reconstruction module necessitates specific technical prerequisites for the input data, particularly:

- a set of RGB images with a resolution of $512 \times 512$ pixels;
- a set of alpha masks (silhouettes) with a resolution of $512 \times 512$ pixels;
- a *poses_bounds.npy* file containing the view matrices of the camera for each image with the specific camera intrinsics.

Given a set of images of size $N$, the *poses_bounds* file is a numpy [5] array of shape $(N, 17)$, in which $N$ is the number of images and 17 is the number of

---

[10] https://min.io/.

[11] https://github.com/google-ar/arcore-android-sdk.

[5] https://numpy.org/

total features for each image. The first 12 columns of each row are the $3 \times 4$ *view matrix* of the camera for the corresponding image, and the last 5 elements represent:

- height of the image obtained from camera intrinsics;
- width of the image obtained from camera intrinsics;
- focal length of the camera obtained from camera intrinsics (we are assuming the focal lengths of both axes are the same);
- scene bounds obtained from depth map of the scene (the minimum and maximum distance from the camera).

It is imperative to maintain a coherent coordinate system throughout the entire process: both the ARCore framework and nvdiffrec adopt the same OpenGL right-handed system convention[12].

**Pose Recorder.** To record the poses during 2D image acquisition, a *pose recorder component* is necessary, wherein each pose corresponds to a single image. We have implemented this workflow as a library in a native Android application, where the management of the anchor lifecycle is a critical aspect, particularly for the *poses compensation algorithm.* Moreover, this library facilitates the selection of a camera with varying resolutions or frames per second (FPS) to initiate the recording process. In the subsequent *preprocessing phase*, the images are resized to $512 \times 512$ pixels to fulfill the input requirements of the machine learning model. ARCore provides a view matrix of the device's pose in the world coordinate system, which is represented by a $4 \times 4$ matrix. The rotation matrix is represented by the first $3 \times 3$ submatrix, while the translation vector is represented by the last column. However, a $4 \times 4$ matrix is not suitable for this particular problem, as a $3 \times 4$ view matrix is required. To address this, the last row of the matrix is removed to obtain the desired $3 \times 4$ matrix. The resulting matrix follows the *column-major order* convention in which the matrix elements are ordered by column[13]. To complete the transformation, a new column of shape $3 \times 1$ that contains the height, width, and focal length of the device is concatenated with the matrix. The resulting matrix is:

$$\begin{bmatrix} r_{11} & r_{12} & r_{13} & t_x & h \\ r_{21} & r_{22} & r_{23} & t_y & w \\ r_{31} & r_{32} & r_{33} & t_z & f \end{bmatrix}$$

in which $r_{ij}$ is the ij-element of the rotation view matrix, $t_i$ is the i-element of the translation vector and $h, w, f$ are the height, the width and the focal lenght respectively extracted from the camera instrinsics. After a matrix flattening operation[14] and a subsequent concatenation, we obtain the final data-flattened

---

[12] https://learnopengl.com/Getting-started/Coordinate-Systems.

[13] https://en.wikipedia.org/wiki/Row-_and_column-major_order.

[14] https://github.com/Fyusion/LLFF/issues/10#issuecomment-514406658.

view matrix. Thus, the following reshaped data entry can be generated for each frame:

$$r_{11}\ r_{12}\ r_{13}\ t_x\ h\ r_{21}\ r_{22}\ r_{23}\ t_y\ w\ r_{31}\ r_{32}\ r_{33}\ t_z\ f\ m\ M$$

in which $m$ and $M$, are respectively the minimum and the maximum scene bounds computed from the depth map in meters. During the recording, a *compensation matrix* is applied in real-time to compensate camera pose jumps. An additional rotational fix is applied to the $3 \times 3$ rotation submatrix of the camera: it consists in a swap of the first and the second column and a sign inversion of the new first column (see footnote 13):

$$\begin{bmatrix} r_{11}\ r_{12}\ r_{13}\ t_x\ h \\ r_{21}\ r_{22}\ r_{23}\ t_y\ w \\ r_{31}\ r_{32}\ r_{33}\ t_z\ f \end{bmatrix} \Rightarrow \begin{bmatrix} r_{12}\ r_{11}\ r_{13}\ t_x\ h \\ r_{22}\ r_{21}\ r_{23}\ t_y\ w \\ r_{32}\ r_{31}\ r_{33}\ t_z\ f \end{bmatrix} \Rightarrow \begin{bmatrix} -r_{12}\ r_{11}\ r_{13}\ t_x\ h \\ -r_{22}\ r_{21}\ r_{23}\ t_y\ w \\ -r_{32}\ r_{31}\ r_{33}\ t_z\ f \end{bmatrix}$$

At the end of recording, different tasks are performed to generate the dataset:

- the compensated *poses_bounds* file is saved in the device's local storage;
- the *compensation matrix* is saved in the device's local storage;
- the images are cropped with an aspect ratio of 1:1 and saved in the device's local storage;
- the whole dataset is compressed and saved in the device's local storage.
- the compressed dataset is uploaded to the S3 bucket.

**Pose Compensation Algorithm.** During experiments we faced a sensor drifting problem, leading to an inconsistent dataset and a jugged surface on the reconstructed model: a comparison was performed between our dataset and the COLMAP's generated one. COLMAP adopts *Structure-from-motion (SfM)* and *Multi-View Stereo (MVS) techniques* [17,18]. The two datasets were generated in two distinct coordinate systems, forcing us to reconcile all the data points though a series of matrix transformations. Finally, the computed difference between the two datasets yields a *difference matrix*, which highlights their deviation (Fig. 2). Consequently, a pose compesation algorithm is required to fix the sensor drifting problem. This relies on a self-made anchor management system to detect real-time variations of positions or rotations of ARCore Anchors while scanning. This avoids trajectory discontinuity by computing and applying a *compensation matrix* to the camera view matrix. The Poses Compensation Algorithm comprises the following components:

- *Anchors*, objects placed in the scene, provided by ARCore;
- *Delta position* from initial pose for each anchor frame by frame;
- *Delta rotation* from initial pose for each anchor frame by frame;
- *Quaternion* products to compute the rotation matrix.

Given a quaternion $q = a + bi + cj + dk$ defined by the following coefficients $< a, b, c, d >$ and the following imaginary components $(i, j, k)$, each delta quaternion can be computed as follows:

$$q_{delta} = q_{target} q_{current}^{-1}$$

(a)    (b)

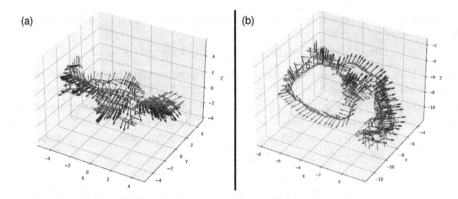

**Fig. 2.** Comparison of our solution's extracted poses (a) with COLMAP's (b). COLMAP lacks of real-world reference during the pose extraction phase resulting in a non-overlapped set of poses between (a) and (b).

in which $q_{delta}$ is the delta quanternion to compute, $q_{target}$ represents the target rotation we want to reach and $q_{current}^{-1}$ represents the inverse of the current rotation. Therefore, because $q_{current}^{-1}$ is the conjugate of quaternion $q_{current}$, it can be computed by an inversion of the imaginary components of the quaternion:

$$conj(a + bi + cj + dk) = a - bi - cj - dk$$

Moreover, given two quaternions $q$ and $r$ having the form:

$$q = q_0 + q_1 i + q_2 j + q_3 k \qquad r = r_0 + r_1 i + r_2 j + r_3 k$$

From [19], the product of two quaternions is a quaternion having the form:

$$n = q \times r = n_0 + n_1 i + n_2 j + n_3 k$$

where:

$$n_0 = (r_0 q_0 - r_1 q_1 - r_2 q_2 - r_3 q_3) \qquad n_1 = (r_0 q_1 + r_1 q_0 - r_2 q_3 + r_3 q_2)$$

$$n_2 = (r_0 q_2 + r_1 q_3 + r_2 q_0 - r_3 q_1) \qquad n_3 = (r_0 q_3 - r_1 q_2 + r_2 q_1 + r_3 q_0)$$

Specifically, the algorithm is composed of three main steps:

- compute the *delta mean pose* starting from the delta pose of each valid anchor (tracked from SDK): this indicates, on average, how much each anchor has moved from the initial pose. More anchors are placed in the scene, more accurate is the estimation;
- combine the current camera pose with the delta mean pose exploiting the *pose composition* method;
- convert the new pose to a $3 \times 4$ matrix and apply the rotational fix.

The values of the compensation matrix change frame by frame resulting in a full matrix of shape $N \times 17$ (Fig. 3).

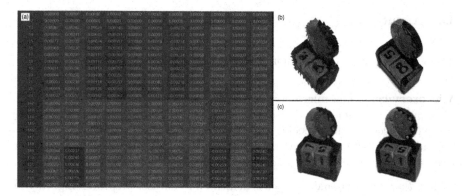

**Fig. 3.** In (a), a partial view of the compensation matrix generated at run-time is illustrated. In (b) and (c), the difference during reconstruction with the implementation of the compensation matrix is presented: in both cases the reference image is placed side by side to highlight the differences.

### 3.3   Preprocessing

In this phase, the images are resized to a resolution of 512 × 512 pixels before starting the alpha masks generation subtask. Thus, we adopted *CarveKit*, a neural networks model to extract the alpha mask starting from the RGB images[15]. To optimize performance, the framework is executed on the GPU. We then refine the silhouettes by applying a threshold to eliminate any ambiguous regions and enhance the edges of the 3D model during the reconstruction phase. Ultimately, we obtain a set of sharpened alpha masks integrated into the initial dataset.

### 3.4   Reconstruction

This phase adopts nvdiffrec tool to reconstruct the 3D model. The input parameters required for this task are:

- a collection of RGB images in PNG format;
- a collection of alpha mask images in PNG format (silhouette);
- a set of camera poses serialized in the *poses_bounds* numpy matrix file.

Finally, upon successful reconstruction, the tool provides as artifacts:

- *mesh.obj* containing the reconstructed mesh, UV mapped;
- *mesh.mtl* containing the material properties;
- *texture_kd.png* file containing the diffuse texture;
- *texture_ks.png* containing the ORM map (-, roughness, metalness);
- *texture_n.png* containing the normal map.

---

[15] https://github.com/OPHoperHPO/image-background-remove-tool.

## 3.5   Architecture

We have designed and implemented the pipeline utilizing microservices architecture standards, specifically tailored to be deployed on a Kubernetes cluster.

**Microservices.** The microservices compose the fundamental constituents of the pipeline. Each microservice, implemented as a Docker image, is purposefully crafted to accomplish a specific task. Specifically, the microservices that have been identified are the *Preprocessing* microservice, the *Reconstruction* microservice, and the *Workloads scheduler* microservice (refer to Fig. 4).

- The *Preprocessing* microservice is dedicated to dataset preprocessing. Its container is based on the *NVIDIA CUDA runtime environment* image, with the necessary dependencies installed to ensure CarveKit to operate properly.
- The *Reconstruction* microservice heavily relies on the nvdiffrec repository. This Docker image is built utilizing specific configurations, dependencies, and environmental variables outlined in the official documentation. The image was modified by adding customized domain-specific code to enable preview image generation, dataset management, and 3D model uploading.
- The *Workloads scheduler* microservice is responsible for job scheduling within the cluster. It operates as a backend service API that oversees the entire pipeline lifecycle for each reconstruction request.

A clear separation between the Preprocessing and the Reconstruction microservices is motivated by the need to preserve the original structure of the nvdiffrec codebase and can ease future updates from the authors. This approach enables code maintenance from the upstream repository, ensuring compatibility with bug fixes and future upgrades. Moreover, the Preprocessing microservice is purposefully crafted to tailor the dataset to fit the specific requirements of the reconstruction tool. In case of necessary changes, a portion of the pipeline can be preserved, while keeping the interface between components unmodified, thus enabling microservice reuse. Consequently, while further subdividing the services into smaller components may seem like an attractive solution, it is important to consider that this could lead to a significant increase in communication overhead, thus negating the efforts to improve system efficiency. The balance between service granularity and communication overhead is critical for ensuring optimal performance in this specific setting.

Each microservice is deployed within the Kubernetes cluster. Specifically, the Workloads scheduler is a resource of type Deployment due to its stateless characteristics. An Horizontal Pod Autoscaler (HPA) is attached to this resource to exploit fault-tolerance and high-availability (HA) to face different traffic-peak times. The Preprocessing and Reconstruction pods are overseen by the upper-level Kubernetes Job resource to attain stateful execution, owing to the presence of isolated reconstruction contexts across different requests. These microservices communicate and exchange unstructured data with the storage layer operated by MinIO through S3 compatible API. It contains both the final 3D model and intermediate stage results. The storage layer and the three microservices represent the *Cloud pipeline workflow*. Furthermore, the *Local pipeline workflow* is implemented in the mobile native app whose goals are to acquire the dataset and view the generated 3D model interactively. Finally, to improve overall performance, data acquisition and visualization phases are executed on the smartphone.

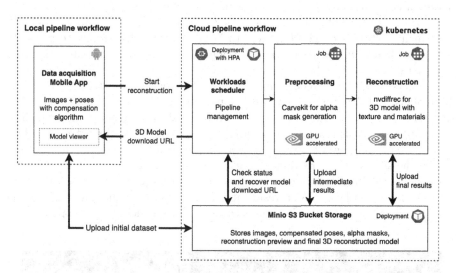

**Fig. 4.** Pipeline architecture with the Workloads scheduler, Preprocessing and Reconstruction microservices. The pipeline workflow is partitioned between local and cloud execution. All the stages communicate with the S3 storage layer to cache intermediate outputs and final 3D reconstructed model.

**Cloud Infrastructure.** The cloud infrastructure consists of a Kubernetes cluster deployed on bare metal, with accelerated machines designated as worker nodes. To support resource-intensive tasks such as dataset preprocessing and 3D model reconstruction, the worker nodes are equipped with an *NVIDIA Quadro M4000 GPU*. However, due to certain specifications associated with the cloud nodes themselves, a *Systemd-enabled Kubernetes worker CUDA-accelerated base image* was crafted leveraging a docker-in-docker execution[16] [17].

## 4    Evaluation

This section accounts the performance and outcomes of the proposed solution, through qualitative and quantitative evaluations. Furthermore, difficulties encountered during the study and prospects for enhancements are presented.

---

[16] https://medium.com/swlh/docker-and-systemd-381dfd7e4628.

[17] https://zauner.nllk.net/post/0038-running-systemd-inside-a-docker-container/.

## 4.1    Qualitative Evaluation

The qualitative evaluation is performed considering user experience in mobile app utilization, alpha masks generation quality, and the real-look feeling of the generated 3D models (Fig. 5). The significance of user experience cannot be understated, especially when it comes to addressing challenges within specific industrial environments. A smartphone user is empowered to scan a variety of equipment, but it is crucial for them to be at ease with the requisite preparatory steps before initiating the model scanning process. In particular, the user must establish anchors by tapping on the screen next to distinguishable reference points. Failing to execute this preparatory process correctly may result in 3D models that are imprecise and of subpar quality. Moreover, it is imperative that the user receives updates on the progress of the reconstruction pipeline through three status indicators, along with a preview of the current model. The generation of alpha masks has a significant impact on the quality of the dataset, due to the silhouette extraction process involved. This procedure relies entirely on machine learning techniques, which are susceptible to errors such as inaccurate segmentation layers. As a result, it is imperative that the masks produced should be carefully examined by the user before commencing the reconstruction

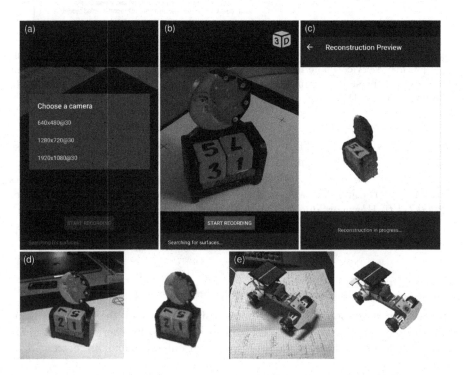

**Fig. 5.** Android application during camera selection (a), data acquisition (b) and reconstruction (c) phases with the proper pipeline workflow status on the User Interface (UI). In (d) and (e) two reconstruction attempts with their respective reference images.

phase. This intermediate step, enables the erroneous alpha masks to be discarded from the dataset. The two aforementioned steps have a significant impact on the overall quality of the dataset. As they are entirely reliant on machine learning techniques, errors may arise due to the lack of operator feedback. This can ultimately result in a reduced level of realism in the 3D models generated.

## 4.2 Performance Evaluation

The performance evaluation of the system takes into account the latency of the pipeline, from the scanning phase to the interaction phase. This latency can be computed using the following formula:

$$T_{latency} = T_{scan} + 2T_{upload} + 2T_{signal} + T_{preprocessing} + T_{reconstruction} + T_{download}$$

Here, $T_{signal}$ denotes the time required for signals to propagate within the infrastructure, while $T_{upload}$ and $T_{download}$ represent the time taken to upload and download assets from the S3 bucket, respectively. Since $T_{scan}$, $T_{preprocessing}$, and $T_{reconstruction}$ take significantly longer than the other steps, we can simplify the formula as follows:

$$T_{latency} = T_{scan} + T_{preprocessing} + T_{reconstruction}$$

The conducted tests consisted in 20 runs with a generated dataset of approximately 100 images each. During the experiments, network latency, denoted by $T_{scan}$, was found to be almost 120 s, while preprocessing time took roughly 30 s. The reconstruction process required approximately 2 h and 30 min (see Table 1). The reconstruction task demands a considerable amount of time, emphasizing the need for ongoing upgrades to this pipeline component. The modular architecture facilitates the integration of more advanced AI models, resulting in streamlined computational processes, improved user experience, and cost savings. Opting for a microservices approach over legacy monolithic 3D reconstruction systems allows for effortless component replacement, while maintaining infrastructure transparency for end user through Kubernetes as middleware. This ensures uninterrupted operational service during upgrades and swift scaling capabilities. Additionally, losses on both training and validation sets were taken into consideration. The calculation of image space loss was performed using nvdiffrast [20], which assesses the difference between the rendered image and the reference one. As shown in Fig. 6, the employment of nvdiffrec resulted in a loss of 0.010540 on the training set and 0.010293 on the validation set.

**Table 1.** List of the performed tasks with frequencies for a single run. Mean execution time over 20 different reconstruction tests with approximately 100 images per run.

| Task | Task frequency | Mean Time (min) |
|---|---|---|
| $T_{scan}$ | 1 | 2 |
| $T_{upload}$ | 2 | $\simeq 0$ |
| $T_{signal}$ | 2 | $\simeq 0$ |
| $T_{preprocessing}$ | 1 | 0.5 |
| $T_{reconstruction}$ | 1 | 150 |
| $T_{download}$ | 1 | $\simeq 0$ |
| **Total** | 8 | $152.5 = T_{latency}$ |

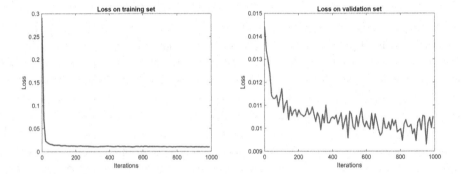

**Fig. 6.** The loss values on the training and validation sets of the 3D reconstructed model performed using nvdiffrec, serving as an evaluation of the model's performance.

## 5    Conclusion and Future Work

This study presents an innovative cloud-native scalable pipeline to reconstruct 3D models of real-world objects, providing a starting point for Digital Twins. The approach offers various advantages related to Industry 4.0, including a faster training process since it employs a 2D smartphone cameras overlaid by Google's ARCore framework for dataset generation, and high-end cloud worker nodes for alpha masks generation and reconstruction tasks. Specifically, nvdiffrec tool by NVIDIA is exploited to perform the effective 3D model reconstruction. This can be interactively viewed on the end user's smartphone. The pipeline complies to microservices architecture standards, enabling scalability in large-scale production environments. Although the proposed solution has achieved the expected outcomes, the modular design allows for future improvements, including:

- adopt a better machine learning model to produce higher quality meshes [21];
- replace or improve the machine learning model to generate the alpha masks;
- decompose the 3D model in layers enabling a more thorough experience;
- implement an in-app feedback gathering feature to collect user experience;

# References

1. Tao, F., et al.: Digital twin-driven product design framework. Int. J. Prod. Res. **57**, 3935–3953 (2019)
2. Moloney, J.: Augmented reality visualisation of the built environment to support design decision making. In: Tenth International Conference On Information Visualisation (IV'06), pp. 687–692 (2006)
3. Schneider, M., Rambach, J., Stricker, D.: Augmented reality based on edge computing using the example of remote live support. In: 2017 IEEE International Conference On Industrial Technology (ICIT), pp. 1277–1282 (2017)
4. Zhang, X., Navab, N., Liou, S.: E-commerce direct marketing using augmented reality. In: 2000 IEEE International Conference On Multimedia And Expo. ICME2000. Proceedings. Latest Advances In The Fast Changing World Of Multimedia (Cat. No. 00TH8532), vol. 1, pp. 88–91 (2000)
5. Cornacchia, G., et al.: Auditing fairness under unawareness through counterfactual reasoning. Inf. Process. Manage. **60**(2), 103224 (2023)
6. Hauswiesner, S., Straka, M., Reitmayr, G.: Virtual try-on through image-based rendering. IEEE Trans. Vis. Comput. Graph. **19**, 1552–1565 (2013)
7. Wiwatwattana, N., Sukaphat, S., Putwanpen, T., Thongnuch, S., Kanokudomsin, P.: Augmenting for purchasing with mobile: Usage and design scenario for ice dessert. In: IISA 2014, The 5th International Conference On Information, Intelligence, Systems And Applications, pp. 446–450 (2014)
8. EL-firjani, N., Maatuk, A.: Mobile augmented reality for interactive catalogue. In: 2016 International Conference On Engineering & MIS (ICEMIS), pp. 1–4 (2016)
9. Hořejši, P.: Augmented reality system for virtual training of parts assembly. Procedia Eng. **100**, 699–706 (2015)
10. Müller, T., Evans, A., Schied, C., Keller, A.: Instant neural graphics primitives with a multiresolution hash encoding. Trans. Graph. **41**, 102:1-102:15 (2022)
11. J. Munkberg, J.: Extracting triangular 3D models, materials, and lighting from images. ArXiv:2111.12503 (2021)
12. Müller, T.: Tiny CUDA neural network framework. https://github.com/nvlabs/tiny-cuda-nn. Accessed 18 Sep 2022
13. Anelli, V.W., Di Noia, T., Di Sciascio, E., Ragone, A.: Semantic interpretation of Top-N recommendations. IEEE Trans. Knowl. Data Eng. **34**(5), 2416–2428 (2022)
14. Müller, T., Rousselle, F., Novák, J., Keller, A.: Real-time neural radiance caching for path tracing. ACM Trans. Graph. (2021)
15. Müller, T.: CUDA templates for linear algebra subroutines (2022). https://github.com/NVIDIA/cutlass
16. Webel, S., Bockholt, U., Engelke, T., Gavish, N., Olbrich, M., Preusche, C.: An augmented reality training platform for assembly and maintenance skills. Robot. Auton. Syst. **61**, 398–403 (2013)
17. Schönberger, J., Frahm, J.: Structure-from-motion revisited. Conf. Comput. Vis. Pattern Recogn. (CVPR) (2016)
18. Schönberger, J.L., Zheng, E., Frahm, J.-M., Pollefeys, M.: Pixelwise view selection for unstructured multi-view stereo. In: Leibe, B., Matas, J., Sebe, N., Welling, M. (eds.) ECCV 2016. LNCS, vol. 9907, pp. 501–518. Springer, Cham (2016). https://doi.org/10.1007/978-3-319-46487-9_31

19. Stevens, B., Lewis, F., Johnson, E.: Aircraft Control and Simulation: Dynamics, controls design, and Autonomous Systems, 2nd Edition. John Wiley & Sons (2003)
20. Laine, S., Hellsten, J., Karras, T., Seol, Y., Lehtinen, J., Aila, T.: Modular primitives for high-performance differentiable rendering. Trans. Graph. **39** (2020)
21. Vicini, D., Speierer, S., Jakob, W.: differentiable signed distance function rendering. Trans. Graph. (Proc. of SIGGRAPH) **41**, 125:1–125:18 (2022)

# Automated Reverse Engineering of the Technology-Induced Software System Structure

Yves R. Kirschner[✉], Jan Keim, Nico Peter, and Anne Koziolek

Karlsruhe Institute of Technology (KIT), Karlsruhe, Germany
{yves.kirschner,jan.keim,anne.koziolek}@kit.edu,
nico.peter@student.kit.edu

**Abstract.** Evolving system architectures can be complex and difficult to understand, leading to problems such as poor maintainability. Automated reverse engineering of system structure models from source code can mitigate these problems and facilitate architectural decisions. However, identifying components with their interfaces can be challenging because components are often implemented in different frameworks and interconnected in complex ways. Our approach aims to create software models using reusable concept descriptions for reverse engineering. We use structural-level mapping rules to reconstruct the static system structure from source code, assuming that the technology used can determine the components with their interfaces and deployment. We evaluate our approach on four public reference systems. The analyses show that technology-specific rules already provide good results, but the addition of project-specific rules further improves reverse engineering.

**Keywords:** Automated reverse engineering · Reusable concept descriptions · Software architecture models · Structure-level mapping rules

## 1 Introduction

Large software systems often become complex and difficult to understand during development, leading to problems such as poor maintainability. To solve these problems, software architects must have a clear understanding of the system's software architecture. Therefore, there is a growing need for automated tools that can extract the static system structure from source code. Automated reverse engineering of models offers benefits such as improved software maintainability and support for architectural decisions. However, reverse engineering the static system structure is challenging due to difficulties in identifying components and their interfaces [4]. Factors such as different programming languages and frameworks used to implement components make it difficult to accurately capture all possibilities. In addition, components may have complex interconnections, making it unclear which interfaces they use to communicate. The goal

© The Author(s), under exclusive license to Springer Nature Switzerland AG 2023
B. Tekinerdogan et al. (Eds.): ECSA 2023, LNCS 14212, pp. 283–291, 2023.
https://doi.org/10.1007/978-3-031-42592-9_19

of our proposed approach is to support the creation and maintenance of models. To reverse engineer models, we want to utilize reusable concept descriptions. To achieve this goal, we formulate the following research questions: *RQ1:* To what extent do a selected framework impact the underlying software static system structure? *RQ2:* How can this impact be implemented as a transformation for reverse engineering? Our new approach aims to use mapping rules at the structural level to reconstruct the static aspects of the system from source code. We assume that components with their interfaces and deployment can often be explicitly determined by the used technology, e. g., application frameworks. Since we want to use knowledge about technologies to discover components, we expect our approach to generate models that are more consistent with the present architecture. We also expect technology-specific rules to provide a better understanding of the relationships between a technology and its underlying concept and the static system structure.

## 2    Foundation

*Web services* are a type of software component that provide a standardized way for communication over the internet [13]. RESTful web services make resources available through a uniform and predefined set of stateless operations, typically HTTP methods [10]. *Reverse engineering* aims to identify structures in the form of elements and relationships within the software system under investigation. This involves analyzing and understanding software systems that may have evolved over time or may not be formally documented [9]. In this way, patterns, relationships, and constraints in the system can be identified, providing insight into the design, implementation, and maintenance of the software. Manual reverse engineering a software architecture can be difficult and time-consuming process, especially for large and complex systems. Automating this process typically involves analyzing the system's code to identify components, interfaces, dependencies, and other architecture elements. This can be accomplished through various techniques, e. g., static analyses, dynamic analyses, or both [5]. Static analyses examine the source code or compiled binary of the software system without running the system. They are fast but may miss certain runtime-related aspects of the system's behavior. Model-Driven Reverse Engineering (MDRE) is the task that focuses on recovering models. Favre et al. define MDRE as the creation of descriptive models from existing systems that have been created in some way [6]. MDRE is about transforming heterogeneous software development artifacts into homogeneous models.

## 3    Approach

Our goal is to automatically extract from existing software development artifacts the structure that represents the static aspects of the system. This structure includes the way a software system is split up into components and shows the dependencies among these components as well as the deployment of these components to nodes. We consider artifacts written during the development of a software system, e. g., source code or other configuration files like deployment descriptors. The idea is to model the knowledge of used technologies in order to reverse engineer this static system structure from artifacts. This approach is an implementation-based reconstruction of the source code based on implementation knowledge and grouping based on deployment. Rules capture how a certain concept is implemented in a technology and how this concept affects the static structure of a system. These rules are expressed as model-to-model transformations. The technology-specific rules are developed by analyzing the patterns of each technology and mapping them to model elements. Rules can be formulated to cover any aspect of a technology that can be identified through static analysis of a software project's artifacts. Although the approach is designed for reuse, it also supports project-specific rules. These rules can be used, for example, to model how components are implemented in a specific software project. To define transformation rules, we use the transformation language Xtend [1]. Listing 1 depicts a simplified form of a extended Backus-Naur form (EBNF) that defines the framework of our approach for such rules. However, the shown EBNF is a simplified version and contains only a subset of the possible solutions. We only include the most relevant production rules.

```
<RulesDocument> ::= {<Rule>}
<Rule> ::= [<Loop>] {<Condition>} {<Detection>}
<Loop> ::= "for" <HelperGet> ":"
<Condition> ::= "if" <HelperBool> ":"
<HelperGet> ::= "getClasses()" | "getMethods()" | ...
<HelperBool> ::= "isAnnotatedWith()" | "isExtending()" | ...
<Detection> ::= "detectComponent()"  | "detectRole()" | ...
```

Listing 1: Simplified EBNF as a conceptual framework for our rules. The example represents non-terminals for helper methods with two methods each.

A `RulesDocument` is a collection of rules and a `Rule` consists of several non-terminals. A rule can start with a loop that iterates over parts of the code model instance. The objects to be iterated are defined in the non-terminal `HelperGet`. The next part of a rule is the `Condition` that is defined as an if-expression with a non-terminal `HelperBool` to select what to inspect. The rule engine provides predefined aspects of what a user might be looking for, such as specific annotations or names. The idea of these `HelperGet` and `-Bool` methods is to discover elements. These methods define queries to the code models that return elements of interest. These query methods need to be defined only once and can be reused without knowing the exact structure of the code models. To associate a model element with the current object, the user performs a detection that can identify, e. g., components, interfaces, and provided or required roles. The methods for these identifications are provided by the rule engine.

The first step in our reverse engineering approach is to create a model from existing artifacts that provides a unified view of the software system. In order for these models to provide a unified view, they must conform to a suitable given metamodel. The structure of these models is realized in MDRE by so-called discoverers that depend on the associated metamodel. The second step is the main step of our reverse engineering approach. The previously created models are used to effectively achieve the desired reverse engineering scenario. During this step, these models are analyzed using rules represented by model-to-model transformations. For this purpose, our approach includes a framework for MDRE that allows for reusable acquisition of this knowledge. These two steps use the proposed rules to identify and compose relevant model elements and their relationships from the collection of code model elements. The first sub-step is for the inner component model and uses the results from model discovery. The defined rules allow the identification of software system elements, e.g., components, interfaces, and communication paths. The second sub-step is for the outer service model. Here, rules for the deployment descriptor artifacts are used to compose components into larger logical units. These composite components can represent services or subsystems.

To generate the static system structure model instance, the first model under-standing sub-step is to create the interfaces by extracting information from the code model instances. To create a model, there need to be several individual rules, each of which helps to identify at least one model element. The previously defined rules are used to identify relevant elements within specific code structures. The rules formulate these structural patterns that define which code artifacts map to relevant components and how to infer provided and required roles. Extracting model information from the code model involves identifying the interface name, signature name, return type, and parameters of each method. The rules define which code artifacts are associated with relevant components and how to derive provided and required roles.

The second sub-step is to compose components based on the information in the deployment descriptor models into services. By associating each component with a service, subsystem boundaries can be inferred, resulting in a more readable and understandable view of the system. Delegation connectors link provided and required interfaces with inner components, while assembly connectors link inner components with each other. Assembly connectors are created for each component that matches the required role of another component in the service.

In the third step, all the information determined by the rules of the previous model understanding is merged into the final static system structure model. For our approach, we use the Palladio Component Model (PCM) [12] as a component-based architecture model, but the concepts are also applicable to others Architectural description languages (ADLs). Our approach can be adapted in this model generation step to use other notations for describing component-based architecture models, e.g., UML component or deployment diagrams.

# 4 Evaluation

For the evaluation, we first create our own reference model for the software system under study in order to compare it with our automated results. To do this, we first analyze the source code and configuration files to identify the components and their roles. We then compare the constructed model with existing documentation or diagrams available in the repository or linked to the software system, and perform a refinement and validation of the constructed model using expert knowledge and domain-specific information. The extraction process involves applying the technology-specific rule set to the system and comparing the resulting model to the expected one. Success is measured using precision $(p)$, recall $(r)$, and $F1$, the harmonic mean of both. True positives are relevant elements that should be found, false positives are falsely extracted elements, and false negatives are missing elements in the extracted model relative to the expected elements. Recall alone does not guarantee correctness as misrecognized elements may still be present. Precision is also necessary to indicate misrecognition. The extracted software architecture is analyzed for possible improvement by adding new rules to the technology-specific rule set. The completeness of the generated model and the effort required to define new rules is measured by the number of newly defined rules and the total lines of code (LOC) required.

*Spring Systems:* The first two case studies are two open source systems implemented primarily based on the Spring framework. PetClinic[1] is a Spring Boot microservices application implemented with Java and Docker that simulates a simple management system for veterinary clinics. Piggy Metrics[2] is a simple financial advisory application developed to demonstrate the microservice architecture model using Spring Boot and Docker. The Spring PetClinic reference system consists of 4 microservices. For these combined, 11 components, 11 interfaces, 11 provider roles, and 9 required roles are evaluated, for a total of 42 elements. The model extracted by our approach with only the technology-specific rules contains all intended components, interfaces, and provided roles. However, 2 required roles are missing, 5 data types are incorrect in the correctly identified roles, and 3 data types are missing in the identified roles. The good results are due to the fact that the system adheres closely to the Spring specifications, providing a solid foundation for defining the technology-specific rule set. The Piggy Metrics reference system consists of four microservices. For these combined, 29 components, 28 interfaces, 28 provider roles, and 22 required roles are evaluated, for a total of 107 elements. The model extracted by our approach with only the technology-specific rules has a total of 116 correctly identified elements, 25 missing elements, and 12 incorrect elements. 23 components are correctly identified, while 5 interfaces and 6 provided roles are missing. In addition, 4 interfaces and 6 provided roles are incorrectly identified. Four required roles are also missing. New project-specific rules are derived to improve the extraction result by analyzing missing and incorrect elements. Two new rules are added, modifying the

---

[1] https://github.com/spring-petclinic/spring-petclinic-microservices.

[2] https://github.com/sqshq/PiggyMetrics.

existing rules with a total of 7 new LOC. These new rules correctly identify the four missing components and their associated roles.

*JAX-RS Systems:* Tea Store[3] is a microservice application implemented in Java and Docker that emulates a simple web store for tea. Acme Air[4] is an application implemented in Java for a fictional airline. The Tea Store reference system consists of six microservices. For these combined, 79 components, 64 interfaces, 79 provider roles, and 10 required roles are evaluated, for a total of 232 elements. The model extracted with only the technology-specific rules has a total of 104 correctly identified elements, 128 missing elements, and no incorrect elements. The system was analyzed to identify missing elements, and new project-specific rules were applied to improve the extraction. In total, four new rules were created and implemented in 29 LOC. Using these new project-specific rules, the new model extracted by our approach produced 15 false positives, 13 false negatives, and 219 true positives out of the expected 232 elements. The Acme Air reference system consists of five services and one package service that define common interfaces. For these, a total of 31 components, 33 interfaces, 31 provider roles, and 30 required roles are evaluated, for a total of 125 elements. The model extracted with the technology-specific rules has a total of 78 correctly identified elements, 47 missing elements, and 4 incorrect elements. With this new project-specific rule set, 30 items are still missing, but no items are incorrect, and 95 items are correct.

**Table 1.** Summary of results. Subscripts indicate the first run with technology-specific rules and the second run with additional project-specific rules. The number of rules (NuR) and LOC are given for the project-specific rules.

| Case Study | $p_1$ | $r_1$ | $F1_1$ | $p_2$ | $r_2$ | $F1_2$ | NuR | LOC |
|---|---|---|---|---|---|---|---|---|
| Spring PetClinic | 93.2% | 93.2% | 93.2% | – | - | – | – | – |
| Piggy Metrics | 90.6% | 82.3% | 86.2% | 91.2% | 88.7% | 89.9% | 2 | 7 |
| Tea Store | 100.0% | 44.8% | 61.9% | 93.6% | 94.4% | 94.0% | 4 | 29 |
| Acme Air | 95.1% | 62.4% | 75.4% | 100% | 76.0% | 86.4% | 3 | 32 |

*Results and Discussion:* The summary of the evaluation results of the four case studies for the technology-specific and project-specific rules is shown in Table 1. Precision values range from 90.6% to 100.0%, recall values from 44.8% to 94.4%, and $F1$-scores from 61.9% to 94.0%. For the Tea Store system, our approach achieves the best overall $F1$-score using the improved project-specific rules. The Spring PetClinic system performs best on the first pass with the technology-specific with a $F1$-score of 93.2% because it strictly follows the Spring framework patterns. The evaluation shows that general technology-specific rules have a higher risk of falsely classifying elements as relevant. However, the results generally improve when these rules are used together with other project-specific

---

[3] https://github.com/DescartesResearch/TeaStore.

[4] https://github.com/acmeair/acmeair.

rules. On average, a new rule improves results by less than 2.0%. Piggy Metrics improved by 3.7% with two rules, while Tea Store improved by 32.1% and Acme Air improved by 11.0% with more rules. JAX-RS systems benefit more from new rules than Spring-based systems due to fewer technology-specific implementation requirements and constraints. The results show that opinionated frameworks like Spring provide a better foundation for technology-specific rule sets than weaker frameworks. Comparing the LOC required for project-specific rule sets reveals differences between Spring and JAX-RS systems. JAX-RS systems required more LOC than the Piggy Metrics system because a single rule covers all discoverable elements. This highlights an area for future improvement to simplify rule implementation. A poor result from the rule engine may indicate a poorly designed system with missing patterns. To address this, architects can implement new project-specific rules. In this way, the rule engine can act as a warning system to check the quality of a relevant system when bad extraction results are given.

## 5   Related Work

Garcia et al. conclude that clustering of software entities is the almost universally used method for automated architecture reconstruction [7]. In most cases, a graph structure is generated based on dependencies in the source code, so that components can be reconstructed using clustering or pattern matching. Although each of these reverse engineering methods has a different principle, they all divide source code entities into mutually exclusive clusters, each based on a dominant principle such as cohesion and coupling or naming patterns. Garzón et al. propose an approach for reverse engineering object-oriented code into a unified language for both object-oriented programming and modeling [8]. Using an incremental and rule-based approach, UML class diagrams and state machines can be mixed with the associated source code. However, these rules cover only the basic object-oriented constructs, not specific technologies. Starting from the assumption that most well-designed systems follow strict architecture design rules, Cai et al. propose a new perspective for architecture reconstruction [3]. Their so-called ArchDRH clustering family allows design rule-based clustering to be combined with other clustering techniques to partition a large system into subsystems. However, these design rules take the form of special program constructs, like shared data structures or abstract interfaces, that are not used by any of the submodules. In their literature review, Raibulet et al. compare fifteen different model-driven reverse engineering approaches and find that the approaches and their application areas are versatile. In this respect, MoDisco [2] is the most related approach in a comprehensive scope [11]. Bruneliere et al. developed the generic and extensible MoDisco approach, which provides support for Java, JEE, and XML technologies to generate model-based views of the architecture. Although MoDisco is extensible with technologies, it does not support direct reuse of a technology's common concepts.

# 6   Conclusion

This paper presents a novel approach for building static system structure models in component-based software systems using reusable concept descriptions for reverse engineering. The approach uses structural mapping rules to reconstruct models from source code, considering technology-specific relationships and concepts. The contributions of the approach include formally defined rules created by technology experts prior to the automatic extraction process, and a rule engine that can apply these rules to produce consistent software models. Evaluation of reference systems using Spring and JAX-RS technologies demonstrated the effectiveness of the approach. The evaluation also showed the potential to improve the rule system by integrating project-specific rules. The automatic model generation enabled by this approach has the potential to improve software maintainability and support architectural decisions in component-based software systems. Future work includes investigating the application of the approach to different types of systems, evaluating its scalability and efficiency, and developing a knowledge base of technology-specific rules to improve its reusability in similar projects.

# References

1. Bettini, L.: Implementing Domain-specific Languages with Xtext and Xtend. Packt Publishing Ltd., Birmingham (2016)
2. Bruneliere, H., Cabot, J., Jouault, F., Madiot, F.: MoDisco: a generic and extensible framework for model driven reverse engineering. In: Proceedings of the 25th IEEE/ACM International Conference on Automated Software Engineering (2010)
3. Cai, Y., Wang, H., Wong, S., Wang, L.: Leveraging design rules to improve software architecture recovery. In: Proceedings of the 9th International ACM Sigsoft Conference on Quality of Software Architectures, QoSA 2013. ACM (2013)
4. Canfora, G., Di Penta, M.: New frontiers of reverse engineering. In: 2007 Future of Software Engineering, FOSE 2007. IEEE Computer Society (2007)
5. Canfora, G., Di Penta, M., Cerulo, L.: Achievements and challenges in software reverse engineering. Commun. ACM **54**, 142–151 (2011)
6. Favre, J.M.: Foundations of model (driven) (reverse) engineering. In: Language Engineering for Model-Driven Software Development (2005)
7. Garcia, J., Ivkovic, I., Medvidovic, N.: A comparative analysis of software architecture recovery techniques. In: ASE 2013 (2013)
8. Garzón, M.A., Lethbridge, T.C., Aljamaan, H.I., Badreddin, O.: Reverse engineering of object-oriented code into Umple using an incremental and rule-based approach. In: CASCON 2014 (2014)
9. Kazman, R., Woods, S., Carriere, S.: Requirements for integrating software architecture and reengineering models: CORUM II. In: Proceedings Fifth Working Conference on Reverse Engineering (Cat. No.98TB100261) (1998)
10. Pautasso, C., Wilde, E.: RESTful web services: principles, patterns, emerging technologies. In: Proceedings of the 19th International Conference on World Wide Web, WWW 2010. ACM (2010)
11. Raibulet, C., Fontana, F.A., Zanoni, M.: Model-driven reverse engineering approaches: a systematic literature review. IEEE Access **5**, 14516–14542 (2017)

12. Reussner, R.H., Becker, S., Happe, J., Koziolek, A., Koziolek, H.: Modeling and Simulating Software Architectures - The Palladio Approach. MIT Press, Cambridge (2016)
13. Roy, J., Ramanujan, A.: Understanding web services. IT Prof. **3**, 69–73 (2001)

# Cloud-Native Architecture for Mixed File-Based and API-Based Digital Twin Exchange

Nafise Eskandani[(✉)][iD] and Sten Grüner[iD]

ABB Corporate Research Center, Ladenburg, Germany
nafise.eskandani@de.abb.com

**Abstract.** Digital Twin technology plays a crucial role in the implementation of Industry 4.0 by providing means of optimizing operations, improving efficiency, reducing costs, and minimizing risks through its ability to simulate and integrate information silos and perform test scenarios in a virtual environment. As industrial enterprises face the need to align themselves with new information technologies (IT) and respond to variable market demands, the role of Digital Twin in enabling the evolution toward smart manufacturing becomes even more significant. This paper provides an overview of Digital Twin technology, identifies the architectural challenges that it encompasses, and proposes a preliminary cloud-native architecture to address these challenges, laying the groundwork for future research in this field.

**Keywords:** Industrial IoT · Digital Twin · Cloud-Native Applications · Software Architecture

## 1 Introduction

Industry 4.0, the combination of industrial practice and Internet of Things (IIoT) technologies, is one of the leading research and development initiatives for transforming and automating traditional manufacturing and process industry enterprises through the integration of modern technologies and tools. The ultimate goal of Industry 4.0 is to create smart manufacturing machines and systems that are connected, automated, and constantly monitored to improve production, reduce costs, and optimize processes [8].

This sector is quickly expanding, pushing a demand for research that explores the new possibilities offered by smart factories: The Industry 4.0 market size is expected to experience significant growth from USD 84.59 Billion in 2020 to USD 334.18 Billion by 2028[1].

Digital Twin (DT) technology is a key enabler of Industry 4.0 [12]. DT enables bridging the gap between physical and virtual systems enabling the exchange of

---

[1] https://www.globenewswire.com/news-release/2022/09/15/2517217/0/en/Demand-for-Global-Industry-4-0-Market-Size-to-Surpass-USD-334-18-Billion-by-2028-Exhibit-a-CAGR-of-19-4-Industry-4-0-Industry-Trends-Share-Growth-Value-Analysis-Forecast-Report-by-.html.

B. Tekinerdogan et al. (Eds.): ECSA 2023, LNCS 14212, pp. 292–299, 2023.
https://doi.org/10.1007/978-3-031-42592-9_20

data and information between them – ultimately facilitating the implementation of Industry 4.0 [15]. The capabilities actually supported by DT are crucial for these systems to be effective. The most important aspects include real-time data acquisition and processing, integration of data from multiple sources, and high fidelity representation [6,17,18]. The importance of such requirements should be reflected into the architectural designs of DT systems.

Especially in the early stages of DT adoption, a mix of different tools and DT access methods, e.g., file-based and API-based DT access, is required due to missing interfaces between the tools and organizations. To date, limited research has explicitly tackled the architectural challenges associated with integrity of DT content when mixing file- and API-based interaction patterns in the implementation of DT. In this paper, we highlight these challenges arising from IT/OT integration and present a cloud-native architecture to facilitate mixed file and API-based exchange of DTs across organizational boundaries.

The remainder of the paper is structured as follows: Sect. 2 introduces the foundations of DTs, in Sect. 3 the cloud-native architecture for DT exchange is presented, Sect. 4 points to related work and in Sect. 5 a summary and an outlook are given.

## 2    Digital Twins in a Nutshell

### 2.1    Scope and Key Concepts

DT applications and their boundaries differ drastically based on the particular use case and industry domain. Applications range from providing static information about products, e.g., supplementary documentation on one end, to real-time monitoring and synchronization of physical activities with virtual space through networked Cyber-Physical Systems [9] on the other end. This state of things leads to a plethora of DT definitions[2] in academic and industrial sources.

For this work, we adopt a use-case-agnostic definition of DT from the Digital Twin Consortium (DTC): "A Digital Twin is a virtual representation of real-world entities and processes, synchronized at a specified frequency and fidelity". Arguably, also non-physical parts of real-world entities may have their digital lifecycle, e.g., product specifications, therefore a definition of the Industry IoT Consortium (IIC) is also applicable: "A Digital Twin is a digital representation sufficient to meet the requirements of a set of use cases". For a discussion of the evolution of industrial DT definitions please refer to [19].

The Asset Administration Shell (AAS) is an interoperable implementation of a DT designed specifically for industrial applications. Developed collaboratively by the Plattform Industry 4.0 consortium and the Industrial Digital Twin Association (IDTA), the AAS aims to establish a standardized and unified approach to accessing information models associated with physical or virtual assets. The AAS is defined using a technology-independent meta-model, enabling integration with various technologies such as RESTful APIs and OPC UA, which can be leveraged at different stages of an asset's lifecycle [2].

---

[2] https://awortmann.github.io/research/digital_twin_definitions/.

AAS are a composite structure comprising multiple submodels, each serving as a coherent and self-contained unit. These submodels encompass information elements and complex data objects such as files and technical functionalities. A technical functionality can refer to diverse range of services such as a configuration management, event logging and monitoring capabilities, or firmware updates. The AAS, the refernced submodels, and the asset AAS is referencing have unique identifiers and can be accessed through dedicated AAS infrastructure. In the area of AAS and related infrastructure, several open-source Software Development Kits (SDKs) have been developed, with Eclipse BaSyx[3] being one of the prominent examples (cf. [3] for an overview of AAS SDKs).

AAS specification differentiates between the so-called "passive" or type 1 AASs and "reactive" type 2 AASs. Passive AASs can be exchanged in a specified packaging format called "AASX" to enable the offline exchange of AAS. The AASX package includes the AAS content, which can be stored as an XML or JSON file. Reactive AASs are typically hosted on a server and accessible using well-defined RESTful APIs. Furthermore, "proactive" type 3 AAS exist, e.g., to facilitate automated negations, which are out of scope of this work.

## 2.2   Architectural Challenges for Digital Twins and AAS

Despite the sophisticated specification of the AAS, its implementation introduces a range of architectural challenges that, to the best of our knowledge, have not been comprehensively addressed in the existing literature. These challenges arise from the complexity of integrating AAS within diverse industrial environments and the need to ensure interoperability, scalability, security, data management, real-time processing, handling heterogeneity, and lifecycle management.

The heterogeneity of assets, technologies, protocols, and interfaces poses a fundamental challenge for the AAS infrastructure. The AAS needs to accommodate a wide range of asset types with varying data formats, communication protocols, and connectivity options. Developing an infrastructure that can effectively handle this heterogeneity requires robust mechanisms for data transformation, protocol abstraction, and interoperability.

As assets evolve over time, the AAS infrastructure must handle updates and upgrades smoothly. It should provide mechanisms for deploying new software versions, firmware updates, and configuration changes to assets. The infrastructure should ensure the integrity and security of updates, coordinate the update process, and manage rollback mechanisms in case of issues or incompatibilities.

Moreover, as the number of assets and data generated within industrial systems grows, scalability becomes a critical challenge for the AAS infrastructure. The infrastructure must be designed to handle increasing data volumes, processing demands, and system complexity without sacrificing performance or reliability. This involves ensuring efficient storage and retrieval of large amounts of data, and providing mechanisms for horizontal and vertical scaling to accommodate evolving system needs. Additionally, scalability should consider the management

---

[3] https://www.eclipse.org/basyx/.

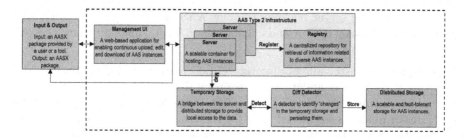

**Fig. 1.** Overview of the proposed cloud-native architecture

of distributed AAS instances, load balancing, and fault tolerance to ensure uninterrupted operation and resource utilization.

We address heterogeneity and scalability challenges with a novel architecture that ensures interoperability and smooth communications, regardless of varying formats of DTs. Moreover, our architecture is designed to accommodate a growing number of participants and increasing volumes of DT data, enabling organizations to expand their DT ecosystem without sacrificing efficiency or performance.

## 3   Cloud-Native Architecture for AAS Implementation

While various vendor-dependent solutions exist for implementing DTs, there is currently no recognized reference architecture for implementing DTs across organizational boundaries from an infrastructural perspective. Figure 1 shows an overview of the proposed cloud-native architecture for mixed use of file-based and API-based DT access. A typical use-case is the import of DTs packaged as type 1 AAS, instantiating and editing them as type 2 AAS via RESTful APIs, and exporting them again as type 1 AAS at some specific event. Type 1 AASs can be generated out of backed systems by means of model transformations has been addressed, e.g., in [7,14]. Mixed file-based and API-based access may be needed in case no direct API-based access is available between organizations, as it is often the case during the introduction of DTs.

Key microservices of the architecture run inside containers. Containers can be deployed on local machines for development and testing, in the cloud for scalable and distributed execution, or on edge devices to bring the system closer to the data source or reduce latency. This flexibility allows manufacturers to choose the most suitable environment based on factors such as cost, performance requirements, data privacy, and network constraints. Also, stateless containers scale horizontally or vertically based on the demand or available resources. Container orchestration platforms like Kubernetes further simplify the scaling process by automating container deployment and management.

In the following, we provide a comprehensive description of each component:

**Server:** The server serves as a provider of AAS and enables dynamic uploading of AAS instances. APIs allow creation new AASs or uploading existing ones.

Once uploaded, the server registers the new AAS instance to the registry. API users can continuously update and enhance the AASs by uploading new versions or modifying existing ones.

*Registry:* The registry allows discovery of information related to diverse AAS instances. It contains metadata and descriptive details about each AAS, including exclusive identifiers, versions, authorship, creation timestamps, and relevant attributes or qualities associated with the represented asset. The registry facilitates exploration, retrieval, and incorporation of AAS instances by providing a centralized catalog comprising the available AASs. Consequently, organizations and systems can seek out particular AASs, extract their corresponding information, and establish connections or interactions with the respective assets.

*Distributed Storage:* The distributed storage serves as a database that stores AAS instances (e.g., AASX files) or their database representation. An AAS typically deals with large volumes of data associated with assets. Distributed storage provides a reliable and scalable solution for storing such data, and enables easy access and retrieval, even in the event of hardware failures or disruptions. Furthermore, the utilization of distributed storage, which incorporates versioning capabilities, facilitates the preservation of diverse iterations of an asset, enabling comprehensive change tracking and the ability to revert back when required.

*Temporary Storage:* The temporary storage serves as a bridge between the server container and the distributed storage. Since containers are stateless, any data or changes made within a container are not preserved when the container is terminated or restarted. By mapping storage outside the container, data persistency can be ensured. The temporary storage stores the mapped data from the container and provides local access to the modified AAS instances.

*Diff Detector:* The change detector allows to monitor the temporary storage and facilitates the transfer of data to distributed storage whenever requested. On request, it identifies any modifications, additions, or deletions to the stored data. When the change detector identifies a change in the temporary storage, it triggers a data transfer process to move the updated data to the distributed storage. This transfer process ensures that the distributed storage remains synchronized and up-to-date with the most recent version of the data. The change detector operates based on predefined rules or algorithms that determine what constitutes a "change" in the context of the monitored data, e.g., based on AAS meta-model.

*Management UI:* The management UI serves as a user interface that facilitates interactions with the registry and empowers users to modify instances of the AAS. It provides a graphical or web-based interface through which users can access and manage various aspects of the AAS, such as properties and attributes of registered AAS instances.

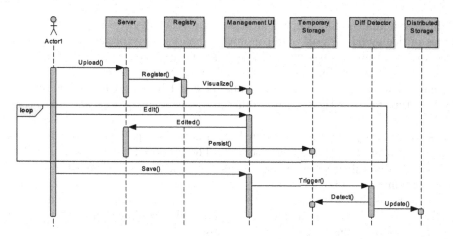

**Fig. 2.** Dynamic view of the typical system use-case

Figure 2 shows a dynamic view of the typical use case for the usage of proposed architecture where type 1 AASs are instantiated into the server for interaction with AAS-enabled tools using RESTful APIs. An actor (user or tool) uploads AASX packages into the AAS server. The latter registers AAS and included submodels in the AAS registry to allow discovery by the AAS-enabled tools. Tools or user interact with the content of DTs and update them using rest API. The server persists the AAS information into the temporary storage. On a specified event, e.g., a user interaction, the content of the AAS is synced into the distributed storage by calculating a difference first and then deploying the changes into the storage allowing a persistent storage and change tracking.

## 4 Related Work

DTs have gained significant attention in recent years and has extensive applications across various industries. As a result, numerous research areas and topics have emerged in the field of DT. These areas cover a broad range, such as modeling and simulation, data integration and streaming, lifecycle management, standardization and interoperability, security, and real-time monitoring and control [4,15,16]. To maintain a focus on infrastructure integrity, this paper will specifically address the relevant studies within this scope.

Malakuti and Grüner [10] discuss the essential architectural decisions when designing DTs. Decisions include the internal structure and content of the DT, APIs and their usage, the bindings between the twins and its physical counterparts, as well as the runtime environment. Our work falls into the API category, while addressing the life cycle of DTs.

Costantini et al. [5] report on defining and deploying a collection of software services designed to serve as a highly distributed computing platform for a hybrid DT model. This platform facilitates the integration of simulative and data-driven models, enabling the incorporation of AI services. In [13] the advantages of deploying DTs on edge computing devices are explored. These advantages range from minimizing manual engineering efforts through IT/OT data integration to improving the reliability of the system by more informed device management and monitoring. Our architecture is deliberately using cloud-native architecture to cover the indicated different deployment options and allow scalability.

Another study [11] presents a four-layer architecture pattern for building DTs and integrating data from diverse sources. The proposed pattern is designed to be highly adaptable, allowing for the integration of new information sources and accommodating both proprietary and standard data formats. Our approach does not focus the the building of DTs, but enables the (intermediate) editing of packaged DT information models and can be used in conjunction with presented pattern to reduce the load on the data sources.

Aheleroff et al. [1] discuss DTs' enabling technologies and reference architecture model, and they introduce Digital Twin as a Service (DTaaS) on top of the proposed reference model. According to the findings of this study, the utilization of Industry 4.0 technologies such as cloud, IoT, and augmented reality enhances the capabilities of DT, thereby driving industrial transformation. Our scalable platform could be used as a component to implement such a DTaaS.

## 5   Summary and Future Work

DT technology emerges as a crucial enabler in the implementation of Industry 4.0, offering significant benefits such as operational optimization, enhanced efficiency, cost reduction, and risk mitigation. The main contribution of this work is an overview of infrastructural integration challenges in implementing DT for mixed file-based and API-based access, and a proposed cloud-native architecture to mitigate those challenges. Such a mixed approach may be especially needed during the gradual introduction of DT tools within an existing tool landscape.

Cloud-native architecture's elastic scalability, containerization, microservices approach, and DevOps practices make it a suitable solution for addressing the integrity interoperability, and scalability challenges of the AAS infrastructure.

Future works includes implementation of more complex interaction patterns, evaluation of scalability and load handling efficiency, as well as piloting the architecture on realistic DT applications.

## References

1. Aheleroff, S., Xu, X., Zhong, R.Y., Lu, Y.: Digital twin as a service (DTaaS) in industry 4.0: an architecture reference model. Adv. Eng. Inform. **47**, 101225 (2021)
2. Bader, S., Barnstedt, E., Bedenbender, H., Berres, B., Billmann, M., Ristin, M.: Details of the asset administration shell-part 1: the exchange of information between partners in the value chain of industrie 4.0 (version 3.0 rc02) (2022)
3. Barnstedt, E., et al.: Open source drives digital twin adoption. IIC J, Innov (2021)

4. Barricelli, B.R., Casiraghi, E., Fogli, D.: A survey on digital twin: definitions, characteristics, applications, and design implications. IEEE Access **7**, 167653–167671 (2019)
5. Costantini, A., et al.: IoTwins: toward implementation of distributed digital twins in industry 4.0 settings. Computers **11**(5), 67 (2022)
6. Glaessgen, E., Stargel, D.: The digital twin paradigm for future NASA and US air force vehicles. In: 53rd AIAA/ASME/ASCE/AHS/ASC Structures, Structural Dynamics and Materials Conference, p. 1818 (2012)
7. Göllner, D., Klausmann, T., Rasor, R., Dumitrescu, R.: Use case driven digital twin generation. In: 2022 IEEE 5th International Conference on Industrial Cyber-Physical Systems (ICPS), pp. 01–06. IEEE (2022)
8. Hermann, M., et al.: Design principles for industrie 4.0 scenarios: a literature review. Technische Universität Dortmund, Dortmund 45 (2015)
9. Lee, J., Bagheri, B., Kao, H.A.: A cyber-physical systems architecture for industry 4.0-based manufacturing systems. Manuf. Lett. **3**, 18–23 (2015)
10. Malakuti, S., Grüner, S.: Architectural aspects of digital twins in IIoT systems. In: Proceedings of the 12th European Conference on Software Architecture (2018)
11. Malakuti, S., Schmitt, J., Platenius-Mohr, M., Grüner, S., Gitzel, R., Bihani, P.: A four-layer architecture pattern for constructing and managing digital twins. In: Proceedings of the 13th European Conference on Software Architecture (2019)
12. Nakagawa, E.Y., Antonino, P.O., Schnicke, F., Capilla, R., Kuhn, T., Liggesmeyer, P.: Industry 4.0 reference architectures: state of the art and future trends. Comput. Ind. Eng. **156**, 107241 (2021)
13. Platenius-Mohr, M., Grüner, S.: An analysis of use cases for the asset administration shell in the context of edge computing. In: 2022 IEEE 27th International Conference on Emerging Technologies and Factory Automation (ETFA) (2022)
14. Platenius-Mohr, M., Malakuti, S., Grüner, S., Schmitt, J., Goldschmidt, T.: File- and API-based interoperability of digital twins by model transformation: an IIoT case study using asset administration shell. Future Gener. Comput. Syst. **113**, 94–105 (2020)
15. Semeraro, C., Lezoche, M., Panetto, H., Dassisti, M.: Digital twin paradigm: a systematic literature review. Comput. Ind. **130**, 103469 (2021)
16. Singh, M., Fuenmayor, E., Hinchy, E.P., Qiao, Y., Murray, N., Devine, D.: Digital twin: origin to future. Appl. Syst. Innov. **4**(2), 36 (2021)
17. Tao, F., Cheng, J., Qi, Q., Zhang, M., Zhang, H., Sui, F.: Digital twin-driven product design, manufacturing and service with big data. Int. J. Adv. Manuf. Technol. **94**, 3563–3576 (2018)
18. Uhlemann, T.H.J., Schock, C., Lehmann, C., Freiberger, S., Steinhilper, R.: The digital twin: demonstrating the potential of real time data acquisition in production systems. Procedia Manuf. **9**, 113–120 (2017)
19. Usländer, T., et al.: Symbiotic evolution of digital twin systems and dataspaces. Automation **3**(3), 378–399 (2022)

# Software Architecture Documentation

# What Rationales Drive Architectural Decisions? An Empirical Inquiry

Klara Borowa[(✉)] [ID], Rafał Lewanczyk, Klaudia Stpiczyńska,
Patryk Stradomski, and Andrzej Zalewski [ID]

Warsaw University of Technology, Institute of Control and Computation Engineering,
Warsaw, Poland
klara.borowa@pw.edu.pl

**Abstract.** Architectural decision-making is a crucial concern for researchers and practitioners alike. There is a rationale behind every architectural decision that motivates an architect to choose one architectural solution out of a set of options. This study aims to identify which categories of rationale most frequently impact architectural decisions and investigates why these are important to practitioners. Our research comprises two steps of empirical inquiry: a questionnaire (63 participants) and 13 interviews. As a result, we obtained a set of rationales that motivated architects' decisions in practice. Out of them, we extracted a list of software quality attributes that practitioners were the most concerned about. We found that, overall, architects prefer to choose solutions which are familiar to them or that guarantee fast software implementation. Mid-career architects (5 to 15 years of experience) are more open to new solutions than senior and junior practitioners. Additionally, we found that most practitioners are not concerned about the quality attributes of compatibility and portability due to modern software development practices, such as the prevalence of using specific standards and virtualisation/containerization.

**Keywords:** Software Architecture · Architectural decision-making · Rationale · Software Quality Attributes

## 1 Introduction

Understanding software architecture as a set of architectural decisions (ADs) [11] draws our attention to the motivation underlying these decisions and - this way - the entire architecture. Design rationale, which is a component of ADs [25], consists of the knowledge and reasoning justifying design decisions [20].

The research on factors (including rationales) [15] that shape architectural decisions in practice is rather scarce and seems still far from being mature. The most recent papers by Weinreich et al. [23], Miesbauer et al. [14] and Tang et al. [20] that explore the motivations underlying practitioners' ADs are at least eight years old. These works are continued in more recent studies that investigate

B. Tekinerdogan et al. (Eds.): ECSA 2023, LNCS 14212, pp. 303–318, 2023.
https://doi.org/10.1007/978-3-031-42592-9_21

what software quality attributes (QAs) are discussed when choosing architectural patterns [4] and what technology features drive technology design decisions [19].

As the software development landscape changes rapidly, the general purpose of this study is to discover what rationales, and why, currently drive ADs in practice. Such results importantly extend our knowledge and understanding of architectural decision-making (ADM)

by allowing researchers to focus their efforts on improving ADM on the basis of current needs and practices of architects. Additionally, we put an emphasis on QAs since they are a rationale subset that has been of major interest for researchers [2,4,5].

Such an aim is expressed by the following research questions:

- RQ1: What rationales most frequently influence architectural decisions?
- RQ2: Which software quality attributes are usually prioritised during architectural decision-making?
- RQ3: Why do practitioners prioritise these rationales?

In order to investigate the above problems we performed a two-phase inquiry. Firstly, we gathered data through a questionnaire. We obtained answers from 63 practitioners. Then, we presented the questionnaire's results to 13 practitioners during interviews. As a result of the questionnaire, we created a list of rationales (including quality attributes as given in ISO 25010 [10]) that practitioners of various experience levels (beginners, mid-career and experts) consider essential. As a result of the interviews, we found out that, depending on experience level, practitioners tend to prioritise different architectural options.

The rest of the paper has been organised as follows: Sect. 2 presents related work, Sect. 3 contains details about our research process and Sect. 4 the study's results. We discuss our findings in Sect. 5, present the threats to validity in Sect. 6 and conclude in Sect. 7.

## 2    Related Work

The notion that software architecture is a set of design decisions [11] has heavily impacted the field of software architecture [2]. To enable better decision-making, researchers have explored such areas as: human factors in ADM [15], AD models [25], mining AK [5], curating AK [3], tools supporting decision-making [13], techniques that can aid designers in the decision-making process [16,21]

and ADM rationale [20].

Numerous aspects make ADM an extremely challenging process. The traditional decision-making process, which includes listing all possible alternatives and their attributes, is impractical for software design decisions [7] because of the number of possible architectural solutions. Furthermore, practitioners can be overwhelmed by the time and effort required to find architectural information [8]. Additionally, an entirely rational design-making process is impossible as long as it depends on human beings, that are impacted by various human factors [15].

While there exist general guidelines [21] and various tools [2] for ADM, empirical research on ADM factors is scarce [15]. On the topic of the practitioners' rationale behind design decisions, several studies must be acknowledged. Firstly, the study of Tang et al. [20], reporting the results of a survey on practitioners' approach to architectural rationale. Researchers had practitioners choose the importance of generic rationales and optionally allowed participants to provide their own rationales. As a result, a list of 12 rationales indicated by practitioners was made. This study's results were later expanded by Miesbauer et al. [14] and Weinreich et al. [23] who performed interview-based studies through which the list was expanded to include 18 rationales in total. Soliman et al. [19] researched what technology features impacted technology design decisions. Bi et al. [4] took a different approach and researched which ISO 25010 software quality attributes [10] were most often discussed in the context of architectural patterns on the StackOverflow platform.

We found no recent empirical research focusing widely on ADM rationale more recent than eight years ago. As software technology evolves rapidly, the rationales could also change.

Additionally, we found no studies on how rationales depend on architects' professional experience, which we believe could be relevant since junior and senior architects find different aspects of ADM challenging [22].

## 3   Method

Our research comprises two phases: questionnaire and interviews. The purpose of the questionnaire was to gather a larger sample of data that would enable us to answer RQ1 and RQ2. The interviews let us delve deeper into the meaning and implications of the questionnaire's results (RQ3). Another reason for using two data-gathering methods was to achieve so-called 'methodological triangulation' [17], which helps to strengthen the validity of our findings. The overview of the study process is presented in Fig. 1. The questionnaire questions, a summary of questionnaire results, the interview plan, and interview coding details are available online [6].

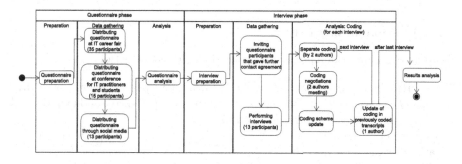

**Fig. 1.** Study phases

## 3.1  Questionnaire: Data-Gathering

The questionnaire's [6] design was simplistic in order to avoid discouraging practitioners from taking part and to avoid biasing the results by suggesting any specific answers. The questionnaire was divided into four main sections:

1. Participant data: age, gender, education, years of experience in software development, role in the company, company size, company domain.
2. An open-ended question to provide a maximum of three most often used rationales for architectural decisions, according to the participant's personal experience.
3. An open-ended question to provide a maximum of three most often used rationales for architectural decisions by the participant's colleagues. We asked this question to investigate if the participants believed that other practitioners have different priorities from them.
4. An optional section containing the option to provide an email and give consent for further contact from the researchers.

In order to obtain samples for the study, we distributed the questionnaires in three different locations:

1. During a 3-day long IT career fair at our faculty, where representatives of over 50 companies were present. We approached each stall and gave a physical copy of the questionnaire to the practitioners that were advertising their companies. We obtained 35 completed questionnaires at this event.
2. During an IT conference for practitioners and students, where representatives from over 60 companies were present. We used the same strategy as the one during the career fair and obtained 15 additional completed questionnaires.
3. We made the questionnaire available online and posted it on our personal social media accounts; this led to additional information from 13 participants.

In total, we obtained data from 63 participants. A summary of the participants' demographic data is presented in Fig. 2, and their employers' companies' domain and size in Fig. 3.

## 3.2  Questionnaire: Analysis

To analyse the questionnaire, we performed the following actions:

1. We divided the participants into the following groups: beginners (under five years of experience), mid-career (5 to 14 years of experience), and experienced (15 or more years of experience) practitioners.
2. We extracted the answers about the participants' as well as their colleagues' rationales and analysed them separately.
3. For each of the six combinations of the above groups (participants' experience level and their own/colleagues' rationales) separately, we classified the rationales (even if they were worded differently) into categories. When applicable,

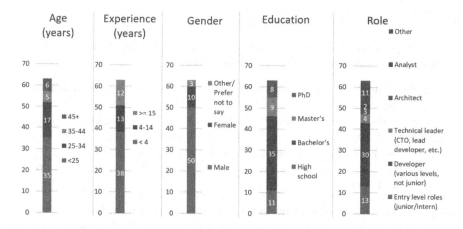

**Fig. 2.** Questionnaire participants

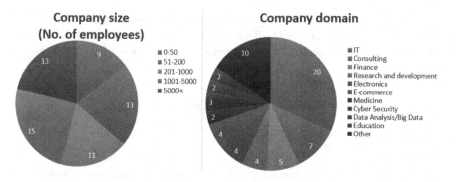

**Fig. 3.** Questionnaire participants companies

we used the ISO/IEC 25010 [10] software quality attributes as the rationale categories. We grouped rationales into categories, since participants often used different words to explain the same factors influencing their decision-making. A rationale category groups rationales that are similar to such a degree that we found them almost indistinguishable. For example, we categorised all of the following as "Time/Deadlines": "time that we will waste on it; how much time there is to do it; time available to create the software; Number of hours required to write the functionality; time-consumption of making the solution; time-consuming; deadline to deliver the project; time available; time". When rationales were only related to each other, like for example "Documentation" and "Maintainability", we did not categorise them together. Table 3 summarises the questionnaire analysis results.

## 3.3 Interviews: Data Gathering

Based on questionnaire data analysis, when creating the interview plan [6], we focused on the following categories of observations:

1. The rationales common for 20% of the participants of each professional experience level.
2. Quality attributes of generally low interest to the architects, namely, attributes mentioned by fewer than 5% of all the participants.
3. Cases in which answers varied among architects of different experience levels. For example, some rationales were over the 20% cutoff score in one group but not in all of them.

We presented the results from the questionnaire in which the above cases occurred to the interviewees. Then, we asked them about the reasons behind the observed level of importance of these rationales for specific architects' experience groups.

All 13 interviewees were recruited from the questionnaire participants. We invited to a follow-up interview all participants that consented to a follow-up interview in the questionnaire. Table 1 presents the overview of the interviewees' characteristics.

**Table 1.** Interview participants

| No. | Gender | Age (years) | Experience (years) | Education | Role | Company size (employees) | Company domain |
|-----|--------|-------------|--------------------|-----------|------|--------------------------|----------------|
| 1 | Male | 23 | 1 | Bachelor's | Software Engineer | 1001–5000 | Infrastructure monitoring |
| 2 | Male | 22 | 1 | Bachelor's | C++ Developer | 51–200 | Power Engineering |
| 3 | Male | 45 | 22 | PhD | Company owner | 0–50 | IT, Data Science |
| 4 | Male | 23 | 1 | Bachelor's | Pythin Backend Developer | 51–200 | Software House |
| 5 | Male | 22 | 1 | High School | Junior Developer | 1001–5000 | E-commerce |
| 6 | Male | 23 | 3 | Bachelor's | Junior Java Developer | over 5000 | Consulting |
| 7 | Male | 24 | 4 | Bachelor's | Software Engineer | 51–200 | Finance |
| 8 | Male | 31 | 5 | Master's | Software Developer | 1001–5000 | Electronics |
| 9 | Male | 45 | 20 | PhD | Architect | over 5000 | Commerce |
| 10 | Female | 25 | 3 | Master's | NLP Engineer | over 5000 | R&D |
| 11 | Male | 41 | 20 | PhD | CTO | 201–1000 | Finance |
| 12 | Male | 28 | 5 | High School | Senior Testing Engineer | 201–1000 | Videogame development |
| 13 | Male | 32 | 6 | Master's | Senior Software Engineering Manager | over 5000 | FMCG |

## 3.4   Interviews: Analysis

The interview recordings have been transcribed. Then we coded the transcripts by following the subsequent steps:

1. Two separate authors coded the same transcript using the descriptive coding method [18]. This means that segments of the transcripts, which contained a relevant piece of information, were labelled with a code that described its type of content. We started with an empty list of codes, to avoid biasing the results towards our own ideas, and allowed the codes to emerge during the coding process.
2. Both coding authors met to negotiate their coding [9] — they made changes to the coding until reaching a unanimous consensus.
3. An updated list of codes was created as a result of the coding meeting.
4. One of the authors re-coded previously coded transcripts with new codes if they emerged during the current analysis step.
5. The above steps were repeated for each interview transcript.

**Table 2.** Codes

| Code | Description | Number of occur-rences | Number of interviews where code occurred |
|---|---|---|---|
| EX | Perspective/performed tasks change with the developer's experience | 58 | 13 |
| CLNT | Recognising client's needs, focusing on the client's benefit. | 31 | 12 |
| EASY | Participant mentions how important ease of use for development/maintenance is in the project | 28 | 13 |
| FUT | Thinking about what effects the choice will have for the project | 29 | 12 |
| D | Focusing on the deadline/ how much time something will take | 23 | 9 |
| FAM | Choosing something based on one's familiarity with it | 25 | 9 |
| IMP | The rationale was omitted because it is 'obviously' important | 18 | 9 |
| EMP | Thinking how the choice will impact other people | 15 | 10 |
| CR | Focusing on personal growth | 15 | 8 |
| OUTDATED | The rationale does not require much thought because it is handled by newer technology | 13 | 8 |
| NEG | The participant disagrees with other practitioners' opinions (from the questionnaire) | 11 | 7 |
| EDU | Described behaviour is an effect of education | 10 | 7 |
| RARE | The participant considers something as niche or unimportant | 9 | 5 |

Codes are summarised in Table 2. After coding all transcripts, we analysed and discussed the coded segments to draw conclusions.

# 4 Results

Table 3 presents the questionnaire results. As explained in Sect. 3.3, we consider the rationale as important to a given group of architects if it was indicated but at least 20% of them. Additionally, we focused on software quality attributes that were mentioned by less than 5% of the participants and the variation in rationale prioritisation in different groups of participants.

## 4.1 RQ1 & RQ2: Most Frequent Rationales and Prioritised Software Quality Attributes

The rationales that most frequently occurred in the questionnaires (over 20% of participants) were:

1. **"Ease of use for development"** was the dominant rationale for almost all groups of participants. Over 40% of the beginner and expert groups believed

**Table 3.** Questionnaire results. ISO/IEC 25010 quality attributes are marked by a bold font.

| No | Rationale category | Sum | | Beginners | | Mid-career | | Experienced | |
|---|---|---|---|---|---|---|---|---|---|
| | | Participants | Colleagues | Participants | Colleagues | Participants | Colleagues | Participants | Colleagues |
| 1 | Ease of use for development | 23 | 11 | 16 | 7 | 2 | 0 | 5 | 4 |
| 2 | **Maintainability** | 15 | 2 | 12 | 1 | 2 | 1 | 1 | 0 |
| 3 | **Performance** | 14 | 6 | 13 | 6 | 0 | 0 | 1 | 0 |
| 4 | Prior knowledge/experience | 14 | 14 | 11 | 9 | 1 | 2 | 2 | 3 |
| 5 | Time/deadline | 12 | 8 | 10 | 6 | 1 | 0 | 1 | 2 |
| 6 | **Reliability** | 10 | 4 | 6 | 3 | 2 | 1 | 2 | 0 |
| 7 | Development Project Environment | 9 | 2 | 4 | 1 | 3 | 1 | 2 | 0 |
| 8 | Cost | 8 | 9 | 5 | 7 | 1 | 0 | 2 | 2 |
| 9 | Popularity | 8 | 8 | 7 | 5 | 0 | 1 | 1 | 2 |
| 10 | Scalability | 7 | 3 | 4 | 3 | 2 | 0 | 1 | 0 |
| 11 | Business/customer requirements | 7 | 5 | 4 | 4 | 1 | 0 | 2 | 1 |
| 12 | Documentation | 6 | 4 | 6 | 4 | 0 | 0 | 0 | 0 |
| 13 | **Usability** | 5 | 0 | 3 | 0 | 2 | 0 | 0 | 0 |
| 14 | **Security** | 5 | 2 | 3 | 2 | 2 | 0 | 0 | 0 |
| 15 | Aesthetics/UX | 5 | 2 | 1 | 1 | 2 | 0 | 2 | 1 |
| 16 | Fit with existing systems/project | 5 | 7 | 4 | 4 | 0 | 1 | 1 | 2 |
| 17 | Decision-making methodology | 5 | 4 | 0 | 0 | 2 | 1 | 3 | 3 |
| 18 | Testability (simplicity of writing tests) | 4 | 0 | 3 | 0 | 0 | 0 | 1 | 0 |
| 19 | Level of complexity of the problem/system | 4 | 1 | 4 | 1 | 0 | 0 | 0 | 0 |
| 20 | Expertise of more experienced colleagues | 4 | 1 | 4 | 1 | 0 | 0 | 0 | 0 |
| 21 | **Functional Suitability** | 3 | 1 | 2 | 1 | 0 | 0 | 1 | 0 |
| 22 | Availability of packages | 3 | 0 | 1 | 0 | 0 | 0 | 2 | 0 |
| 23 | Team members' preferences | 3 | 4 | 2 | 4 | 0 | 0 | 1 | 0 |
| 24 | **Portability** | 2 | 2 | 2 | 1 | 0 | 0 | 0 | 1 |
| 25 | System life expectancy | 2 | 0 | 0 | 0 | 0 | 0 | 2 | 0 |
| 26 | I want to add new skill to my resume | 2 | 1 | 2 | 1 | 0 | 0 | 0 | 0 |
| 27 | **Compatibility** | 1 | 2 | 0 | 0 | 0 | 0 | 1 | 2 |
| 28 | Return on Investment (ROI) | 1 | 1 | 1 | 1 | 0 | 0 | 0 | 0 |
| 29 | Market expectations | 1 | 0 | 1 | 0 | 0 | 0 | 0 | 0 |
| 30 | Available human resources/money | 0 | 4 | 0 | 2 | 0 | 2 | 0 | 0 |
| 31 | Bus factor | 0 | 1 | 0 | 1 | 0 | 0 | 0 | 0 |
| 32 | "It works so I should use it" | 0 | 1 | 0 | 1 | 0 | 0 | 0 | 0 |
| 33 | My colleagues have the same rationales as me | 0 | 19 | 0 | 13 | 0 | 4 | 0 | 2 |

that it was important. However, this was not the case for mid-career practitioners, where only 15% mentioned this rationale.

2. The quality attribute of **"Maintainability"** was the second most often indicated rationale, which was mentioned by 24% of the participants. This was due to the beginners' insistence that this rationale is important (30% of them), though it was not similarly prioritised by mid-career practitioners (15%) and experts (8%).

3. Both the quality attributes of **"Performance"** and **"Prior knowledge/experience"** were mentioned by the same number of practitioners overall (22%). **"Performance"**, similarly to **"Maintainability"**, was important to beginners (33%) but not to mid-career (0%) and to expert practitioners (8%). **"Prior knowledge/experience"** of the solution, in the same way as **"Ease of use for development"**, was prioritised by both beginners and experts (over 20% in both groups) but not by mid-career practitioners (only 8%).

Rationales that were overall mentioned by less than 20% of the participants but were important for a particular group of practitioners (over 20% of that group):

1. **"Time/deadline"** is a rationale that was mentioned by 26% of beginners but less often by mid-career and expert practitioners (8% in both groups).

2. **"Development Project Environment"**, which refers to various aspects of management and organisation of development project (e.g. company standards, client specifics) or current possibilities (available technologies), was important to mid-career practitioners (23%) but less so to beginners (10%) and experts (16%).

3. A **"decision-making methodology"** was by experts (25%) but only a few mid-career practitioners (8%) and no beginners.

Three software quality attributes were mentioned by less than 5% of the participants: **Compatibility** (1 participant), **Portability** (2 participants) and **Functional Stability** (3 participants).

Finally, when asked about their colleagues' rationales, most participants wrote unprompted in their questionnaires that **their colleagues are motivated by the same rationales as they are themselves** (30%). These were not cases of copying the same answers from one question to another but literally writing a statement about one's colleagues. This answer dominated the beginner (33%) and mid-career (31%) groups but occurred less frequently in the expert group (17%).

## 4.2    RQ3: Rationales' Origins

By analysing the interviews, we found a key set of rationales' origins. Some rationales and rationale origins may slightly overlap (e.g. "Time/deadlines" rationale and "fear of deadlines" rationale origin). This was the case when participants listed both a rationale in the questionnaire and a rationale's origin in the interviews. The rationale's origins include (number of code occurrences over-all/number of interviews where code occurred):

1. **Practitioner's experience(58/13)**: The primary origin of the practition-ers' rationales were their previous experiences. Beginners had limited expe-rience, and to avoid the risk of not performing their duties efficiently, they preferred the solutions which they had used previously - because of that, "Ease of use for development" and "Prior knowledge" turned out to be the prevailing rationale for them. As one of the participants stated: "(...) [junior developers] are such fresh people, it is certainly much more conve-nient. Because, well, since it's easy to learn something [how to use a solution], it's easy to reach the right level quite quickly."

   Experts with significant experience also prioritised these rationales but for different reasons – they already had knowledge that they were confident in, so they did not feel the need to try new solutions and leave their comfort zone, e.g. "Maybe more experienced people who worked a long time with a certain technology change it less often than people who are just entering the IT market (...), but feel comfortable with certain technologies and have been comfortable working with them for many years."

   The exception to this effect were mid-career practitioners who were most likely to possess the knowledge and willingness to discover new solutions. As a participant said: "Maybe the moderately experienced people are nei-ther those very experienced people who have been working in a particular technology for a longer period of time, but those who change it more often and maybe they see that it is not that difficult, they are used to changing technologies."

   The practitioner's experience influence was also crucial for choosing the "Time/deadline" and "decision-making methodology" rationales. Beginners feared the possible consequences of missing a deadline more than other practitioners. Hence, they indicated the "Time/deadline" rationale more frequently than more experienced architects, e.g. "People with more experi-ence are more assertive when it comes to deadlines and are able to say 'no' when they know that it is simply impossible to do something in a certain time, and those with less experience may also not be so sure that this is the moment that it is worth saying 'no' and not doing something, they are afraid of the deadline."

   However, using a "decision-making methodology" as their rationale's foun-dation was only possible to experienced practitioners due to their greater knowledge, e.g. " (...) we [the architects] are just getting used to such methodologies, acquiring them, so we will only use them after some time."

2. **Client focus (31/12)**: Various rationales originated from the endeavour to meet the client's needs. Practitioners often prioritised "Ease of use for devel-opment" and "Time/deadline" rationales because they strived to deliver new functionalities to the client as soon as possible, e.g. "(...) recently there has been a lot of emphasis on time to market and deadlines for implementing individual functionalities, which are usually short."

Similarly, the "Development Project Environment" had to be considered to satisfy the client's needs. Even if two projects appeared to be the same, the environment often made a difference in its development. As one participant stated: "Otherwise, seemingly the project sounds the same, but in practice, the client often wants something completely different than the previous one." Additionally, "Performance" was seen generally as a key software quality attribute from the client's perspective, since weak software performance (software freezes, long waiting times, etc.) was seen as very problematic to the clients, e.g. "(...) usually the performance of the system is related to the comfort of use, so it seems to me that this is also the reason why performance is an important criterion."

3. **Making one's life "easy" (28/13)**: Generally, practitioners choose solutions that they believed would make their work as effortless as possible. This was not only related to the "Ease of use for development" rationale but also "Prior knowledge" (the source of information about what is "easy") and "Maintainability" (minimisation of future work). As one participant stated: "Some developers are lazy, which means that solutions that are easier to maintain often scale easier and perhaps require less work or less mental effort to add a new feature or to fix a bug."

4. **Thinking of the project's future (29/12)**: In general, practitioners were aware of the software life-cycle and knew that "Maintainability" could impact the amount of effort they would have to put into maintaining the system in the future. However, "Ease of use for development" was also a rationale impacted by this factor. Practitioners believed that if it is easy to use a given solution, it will also be easier to find, hire and train new employees that would work on the project in the future, e.g. "(...)the ease of training new employees to work, whenever the software is easier to develop and is based on popular technology or the code is transparent, it is easier to introduce someone new here."

5. **Fear of deadlines (23/9)**: The fear of missing a deadline had a major impact on beginner practitioners. This was not the case for mid-career and expert practitioners since they already had experiences with missed deadlines in their careers and had the capacity to imagine how such a situation could be handled. For example: "I think it's because the more experienced ones, I also know that this is how managers and programmers work, as well as project managers, that they know that this deadline is set with some reserve."

6. **Familiarity with a particular solution(25/9)**: Prior experience with a particular solution was the main source of architectural knowledge. Since it is rarely possible to explore all the possible alternatives, prior experiences are the primary source of information, e.g. "Architecture, all engineering, in general, is based on experience, and experience means things that we brokne in previous designs, in previous products. And on this experience, which looks so negative, but is nevertheless building our knowledge, we base what we create in the future.".

7. **"Obviousness" (18/9):** In the case of the "Functional Stability" quality attribute, some practitioners expressed the opinion that the importance of this rationale is simply obvious, and as such, there was no need to mention it in the questionnaire, e.g. "It's [Functional Stability] also so mundane and part of such day-to-day work that maybe we don't tie it to the architecture.".

8. **Empathy (15/10):** "Ease of use for development" and "Maintainability" were often prioritised because of the practitioners' awareness that their colleagues will have to maintain and further expand a system in the future, e.g. "It should be done in such a way that I would not hurt myself or that it would not be painful for my colleagues to maintain. I see in this perhaps some form of empathy.".

9. **Personal growth (15/8):** Mid-career practitioners did not prioritise "Ease of use for development" and "Prior knowledge" rationales, as beginners and experts did. Our participants pointed out that mid-career practitioners are in a specific professional situation where they can already feel confident in their basic knowledge (unlike beginners) but strive to learn about new solutions to further develop their careers (unlike experts). As one participant stated: "(...) resume driven development, i.e. we choose those technologies that will look nice in the CV, or that will make us learn something.".

10. **New technology handles the problem (11/7):** In the case of the "Compatibility", and "Portability' quality attributes, practitioners believed that new technologies already solved most problems related to these rationales. In the case of "Compatibility", currently, existing standards are widely used, and compatibility problems are rare. As a participant stated: "(...) because everything is somehow compatible with each other, only a matter of certain calling some services(...)".
Similarly, the widespread use of virtualisation and containerisation solved most problems with "Portability", as a participant stated: "(...) because practically everything can be uploaded, containerized".

11. **Practitioner's education(10/7):** "Performance" was stated to be a rationale prioritised by beginner practitioners that recently finished their degrees in a field related to Software Engineering. This was due to the focus on the use of optimal data structures and algorithms during their studies, e.g. "(...) during studies and in earlier educational programming, a lot of emphasis was placed on making these solutions work quickly. I even had one subject where we were judged on how many minutes it took to run a program, so it stuck in my head a bit.".

12. **Perception of the quality attribute as unimportant(9/5):** Some participants stated that in the case of the projects that they worked on, "Compatibility" and "Portability" quality attributes were not important. For example, the project was targeted to work on a very specific platform, as the participant stated: "(...)projects are created, for specific hardware or for specific platforms, not multi-platform solutions."

# 5   Discussion

Two top rationales that were not quality attributes were "Ease of use for development" and "Prior knowledge/experience". This result is similar to the findings of Miesbauer et al. [14] and Weinreich et al. [23] who found that the most influential rationale was "Personal experience/Preferences". This implies that the current trend of researching human factors in ADM [2,15] is appropriate for further understanding and improving ADM. To be more specific, it seems that practitioners prioritise minimising their own and their colleagues' workload, both in the short and the long term. This fits with the principle of "Simplicity – the art of maximising the amount of work not done" [1] from Agile software development. However, if done inappropriately, this can lead to consequences such as incurring architectural technical debt [12].

The quality attributes of "Maintainability" and "Performance" were perceived as the most important out of the set of ISO 25010 software quality attributes [10]. This matches the findings of Bi et al. [4] who found these to be the most often discussed quality attributes in the context of architectural patterns. We further explain this phenomenon since we found that beginner practitioners emphasise these rationales more than experts. In the case of "Maintainability", it seems that they wanted to avoid their own future workload, which may be perceived as an intimidating perspective. In the case of "Performance", beginners followed the knowledge acquired during their formal education and the emphasis of scholars on algorithmic efficiency.

Additionally, we found that practitioners in general do not put an emphasis on the quality attributes of "Portability" and "Compatibility". Modern technologies deliver solutions that well-address both these issues. In the case of "Portability", there are many efficient tools that resolve such problems: virtualisation, containerisation or frameworks for building multi-platform applications. Furthermore, in some fields (like developing console video games), the hardware on which the software will be run can be accurately predicted. Challenges with "Compatibility" have been overcome mostly through the standardisation of the technologies used by practitioners; for example, in the case of web applications, a REST API between the front-end and back-end layers is a predictable solution that most would choose by default.

Finally, we discovered that depending on experience level, practitioners have a significantly different mindset when it comes to ADM. Beginners are greatly influenced by a fear of the unknown: they fear that it would be too hard to develop the software, or to maintain it later, to learn new solutions during the projects, and the consequences of unmet deadlines. Experts experience less fear of deadlines but put an emphasis on ease of development to make their colleagues' work easier and feel comfortable with their current practices. They were also the only group to use any decision-making methodologies, which they found natural if they gained enough knowledge. Lastly, mid-career practitioners are the most open to learning about new solutions and attempting not to use ones that are not considered "easy", to create bespoke solutions that would fit their clients the best.

# 6   Threats to Validity

In this Section we describe three main kinds of threats to validity [17]:

**Construct Validity** To find the participants' rationales for architectural decisions, the possible methods of enquiry are either methods based on self-reporting or observation of the participants' work. We have chosen self-reporting methods (questionnaires and interviews) since that enabled us to obtain data from a greater number of practitioners. However, it is still possible that the participants' actual rationale may differ from those that they reported. For example, they may be impacted by cognitive biases [24] that they are not aware of.

**Internal Validity** To maximise the internal validity of our findings, the coding of the transcripts was always done independently by two authors. Then, both discussed the coding until they unanimously agreed on all codes. This was done to minimise the impact of the researcher's bias on the findings. However, it is possible that factors that we did not consider could play a role in practitioners' approach to decision-making, such as their company's size or domain.

**External Validity** We used convenience sampling since it is an extreme challenge to obtain a random generalisable sample of software practitioners. However, we strived to overcome this by providing data source triangulation [17]: we searched for participants from three different sources (two in-person events and one on social media). This resulted in a varied group of participants.

Though, worth noting is that the sample may be biased towards less experienced practitioners, due to the majority of participants having less than 4 years of professional experience. Additionally, since our results partially match results from previous studies [4, 14, 23], it seems that our sample was big enough to give us outcomes also noticeable to other researchers.

# 7   Conclusion

In this study, we performed a mixed methods two-step empirical inquiry into the practitioners' rationale behind their architectural decisions. The three main contributions of this study are as follows:

1. A list of the most impactful rationales that influence practitioners' architectural decision-making;
2. An exploration of these rationales' origin;
3. The finding of how a practitioner's experience has a significant impact on how they make architectural decisions.

Future research could employ different research techniques to further confirm or disconfirm our findings. A survey on a random generalisable sample would be beneficial, as well as observational studies on practitioners that would explore their decision-making in real-time. In accordance to our findings, since experience level seems to be a major factor shaping who architects make their decisions researchers should take it into account during future research on ADM.

Practitioners could benefit from our study by understanding better the way they and their colleagues develop software architectures. The observation on the influence of experience on ADM should also be reflected in shaping a team's structure, e.g. it would be prudent to focus on having mid-career (between 5 and 14 years of experience) practitioners in their teams when working on an innovative project.

# References

1. Beck, K., et al.: Principles behind the Agile Manifesto (2001). https:// agilemanifesto.org/principles.html
2. Bhat, M., Shumaiev, K., Hohenstein, U., Biesdorf, A., Matthes, F.: The evolution of architectural decision making as a key focus area of software architecture research: a semi-systematic literature study. In: 2020 IEEE International Conference on Software Architecture (ICSA), pp. 69–80. IEEE (2020)
3. Bhat, M., Tinnes, C., Shumaiev, K., Biesdorf, A., Hohenstein, U., Matthes, F.: ADeX: a tool for automatic curation of design decision knowledge for architectural decision recommendations. In: 2019 IEEE International Conference on Software Architecture Companion (ICSA-C), pp. 158–161. IEEE (2019)
4. Bi, T., Liang, P., Tang, A.: Architecture patterns, quality attributes, and design contexts: how developers design with them. In: Proceedings - Asia-Pacific Software Engineering Conference, APSEC 2018-Decem(61472286), pp. 49–58 (2018)
5. Bi, T., Liang, P., Tang, A., Xia, X.: Mining architecture tactics and quality attributes knowledge in stack overflow. J. Syst. Softw. (May) (2021)
6. Borowa, K., Lewanczyk, R., Stpiczyńska, K., Stradomski, P., Zalewski, A.: What rationales drive architectural decisions? An empirical inquiry - Additional material (May 2023). https://doi.org/10.5281/zenodo.7946764
7. Burge, J.E.: Design rationale: Researching under uncertainty. Artif. Intell. Eng. Design, Anal. Manuf.: AIEDAM **22**(4), 311–324 (2008)
8. De Dieu, M.J., Liang, P., Shahin, M.: How do developers search for architectural information? An industrial survey. In: Proceedings - IEEE 19th International Conference on Software Architecture, ICSA 2022 (December 2021), pp. 58–68 (2022)
9. Garrison, D.R., Cleveland-Innes, M., Koole, M., Kappelman, J.: Revisiting methodological issues in transcript analysis: negotiated coding and reliability. Internet Higher Educ. **9**(1), 1–8 (2006)
10. ISO/IEC 25010: ISO/IEC 25010:2011, systems and software engineering - systems and software quality requirements and evaluation (square) - system and software quality models (2011)
11. Jansen, A., Bosch, J.: Software architecture as a set of architectural design decisions. In: 5th Working IEEE/IFIP Conference on Software Architecture (WICSA'05), pp. 109–120. IEEE (2005)
12. Kruchten, P., Nord, R., Ozkaya, I.: Managing Technical Debt. Addison-Wesley Professional (2019)
13. Liu, M.X., et al: Unakite: scaffolding developers' decision-making using the web. In: Proceedings of the 32nd Annual ACM Symposium on User Interface Software and Technology, pp. 67–80 (2019)
14. Miesbauer, C., Weinreich, R.: Classification of design decisions – an expert survey in practice. In: Drira, K. (ed.) ECSA 2013. LNCS, vol. 7957, pp. 130–145. Springer, Heidelberg (2013). https://doi.org/10.1007/978-3-642-39031-9_12

15. Razavian, M., Paech, B., Tang, A.: Empirical research for software architecture decision making: an analysis. J. Syst. Softw. **149**, 360–381 (2019)
16. Razavian, M., Tang, A., Capilla, R., Lago, P.: Reflective approach for software design decision making. Proceedings - 1st Workshop on Qualitative Reasoning about Software Architectures, QRASA 2016 pp. 19–26 (2016)
17. Runeson, P., Höst, M., Rainer, A., Regnell, B.: Case study research in software engineering: guidelines and examples (2012). https://www.wiley.com
18. Saldaña, J.: The coding manual for qualitative researchers, pp. 1–440 (2021)
19. Soliman, M., Riebisch, M., Zdun, U.: enriching architecture knowledge with technology design decisions. In: Proceedings - 12th Working IEEE/IFIP Conference on Software Architecture, WICSA 2015, pp. 135–144 (2015)
20. Tang, A., Babar, M.A., Gorton, I., Han, J.: A survey of architecture design rationale. J. Syst. Softw. **79**(12), 1792–1804 (2006)
21. Tang, A., Kazman, R.: Decision-making principles for better software design decisions. IEEE Softw. **38**(6), 98–102 (2021)
22. Tofan, D., Galster, M., Avgeriou, P.: Difficulty of architectural decisions - a survey with professional architects. In: Drira, K. (ed.) Softw. Architect., pp. 192–199. Springer, Berlin Heidelberg (2013). https://doi.org/10.1007/978-3-642-39031-9_17
23. Weinreich, R., Groher, I., Miesbauer, C.: An expert survey on kinds, influence factors and documentation of design decisions in practice. Future Gener. Comput. Syst. **47**, 145–160 (2015)
24. Zalewski, A., Borowa, K., Ratkowski, A.: On cognitive biases in architecture decision making. In: Lopes, A., de Lemos, R. (eds.) Softw. Architect., pp. 123–137. Springer International Publishing, Cham (2017). https://doi.org/10.1007/978-3-319-65831-5_9
25. Zimmermann, O., Koehler, J., Leymann, F., Polley, R., Schuster, N.: Managing architectural decision models with dependency relations, integrity constraints, and production rules. J. Syst. Softw. **82**(8), 1249–1267 (2009)

# Learning from Each Other: How Are Architectural Mistakes Communicated in Industry?

Marion Wiese(✉) ⬛, Axel-Frederik Brand, and André van Hoorn ⬛

Universität Hamburg, Department of Informatics, Hamburg, Germany
marion.wiese@uni-hamburg.de

**Abstract.** *Context.* Own experiences and faulty decisions can be an important source of information for software architects. The experiences and mistakes of other architects can also be valuable information sources. *Goal.* Under the assumption that the knowledge about faulty decisions, i.e., mistakes, regarding software architecture is not shared adequately in practice, this work qualitatively investigates the handling and particularly communication of those mistakes by software architects. *Method.* We conducted a grounded-theory study in which we interviewed ten German software architects from various domains. *Results.* We identified software architects' definitions of architectural mistakes, their handling of these mistakes, and their preferred communication strategies regarding these mistakes. We found that architects communicate mistakes mainly within their project teams and seldom within or across companies. *Conclusions.* We derived strategies to make learning and prevention of mistakes more effective. To share experiences and knowledge beyond architects' peer groups, companies should invest more effort in discussing mistakes more consciously and create an environment where mistakes can be discussed openly.

**Keywords:** Software Architecture · Software Architecture Knowledge · Software Architecture Decisions · Software Architecture Communication

## 1 Introduction

"Errare humanum est" —to err is human, is common knowledge since ancient times [10]. In software architecture, we also make mistakes. By sharing our experiences with mistakes, we enhance the chance of not repeating them. In other domains, e.g., economics, it has become common to learn from each other's mistakes by sharing experiences, e.g., by conducting "Fuck up nights" [1]. However, in software architecture (SA), it seems that mistakes are not a commonly discussed topic. Even using the term "mistake" in the context of SA may seem offensive.

© The Author(s), under exclusive license to Springer Nature Switzerland AG 2023
B. Tekinerdogan et al. (Eds.): ECSA 2023, LNCS 14212, pp. 319–336, 2023.
https://doi.org/10.1007/978-3-031-42592-9_22

Technical debts are constructs in software systems that are beneficial in the short term but hinder changes in the long term [2]. Technical debt in SA was identified as one of the most dangerous types [13] because there is a lack of refactoring strategies [3].

One goal to avoid architectural technical debt is to amass knowledge and have at least some experience before deciding on an SA issue. A lot of research focuses on the optimization of SA processes, particularly with regard to SA decision-making [4,21] and gathering SA knowledge [22]. Soliman et al. found that when searching for SA knowledge on Google, experience reports on design decisions and drawbacks of solution options are relevant to a decision but are underrepresented in search results [20].

Architects deal with mistakes, i.e., design decisions that turn out to be sub-optimal,
by doing "post-mortems" [5] or by defining anti-patterns [17], and architecture smells [14]. However, the question of how to communicate the mistakes between architects is not yet researched systematically to the best of the authors' knowledge.

Our goal is to fill this gap by conducting a grounded theory study. We interviewed ten software architects to gather their approaches to sharing bad experiences regarding decisions in SA, i.e., SA mistakes (SAMs). To follow this goal, we answer the following research questions (RQs):

- **RQ 1: *How do architects define a SA mistake?*** This question lays the foundation for our work, as the term mistake is not yet commonly used or defined in relation to SA.
- **RQ 2: *How do architects manage SA mistakes?*** We explain how the architects identify and handle SAMs. It is relevant to understand the overall management of SAMs to identify communication within these processes. Furthermore, we created a comprehensive model of the SAMs' management.
- **RQ 3: *How do architects communicate SA mistakes?*** We identified the ways architects communicate SAMs and particularly on which level, i.e., personal, team-wide, company-wide, or even outside of their company. Furthermore, we identified factors that suppress or promote the communication of SAMs. Thereby, we uncovered opportunities for process improvements.

As the contribution of our study, we answer the research questions and provide:

- A definition of SA mistakes
- A theory of a model of SA mistakes' management
- SA mistakes communication issues and potential for improvement

In Sect. 2, we explain our research methodology. We present the results and answer the research questions in Sect. 3. In Sect. 4, we discuss our findings. We compare our study with related work in Sect. 5 and discuss the threats to validity of our study in Sect. 6. With Sect. 7, we conclude our paper and summarize the contributions for practitioners and researchers. Additional material is available [24].

# 2 Method

To answer our research question, we did a grounded theory study. Grounded Theory was first introduced by Glaser & Strauss [7]. In grounded theory, the collected data is analyzed interpretatively, and identified concepts are comprehensibly collected. The concepts are compared, structured, and summarized into categories. From these categories, theses are derived that are valid across the data. The final goal of Grounded Theory is to develop a theory on the researched topic. This theory must then be validated by further studies, e.g., surveys. The coding and analysis process takes place in parallel to the collection of new data, whereby the categories are iteratively reconsidered, compared, and questioned. This is referred to as the method of constant comparison. The process of collecting and analyzing data is carried out until the theory is saturated. Saturation is reached when new data hardly generate any new insights in the form of new concepts and categories.

We collected and analyzed data in three phases that merged into one another. In each phase, we adapted the interview guide, did the interviews, and analyzed the corresponding data.

## 2.1 Data Collection

We conducted ten interviews with architects selected according to our sampling strategy and in accordance with our interview guide. We transcribed the recordings of the interviews for further analysis. All interviews were held in the German language.

*Sample.* We recruited software architects from our personal network, via social media and speakers from conferences in three phases. All participants completed a survey about their personal background, e.g., domain, company size, and experience level (see [24]). With this information and the iterative approach, we ensured to gather participants from different domains, with different levels of experience, and consulting and company architects. A variety of participants is important to validate that code saturation is reached for the given context, i.e., German software architects. An overview of the participants can be seen in Table 1.

*Interview Guideline.* We adapted the guideline before each of the three phases to iteratively focus on the emerging theory. All guidelines are available on Zenodo [24] In the end, i.e., in phase three, this led to the following nine questions:

1. What is a SAM or faulty decision in this context?
2. Can you give me examples from your own experience of a SAM or faulty decision? (plus sub-questions regarding the handling of this specific example)
3. What is the role of communicating bad decisions and mistakes for software architects?
4. How do you talk about bad decisions with your colleagues or other architects?
5. How do you talk about SAMs with your team lead or other managers? Does your communication style differ from your colleagues?

**Table 1.** Study Participants

| Participant | Company Domain | Company size (#employees) | Team organization | Years in IT | Years as architect | Gender |
|---|---|---|---|---|---|---|
| P1 | Media | 1000-5000 | agile | >20 | 5-10 | f |
| P2 | Consulting | >5000 | agile | 10-15 | 10-15 | m |
| P3 | Consulting | >5000 | agile | >20 | 10-15 | m |
| P4 | Aviation | >5000 | agile | 15-20 | 10-15 | m |
| P5 | Industry | >5000 | mix (agile/classic) | 10-15 | 2-5 | m |
| P6 | Consulting | 0-100 | agile | 15-20 | 5-10 | m |
| P7 | Consulting | 100-1000 | agile | 5-10 | 5-10 | m |
| P8 | Consulting | 1000-5000 | agile | >20 | 15-20 | m |
| P9 | Consulting | 0-100 | agile | >20 | >20 | m |
| P10 | Insurance | >5000 | agile | >20 | >20 | f |

6. How do different error cultures (e.g. through in-sourcing/out-sourcing or international work/different companies) influence you in dealing with SAMs or faulty decisions?
7. How are faulty decisions or SAMs dealt with in your company for the purpose of knowledge transfer?
8. How has the way you deal with and communicate mistakes changed over time?
9. With regard to concrete faulty decisions — how and with whom should software architects communicate them?

## 2.2 Data Analysis

We coded the transcriptions according to Charmaz's guidelines and reached theoretical saturation after ten interviews [6].

***Coding.*** According to Charmaz [6], the process of coding consists of two phases: initial coding and focused coding. *Initial coding* is an inductive approach. Data segments are considered word-by-word and sentence-by-sentence, and all initial analytical concepts are collected without further comparison. *Focused coding* describes hierarchical sorting and abstracting, i.e., merging of concepts or categories as well as the selection of core categories on which the analysis is focused. The process no longer focuses on the raw data but only on the codes.

Furthermore, through cross-coding phases, during which we constantly compared the codes and coded segments, we iterated through every interview multiple times to make sure that the codes were comparable and identical in meaning (Code list see [24]).

***Theoretical Saturation.*** The goal of the methodology is to achieve theoretical saturation. Theoretical saturation means that the evaluation of new data, for example, through further interviews, no longer fundamentally changes the existing structure of the category system. To evaluate saturation, the number of new codes in each new interview is evaluated, and the goal is to amass fewer codes with each interview's evaluation, particularly focus codes.

As we used cross-coding, the number of codes varied a lot and even got smaller if codes were merged in the process. During our last three interviews, we reduced the codes from 291 codes to 264 codes. During the last interview, we still gained 13 codes (see [24]). However, all these new codes were initial codes and did not provide new insides for the report of the results. Therefore, we assume theoretical saturation for the results presented in this paper.

# 3 Results

In this section, we give a detailed overview of the definition and characteristics of SA mistakes and how to detect them. We present how architects handle detected SAMs and, finally, summarize how they communicate the detected SAMs. Each section concludes with a summary.

## 3.1 RQ1: Definition and Characteristics of SA Mistakes

From the transcripts, we extracted the following definition of SAMs and their characteristics.

*Definition.* A SA decision is classified as a mistake if, for a given problem, an alternative solution exists that solves the problem better than the implemented solution. The choice of an architect is always associated with trade-offs and considerations. Whether a problem is solved "better" is not easy to judge objectively. Therefore, some participants describe SAMs by their negative impact on non-functional quality attributes. *"When it comes to architectural decisions, that [a mistake] is if something doesn't work, I mean more the non-functional [if] you will not meet a non-functional requirement."*

The effects of a SAM are often noticed particularly late, i.e., they have a long feedback cycle. *"The question is, however, after some time, when you reach an appropriate scale, and the application has a corresponding scope, whether you then realize: Yes, you've got it working, but it's not really running ideally."*

SAMs are considered difficult to identify because the alternatives are not directly known to the architects. Even if the architects know the alternatives, the effects of SA decisions are difficult to assess. *"However, you often do not see what an alternative implementation would have brought and what difficulties it would have brought with it."*

SA is an overarching topic because SA should fulfill many different, conflicting goals with many influencing factors and constraints. Therefore, problems are not simply attributable to individual decisions: *"So I think with architecture mistakes, it's often the case that you can't even say that they did something wrong at that point, but it is rather that somehow the realization arises that something is not going right."*

> The goal of SA is to meet non-functional requirements. A SAM is defined as the non-fulfillment of these requirements. SA pursues many different and contradictory goals, and alternatives are often not obvious, which makes the evaluation difficult. A wrong decision often becomes apparent only after a long time.

*Characteristics.* For the participants, a SAM results from the comparison of an actual state with a target state. One participant explained that a SAM is *"everything that turns out afterward that it somehow doesn't work out the way you imagined it."* This comparison between the actual and target state is a subjective evaluation. The subjective approach results in subjective error levels. The situations are classified as acceptable or not acceptable, which in situations with several actors can result in a different understanding of the situation. *"We use our own developed framework, which is already twelve years old because Person C wants it that way, and he gets in the way when we use something else. . . . these are not only wrong decisions, this is almost wanton destruction.".*

The term "mistake" is subjectively perceived in different ways, i.e., there are different connotations associated with the term. Some architects mentioned that making SAMs is normal. *"I think making faulty decisions is okay. It can happen, and you have to deal with that somehow."* Some participants also mentioned the positive aspect of making SAMs and learning from them. *"It's that feeling that to do something really well, you have to have failed at it at least once."* However, much more frequently, the participants mention negative aspects of making SAMs: *"However, it is unfortunately often the case that due to the fact that SA [decisions] are the expensive decisions, mistakes very often cannot be communicated . . . because then it often looks as if people have wasted a lot of money out of stupidity."*

Another characteristic of mistakes is that they are avoidable. We already established that architects think "making mistakes is normal". This can be interpreted as "making mistakes is unavoidable". Yet, this inevitability only applies to mistakes in general. *"I don't think we could have actually done much differently about the situation. . . . That falls under [can be considered as] 'shit happens."'* However, on the level of a single mistake, mistakes are considered to be avoidable. *"If you had trusted the expertise [of the people involved], this wouldn't have happened."*

Finally, another characteristic of a SAM is that we often don't know whether a decision is a mistake until a certain amount of time has passed. *"I think, overall, it came to light too late that this was even a problem at all."*

---

- A SAM is a subjective evaluation of a situation.
- A SAM may be viewed as acceptable by some and unacceptable by other persons.
- The term SAM can be given positive or negative connotations.
- The single SAM can be seen as avoidable.
- In general, the occurrence of SAMs is regarded as unavoidable.
- A SAM is often recognized retrospectively after a certain period of time.

---

## 3.2   RQ2: Management of SA Mistakes

We asked the participants questions about their example situation, particularly how and when they came to the conclusion that the situation was a SAM and how the situation was handled afterward. The results are clustered into four subsequent actions:

1. Detecting SAMs
2. Handling SAMs
3. Learning from SAMs
4. Preventing SAMs

We created a theory of a model to visualize the communication-based inter-dependencies between these categories and their sub-categories, depicted in Fig. 1.

*Detecting SAMs.* Mistake detection is typically initiated by a trigger. These triggers can be driven by the architects themselves, e.g., dissatisfaction with the situation or questioning of requirements. *" If I look at it [the decision] like this, to what extent is this decision that was made in management supported by the teams that use it [the system] . . . ? There was a moment when I realized: Not at all."* More often, however, triggers from outside were mentioned, e.g., changes in project team structure, functional tests with users, changes in technical conditions, architecture reviews, or new requirements. *"So you suddenly have certain load situations and realize that you have now found the bottleneck. You made a decision back then that now presents you with extreme problems."*

In the next step, the trigger is used to try to understand the situation. It is not always apparent whether there is a mistake or exactly where the mistake is. *"If you notice a problem somewhere and you ask the swarm [all colleagues combined], then the first question is: Where does it come from? What is the cause? And then you come to the conclusion that at some point you made a wrong decision or a wrong assessment."*

To evaluate the situation, the effects of the SAM are analyzed, alternatives are examined, and, if possible, reasons for decisions are reconciled. *"Often the question is: Was this the best, the second best, or the fourth best solution for something? Nevertheless, the question is: Does it work? Or does it not?"*

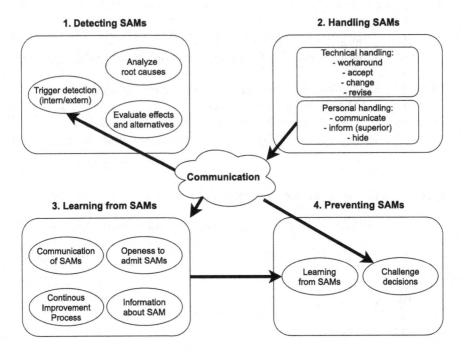

**1. Detecting SAMs**

Analyze root causes

Trigger detection (intern/extern)

Evaluate effects and alternatives

**2. Handling SAMs**

Technical handling:
- workaround
- accept
- change
- revise

Personal handling:
- communicate
- inform (superior)
- hide

Communication

**3. Learning from SAMs**

Communication of SAMs

Openess to admit SAMs

Continous Improvement Process

Information about SAM

**4. Preventing SAMs**

Learning from SAMs

Challenge decisions

**Fig. 1.** Theory of a model of SAM's Management

A SAM is detected when a trigger causes the re-evaluation of a situation. These triggers can originate from the architects themselves (internal) but also from external triggers such as changes in the project team, new requirements, functional tests, or external audits. After detection, the situation is analyzed, and alternatives are examined, which triggers a follow-up action.

***Handling SAMs.*** The SAM's handling describes the follow-up action resulting from the evaluation. This corresponds to the technical handling of the SAMs. Other actions are directly performed by the people involved, which corresponds to the personal SAM handling. The core of SAM handling is often the intention to do something different in the future. *"Well, I wouldn't do it that way again. I would try it differently."*

Regarding technical handling, sometimes a workaround can be created to restore functionality. The most common handling approaches are to accept a sub-optimal situation or to develop the architecture further. *"And if it [the SA] does [work], then it is probably more sensible to live with it than to switch everything to the best solution, come hell or high water."* Only rarely do architects revise their architecture completely. *"This project completely failed. We came in there as a different consulting company and had to stop everything, redo everything, and set everything up again."*

As personal SAM handling, all participants report that as a result of a SAM's assessment, the SAM must be communicated, e.g., *"We have highlighted these problems over and over again. We have said this again and again."* Furthermore, it is important to communicate with superiors to get their support. *"I talk very openly with my direct superiors if I think something is right or wrong. Then we usually think about whether we want to change it or not."* Interestingly, many participants reported that they did not use to communicate SAMs in the past, and this changed over time. *"In the past, I was much more defensive about admitting my own mistakes."* The topic of SAMs' communication will be studied in more detail in the following Sect. 3.3.

> SAMs are handled on a technical and personal level. The technical handling comprises creating workarounds and accepting, changing, or revising the SA. Often the sub-optimal solution is accepted with the intention of deciding differently next time. Personal handling comprises communication with colleagues and superiors. The participants conceded their openness to communicate SAMs did develop over time.

***Learning from SAMs.*** We asked the architects if and how they learn from SAMs, i.e., we asked them about the requirements to learn from SAMs.

Firstly, all participants consider that communication is an effective strategy for gaining knowledge from a SAM. They talk about how, in their assessment, a particular situation is a mistake in order to challenge that assessment through the perspective of others. Talking about mistakes means a common evaluation of a situation, the comparison of ideas about an ideal situation, and thinking about further possibilities for action. *"Yes, mistakes need to be talked about. ... It's only through communication and discussion that you come to a good alternative solution that you want to apply."*

Secondly, whether architects are able to learn from SAMs depends on their personal openness to SAMs and the openness of the environment to SAMs. On a personal level, we classified the attitude of all participants as constructive. The participants were open to and aware of their own mistakes without seeing them as a defeat. Similar to the personal level, mutual acceptance of mistakes in the environment is also important The expectation should not be "It is bad to make mistakes" but "It is bad not to learn from mistakes." *"We're all human, we all make mistakes, that's okay. You have to accept that in order to get better. Actually, it's not a mistake, but you learn something from it."*

Thirdly, the participants stated that an established continuous improvement process (CIP) [11] is essential for the learning process. A CIP should specifically try to increase the triggers for SAM detection and make detection a regular process. Furthermore, the SAM's detection is promoted by refining the idea of the ideal solution and the collection of information that can be used in the evaluation. The CIP tries to derive concrete actions that prevent SAMs in the future. *"[After a SAM situation,] I directly asked: What could have been done better? Could this have been foreseen beforehand? What is being done to avoid it in the future?"*

Finally, it is considered important to have the necessary information to classify the SAM situation. For SAMs, the focus is on the context of the decision. What were the reasons for the decision? What were the goals? The documentation of decisions, e.g., by Architecture Decision Records (ADR) [9], is mentioned but not considered to be widespread. *"I am a big fan of Arc42 and also ADR . . . I often start a system design with quality scenarios and quality metrics, especially with new customers. . . . I also do a lot of architecture reviews."*

> Architects need to communicate the mistake with other stakeholders to be able to learn from SAMs. The ability to learn from SAMs depends on the openness to admit SAMs on a personal and organizational level. An established CIP helps with SAM detection, communication, and information gathering. Important information regarding a SAM are SA decisions and their rationale, which should be documented.

**Preventing SAMs.** Learning from mistakes is one form of preventing further mistakes. *"Even if it is a mistake, it is, of course, important, especially in the architecture, that you try to prevent it in other areas that might run into this same mistake."*

Furthermore, the architects approach people to challenge their decisions before implementing them. *"We had meetings, I presented the advantages and disadvantages from my point of view, and we did not get together afterward."*

The architects also mentioned other means of preventing SAMs, e.g., taking responsibility for SA, making group decisions, and making more conscious decisions. However, these topics are already discussed in detail in many other research papers.

> To prevent SAMs, we should communicate and learn from past SAMs. Challenging SA decisions, i.e., communicating them in advance, is a way of preventing SAMs.

### 3.3   RQ3: Communication of SA Mistakes

Communication is used as a strategy for SAM detection, for learning from SAMs, and for SAM prevention (see Fig. 1). This section presents the communication partners, communication facilitating and hindering factors, and the structures in which communication takes place.

**Communication Partners.** All interviewees work in agile project teams, and their most mentioned form of communication is communication on the team level, i.e., with team colleagues. The colleagues are often directly affected by and interested in resolving the situation. It is a common practice in their teams to discuss a solution in a group. A special kind of group communication is discussions in the context of retrospectives. *" This has led to retrospectives in which people have said: 'That's annoying, and it keeps coming back. Can we do something about it or not?' . . . Then we had a special meeting about it with the topic: Where are we? Where do we stand? Where do we have to go?"*

The client is also a frequent target of communication, especially due to the need to coordinate further action and the financial impact of decisions. Involving the client in retrospectives or debriefings is perceived as valuable. Likewise, in acute SAM situations, the client is usually involved. In such a situation, some architects considered communication to be more difficult in some companies. " *[I]f you point out mistakes in a project team with other external people or even with customer employees, particularly in a customer environment where you also have other [consulting] companies, you really have to be very sensitive and really think twice about what you say.* "

In the context of SA decisions, communication with direct superiors was not considered to be difficult, e.g., *"I would assess myself in such a way that I can admit mistakes, even to my boss."* One participant even stated: *"My boss gets to listen to a lot. And my boss's boss and my board. So, I'm really there – I have a big mouth. I so don't care."*

The participants rarely mentioned talking about SAMs with architects outside the team. This is only done if necessary by asking specific questions or in the context of an architecture board. *"[T]here is a regular meeting once a month, called the architecture circle. And then all the brains of my employer sit there and give their suggestions."*

Concrete examples of active company-wide communication of SAMs are scarce. Special formats for the presentation of mistakes, such as 'Fuckup Nights,' are mentioned only once. Open spaces and all-hands workshops are also mentioned as spaces with the possibility that SAMs are discussed. *"We do a lot of 'Open Spaces,' including technical 'Open Spaces.' Half of them are not about how cool something is that you built but to look at the mistakes I made."*

Very occasionally, SAMs are discussed with outsiders, e.g., in the form of conference talks or networking events. The personal conviction that SAMs present valuable knowledge is the motivation for this. *"I think I can teach people more when I talk about [SA] mistakes than how to do it right."*

> SAM communication takes place on six different levels: with team colleagues, with the clients, with the superiors, with other architects, company-wide, and with outsiders. The most common form is communication within the team. Company-wide discussions of SAMs or communication with outsiders rarely occur.

*Communication Facilitating and Hindering Factors.* The communication preferences and observed communication patterns can be divided into facilitating and hindering factors. However, some of these factors can be seen as both facilitating and hindering, depending on the architects' characteristics, e.g., professional status and self-confidence, and psychological safety.

The biggest facilitating factor in communicating SAMs successfully is ensuring access to information. This access to information is influenced by the diversity of experiences, i.e., multiple cultural backgrounds but also different domains of IT experience. Diversity ensures that many requirements are represented. *"We have a regular meeting in development. ... Anyone can bring in any topic, be it from testers or other teams. Not development teams, but other teams. That's when a few problems come to light."*

However, this also means a diversity of communication preferences. Responding to these preferences or even being aware of differences between team cultures can further facilitate communication. *"I am also someone who is not afraid of*

*speaking in large crowds. There are also people who perhaps have relevant expe-*
*rience who don't want to speak in front of a large crowd right away, where [for*
*whom] you would then perhaps have to find other means to communicate that."*

Transparent communication promotes exchange. Having access to or being
exposed to SAMs information enables the absorption of information, which
means that learning from the mistakes of others is possible. In the office, you
inevitably run into other people. In times of remote work, teams need to communicate in open channels rather than in private. *"Otherwise, I often ghost around*
*[roam around] in some channels, i.e., Microsoft Teams channels, in order to also*
*capture topics that are being discussed."*

The biggest hindering factors are potential negative consequences. The communication of SAMs can generate costs, e.g., in contracting situations or raise
the question of guilt. *"Unfortunately, it is often the case that software architec-*
*ture is the most expensive decision and that mistakes are often not communica-*
*ble."* Additionally, the personal expectation of the outcome of communication
can trigger negative consequences in individuals, such as disappointment. *"With*
*younger colleagues, the disappointment is usually great when this [developed SA*
*proposal] decision is not followed."*

The participants also consider the environment to be of decisive importance
for the willingness to communicate SAMs. *"If you're in the corporate bubble, then*
*most people … can admit mistakes and reflect on them. In other environments,*
*I have experienced different situations where people can't admit it [mistakes]."*
This is called psychological safety in the domain of psychology, which promotes
information sharing [16]. *"[My] Superiors always say that reflection is important;*
*admitting mistakes is important."* A lack of psychological safety hinders SAM
communication.

Furthermore, discrepancies among communication participants in reputation,
status, or hierarchy seem to make communication more difficult. *"That was a*
*challenge, to do a [meeting] format with a developer from a customer and his*
*board of directors ."*

The participants also mentioned that as one's own professional status and
self-confidence grow, the willingness to communicate SAMs increases, particularly in unclear situations. This, however, means that stakeholders with less
status and self-confidence might not share their experiences with mistakes. *"So*
*that you can admit mistakes openly, you also need a certain standing. And if you*
*don't feel confident, you won't do it."*

People do not only act rationally, either. The exchange of SAM information is
hindered by human characteristics such as emotional bias, e.g., human conflicts
may hinder communication. Seeking direct conversation does not work if there
is no access or willingness to talk. *"So the question is, as an employee, how do*
*I get the board to listen to me? That's very difficult."*

Finally, communication is complicated by conflicts of interest between the
role in the project context and personal goals. Even if there is no fear of dis-
missal, communicating SAMs could damage one's own reputation or that of the
company, no further assignment may follow, or conflicts may arise. *"But some-*

*times that is not the right architecture at all. Nevertheless, you might defend it that way. You're not going to admit that mistake and say, 'I did that because it helps me sell my people [consultants].'"*

Facilitating factors for SAM communication are access to information, i.e., transparent communication and diverse teams in terms of cultures and expertise, as well as supportive communication structures. Hindering factors are potential negative consequences, a missing psychological safety, discrepancies in reputation, status, or hierarchy, a missing professional status and self-confidence, a missing psychological safety in the environment, emotional biases, and conflicts of interest.

***Communication Structures and Strategies.*** The participants' preferred communication structure is to talk directly with others. *" In a team, we are closer to each other, and we sit down together when there are issues."*

While the participants seek direct communication for acute problems, regular appointments are nevertheless a frequently observed pattern for active exchange. These appointments take place regularly and for various purposes. They shape communication not just in response to problems but proactively: *"These classic escalation issues have become fewer because we have managed to have regular appointments. As overarching architects, we have 'Face To Faces' with all the teams ... to sit down and identify and discuss issues."*

During these conversations, participants pursue the strategy of communicating constructively and explaining their own points of view in a well-founded manner. In this context, the participants perceive it as helpful not only to communicate problems and not to create accusations. *"You have to say, 'I don't think this is well designed, for such and such reasons, we have such and such disadvantages.' ... It's not about, 'Peter, you wanted to do it then, and this is bad now."*

Predominantly, architects try to convince their colleagues rather than overrule them. By this, they hope that the other person will adopt the values in the long term rather than simply accept them without understanding them. *"So they might do it then, grudgingly accept it. But they do not understand it. And without understanding, they won't do it any better next time."*

Architects prefer direct communication with colleagues. Regular appointments are important and have the advantage of addressing problems proactively. Communication should be constructive and personal positions should be explained in a well-founded manner. It is important to convince people rather than overrule them.

## 4   Discussion

In retrospect, the initial hypothesis that SAMs are typically not sufficiently communicated has been only partially confirmed. In the project teams and the peer groups of the participants, there is an active exchange about SAMs. However, the situation changes on the company level or outside the company. Despite a high level of commitment on the part of the participants, there are only a few examples in which SAMs are discussed outside the involved project teams. In terms of the participants' companies' size, this means that many employees do not have access to the learned information.

Obviously, the processing of information in a larger circle must be approached differently and requires more effort than in a small circle of individuals. The information and facts must be prepared more systematically, and there is less time for individual questions. However, making an information exchange process publicly accessible within the company, e.g., in open spaces or all-hands workshops, would counteract information silos.

Practical indications can be derived from the action strategies of the participants. Regarding the process model presented in Fig. 1, goals can be formulated, which are discussed below.

### 4.1    Increase Detection Trigger

People and organizations can influence the triggers for SAM detection in the process shown in Fig. 1. More triggers mean more opportunities for the SAMs' detection.

On a personal level, a constructive mindset is most crucial. A different personal attitude may cause SAM detection to be blocked. The point perceived as most important is the change in expectations mentioned in Sect. 3.2. "It is bad to make mistakes" changes to "It is bad not to learn from mistakes."

On a personal and organizational level, formalized and regular CIPs should be established. They can be used to check the validity of SA ideas and implementations and is thus a trigger for SAM detection. The participants report regular architecture reviews or exchanges with architects as one way to achieve continuous improvement, but they require lightweight approaches.

### 4.2    Ensure Communication Opportunities

Our results show that it is extremely important that SAMs are communicated. Successful communication involves not only talking but also listening. The stigma of failure must be removed so that open discussion, rapid learning, and innovation can occur instead of employees hiding failures in order to protect themselves. Conditions for open discussion should be created, and invitations to participate should be formulated and responded to productively.

The negative connotation of SAMs was discussed in Sect. 3.1. Therefore, some people try to portray SAMs in a positive or euphemistic way. A constructive mindset also means learning from mistakes. However, this should not lead to a euphemistic presentation of SAMs. SAMs, in general, are not positive but have negative consequences and are avoidable. The fact that they also have positive consequences does not make them positive as a whole.

Firstly, these findings can be taken as an impetus for an analysis of one's own handling of SAMs. Secondly, they are also a call for companies to further enable and support SAMs communication among their employees, e.g., by creating company-wide communities of interest. Finally, there should be more open communication about SAMs outside of companies or across companies. For example, governments or chambers of commerce could support this information exchange across companies.

## 5  Related Work

Our related work section focuses on the main topics of our work, which are SAMs and their communication.

**Software Architecture Mistakes.** The topic of SAMs is highly related to SA decision-making. A variety of research has been done in this research field, e.g., [4]. However, most of this research focuses on the decision-making process when deciding on an SA or a part of a SA.

Tang et al. did a systematic literature review of the human aspect in decision-making [21]. One of the mentioned decision-making practices is "knowledge management", i.e., knowledge capture, sharing, and communication, which are also important aspects of our work. Yet, all mentioned studies focus on knowledge documentation. While Tang et al. acknowledge that "experience and knowledge play a role in decision making," all identified studies focus on the knowledge aspect [21]. The experience aspect, which includes learning from other people's experiences, is not mentioned. In their semi-systematic literature review, Bhat et al. [4] also identified different studies stating the relevance of experience and knowledge, e.g., [8]. Yet, no work seems to explore how to improve the experience of architects.

Less research has been done on how to deal with bad decisions after they have been made. Some of these aspects are discussed in the research field of architectural technical debt, e.g., [3]. For example, Kruchten et al. present a guideline on how asking about SAMs might lead to the root causes for some architectural technical debts [12]. However, in their recent interview study, Wiese et al. still identified a lack of refactoring strategies for old legacy systems as IT managers' main concern [23].

**Software Architecture Mistake Communication.** In the field of SA Communication, a wide range of work has been done, e.g., regarding documentation [9], visualization [18], or stakeholder communication [15]. Smolander et al. argue the importance of organizational and inter-organizational communication between architects [19]. However, regarding the communication of SAMs between architects, we were not able to find related studies.

We argue that communication is essential to amass SA knowledge. In their study about SA knowledge in search engines, i.e., Google, Soliman et al. identified a lack of knowledge on bad decisions in the search engine results [20]. Our study supports the idea that this lack is not caused by a faulty search strategy but by a lack of willingness to share this knowledge. However, we did not find research on if or how communication of SAMs might enhance knowledge gathering.

# 6   Threats to Validity

We present threats to validity for our qualitative study by addressing the construct, internal and external validity.

*Construct Validity.* For an interview study, the selection of participants and interview questions have a great impact on the validity of the study. In our study, we only interviewed architects working in an agile environment. As we did not enforce this as a precondition, we suspect that an agile team organization is state-of-the-art. We, therefore, suggest using our study's results specifically for agile working companies.

Furthermore, architects that are more open to discussing their SAMs might be more willing to participate in our study, which might bias our study. We also recruited participants from our personal network. These participants might not be as open regarding their SAMs but might still participate for our sake.

Finally, we interviewed ten architects, which might seem too few. However, we reached code saturation on the focus code level, i.e., codes that were reported in this paper did not change during the last three interviews. Further studies in other countries and with more participants, e.g., surveys, should validate our theories.

*Internal Validity.* In the case of our study, internal validity means the possibility of wrongly interpreting and misunderstanding the interview transcripts. To avoid such misconceptions, the coding was done by two researchers. Furthermore, we were able to ask the participants for clarification in cases we were unsure about a statement.

*External Validity.* External validity concerns the generalization of the result. However, the ability to generalize the results is not the goal of a qualitative study such as ours. Nonetheless, we only surveyed German architects, and architects in other countries might have different insights, particularly as cultural aspects are important in our study. The generalizability of our results could be enhanced by further studies, e.g., by surveys generating quantitative data and by interview studies in other countries.

# 7   Conclusion

In our study, we analyzed the communication of SAMs in the industry by performing an interview study with ten architects. We derived their definition and list of characteristics of SAMs, their handling of such SAMs after their detection, and finally, their ways of communicating SAMs. We identified optimization potential regarding the enhancement of SAM's detection triggers.

While the communication of SAMs takes place on the team level, we identified optimization potential on a company and cross-company level. Furthermore, we identified communication partners, structures, and strategies, and we presented communication facilitating and hindering factors.

**For practitioners,** our study could spark the company-wide exchange of SAMs. Furthermore, we provided many ideas on how to optimize communication on a personal level, e.g., by visiting public communities of interest and changing our own mindset from "It is bad to make mistakes" to "It is bad not to learn from mistakes."

**For researchers,** we provided the theory of model on how practitioners manage SAMs. This, in turn, forms the question of how to decide whether to accept a SAM, change the architecture, or revise the architecture completely. Furthermore, we identified the research question on how to optimize the communication of SAMs on the enterprise level besides the ideas mentioned by our participants. For these ideas, an evaluation of their effects is also still missing.

**For future work,** we suggest performing a subsequent survey study to validate our theories and refine them by taking the different contexts, e.g., domains, countries, and cultural environments, into account. In addition, this could help to generalize our results. After that, the aforementioned research questions on how to optimize SAM communication should be addressed by solution-seeking studies.

# References

1. Fuckup Nights (2023). https://en.fuckupnights.com/
2. Avgeriou, P., Kruchten, P., Ozkaya, I., Seaman, C.: Managing technical debt in software engineering. Dagstuhl Reports **6**(4) (2016)
3. Besker, T., Martini, A., Bosch, J.: Managing architectural technical debt: a unified model and systematic literature review. J. Syst. Softw. 135 (2018)
4. Bhat, M., Shumaiev, K., Hohenstein, U., Biesdorf, A., Matthes, F.: The evolution of architectural decision making as a key focus area of software architecture research. In: Proceedings of the IEEE 17th International Conference on Software Architecture, ICSA 2020 (c) (2020)
5. Bjørnson, F.O., Wang, A.I., Arisholm, E.: Improving the effectiveness of root cause analysis in post mortem analysis: a controlled experiment. Inf. Softw. Technol. **51**(1) (2009)
6. Charmaz, K.: Constructing grounded theory. Sage Publications (2014)
7. Glaser, B.G., Strauss, A.L.: The discovery of grounded theory: strategies for qualitative research. Nurs. Res. **17**(4), 364 (1968)
8. Hassard, S.T., Blandford, A., Cox, A.L.: Analogies in design decision-making (2009)
9. van Heesch, U., Avgeriou, P., Hilliard, R.: A documentation framework for architecture decisions. J. Syst. Softw. **85**(4) (2012)
10. Hieronymus, S.E.: Errare humanum est. In: Seneca, Epistulae morales VI,57,12; Cicero, Orationes Philippicae 12,2, vol. VI,57,12 (2023)
11. Imai, M.: Kaizen. No. 201, Random House Business Division, New York (1986)

12. Kruchten, P., Nord, R., Ozkaya, I.: Managing technical debt: reducing friction in software development. Carnegie Mellon University, Software Engineering Institute (2019)
13. Martini, A., Bosch, J.: The danger of architectural technical debt: contagious debt and vicious circles. In: Proceedings of the 12th Working IEEE/IFIP Conference on Software Architecture, WICSA2015 (2015)
14. Mumtaz, H., Singh, P., Blincoe, K.: A systematic mapping study on architectural smells detection. J. Syst. Softw. 173 (2021)
15. Márquez, G., Taramasco, C., Astudillo, H., Zalc, V., Istrate, D.: Involving stakeholders in the implementation of microservice-based systems. IEEE Access 9 (2021)
16. Newman, A., Donohue, R., Eva, N.: Psychological safety: a systematic review of the literature. Hum. Resour. Manage. Rev. 27(3) (2017)
17. Richards, M.: Software architecture patterns. O'Reilly Media (2015)
18. Shahin, M., Liang, P., Babar, M.A.: A systematic review of software architecture visualization techniques. J. Syst. Softw. 94 (2014)
19. Smolander, K., Päivärinta, T.: Describing and communicating software architecture in practice: observations on stakeholders and rationale. In: Pidduck, A.B., Ozsu, M.T., Mylopoulos, J., Woo, C.C. (eds.) CAiSE 2002. LNCS, vol. 2348, pp. 117–133. Springer, Heidelberg (2002). https://doi.org/10.1007/3-540-47961-9_11
20. Soliman, M., Wiese, M., Li, Y., Riebisch, M., Avgeriou, P.: Exploring web search engines to find architectural knowledge. In: International Conference on Software Architecture (ICSA2021) (2021)
21. Tang, A., Razavian, M., Paech, B., Hesse, T.M.: Human aspects in software architecture decision making - a literature review. In: International Conference on Software Architecture (ICSA2017) (2017)
22. Weinreich, R., Groher, I.: Software architecture knowledge management approaches and their support for knowledge management activities: a systematic literature review. Inf. Softw. Technol. 80 (2016)
23. Wiese, M., Borowa, K.: IT managers' perspective on technical debt management. J. Syst. Softw. 202 (2023)
24. Wiese, M., Brand, A.-F., van Hoorn, A.: Additional material for learning from each other: how are architectural mistakes communicated in industry? (2023). https://doi.org/10.5281/zenodo.7924700

# A Query Language for Software Architecture Information

Joshua Ammermann[1]([⊠])([iD]), Sven Jordan[2], Lukas Linsbauer[3],
and Ina Schaefer[1]([iD])

[1] Karlsruhe Institute of Technology (KIT), Karlsruhe, Germany
{joshua.ammermann,ina.schaefer}@kit.edu
[2] Volkswagen AG, Wolfsburg, Germany
sven.jordan@volkswagen.de
[3] Technische Universität Braunschweig, Braunschweig, Germany

**Abstract.** Software maintenance is important, but suffers from architecture information that is diverging over time (architectural drift). The Digital Architecture Twin (DArT) can support software maintenance by providing continuously recovered architecture information. But the crucial link for stakeholders to retrieve this information is missing. To fill this gap, we contribute the Architecture Information Query Language (AIQL), which enables stakeholders to access up-to-date and tailored architecture information. We derived two application scenarios in the context of continuous reverse engineering. We showed that the AIQL provides the required functionality to formulate queries for the application scenarios. In a user study, stakeholders agreed that the language is easy to understand and assessed its value to the specific stakeholder for the application scenarios.

**Keywords:** Software architecture · Query languages · Software architecture recovery

## 1  Introduction

As software systems evolve over time, architecture documentation is getting increasingly important. In many cases, the architecture documentation is not kept up-to-date due to cost and time restrictions [8]. This divergence is called architectural drift and leads to increased maintenance effort [14]. To mitigate architectural drift, Software Architecture Recovery (SAR) methods emerged [4, 5]. SAR methods enable the recovery of architecture information but only target isolated views (e.g. structural or behavioral views) of a software system from specific information sources (e.g. source code). Further, architecture information is only recovered at a single point in time.

To solve all of the aforementioned issues, Jordan et al. [7] recently developed the Digital Architecture Twin (DArT), an architectural data model that co-evolves with a software system. A DArT incorporates several SAR methods to

B. Tekinerdogan et al. (Eds.): ECSA 2023, LNCS 14212, pp. 337–345, 2023.
https://doi.org/10.1007/978-3-031-42592-9_23

automatically generate up-to-date architecture information from multiple information sources (e.g. source code, build and deployment scripts, and views). The DArT enables integration into the development process in the form of continuous reverse engineering [3]. Further, the DArT provides up-to-date, tailored architecture information for stakeholders enabling design decisions on the current software architecture of the software system. However, the crucial link between stakeholders and extensive architecture data models, i.e., a tailored Architecture Query Language (AQL) for the DArT, is missing.

This ability to query an architecture information base is a challenge in reverse engineering [3]. The term AQL was proposed by Sartipi [12] in the context of their reverse engineering approach. Sartipi's AQL is not suitable for querying the DArT as it is constrained to a specific recovery process [12] and limited in the supported views. Accessing the vast amounts of information in architecture data models becomes harder, the fewer views exist in the query language. In fact, some information may be irretrievable if there is no suitable view to query it. The AQL by Wang et al. [15] is tailored to information exchange between Architecture Description Languages (ADLs), which document software architectures [9,14], so the query results are ADL instances themselves [15]. This is inconvenient to stakeholders because for each view a suitable ADL has to be known and used.

To counter those shortcomings of existing AQLs, we propose the Architecture Information Query Language (AIQL)[1] that is process-agnostic, typed and supports querying architecture information of various software architecture views. The AIQL is easily extensible to support additional views and has an easy-to-use syntax. Architecture information can be queried by defining and restricting query templates. Composition of query templates is a key element of the AIQL, that strongly encourages reuse. The AIQL provides stakeholders with efficient access to the architecture information in extensive architecture data models. To demonstrate this, we present two application scenarios in the context of continuous reverse engineering, which now can be realized by accessing a DArT using the AIQL. In a user study with eight experts, they agreed that the AIQL is easy to understand and use. They further confirmed that AIQL queries enable drilling down into the architecture information in the DArT.

## 2    The Digital Architecture Twin (DArT)

The DArT [7] is an digital representation of a software system. The DArT automatically recovers and integrates architecture information of multiple views and versions. Figure 1 displays how the DArT is filled with information. First, in an Architecture Recovery step (①), architecture data is continuously gathered from heterogeneous sources by Data Collection Agents. Architecture Information Recovery Services apply different architecture recovery approaches on the gathered data to recover architecture information. The recovered architecture information is then integrated into the DArT as a representation of a software

---

[1] This work briefly summarizes the author's master thesis [1]. Further details and evaluation is provided in the extended version of this paper in the arXiv [2].

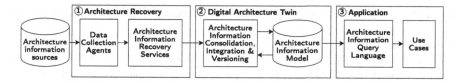

**Fig. 1.** Architecture Information Processing using the DArT [7]

system's architecture (step ②). The architecture information is versioned and stored in a unified and persistent Architecture Information Model. In step ③ stakeholders want to access tailored parts of this information to fulfill specific tasks. For this, an easy-to-use language is required to make the information accessible to various kinds of stakeholders, such as developers or enterprise architects.

## 3   Application Scenarios

Frequent challenges in the industry are understanding and evolving as well as harmonizing software systems. This implies making architecture decisions for existing and new software systems using tailored and up-to-date architecture information, which supports the design decision process. We identified two application scenarios addressing these challenges, which are refined into concrete use cases and are part of the user study to evaluate the language.

*Sce. 1: Tailored documentation.* Analyzing an architecture is a necessity to make design decisions. To ease this, the language should support tailored architecture documentation in the form of different views for specific stakeholders. Thus, querying for different views from an architecture information base needs to be supported. The retrieved information may be used to strengthen the understanding of the system by visualizing it. Examples for this scenario are an enterprise architect, who wants to list all interfaces to another specific sub-system, or a product owner, who wants to create a comprehensive structural diagram, or a developer, who wants to create a class diagram of a system component.

*Sce. 2: Recommendation system for architectural design decisions.* A recommendation system for architectural design decisions enables the reuse of good design decisions of existing systems. Such a recommendation system uses a knowledge base of previous design decisions to propose architectural designs that may benefit another software system. For this, relevant system properties as well as design decisions, have to be accessible via a query language. Furthermore, a system architect might want to browse the knowledge-base using exploratory queries.

## 4  The Architecture Information Query Language (AIQL)

The AIQL was designed to enable the application scenarios. In this section, we demonstrate the AIQL's main language features by an example.[2] Our running example consists of a client and a server component connected via Remote Procedure Call (RPC) (see Fig. 2a). After the architecture recovery step, this system is represented in the DArT's technical component view as depicted in Fig. 2b. A *SoftwareSystem* component, representing the system, and for each component from the running example, a corresponding *TechnicalComponent* was created.

*Language Design.* Imagine a software architect who wants to generate tailored documentation for server components (see scenario 1). Figure 3 shows an example AIQL query to retrieve server components from the DArT (for simplicity, we assume that such components could be identified by their name). Using this example, we demonstrate the AIQL's main language features.

In general, an AIQL query consists of three parts: header, body, and output. The header contains information for the whole query, so no information has to

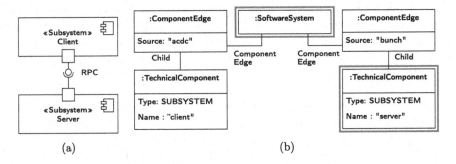

(a)                                                    (b)

**Fig. 2.** Unified Modeling Language (UML) component diagram of a client-server example system (a). The UML object diagram shows the system recovered in the DArT (b). Highlighted are the objects that the AIQL query in Fig. 3 returns for this example system.

```
1   MODEL "system.model";
2   VERSION LAST;
3
4   LIST TechnicalComponent serverComponent RESTRICTIONS:
5       (Name 'server');
6
7   LIST SoftwareSystem system RESTRICTIONS:
8       (EXISTS Children serverComponent);
9
10  OUTPUT serverComponent;
11  OUTPUT system;
```

**Fig. 3.** AIQL query for client-server entities of the technical component view.

---

[2] Detailed description of the language's syntax in Extended Backus-Naur Form (EBNF) and its semantics are provided in the extended version [2].

be provided externally. In the header (lines 1-2), the location of the **MODEL** from which the architecture information will be queried, and the **VERSION**(s) of the model are defined. Static keywords for the **FIRST** and **LAST** versions are provided, and multiple versions can be accessed through appropriate expressions.

In the query body, query templates for elements of the architecture information model can be defined, which a stakeholder either wants to output or further specify the query. A query template is declared using the **LIST** directive (line 4) followed by the unique name of the type of the element, that should be queried (e.g. *TechnicalComponent*), and a user-defined identifier (e.g. *serverComponent*). A query template matches the model elements satisfying the specified **RESTRICTIONS**. Multiple restrictions can be defined in one query and are implicit conjunctions except if the **OR** keyword is used. Restrictions can be used on element attributes (e.g. *Name* in line 5) for which a static expression language is provided. For our example, the attribute *Name* has to match *'server'*.

The composition of query templates is a key element of the AIQL, that strongly encourages reuse. References to other model elements can be restricted through a combination of a quantifier (such as **EXISTS** or **FORALL**), the name of the reference, and the identifier of another query template. Quantifiers are only required for one-to-many or many-to-many references. Entities of different views may be connected through relations and, thus, a stakeholder's queries can span multiple views. In line 8 the one-to-many reference *Children* from *SoftwareSystem* to *TechnicalComponent* is restricted by the **EXISTS** quantifier and the *serverComponent* template. Only software systems that have a server component are matched. The reference *Children* in this case is a shortcut defined in the AIQL as the DArT in this example contains *ComponentEdges* (see Fig. 2b) which are resolved internally. User-defined shortcuts allow more concise queries.

Finally, architecture model elements can be output using multiple **OUTPUT** directives and the query template identifier. Output directives support tailoring of the output format (e.g., to only output specific attributes).

## 5   User Study

We performed a user study at an industry partner to evaluate the AIQL's usability. The eight participants (Enterprise-, Solution-, and Domain Architects, former business stakeholder, IT Project managers, and developers) ranged from 7 to 21 years of work experience. In the user study, we asked participants about the comprehensibility of the AIQL (**RQ1**), the comprehensibility and usability of the output (**RQ2**) and the complexity of example queries (**RQ3**). We presented the AIQL in-depth (i.e., theoretical and practical) to the participants and allowed them to use the AIQL. Furthermore, we showed participants the application scenarios and relevant example queries and asked them to assess the value of the AIQL for both application scenarios (**RQ4**).

**RQ1** All participants stated that the AIQL is easy to understand. In comparison to other languages (e.g. the Structured Query Language (SQL)), the AIQL was deemed equally easy. 62.5% of participants found the language intuitive and the keywords meaningful. 37.5% of participants mentioned difficulties using the AIQL, due to the short timeframe of the user study, they were not able to memorize all keywords of the AIQL. More time to familiarize themselves with the AIQL as well as with the DArT was needed. Three participants (solution and enterprise architects) preferred the accessible language design, whereas one participant did not immediately grasp the composition of sub-queries. It was also noted that the comprehensibility is limited for non-technical experts and that the language may be hard to understand for business users. Detailed responses by the participants mentioned missing an "Aggregate"-keyword to automatically filter the highest-level sub-systems. The current editor support was praised to ease getting started with the AIQL.

*RQ2* All participants stated that the AIQL is useful for extracting architecture information about a software system, but it is restricted by the underlying data model. 50% of participants noted that the AIQL, if not used to full power is not necessarily more useful than a static view, but the AIQL is more useful when used in an exploratory approach. It was debated that the AIQL is more useful, when adding information about frequency of class calls and when the stakeholder knows the system to some degree. A supplementing static/dynamic view would help for an initial overview of the software system. 37,5% of participants found the AIQL more useful for drilling down into the architecture information. It was noted that the AIQL does not provide more information than a static visualisation as it only displays recovered architecture information. Participants mentioned that the output format (in JavaScript Object Notation (JSON)) is hard for humans to read, but useful for further use and automation.

*RQ3* Participants stated that the complexity of shown example queries varied from trivial to complex. An easy example query was perceived as very simple. An example query in the complexity of the running example was still perceived as easy. Participants mentioned that linking queries using the sub-query templates was perceived as doable. A complex query using four nested sub-queries was deemed as complex, leading participants to express concerns about the complexity of queries containing more nested sub-queries. Some participants also criticized the lack of self-contained queries (i.e. no sub-query composition).

*RQ4* 50% of participants stated that the AIQL is useful to extract tailored architecture information. Depending on the participant's background, some find the AIQL to be potentially more useful. Developers or solution architects assessed the AIQL as more useful for extracting tailored architecture information for specific use cases than enterprise architects. The participants believed that the AIQL can be helpful in understanding the source code, from an unknown software system. All participants stated the use of a recommendation system or wizard-based queries for finding similar software systems based on requirements and architecture is very interesting and "incredibly useful".

# 6   Related Work

Querying of software systems is frequently used in the context of software architecture recovery. Relational queries are used by tools such as *ArchView* [11], *ARM* [6], and *Dali* [8] [4]. Dali and ArchView directly use SQL on an architectural database [4], which is used to persist the recovered architecture information. ARM allows the definition of pattern descriptions and rules in the commonly used Rigi Standard Format, which are translated into pattern queries exploitable in Dali via SQL [6]. However, the architecture information in the database is not correlated with other architecture information. Our proposed AIQL is a Domain-Specific Language (DSL) instead of a general-purpose query language. DSLs leverage the restriction to a particular problem domain - the software architecture domain in our case - to gain expressive power by providing domain-tailored notations and abstraction.

*Architectural Query Languages (AQLs).* AQLs are tailored for architecture information retrieval. The term AQL was proposed by Sartipi for an interactive pattern-based architecture recovery method [13] implemented in *Alborz* [12]. Achitecture information is incrementally recovered by refining patterns defined in the AQL, which are matched against a database of architectural information. An AQL query consists of abstract connectors and components inspired by ADLs. The tight coupling of Sartipi's AQL to the manual recovery process using special syntactic elements makes it difficult to reuse aspects for a language that is not driven by the proposed process, whereas the AIQL is independent of the architecture recovery process. Wang and Gupta defined the query language *ADLQL* [15], which is inspired by SQL. They aim to enable information exchange between ADLs, which are not expressive enough by themselves. Thus, a framework enabling integration of ADL is introduced. ADLQL allows the definition of queries that can be executed against predicates, representing architectural information, using denotational semantics. ADLQL is limited to ADLs, which have to be integrated and do not account for other relevant artifacts, such as a system's source code, whereas the AIQL is capable of handling source code. Monroy et al. introduced a query mechanism for recovered architecture models using natural language (Spanish) in the *ARCo* framework [10]. An advantage of the natural language is its richness benefiting inexperienced stakeholders, for example, students, but on the other side, it is ambiguous [10,14]. The use of more semantically narrow and formal languages is more suitable, as we expect our stakeholders to have a decent amount of domain knowledge.

# 7   Conclusion and Future Work

This work aimed to provide the AIQL to access the information present in extensive architecture data models such as DArTs. The language encourages reuse through the composition of templates and supports querying information of different views and levels of abstraction along with different versions of a system's architecture over time. In a user study, we showed that the AIQL is easy to understand, but also identified two aspects to improve our language: providing additional language constructs and providing other output formats. The user study also highlighted the demand for a supporting static view. Future work is concerned with the realization of further application scenarios using the AIQL.

# References

1. Ammermann, J.: An architecture information query language for the digital architecture twin. Master Thesis, TU Braunschweig (2022). https://doi.org/10.24355/dbbs.084-202209301202-0, https://leopard.tu-braunschweig.de/receive/dbbs_mods_00071363
2. Ammermann, J., Jordan, S., Linsbauer, L., Schaefer, I.: A query language for software architecture information (extended version) (2023). https://doi.org/10.48550/arXiv.2306.16829
3. Canfora, G., Di Penta, M., Cerulo, L.: Achievements and challenges in software reverse engineering. Commun. ACM 54(4), 142–151 (2011). https://doi.org/10.1145/1924421.1924451
4. Ducasse, S., Pollet, D.: Software architecture reconstruction: a process-oriented taxonomy. IEEE Trans. Softw. Eng. 35(4), 573–591 (2009). https://doi.org/10.1109/TSE.2009.19
5. Garcia, J., Ivkovic, I., Medvidovic, N.: A comparative analysis of software architecture recovery techniques. In: Proceedings of the 28th IEEE/ACM International Conference on Automated Software Engineering, pp. 486–496. ASE'13 (2013). https://doi.org/10.1109/ASE.2013.6693106
6. Guo, G.Y., Atlee, J.M., Kazman, R.: A software architecture reconstruction method. In: Donohoe, P. (ed.) Software Architecture, TC2 First Working IFIP Conference on Software Architecture (WICSA1), 22–24 February 1999, San Antonio, Texas, USA. IFIP Conference Proceedings, vol. 140, pp. 15–34. Kluwer (1999)
7. Jordan, S., Linsbauer, L., Schaefer, I.: Autoarx: Digital twins of living architectures. In: ECSA 2022, Prague, Czech Republic, September 19–23, 2022, Proceedings. Lecture Notes in Computer Science, vol. 13444, pp. 205–212. Springer, Cham (2022). https://doi.org/10.1007/978-3-031-16697-6_15
8. Kazman, R., Carrière, S.J.: Playing detective: reconstructing software architecture from available evidence. Autom. Softw. Eng. 6(2), 107–138 (1999). https://doi.org/10.1023/A:1008781513258
9. Medvidovic, N., Taylor, R.N.: A framework for classifying and comparing architecture description languages. SIGSOFT Softw. Eng. Notes 22(6), 60–76 (1997). https://doi.org/10.1145/267896.267903
10. Monroy, M., Pinzger, M., Arciniegas, J.: Arco: Architecture recovery in context. J. Xi'an Univ. Archit. Technol 13(2), 128–143 (2021)
11. Pinzger, M.: ArchView - analyzing evolutionary aspects of complex software systems. Ph.D. thesis, TU Wien (2005)
12. Sartipi, K.: Alborz: A query-based tool for software architecture recovery. In: 9th International Workshop on Program Comprehension (IWPC 2001), 12–13 May 2001, Toronto, Canada, pp. 115–116. IEEE Computer Society (2001). https://doi.org/10.1109/WPC.2001.921721
13. Sartipi, K.: Software architecture recovery based on pattern matching. Ph.D. thesis, University of Waterloo, Waterloo, ON, Canada (2003)

14. Taylor, R.N., Medvidovic, N., Dashofy, E.M.: Software Architecture - Foundations, Theory, and Practice. Wiley (2010). https://eu.wiley.com/WileyCDA/WileyTitle/productCd-EHEP000180.html

15. Wang, Q., Gupta, G.: A logic programming-based environment for integrating architecture description languages. In: WLPE 2004: 14th Workshop on Logic Programming Environments, pp. 67–86 (2004)

# Extracting the Architecture of Microservices: An Approach for Explainability and Traceability

Pierre-Jean Quéval[1,2(✉)] and Uwe Zdun[1]

[1] University of Vienna, Vienna, Austria
pierre-jean.queval@univie.ac.at
[2] Doctoral School Computer Science, Vienna, Austria

**Abstract.** The polyglot nature of microservice architectures and the need for high reliability in security analyses pose unique challenges that existing approaches to automatic architecture recovery often fail to address. This article proposes an approach for extracting detailed architecture models from polyglot microservice source code focusing on explainability and traceability. The approach involves abstracting code navigation as a tree structure, using an exploratory algorithm to detect architectural aspects, and providing a set of generic detectors as input. The architecture models are automatically annotated with detailed information that makes them useful for architecture conformance checking and violation fixing. Our case studies of microservice software systems validate the usefulness of our approach, providing insights into its completeness, accuracy, and effectiveness for software architecture tasks.

**Keywords:** Architecture · Explainability · Microservices · Polyglot

## 1 Introduction

Understanding software architecture is essential for ensuring software systems' maintainability, scalability, and evolution. However, with the increasing complexity and diversity of modern software systems, extracting a comprehensive view of the architecture has become challenging. This is particularly true for polyglot microservice architectures [5,6], which are becoming more prevalent in the industry. Existing approaches to automatic architecture recovery [3,11] must address the unique challenges such architectures pose, leading to incomplete or inaccurate architecture models. In addition, existing approaches often need more explainability and traceability for extracting models from the source code.

To address these challenges, we present an approach for extracting detailed architecture models with security annotations from polyglot microservice source code, focusing on explainability and traceability, making them useful for tasks such as architecture conformance checking [9] and violation fixing [7] concerning microservice-specific patterns and best practices.

© The Author(s), under exclusive license to Springer Nature Switzerland AG 2023
B. Tekinerdogan et al. (Eds.): ECSA 2023, LNCS 14212, pp. 346–353, 2023.
https://doi.org/10.1007/978-3-031-42592-9_24

## 2   Related Works

Software architecture reconstruction is particularly challenging for decentralized and polyglot systems such as microservices [2]. Static analysis can be performed on a system before deployment, extracting information from existing artifacts [2,3]. Such analyses can help to provide formal verification, generate test cases, support program or architecture comprehension (e.g., by generating UML models [10]), and maintain programs (e.g., by identifying code clones [12]). Rademacher et al. [11] propose a model for microservices that address their increased architectural complexity. Bushong et al. [1] present a method to analyze a microservice mesh and generate a communication diagram, context map, and microservice-specific limited contexts. Granchelli et al. [4] introduce MicroART, an architecture recovery approach for microservice-based systems. Ntentos et al. [8] extract an accurate architecture model abstraction approach for understanding component architecture models of highly polyglot systems. Like these studies, our study focuses on static analyses and polyglot systems, but in contrast, our approach aims to support traceability and explainability.

## 3   Our Approach

Our approach splits the process of extracting a software architecture model into three independent and decoupled steps. It allows us to work on the different concerns involved in each step separately and achieve better control and accuracy:

1. **Tree abstraction:** By abstracting ubiquitous structures, like folder hierarchies, lines in a text file, nested brackets inside a code file, or widespread file formats like XML or YAML, the detection logic can be expressed agnostically and applied to various languages and paradigms.
2. **Exploration:** The core of our approach is the exploration of the source code based on a minimal set of generic and configurable detectors representing the knowledge about the project in a concise and readable manner.
3. **Scan:** By decoupling the generation of a specific representation from the detection, the detection logic is focused on architectural and security features common to many projects rather than on the specific concerns of a single analysis.

### 3.1   Tree Structure Abstraction

In the tree structure abstraction approach, we use a TreeReader class to represent the tree's current position and navigate to other nodes in the tree. The TreeReader class has three public methods: MoveDown() moves the reader to the first child of the current node, ReadNext() reads the next sibling, and MoveUp() moves the reader to the parent node. The Value property holds the content of the current node as a string, which works well for handling string-based elements in source code.

The Path property represents the path to the current node from the root. A Path itself consists of two attributes. The Name attribute serves as an identifying value for a specific type of navigation, e.g., a folder hierarchy. The Children attribute represents which child node was selected from the current node in the path. For example, a path $P = \{$ *"Directory" [2, 1, 2]*$\}$ means, from the root of a folder hierarchy, move to the second child node, then move to the first child node of the previous node, and finally move to the second child node of the previous node.

## 3.2   Generic Exploratory Algorithm

**Overview.** Rather than directly generating a diagram, our generic exploratory algorithm aims to create a model of the source code that captures its architectural aspects. The model is represented as a tree structure, where each node in the tree corresponds to a localized part of the source code, known as an "Instance." An instance can be a function, a class, a file, or any specific part of the source code with a specific location. A branch in this tree is the Path from a parent Instance to its children. An Instance can have many Aspects associated with it. Aspects are semantic elements representing a particular characteristic or property of the Instance that are relevant to the analysis.

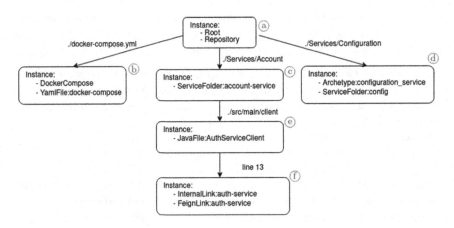

**Fig. 1.** Simplified model of a Repository

Figure 1 is an example of a simple model. It pinpoints six locations of interest in the source code:

- the root folder of the repository (a),
- a docker-compose file (b),
- two folders corresponding to a specific service. (c, d),
- a Java file (e), and
- a specific line in the Java file that declares a link (f).

An Aspect is a simple label that may contain a value. For instance, (e) has the aspect "JavaFile:AuthServiceClient," which can be understood as: "Here is an instance of a Java file named AuthServiceClient." An instance can exhibit more than one Aspect, e.g., as it is the case for the Instance (d), which is both the folder of a service called "config" and the root of a specific archetype called "config_service." An Instance is automatically created for the root repository with the Aspect "root". Still, apart from this, labels and values of Aspects have no further meaning for the algorithm. They only serve as inputs and outputs for the detectors.

If the location of an Instance is contained within the location of another Instance, it is considered its child, and the branch contains the Path from the parent Instance to the child. The Paths in Fig. 1 are written in a readable format for better reading, such as the link "line 13" between (e) and (f), which would be a Path structure $P = \{$ "Text file," [12]$\}$ with zero-based indexing.

**Detector-Based Algorithm.** The purpose of a detector is, from an Instance with a given Aspect, to detect another Instance with another Aspect. Using Fig. 1, creating the Instance (f) from the Instance (e) could be done with a detector like "From a *JavaFile*, detect a *FeignLink* by using a *Text File* Tree Reader and detect a node whose value satisfies *a regex expression*."

The algorithm in Fig. 2 can thus extract a complete model, starting from a root instance. Note that the detectors are automatically ordered according to their dependencies. The exploratory algorithm also makes tracing how each aspect was detected straightforward. When an aspect is detected, our tool keeps a trace of the originating detector in the instance.

### 3.3   Scanner

The next step is to scan the model into a specific format. The Component and Connector (C&C) view is generated from the model, a high-level abstraction of the system's components and their relationships. The C&C view clearly and concisely represents the system's architecture, allowing for more straightforward analysis and evaluation. The scanner for the C&C also receives parameters in input, such as which aspects to include or what constitutes a component. This two-step process maintains a decoupling between the detection of architectural aspects and the specific view of the architecture.

## 4   Case Study

We based our study on our prior work [13], which studies case studies of 10 microservices from Github repositories to automatically assess their conformance to a set of Architectural Design Decisions. The Component & Connector views were manually modeled based on line-by-line inspection of their source, and industrial experts confirmed the assessment scheme conformed to the most widely used security tactics for microservices today. Using the Component &

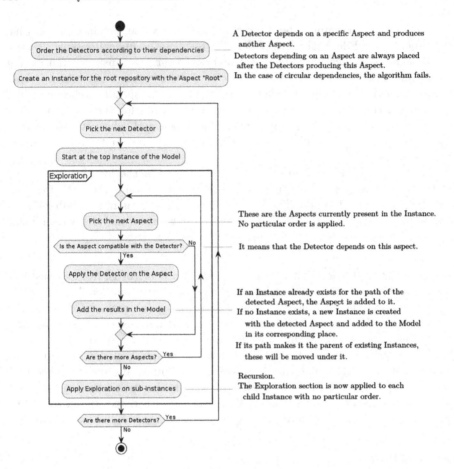

A Detector depends on a specific Aspect and produces another Aspect.
Detectors depending on an Aspect are always placed after the Detectors producing this Aspect.
In the case of circular dependencies, the algorithm fails.

These are the Aspects currently present in the Instance. No particular order is applied.

It means that the Detector depends on this aspect.

If an Instance already exists for the path of the detected Aspect, the Aspect is added to it.
If no Instance exists, a new Instance is created with the detected Aspect and added to the Model in its corresponding place.
If its path makes it the parent of existing Instances, these will be moved under it.

Recursion.
The Exploration section is now applied to each child Instance with no particular order.

**Fig. 2.** Exploration

Connector views of the study[1], we ensure that we have a ground truth of models that are accurate and relevant to the security analysis of the given repositories. The study's full results cannot be directly presented within the scope of this short paper but a replication package is provided online[2].

Our case study focuses on analyzing the architecture of the Piggymetrics application, a widely known microservices-based system. Piggymetrics is a financial management platform demonstrating the complexities and challenges associated with polyglot microservice architectures. We aim to answer the following questions:

– **RQ1** *Can the approach extract an accurate Component & Connector View?* This would mean extracting the same components and connectors as the manual view.

---

[1] https://zenodo.org/record/6424722.
[2] https://zenodo.org/record/8100928.

- **RQ2** *Can the approach extract accurate security annotations?* This would mean extracting the same annotations as the manual view.
- **RQ3** *Can the approach explain its result?* This would mean providing each annotation a link to a location in the source code.

### 4.1  Comparison of Manually Derived and Automatically Extracted Views

The automatic extraction detected the same components as the manual one, but the names are less informative. For instance, a component referred to as "Oauth2 Server" in the manual model becomes "auth-service" in the automatic one. This is an interesting finding since formalizing the naming conventions was not considered when starting this study, but it would be beneficial in improving the usefulness of the generated views. This work would primarily affect the scanner transforming the model into a Component & Connectors view. The extracted annotations for the components are the same, which is not highly significant since we used the manual view as a reference for the desired features. However, it shows that these features could be translated neatly into our detectors.

Our automatic tool detected an additional link among the connectors, from "auth-service" to "config", compared to the manual one. Since it was adequately justified in the traces, we consider this a correct result by our automatic extractor. The most noteworthy difference lies in the security annotations on the connectors. The manual view presents not only the intrinsic attributes of the connector, e.g., that a given connector is a database connection and uses plain text credentials, but also contextual information, like "authentication scope/all request" that was often missing in the automatic view.

The automatic extraction of features that can be traced back to a location in the source code is more straightforward than identifying features deduced from multiple sources of information in the repository. While some of these contextual features are also automatically extracted, e.g., to identify internal links between services or external configuration files, these rely on multiple detectors and require more fine-tuning.

### 4.2  Detectors

The automatic generation of a model for Piggymetrics requires 65 atomic detectors, not counting the one required to transform the model into a Component and Connector View. Most are very generic, for instance, identifying an XML file or an ArtefactId inside a POM file. While not each of these detectors will be relevant to every single source code, they are, as a whole, describing patterns widely prevalent among microservices projects.

20 detectors were more specific, encoding information related to the Spring framework used in Piggymetrics. For instance: "*@EnableDiscoveryClient* in a Java file denotes a registry link." These specific detectors were of two types: (1) recognizing one or more specific values in a single node; (2) recognizing a specific path for a node. That detecting specific features is so straightforward is promising since it opens the possibility of generating these detectors automatically.

### 4.3   Traces

The purpose of the trace is to allow a human to quickly verify a specific element of the view. Each annotation, whether from a component or a connector, is listed with the locations in the source code explaining it. Traces are exported as a Json file, which list the code location for each element's annotation (component or link.) For instance: "*element:* gateway {*annotation:* csrf_scope_all_requests {*location:* /piggymetrics/auth-service/[...]/auth/config/WebSecurityConfig.java, line 28"

These work well for most annotations but would become cumbersome for those requiring multiple detectors, as the number of concerned locations can quickly become combinatorially too important; therefore, these annotations are currently not traced.

## 5   Discussion

As of **RQ1**, the case study demonstrated the ability of our approach to extract a component and connector view from the source code. Our approach provided the needed detectors to produce an accurate component and connector view of the system's architecture. The only shortcoming here is the absence of a naming system that makes the names less informative than in a manual view.

Considering **RQ2** and **RQ3**, while we achieve promising results, they are less satisfying. Some security features can only be detected by analyzing multiple locations in the source code. It makes the definition of detectors and the tracing less straightforward.

Future research could explore ways to address the limitations of our approach and further improve its accuracy and scalability. One promising direction is to rely on a common core of generic detectors and automatically produce the specifics with an analyzer and a higher-level description of the expectations. Such an improvement could reduce the dependence on manually crafted detectors and increase the system's coverage under study.

## 6   Conclusion

This paper presented an approach for extracting a component and connector view from source code. We evaluated our approach using case studies in microservices and demonstrated its effectiveness in extracting a clear and understandable representation of the system's architecture. Our approach has limitations, particularly its dependence on the quality of the detectors provided as input. Future research could address these limitations by automatically generating the detectors from a higher-level expectation description and may make our approach a helpful tool for software architects and developers.

**Acknowledgements.** Our work has received funding from the European Union's Horizon 2020 research and innovation programme under grant agreement No 952647 (AssureMOSS project). This work was supported by: FWF (Austrian Science Fund) project API-ACE: I 4268; FWF (Austrian Science Fund) project IAC: I 4731-N.

# References

1. Bushong, V., Das, D., Al Maruf, A., Cerny, T.: Using static analysis to address microservice architecture reconstruction. In: 2021 36th IEEE/ACM International Conference on Automated Software Engineering (ASE). IEEE (2021)
2. Cerny, T., Abdelfattah, A.S., Bushong, V., Al Maruf, A., Taibi, D.: Microservice architecture reconstruction and visualization techniques: a review. In: 2022 IEEE International Conference on Service-Oriented System Engineering (SOSE). IEEE (2022)
3. Ducasse, S., Pollet, D.: Software architecture reconstruction: a process-oriented taxonomy. IEEE Trans. Software Eng. **35**(4), 573–591 (2009)
4. Granchelli, G., Cardarelli, M., Di Francesco, P., Malavolta, I., Iovino, L., Di Salle, A.: Towards recovering the software architecture of microservice-based systems. In: 2017 IEEE International conference on software architecture workshops (ICSAW). IEEE (2017)
5. Hasselbring, W., Steinacker, G.: Microservice architectures for scalability, agility and reliability in e-commerce. In: 2017 IEEE International Conference on Software Architecture Workshops (ICSAW). IEEE (2017)
6. Newman, S.: Building Microservices. O'Reilly Media Inc., Sebastopol (2015)
7. Ntentos, E., Zdun, U., Plakidas, K., Geiger, S.: Semi-automatic feedback for improving architecture conformance to microservice patterns and practices. In: 2021 IEEE 18th International Conference on Software Architecture (ICSA). IEEE (2021)
8. Ntentos, E., et al.: Detector-based component model abstraction for microservice-based systems. Computing **103**(11), 2521–2551 (2021)
9. Ntentos, E., Zdun, U., Plakidas, K., Meixner, S., Geiger, S.: Assessing architecture conformance to coupling-related patterns and practices in microservices. In: Jansen, A., Malavolta, I., Muccini, H., Ozkaya, I., Zimmermann, O. (eds.) ECSA 2020. LNCS, vol. 12292, pp. 3–20. Springer, Cham (2020). https://doi.org/10.1007/978-3-030-58923-3_1
10. Papotti, P.E., do Prado, A.F., de Souza, W.L.: Reducing time and effort in legacy systems reengineering to MDD using metaprogramming. In: Proceedings of the 2012 ACM Research in Applied Computation Symposium (2012)
11. Rademacher, F., Sachweh, S., Zündorf, A.: A modeling method for systematic architecture reconstruction of microservice-based software systems. In: Nurcan, S., Reinhartz-Berger, I., Soffer, P., Zdravkovic, J. (eds.) BPMDS/EMMSAD -2020. LNBIP, vol. 387, pp. 311–326. Springer, Cham (2020). https://doi.org/10.1007/978-3-030-49418-6_21
12. Rattan, D., Bhatia, R., Singh, M.: Software clone detection: a systematic review. Inf. Softw. Technol. **55**(7), 1165–1199 (2013)
13. Zdun, U., et al.: Microservice security metrics for secure communication, identity management, and observability. ACM Trans. Softw. Eng. Methodol. **32**(1), 1–34 (2023)

# A Comparison of Static and Dynamic Analysis to Identify Microservices in Monolith Systems

Bernardo Andrade, Samuel Santos, and António Rito Silva(✉)🅭

INESC-ID/Department of Computer Science and Engineering, Instituto Superior
Técnico, Av. Rovisco Pais 1, 1049-001 Lisboa, Portugal
{bernardo.andrade,samuel.c.santos,rito.silva}@tecnico.ulisboa.pt

**Abstract.** One of the most challenging problems in migrating a monolith to a microservice architecture is the identification of the microservices boundaries. Several approaches have recently been proposed for the
automatic identification of microservices, which, even though following
the same basic steps, diverge on how data from the monolith system are
collected and analyzed. In this paper, we compare the decompositions
generated for two monolith systems into a set of candidate microservices, when static and dynamic analysis data collection techniques are
used. As a result of the analysis, we conclude that neither of the analysis
techniques, static or dynamic, outperforms the other, but the dynamic
collection of data requires more effort.

**Keywords:** Microservices · Software Evolution · Static Analysis ·
Dynamic Analysis · Software Architecture

## 1  Introduction

Microservice architecture [6] has become the main stream in the development of
large-scale and complex systems when companies, such as Amazon and Netflix,
faced constraints on their system evolution due to the coupling resulting from
the use of a large domain model maintained in a shared database. However,
the adoption of this architectural style is not free from problems, where the
identification of microservice boundaries is one of the most challenging, because
a wrong cut results in the need to refactor between distributed services, which
affects service interfaces and cannot have the support of integrated development
environments.

The identification of microservice boundaries has been addressed by
research [1] in the context of the migration of monolith systems to a microservice
architecture. Some approaches take advantage of the monolith's codebase and

This work was partially supported by Fundação para a Ciência e Tecnologia (FCT)
through projects UIDB/50021/2020 (INESC-ID) and PTDC/CCI-COM/2156/2021
(DACOMICO).

runtime behavior to collect data, analyze it, and propose a decomposition of the monolith. Although each of the approaches uses different techniques, they follow the same basic steps: (1) collection: collect data from the monolith system; (2) decomposition: define a decomposition by applying a similarity measure and an aggregation algorithm, like a clustering algorithm, to the data collected in the first step; (3) analysis: evaluate the quality of the generated decomposition using a set of metrics.

However, the approaches differ in the techniques applied in each of the steps. In terms of data collection, they differ in whether the data is collected using static analysis of the code [9], or whether it is collected through the execution of the monolith [4].

In this paper, we analyze two monolith systems to study whether these two data collection techniques provide significant differences when identifying candidate decompositions. The analysis framework is built on top of what the gray literature considers as one of the main difficulties in the identification of microservices boundaries in monolith systems: the transactional contexts. Therefore, the decomposition to a microservice architecture should minimize the number of distributed transactions implementing a functionality, i.e., minimize the cost of redesigning the functionality in the microservice architecture.

Taking into account this analysis framework, we address the following research question: **Which collection of monolith behavior data, static or dynamic analysis, generates better decompositions?**

## 2   Related Work

In recent years, a myriad of approaches have been proposed to support the migration of monolith systems to microservice architecture [1], which use the monolith specification, codebase, services interfaces, runtime behavior, and project development data to recommend the best decompositions.

In this paper, we address approaches that use the monolith codebase or runtime behavior. These approaches follow the same steps, but can diverge on the similarity measures they use, such as accesses [4], reads and writes [9], and sequences [2]. On the other hand, there is no empirical evidence on whether the use of execution traces to collect the behavior of the monolith, e.g. [4], provides better results than static code analysis collection and what is the required effort to collect the data. As far as our knowledge goes, there is no work on the comparison between the use of static and dynamic analysis in the migration of monolith systems to a microservice architecture.

## 3   Monolith Microservices Identification

Different approaches to the migration of monoliths to microservice architecture apply, in the *Collection* step, static or dynamic techniques, but there is no evidence in the literature on whether one of them subsumes the other, whether they are equivalent, or even whether they are complementary. Therefore, we collected data using both techniques to address this open problem.

Data was collected from two monolith systems, LdoD[1] (122 controllers, 71 domain entities) and Blended Workflow (BW)[2] (98 controllers, 52 domain entities), which are implemented using the Model-View-Controller architectural style, where the controllers process the request by triggering transactional changes in the model, thus corresponding to monolith functionalities. The monolith is designed considering its controllers as transactions that manipulate a persistent model of domain entities.

As a result of the collection, the functionalities accesses are stored in a JSON format file, which consists of a mapping between functionality names and functionality traces. Each functionality trace is characterized by a unique identifier and a (compressed) list of accesses observed for the execution of a specific functionality. An *Access* is composed of the domain entity and the type of access, read, or write.

During the *Decomposition* step of the migration process, our tool uses hierarchical clustering (Python SciPy) to process the collected data and, according to 4 similarity measures [8], generate a dendrogram of the domain entities. The generated dendrogram can be cut to produce different decompositions, given the number of clusters.

For the *Analysis* step, our tool generates multiple decompositions, by varying the weights of the similarity measures and the number of clusters, and compares them according to a complexity metric. The complexity metric measures the development effort to migrate a monolith to a microservice architecture due to the introduction of distributed transactions [7]. Furthermore, for each monolith system, we compare the decompositions obtained using the statically collected data vs the decompositions obtained using the dynamically collected data using the MoJoFM [10] distance metric.

## 3.1   Data Collection Tools

Two data collection tools were developed. The static collection tool is built on top of Spoon [5] and is capable of, through codebase introspection, identifying Spring-Boot controllers, which represent monolith functionalities, and persistent domain entities implemented using an Object-Relational Mapper (ORM) framework. The dynamic collection tool processes execution traces to identify runtime accesses to the domain entities. Execution traces were obtained by using Kieker [3] on a running instance of the monolith under analysis. Monolith systems were instrumented using AspectJ to intercept calls to ORM data access methods, the ones responsible for manipulating the persistent state.

---

[1] https://github.com/socialsoftware/edition.

[2] https://github.com/socialsoftware/blended-workflow.

## 3.2  Monolith Monitoring

While for the static data collection it was enough to run our static analysis tool on the monolith codebases, for the dynamic data collection three different monitoring strategies were followed: in production, through functional testing, and by simulation.

Regarding the LdoD system, it was monitored in three different environments: production, functional testing, and simulation. Production monitoring lasted 3 weeks and a total of 490 GB worth of data was collected. Throughout this period, tight supervision was necessary to oversee the impact the monitoring had on the performance of the system's functionalities. Since the server hosting the application had a small free disk space (around 20 GB) and a massive performance drop was observed if it was full, it was mandatory to collect the generated logs from time to time (2–3 days) to not harm the user experience and to collect fresh logs instead of discarding them.

Analyzing the data collected, only 44% of the controllers were used in production, compared to the total number of controllers identified by static analysis. Therefore, further processing and evaluation of these data was abdicated due to the substantial effort required to process them and the relatively low coverage. Regarding functional testing, it was achieved by running a suite of 200 integration tests (4.207 lines of code) that exercised 96% of the controllers and 82% of the domain entities, generating a few megabytes (<200 MB) of data, while the instruction coverage, reported by JaCoCo[3], was 72% for domain entities and 82% for controllers. The reduced size of the collected data is explained by the usage of small subsets of the original database's data, and so the traces associated with the execution of functionalities were much shorter. Finally, a system expert simulated, for one hour, the use of functionalities, using a database with a minimal set of data, and 200 MB of the data was collected and 84% of the controllers and 80% of the domain entities were exercised.

Concerning the BW system, it was only simulated by an expert for one hour and 86% of the entities and 68% of the controllers were exercised. In this case, the reduced number of exercised controllers is justified by the deprecation of several controllers that are not reachable through the user interface.

Due to the low coverage of the data collected in production, this set of data is not used in the next steps of the research.

## 3.3  Static vs Dynamic Data Collection

The data collection process obviously differs in the coverage of controllers between static and dynamic collection, and they also differ in the identification of the domain entities that each controller accesses.

Therefore, we computed the percentage (average) of domain entities that each controller accesses when comparing the different data collection strategies.

In LdoD, static analysis identifies 95% of the domain entities, when compared with those identified through tests, while tests identify 71% of the domain

---

[3] https://github.com/jacoco/jacoco.

entities, when compared with those identified through static analysis. For static analysis and simulation the relation is 91% and 77%. On the other hand, in BW it is 93% and 78%, for static analysis and simulation.

Therefore, we can observe that for the coverage of the accesses to domain entities in the context of the controllers, in some cases, dynamic analysis can identify accesses to domain entities in the context of a controller execution, which the static collection does not, due to late binding. This is one of the limitations of static analysis that may not be able to statically infer the type of domain entity in the case of polymorphic inheritance. The opposite also occurs; static analysis can identify accesses to domain entities that dynamic analysis cannot. This can occur due to a reduced dynamic analysis coverage.

# 4    Evaluation

The goal of evaluation is to assess which technique, static or dynamic, provides the best results. First, we evaluate whether the use of static or dynamic analysis allows identifying a combination of similarity measures that provides better decompositions in terms of the complexity metric. Then, we assess whether the dynamic analysis produces significantly different decompositions, when compared to the ones statically generated and with an expert decomposition.

In both analyzes, the *Decomposition* step is applied to the statically and dinamically collected data. Several dendrograms are produced, by varying the weights of four existing similarity measures [8] - Access (A), Write (W), Read (R) and Sequence (S) - in intervals of 10 in a scale of 0 to 100. For instance, (40, 20, 20, 20) represents a combination of similarity measures in which a dendrogram is generated using hierarchical clustering for 40% access, 20% write, 20% read, and 20% sequence. Then several cuts are made on each dendrogram. Each cut results in a candidate decomposition of the monolith with a specific number of clusters, ranging from 3 to 10. For each generated decomposition, the complexity metric [7] values are calculated.

## 4.1    Complexity and Similarity Measures Correlation

To assess the correlation between the complexity metric, the weights given to each similarity measure, and the number of clusters, a linear regression model was employed using the Ordinary Least Squares method.

For LdoD and BW, the regression results on the impact of the combination of similarity measures and the number of clusters on the complexity metric show that both dynamic and static analysis have a statistically significant positive correlation with complexity for the number of clusters coefficients.

Regarding the similarity measures, the analysis shows that, independently of using statically or dynamically collected data, it is not possible to infer that one similarity measure by itself is determinant to generate a decomposition with the lowest complexity, because the magnitude of the coefficients is not pronounced and some confidence intervals contain zero.

The obtained $R^2$ values were considerably high, with the exception of the functional testing environment in the LdoD system with only 0.176. This means that, apart from this specific environment, the regression model explains most of the data set (low variability).

## 4.2  Best Complexity Decomposition

Although it seems that both collection techniques provide similar insight in terms of the correlation between the similarity measures and the complexity metric, we want to know whether they produce significantly different decompositions.

To assess the results of the two techniques, we compare the highest-quality decompositions, in terms of complexity, of each approach with a decomposition proposed by a domain expert for both systems. In this analysis, we consider the expert decompositions as a reference and evaluate, using the MoJoFM metric, which approach provides closer results to it. Since the two techniques may miss some domain entities during the collection phase, we decided that all unassigned entities would be placed in the largest cluster, as this strategy is in accordance with the rationale of the incremental decomposition strategy [6, Chapter 13].

**Table 1.** Comparison of the best automatically generated decompositions with expert decompositions. N is the decomposition number of clusters.

|   |    | LdoD | | | BW | |
|---|----|--------|-------|------|--------|-------|
|   |    | Static | Tests | Sim  | Static | Sim   |
| N | 3  | 62.12  | 65.15 | 68.18 | 46.67 | 44.44 |
|   | 4  | 60.61  | 69.7  | 66.67 | 44.44 | 46.67 |
|   | 5  | 56.06  | 68.18 | 66.67 | 44.44 | 60.00 |
|   | 6  | 78.79  | 66.67 | 66.67 | 62.22 | 57.78 |
|   | 7  | 77.27  | 74.24 | 68.18 | 66.67 | 64.44 |
|   | 8  | 83.33  | 72.73 | 59.09 | 66.67 | 62.22 |
|   | 9  | 81.82  | 74.24 | 57.58 | 71.11 | 62.22 |
|   | 10 | 45.45  | 74.24 | 56.06 | 71.11 | 62.22 |
| avg |  | 68.18  | 70.64 | 63.64 | 59.17 | 57.5  |

**Table 2.** Comparison of the best automatically generated decompositions with expert decompositions, considering only common controllers and entities.

|   |    | LdoD | | | BW | |
|---|----|--------|-------|------|--------|-------|
|   |    | Static | Tests | Sim  | Static | Sim   |
| N | 3  | 62.12  | 65.15 | 68.18 | 46.67 | 44.44 |
|   | 4  | 60.61  | 69.7  | 66.67 | 44.44 | 46.67 |
|   | 5  | 56.06  | 68.18 | 66.67 | 44.44 | 60.00 |
|   | 6  | 78.79  | 66.67 | 66.67 | 62.22 | 57.78 |
|   | 7  | 77.27  | 74.24 | 68.18 | 66.67 | 64.44 |
|   | 8  | 83.33  | 72.73 | 59.09 | 66.67 | 62.22 |
|   | 9  | 81.82  | 74.24 | 57.58 | 71.11 | 62.22 |
|   | 10 | 45.45  | 74.24 | 56.06 | 71.11 | 62.22 |
| avg |  | 68.18  | 70.64 | 63.64 | 59.17 | 57.5  |

The results of the comparisons are represented in Table 1, where each cell indicates the percentage value of MoJoFM (0–100%) between the lowest complexity decomposition with N clusters, using a particular collection technique, and the expert decomposition of the system. Overall, the MoJoFM values obtained for the different collection approaches were very similar for both systems, which led us to conclude that there is no collection technique that provides better results. However, note that, especially in the simulation technique, the dynamic analysis did not cover all controllers during the collection phase and also missed more entities than the static approach. Therefore, we decided to assess whether the dynamic analysis approach could surpass static analysis if only the controllers and entities that are identified by both approaches were considered.

To evaluate this scenario, we ran the static analysis on the two monoliths considering only the common controllers and domain entities, for each dynamic technique. For the LdoD system, there are two *Static* columns because the static collection needs to be evened for the two types of dynamic collection, *Tests* and *Sim*. The results are represented in Table 2, where we can observe that, on average, both approaches continue to generate decompositions almost equally distant to the expert for both systems. The main difference observed (7–9%), for the LdoD system, is the average MoJoFM values obtained for the static approach when *evened* with dynamic analysis using the simulation approach. However, a similar impact is not seen for the BW system.

Based on these results, we conclude that, for both systems, we do not see significant differences between the lowest complexity decompositions obtained using statically and dynamically collected data, and that none of the approaches achieves identical decompositions to the expert's, since the average MoJoFM values obtained vary around 60–70%.

Given the similarities, when compared to the expert, we decided to assess how far apart the static and dynamic decompositions were from each other, considering the common controllers and entities.

For LdoD, the average MoJoFM between the evened static and tests approaches is 75%, while between the evened static and simulation approaches it is 69%. For BW, the average MoJoFM between the evened static and simulation approaches was 56%. Therefore, we can observe that the best decompositions generated by the collection techniques tend to be closer to each other than to the expert decomposition for monolith LdoD. However, the same conclusion cannot be drawn for the BW monolith.

We have done an additional analysis, by inspecting the best decomposition for each one of the evened techniques, and we could observe that the clusters in the experts decomposition were more balanced in terms of the number of domain entities per cluster. This may be an indication that the expert cut was driven by the structural qualities of the monolith (modularity), which drive the domain model design. Additionally, when comparing the generated decompositions, we found similarities between the semantic intent of each of the clusters.

Overall, this suggests that neither of the analysis techniques outperforms the other, although there is room for future research.

### 4.3  Lessons Learned

From this research, we have learned the following lessons: (1) It is not possible to conclude that the decompositions generated using one of the analysis techniques, static or dynamic, outperform the other. (2) The effort to collect data dynamically is significantly superior to static collection. Collecting and evaluating data from production, results in a large amount of data and very low coverage. On the other hand, the use of integration tests, despite requiring higher development costs, achieves better coverage This is because integration tests are usually designed to verify the integration of the modules, not the execution of all paths, which is the aim of unit tests. Integration tests are also harder to develop and maintain because they often break.

## 5 Conclusions

In this paper, two monolith systems were analyzed to study the impact of applying static and dynamic analysis on the quality of the automatically generated decompositions as well as whether a particular combination of similarity measures provides better decompositions.

As a result of the experiments and analysis, we conclude that different monolith analysis techniques generate decompositions that do not outperform each other, but, it was clear that the effort required by the dynamic analysis is much superior and resulted in less coverage. In particular, the data collection done in production revealed to have a very low coverage and generated a large amount of data.

The data used and produced in this research is available at http://doi.org/10.5281/zenodo.5675593.

## References

1. Abdellatif, M., et al.: A taxonomy of service identification approaches for legacy software systems modernization. J. Syst. Softw. **173**, 110868 (2021)
2. Amiri, M.J.: Object-aware identification of microservices. In: 2018 IEEE International Conference on Services Computing (SCC), pp. 253–256 (2018)
3. Hasselbring, W., van Hoorn, A.: Kieker: a monitoring framework for software engineering research. Softw. Impacts **5**, 100019 (2020)
4. Jin, W., Liu, T., Cai, Y., Kazman, R., Mo, R., Zheng, Q.: Service candidate identification from monolithic systems based on execution traces. IEEE Trans. Software Eng. **47**(5), 987–1007 (2021)
5. Pawlak, R., Monperrus, M., Petitprez, N., Noguera, C., Seinturier, L.: Spoon: a library for implementing analyses and transformations of Java source code. Softw. Pract. Exp. **46**(9), 1155–1179 (2016)
6. Richardson, C.: Microservices Patterns: With Examples in Java. Manning Publications (2019)
7. Santos, N., Rito Silva, A.: A complexity metric for microservices architecture migration. In: 2020 IEEE International Conference on Software Architecture (ICSA), pp. 169–178 (2020)
8. Santos, S., Silva, A.R.: Microservices identification in monolith systems: functionality redesign complexity and evaluation of similarity measures. J. Web Eng. **21**(05), 1543–1582 (2022)
9. Tyszberowicz, S., Heinrich, R., Liu, B., Liu, Z.: Identifying microservices using functional decomposition. In: Feng, X., Müller-Olm, M., Yang, Z. (eds.) SETTA 2018. LNCS, vol. 10998, pp. 50–65. Springer, Cham (2018). https://doi.org/10.1007/978-3-319-99933-3_4
10. Wen, Z., Tzerpos, V.: An effectiveness measure for software clustering algorithms. In: Proceedings of 12th IEEE International Workshop on Program Comprehension, pp. 194–203. IEEE (2004)

# Author Index

B. Tekinerdogan et al. (Eds.): ECSA 2023, LNCS 14212, pp. 363–364, 2023.
https://doi.org/10.1007/978-3-031-42592-9

Printed in the United States
by Baker & Taylor Publisher Services